I0896330

"Kessler creatively engages a topic that often mystifies modern readers. He showcases responsible, yet accessible, readings of particular passages as he traces the theme of silence throughout the Hebrew Bible. By providing implications for contemporary theology and life he reveals the relevance of this theological concept and these biblical texts for confessional communities today. A must-read."

—**Mark J. Boda**, *Professor of Old Testament, McMaster Divinity College*

"Kessler offers an excellent discussion of the concepts, functions, contexts, and ethos of silence in the Hebrew Bible. With exegetical rigor and keen theological discernment, he shows how and why the dialectic between sound and silence, and more specifically the fraught space between the two, is often where our most profound experiences with God are to be found. This is clearly a book written with close attention to our contemporary situation; it invites and rewards serious reflection."

—**Samuel E. Balentine**, *Professor of Old Testament Emeritus, Union Presbyterian Seminary*

"Kessler is a perceptive reader of the Hebrew Bible, calling attention to exegetical and literary matters, as well as to theological significance. His comprehensive analysis of the motif of silence in the Hebrew Bible is remarkable. Readers will be surprised by how much is said about silence, how meaningful silence is, and how the biblical text communicates important concepts even through silence. With great confidence and ease, Kessler leads the reader into the depths of this important biblical theme—a pleasure to read."

—**Elie Assis**, *Dean of the Faculty of Jewish Studies, Bar Ilan University*

"In the Hebrew Bible, silence is much more than the absence of sound. It is an exceptional phenomenon that can presage divine abandonment or conversely God's mercy and forgiveness. John Kessler's study traverses the full range of peak human experiences grounded in silence, and careful exegesis of these biblical accounts brings forth their deeper meaning. A fitting climax is a meditation on the silence of the sacred, not only at the Holy of Holies in the Jerusalem Temple but as well in the experiences of everyday people, with Sabbath observance a rich example."

—**Richard Bautch**, *Professor of Humanities and Associate Dean of The School of Arts and Humanities, St. Edward's University*

BETWEEN HEARING AND SILENCE

A Study in Old Testament Theology

John Kessler

BAYLOR UNIVERSITY PRESS

Cover and interior design by Kasey McBeath
Cover image: Photo by Madhu Shesharam on Unsplash

Library of Congress Cataloging-in-Publication Data

Names: Kessler, John, 1951- author.
Title: Between hearing and silence : a study in Old Testament theology / John Kessler.
Description: Waco : Baylor University Press, 2021. | Includes bibliographical references and index. | Summary: "A thematic survey of the various scenarios in the OT wherein silence, both divine and human, play a significant role, and an exploration of the latent theological meaning behind these varied situations"-- Provided by publisher.
Identifiers: LCCN 2020041151 (print) | LCCN 2020041152 (ebook) | ISBN 9781481313766 (paperback) | ISBN 9781481314190 (pdf) | ISBN 9781481313759 (epub)
Subjects: LCSH: Silence in the Bible. | Bible. Old Testament--Criticism, interpretation, etc. | Silence--Religious aspects.
Classification: LCC BS1199.S53 K47 2021 (print) | LCC BS1199.S53 (ebook) | DDC 221.6--dc23
LC record available at https://lccn.loc.gov/2020041151
LC ebook record available at https://lccn.loc.gov/2020041152

Printed in the United States of America on acid-free paper with a minimum of thirty percent recycled content.

To Père Jean Lévêque O.C.D.
With profound gratitude

אך אל אלהים דומיה נפשי ממנו ישועתי

For God alone my soul waits in silence; from him comes my salvation. (NRSV)
Ps 62:1

CONTENTS

Acknowledgments ix
Abbreviations xiii

1 Understanding Silence 1
Foundational Issues

2 Silence as Alienation 13
When Relationships Break Down

3 Silence as Catastrophe 33
When Everything Falls Apart

4 Silence as Repentance and Renewal 55
Dwelling in the Space between Loss and Restoration

5 Silence as Security 71
God Our Rock

6 The Two Silences 87
The Silence of the Grave and the Silence of the Sacred

7 How Long O Lord? 107
God's Silence and Human Suffering

8 Finding God between Sound and Silence 131

Epilogue 159

Playlist for Silence 163
Notes 167
Bibliography 221
Author Index 241
Subject Index 245
Scripture Index 255
Hebrew Index 273

ACKNOWLEDGMENTS

I wish to express my sincere gratitude to the numerous people who have contributed to the writing of this book. I am thankful to the president, Dr. Gary Nelson, and to the board of governors of Tyndale University, Toronto, for granting me sabbatical leaves from January 2017–July 2017 and January 2019–July 2019. Without these times of focused research, I could not have completed this project. Thanks are also especially due to our former dean, Dr. Janet Clark, who supported my sabbatical applications and tirelessly encouraged me along the way. I similarly wish to express my great appreciation to the Tyndale library, most especially to Hugh Rendle, head librarian, and to Monica Duce and Leah Vetro, his assistants, who helped with my almost daily requests for materials. As well I wish to offer special thanks to my colleagues in the Biblical Studies department of Tyndale Seminary in Tyndale University, Drs. Rebecca Idestrom, Ian Scott, and Duncan Reid. Many other friends and colleagues at Tyndale offered their support and encouragement. I would address a special word of gratitude to Drs. Dennis Ngien and John Wilkinson in this regard.

Thanks are also due to Cade Jarrell, David Aycock, Jenny Hunt, and the team at Baylor University Press for their patience, encouragement, expertise, and tireless support. I wish to similarly express my appreciation to the two "blind" reviewers who read portions of the text for Baylor, and whose insightful comments were of great assistance. Professor William Morrow of the School of Religion, Queen's University, Kingston, Ontario, provided superb insights regarding the theme of protest in the Psalms, which I address in chapter 7, in personal communication. Over the past few years, my conversations with Dr. Sonja Noll, now of the Pontificia Universidad Católica de Chile, have similarly stimulated my thought and reflection. Many colleagues from various institutions, too numerous to mention individually here, offered their support and encouragement. I also offer particular thanks to Professors Konrad Schmid (Zurich) and Manfred Oeming (Heidelberg) for their insightful comments in the course of our conversations. Annual breakfast discussions at SBL with Dr. Richard Middleton of Northeastern Seminary at Roberts Wesleyan College were both stimulating and refreshing. I wish to thank Dr. Peter Williams, principal of Tyndale House, Cambridge, and librarian Simon Sykes, as well as the rest of the library staff, for their invaluable assistance during my time there in 2017.

I have had the privilege of presenting some of the material contained in this monograph on various occasions. I have taught seminar courses on "Silence in the Bible" at Tyndale Seminary, and am deeply indebted to my students for their comments, questions, and most of all their objections and challenges. My long-time research assistant Simon Pan also helped me at numerous points in the preparation and presentation of these seminars. I am extremely grateful for his help over many years. Some of the material in this monograph was included in two SBL presentations. In the 2017 SBL Meetings in San Antonio, TX, I delivered a paper entitled "Silence in the Hebrew Bible: An Overview of Key Issues and Debates" in the joint session of the "Speech and Talk in the Mediterranean World" and "Senses and Culture in the Biblical World" sections. I am grateful to Yael Avrahami and Greg Goering for their kind invitation to participate. This was followed in 2019 by a paper entitled, "The 'Calls to Silence' in Zeph 1:7; Hab 2:20; and Zech 2:17[ET 13]: A Form- and Redaction-Critical Reassessment" in the Book of the Twelve section in the 2019 Meeting in San Diego, CA. I thank Jakob Wöhrle and Lena-Sofia Tiemeyer for including me in the program, and for their ongoing interest in my work.

I must express a very special word of thanks to Dr. Charles Meeks, Adjunct Professor of Theology, Northeastern Seminary at Roberts Wesleyan College, Rochester, NY, and to Jenny Hunt, Production Manager at Baylor University Press, who helped with much of the editing for this project, as well as undertaking the formatting and processing of the files. Their expert assistance was utterly invaluable in bringing this book to completion. I am deeply grateful to them for their patience and care. Any remaining errors are my own.

I am thankful to Cade Jarrell at Baylor for his support and enthusiasm regarding this project, and for allowing me to include a "playlist" to accompany the text of the book. As will become apparent to my readers, silence can be as meaningful as speech. Often, the deep emotions that lie beyond words are best expressed through music. The musical selections on the list reflect various aspects of silence and its many meanings, and are drawn from many musical genres. Many of the selections manifest the ability of certain pieces of music to contain silences within them. I am profoundly grateful to my longtime friend, jazz lover, former student, and fellow parishioner Dr. Laurence Wedderburn, M.D. for our numerous conversations about silence, music, and for his suggestions as I assembled the playlist. Many more musical compositions could have been included, but these will, I hope, give my readers some suggestions for further listening.

On a more personal note, words cannot express my profound gratitude to my beloved wife Sandra, who has patiently supported and encouraged me through this long and arduous journey. I am deeply indebted to her. Thanks are also due to my daughter Andrea and her husband Phil for their support and their suggestions for the playlist, to my son Jeremy for his words of encouragement, and to my son James, who has personally and patiently observed much of the process of the writing of this book, and who will be very glad to see me out of my study and away from my desk more often.

Finally, I pause to give thanks to the Triune God, whose great goodness has once again preserved me in life over the writing of the book, despite significant and ongoing challenges to my health. Words simply cannot express my gratefulness for this gift, in addition to so many others.

I dedicate this book to my *Doktorvater* at the Institut Catholique de Paris, Fr. Jean Lévêque, O.C.D. Père Lévêque's incarnation of the depths of divine silence embodies the wonder of the knowledge of God reflected in the Scriptures, especially those passages that relate to silence, stillness, and waiting on God. He has been—and continues to be—an inspiration to so many.

John Kessler
Toronto, July 30, 2020

ABBREVIATIONS

Unless noted in the list below, all the abbreviations in this book follow the form in the *Society of Biblical Literature Handbook of Style*, 2nd ed. (Atlanta: Society of Biblical Literature, 2014).

ASBT	Acadia Studies in Bible and Theology
BeOl	Berit Olam
BibG	Biblische Gestalten
CBSC	Cambridge Bible for Schools and Colleges
CSQ	*Cistercian Studies Quarterly*
ConJ	*Concordia Journal*
CSHebB	Critical Studies in the Hebrew Bible
DSB	Daily Study Bible
DOTHB	*Dictionary of the Old Testament: Historical Books*
DOTP	*Dictionary of the Old Testament: Prophets*
DOTWis	*Dictionary of the Old Testament: Wisdom, Poetry and Writings*
DlD	*Dor leDor*
EDEJ	*Eerdmans Dictionary of Early Judaism*
EBS	Encountering Biblical Studies
EncPhil	*Encyclopedia of Philosophy*
EMQ	*Evangelical Missions Quarterly*
HBM	Hebrew Bible Monographs
JPSTC	Jewish Publication Society Torah Commentary
JEBS	*Journal of European Baptist Studies*
JMD	*Journal of Multicultural Discourses*
KJCS	*Korean Journal of Christian Studies*
MT	*Modern Theology*
NCamBC	New Cambridge Bible Commentary

NCBC	New Century Bible Commentary
NVBS	New Voices in Biblical Studies
NIVAC	New International Version Application Commentary
OEBE	*Oxford Encyclopedia of the Bible and Ethics*
OxTM	Oxford Theological Monographs
PeP	*Parole et Pain*
PT	*Philosophy Today*
RRJ	*Review of Rabbinic Judaism*
StMR	*St. Mark's Review*
SSR	Studies in Semitic Languages and Linguistics
THOTC	Two Horizons Old Testament Commentary
VEccl	*Verbum et Ecclesia*

1
UNDERSTANDING SILENCE

Foundational Issues

What is silence? And why is it worth considering? Even a moment's reflection reveals how elusive a concept silence actually is. Why is it so difficult to define? Unlike many topics that can be dealt with more objectively, most if not all discussion of silence necessarily proceeds from its *experiential* dimension. Like hunger, fatigue, thirst, or love, we are able to speak of silence because we have experienced it. As children we hear the sound "shhh" and learn something of silence by being called to enact it, to cease what we are doing, and "not make a sound." Or we may have experienced silence lying fearfully in our beds in the dead of night, attentive to every creak or thump. As we proceed through life, we learn that silence is closely related to concepts such as stillness, calm, peace, and quiet. We discover as well that it can be something external, such as a calm or silent place, or relate to more internal states, such as a serene or peaceful heart. We learn that it can describe intentionally adopted behaviors. Someone appears upset and we ask, "why are you so quiet?" However, it can also refer to imposed behaviors—"the teacher forbade all discussion of the subject." It can describe how actions should be performed—"leave quietly when you go"—or characteristics of persons or things. We sing the carol *Silent Night* or hear talk of a "quiet child." We quickly become aware that the concept of silence is multiform, relating to numerous interrelated ideas and experiences.

As we shall see, silence may mean many things, but rarely, in our common use, does it refer to a total absence of all sound. A silent night is not a time of absolutely no sound, nor is a taciturn person one who never speaks at all. When a person or group is said to have been forced into silence, that silence does not concern *all* speech, but only to certain, prohibited topics. The title of Rachel Carson's famous monograph *Silent Spring* alludes not to the absence of all sound, but to the customary noises of birds and insects lost due to environmental pollution.[1] Composer John Cage, famous for his piece *4'33"* in which the audience sits in silence while the musicians do not play a note, declared after its premiere performance, "There's no such thing as silence." He was referring to the audience's experience of becoming aware of the numerous sounds other than musical notes that were audible to them.[2] In fact, it is not altogether certain whether a total absence of sound is actually perceptible by the human person. Cage once described being placed in a totally soundproofed room and yet being able to hear two sounds, one low and the other high. He was subsequently informed that the low sound was the circulation of his blood, and the higher one emanated from his nervous system.[3]

We generally understand silence as *expressive of meaning*. A person who chooses to remain silent may be communicating a wide range of sentiments or making any number of declarations: anger or peace, assent or dissent, acceptance or rejection. Furthermore, silence relates not only to speech and sound, but also to actions. To fail to intervene is to remain silent. But silence does more than simply convey meaning. It is deeply connected to affect, ethos, and context. Specific geographic settings seem to exude a silence of their own.[4] Silence is sometimes associated with buildings. Alain Corbin describes certain edifices, both real and literary, that seem to be infused with it.[5] Silence may also depict the inner attitude of a person who is attentive and waiting for that which another may say or do. Mystic and religious philosopher Simone Weil famously writes of *Waiting for God*.[6]

Moreover, silence may also have an active dimension. As one philosopher has stated, one may *do* things by means of it.[7] Silence has effects, and may create possibilities. A sudden diminution of sound may draw one's attention away from distractions and preoccupations, and create a context for speech and hearing. In A. A. Milne's famous children's book *The House at Pooh Corner*, Winnie the Pooh, a bear, and his companions Piglet and Rabbit, are lost in the fog, and cannot find their way home. It is only when they become separated, and Pooh is away from Rabbit's incessant banter, that he can "hear" his honey pots calling him and leading him home.[8] On a more sombre note, the films of Ingmar Bergman illustrate silence's ability to create a context or a space within which words or actions take on special poignancy.[9] Edgar Lee Masters' poem *Silence* (Feb 1915) sets forth the many ways silence may express that which lies beyond words.[10]

Silence frequently pulls us in two opposing directions. On the one hand, in our frenetic world we desperately crave the peaceful silence of solitude, stillness, and undisturbed rest.[11] Images of glass-like lakes, mountain vistas, or deep green forests come to mind and offer us respite. On the other hand, silence may speak to us of death, separation, and sorrow. The realities of a telephone that no longer rings, a silent room where no one enters, or an aching emptiness within speak to us of silence. Hamlet, just before his tragic death, utters the words, "the rest is silence."[12] Bob Dylan once observed, "experience teaches that silence terrifies people the most."[13] As we go on in life, we encounter silence in various contexts and see it enacted numerous ways. And, at one time or another, silence affects us most profoundly, for good or for ill.

In recent years there has been a great proliferation of books, articles, and films on silence, written from various perspectives: religious and secular, theoretical and applied.[14] Discussions of silence frequently take one specific dimension of it as their starting point. Some studies focus on its more philosophical and theoretical aspects.[15] Others examine the phenomenon of silence cross-culturally.[16] Some works decry the deleterious effects of noise, and its proliferation in modern society and call for resistance to it.[17] More theologically oriented works frequently focus on silence as a spiritual discipline, and provide counsel on its practice.[18] The life and practices of the Carthusian monastery in the French Alps are often of special interest in this regard.[19] Others examine the place of silence in Christian traditions, or world religions more broadly.[20] Still others have pointed to the culpable silences of religious communities at moments when there ought to have been speech or action, and called for an end to such silence today.[21]

Silence in the Hebrew Bible: Foundational Concepts

In the midst of this rich and diverse body of literature and other media, the specific focus of the present monograph is upon silence in the Old Testament (or, as I will be referring to it, the Hebrew Bible, or HB). A great wealth of scholarly material on silence in the HB has appeared in recent years. Before 2010, this area of investigation had received relatively little attention from scholars, especially in the English-speaking world. Many significant studies had appeared in Italian, Spanish, French, and German, often consisting of encyclopedia and dictionary entries and specialized articles. In 2004, Paolo Torresan provided an extensive bibliography of such works.[22] Silvio Báez's monographs on silence in the HB also constituted an important contribution to the field.[23] More recently, several significant English-language studies have appeared. In 2011, Marjo Korpel and Johannes de Moor published *The Silent God*, a work examining the motif of divine silence both in the arts and philosophy, and most especially in the biblical and comparative materials from the ancient Near East (ANE).[24] Göran Eidevall's important 2012 semantic study examined various lexemes related to silence, as well as the relationship between silence as the absence of speech and the related concepts of stillness or calm.[25] Most recently, Sonja Noll has produced a magisterial analysis of the semantics of silence in the HB.[26] As the book's title suggests, Noll's work is highly technical and focuses on "the lexical representation of silence."[27] In pursuit of this objective, she seeks to determine the semantic field of the various Hebrew terms that are frequently understood by most translations and lexicons as related to silence, then proposes revisions of various traditional translations of these terms, and establishes broader categories for the Hebrew understanding of the concept of silence.

The study of silence in the HB must take as its point of departure the understanding of silence present within its own linguistic, sociological, and ideological world.[28] The HB employs various rich and multifaceted means of speaking of silence. However, despite this diversity, a single foundational assumption lies at its core. Similar to its meaning in English, for the biblical writers silence is *not the total absence of sound or actions* but rather the absence of (or, alternatively, the cessation or restraint of) those sounds or actions that would *normally be expected in a given circumstance*. Moving one step further, in the HB, where such silences occur, they are generally *communicative*. Quite the opposite of Macbeth's sorry verdict that life "is a tale told by an idiot, *full of sound and fury, signifying nothing*," the HB views the *absence of expected sounds or actions* as meaningful and significant.[29]

I write these lines in the midst of the COVID-19 pandemic in 2020. I live in Toronto, a large, noisy, urban center. Normally, aircraft destined for or departing from Toronto's Pearson International Airport pass overhead day and night. Nearby roads are clogged with traffic. But in March the skies and roads became "silent." Images of normally crowded sites in Paris, Venice, London, Jerusalem, Tokyo, Hong Kong, and New York, now eerily silent, were displayed across the globe. Pollution diminished as air and road traffic were stilled. In some locations animals emerged from forests and walked about freely. For many, the silence in the skies and calm in the streets was a welcome relief. But to others it represented an aberration, a reflection of the threat posed by the pandemic ravaging the world. But whether the conspicuous silence was welcomed or not, the reason *why* the skies and streets were silent was not generally in doubt. However, someone with no idea of COVID-19 or the world's response to it, upon emerging from a long hiking journey in the Andes and having been entirely "off the grid," would be stupefied. Why had the world gone silent? What did this mean? What was happening?

These questions point to a core element of our study: silence, either human or divine, is generally a form of communication, and when present, calls for an *explanation*.[30] We live in a world of sound, or a "soundscape," in which we encounter speech, sound, as well as various kinds of silence. Indeed, as will be explained below, the concept of a *soundscape*—that is, the sounds depicted in a biblical text or the sounds hearers would encounter as the text was read aloud—will form a critically important component of the biblical passages we will study.[31] Some silences are normal parts of daily life. They are as essential to communication as rests are to music. The silences of politeness in everyday interactions, or of brief pauses in speech, are entirely unremarkable.[32] When such silences are not present, we become irritated or annoyed. However, when silence moves beyond these more basic roles, it draws attention to itself and is almost always meaningful. We become aware of its presence, ask why it has occurred, and what it means.[33]

Silence: Meanings, Functions, Contexts, Ethos

Generally speaking, a given context and culture will possess *a range of socially acknowledged possibilities* that can account for silence in a given context. As just noted, some silences are expected and unremarkable. Although meaningful, the significance of such silences is not difficult to ascertain. The concert hall is full. The lights are dimmed. Silence descends upon the room. The telephone rings, a child learns that an expected event has been cancelled and returns silently to her room. Such silences are easily interpreted. At other times, the meaning of the silence is unclear. We expect those close to us to respond to us, and if they do not, we wonder why: "Is there something wrong? Are you upset? Are you angry with me? Are you not well?" Or, in the midst of a crowded restaurant, a sudden silence sweeps over the diners. Why, we wonder. Has someone had a heart attack, or choked on their food? Or has a well-known celebrity entered the room? Or is some kind of argument about to erupt?

Moving one step further, expressions of silence may be both *trans-cultural* (i.e., relatively stable across cultures) and *culturally specific*. Silence in the presence of a superior or honored person is widely understood as a sign of respect. However, many greater subtleties exist within specific cultures and contexts, as well as from one historical period to the next.[34] Thus, as intimated above, the meaning of silence in a biblical text must be determined in terms of the social, literary, and theological world of the HB itself.

Approached this way, biblical silences prompt important questions: Why does God stop speaking to Saul (1 Sam 28:6, 15)? Why, following the destruction of Jerusalem, do its elders sit in silence (Lam 2:10)? Why does Elisha command the prophets to be silent, just before Elijah is about to be taken up (2 Kgs 2:3, 5)? What is the significance of the silence that follows the wind, earthquake, and fire in 1 Kings 19:12? To speak of silence in the biblical text is thus to raise questions of meaning and significance. And in the present monograph, we will examine several series of texts within the HB dealing with silence, and seek to discern its meaning and significance within them.[35]

Although silence can serve as a bearer of meaning, its significance is not limited to this role. In fact, there are three other facets of silence in the HB that are highly relevant for the present study. First, the silences of a text may create an *ethos* or *ambiance* in which its action takes place. Genesis 22, to be studied in detail in chapter 8, is a significant example. Abraham's inner sentiments are not revealed. His words are ambiguous. The repeated phrase "the two [Abraham and Isaac] walked on together" contains within it an oceanic depth of silence. E. A. Speiser has described the phrase as the "most poignant and eloquent silence in all literature."[36] Second, silence may have a profoundly *active* dimension. For example, silence enacts resistance in 2 Kings 18:36, where, in obedience to Hezekiah's command, the people remain silent in the face of the Assyrian commander's argument that they surrender. A similar active role of silence appears in 1 Kings 19:12, where the Lord replaces loud sounds with silence to draw human attention to that which God will say or do. Silence thus becomes a *precursor* for hearing the divine word. Samuel's nighttime experience at Shiloh manifests a similar pattern. Third, silence may serve as a descriptor of a human state of heart when *words might seem inadequate for such a task*, especially in cases of trauma.[37] This appears in Leviticus 10:3, where Aaron is silent following the death of his sons, and in Lamentations 2:10, where the elders of Jerusalem are silent following its destruction. In a more positive vein, Psalm 62:1-2 describes the psalmist as waiting attentively for God's response. In such passages silence describes a state of waiting and expectancy. In sum, silence in the HB functions in various ways: as a bearer of meaning of various sorts; as a means of creating an ambiance within a text; as an active statement; as a phenomenon in the external world, creating space to hear God's voice; and as a reflection of various states of the human spirit, many of which might become truncated if put into words. Thus, over the course of our study, in pursuit of a closer understanding of the dynamics of the divine-human relationship, we will frequently find ourselves "between silence and hearing."

A few qualifications are in order at this point. Although my discussion touches upon a number of aspects of silence often discussed in biblical studies and theology, space precludes a full investigation of them.[38] Thus, I will engage matters of semantics and lexicography, but only briefly. Similarly, although matters of theodicy and the "silence of God" are indeed relevant to aspects of my topic, I cannot undertake an in-depth analysis of such matters. Again, although I will touch upon the important issue of illegitimate or culpable silence—that is, those times when persons remain silent when they should speak, or are reduced to silence by those more powerful than themselves—I cannot pursue this matter exhaustively. Similarly, the issues of silence at Qumran, in the intertestamental literature, and in the New Testament (NT) lie outside my purview.[39] Finally, although my study has implications for various spiritual practices in Christian and other traditions (and indeed I will in the course of this study refer to them from time to time), this is not its primary goal. This does not mean, however, that my study has no relevance for Christian theology and spirituality. On the contrary, I will describe my understanding of how readers may move from the world of the HB to that of Christian experience today near the conclusion of this chapter.

This study is an investigation of silence rooted in the disciplines of *exegesis* and *biblical theology*. As such, we will engage in careful exegetical readings of various HB passages involving silence and seek to understand the meaning borne by silence in each text. Moreover, as we shall see, quite frequently various texts coalesce and form consistent patterns of meaning which flow through various sections of the HB.[40] Then, having performed our task of exegesis, we shall seek to discover their theological significance and reflect upon their contemporary relevance.

How Does the HB Denote Silence?

The HB has four principal ways of referencing silence: (1) specific terminology; (2) narrative descriptions of persons not speaking or acting; (3) nonverbal indications of keeping silent; and (4) complex images, motifs, and conceptualizations in which silence is a key element. A fifth consideration, Masoretic scribal designations, usually via a gap (*parashah setumah*) or line break (*parashah petuchah*), could be included, but these were added subsequent to the writing of the text itself, and, apart from a few instances, will not be discussed here. Without entering into great detail, let us briefly examine these means of referring to silence.

Specific Terminology

Noll's recent monograph presents a comprehensive analysis of the key terms and semantic field relating to silence.[41] She identifies eight primary verbal roots relating to silence, categorizing them broadly as denoting either restraint or cessation. The roots she identifies as indicating restraint are **ḥarash*, **'ilem*, and **hashah*, while cessation is referenced by the root **damam*-1 (and various associated terms: **doum*, **damah*, *dumiyah*, *demamah*), *has*, **shataq*, and **sakat*. Finally, she identifies **shaqaṭ* as standing on the periphery of the semantic field of silence. As an overall conclusion, she states: "The lexemes studied do not, in fact, refer primarily to a lack of noise, but instead more broadly to a lack of action, a failure to do what is expected, a cessation of commotion, the cessation of life, or the presence of rest. *Most of the lexemes have surprisingly little to do with the absence of sound*, having more to do with unmet social expectations or the quieting of chaos in the natural world."[42] Three lexemes will be of special interest in our analysis: (1) **ḥarash*, a verbal root that frequently indicates restraint or cessation of speech, movement, or actions (Exod 14:14; Num 30:4; 2 Sam 13:20; 2 Kgs 18:36; Isa 42:14; Mic 7:16; Pss 28:1; 50:21; Job 13:13); (2) **damam*-1 (and its related nouns, verbs and adjectives, noted above), terms that frequently denote stillness, peace, silence, or calm (Exod 15:16; Lev 10:3b; Josh 10:12; Pss 37:7; 62:1; 131:2; Isa 23:2; Amos 5:13);[43] and (3) *has*, an interjection similar in meaning to the English "shh," used as an urgent demand for silence (Judg 3:19; Amos 6:10; 8:3; Hab 2:20; Zeph 1:7; Zech 2:13; Neh 8:11). As we encounter these terms, we will explore their significance in their various contexts.

Narrative Descriptions

Quite frequently, the concept of silence, especially as inaction or indifference, is depicted through narrative without recourse to the lexical stock above. Thus the refusal to speak or act becomes a means of expressing silence.[44] As noted above, Genesis 22 is a prime example of narrative silence. Narrative descriptions of reprehensible silence appear in Jacob's failure to respond to the sexual violation of his daughter Dinah (Gen 34:5, 25-31) and David's similar lack of response to the victimization of his daughter Tamar (2 Sam 13:21). Narrative silence also figures in passages such as 1 Samuel 10:16 and 2 Kings 18:36.

Nonverbal Expressions

The HB depicts certain nonverbal expressions of silence. These include placing one's hand over one's mouth (Judg 18:19; Job 21:5; 40:4), or shutting one's mouth (Isa 52:15).[45]

Complex Images and Conceptualizations

Much like the ingredients in a recipe or the soundtrack of a film, silence plays an indispensable yet at times complex and ambiguous role in certain depictions and motifs within the HB. For example, Sheol, the realm of the dead, is said to be characterized by silence (Ps 115:17; Isa 47:5). However, at times its inhabitants are depicted as speaking (Isa 14:12-17). Similarly the temple is associated with silence (see esp. 1 Kgs 6:7). But why is this so? Silence is frequently associated with repentance. The penitent sit before God in silence (Lam 2:10; 3:25-26). Yet penitence is frequently depicted as involving wailing and tearing one's clothes (Lam 2:11, 18-19; 3:49-50; Joel 2:12-14). Thus, in many instances, silence forms one strand in a more wide-ranging and complex tapestry.

Our Journey into Silence and Hearing

In the chapters to follow we will journey into the HB's portraits of silence and hearing. Chapters 2–4 form a unit. In chapter 2, we will encounter the deterioration of the divine-human relationship as human unfaithfulness leads to God's silence, reflecting the *alienation* that has now come between the two parties. This is followed in chapter 3 by a study of the silence of *catastrophe* as judgment comes upon the people and land. Happily, however, judgment is not the last word. In chapter 4, the silence of *repentance* opens the door for relational renewal and hope. In chapters 5–7, we turn our attention to several key collocations involving silence. Chapter 5 explores the theme of silence as an expression of the *security* that the people of God have in the Lord as their rock and hiding place, most especially in times of crisis and threat. Chapter 6 examines two seemingly contradictory expressions of silence: the silence of Sheol, or death, frequently associated with severe uncleanness, and the silence of sacredness, especially that silence associated with Israel's most holy places, the inner sancta of the tabernacle and the temple. Chapter 7 wrestles with the motif of God's silence in the Psalms, specifically as it relates to divine unresponsiveness to the cries and sufferings of the Lord's people. Finally, chapter 8 explores the interplay between speech, sound, and silence in three well-known texts, Genesis 22, 1 Kings 19, with its allusion to the famous "still small voice," and the Book of Job, tracing the journey of those whom the Lord has called through doubt and perplexity to greater clarity. A concluding epilogue draws out the implications of our study.

From Then to Now

As intimated above, this monograph is not simply a description of silence in the HB or in the life of the ancient Israelite community. These pages are written out of the conviction that the spirituality reflected in these HB passages has ongoing meaning for the synagogue, for the church, and beyond. It is my sincere desire that readers, whether of Jewish, Christian, or any other commitment, may read them with profit. More specifically, I write out of the conviction that the spiritual dynamics in evidence in these passages are essentially the same as those that are present in the divine-human relationship as represented in the NT.[46] Both bodies of literature depict the same God engaging in an ongoing and interactive relationship with a community of faith (1 Cor 10:1-11; 1 Pet 2:1-10; 3:10). Movement between the testaments, in my view, hinges upon the apprehension of the *relational dynamics* in evidence in the texts under consideration. I have explored this in detail in my *Old Testament Theology*. Thus, the issue is not "is this text still relevant?" but rather, in any given passage, what are the character qualities that the Lord desires to see incarnated by the people of God? What are the values and virtues that are most central to the Lord's purposes, and how ought they be lived out? What kind of world does God desire the community of faith to enter into and to bring into being through obedience to the demands of the passage? What does the passage under consideration have to say about the relationship between the Lord and the people of God, between the members of the community of faith, between God and those outside the visible community of faith, and between God and the creation, and the place of the people of God vis-à-vis the creation?[47] It seems to me that by foregrounding such questions, readers today may quite rapidly see the implications of the HB texts we will be studying.

Conventions and Limitations

In the course of this study I will observe the following conventions. All biblical citations are from the NRSV. Out of a desire to enable non-specialist readers to pronounce and discuss key Hebrew words, I have used a simplified phonetic system of transliteration. I have provided full phonetic equivalents for nouns (thus, Heb *melek*, king). Verbal roots will be generally be given in the third masculine singular of their most commonly appearing stem, and preceded by an asterisk (e.g., **paqad*). The *shureq* of hollow verbs will be represented by *ou* (thus, **qoum*). Consonantal *waw* is transliterated by *w*. *Shin* and *tsade* are rendered as sh and tz, respectively, for ease of pronunciation. However, *chait* is designated by *ḥ*, rather than ch, so as to avoid the normal English pronunciation of ch as in cheese. The letter *tet* is transliterated with a diacritical (thus *ṭ*) to distinguish it from *tav*. I have not distinguished between *sin* and *samek*. The presence or absence of the *dagesh lene* is reflected with reference the letters *beth* and *pe*, but not elsewhere. I have avoided gender-specific pronouns for the God of Israel, but I have retained them in the NRSV and the authors I quote. I will render the Tetragrammaton into English either by "Yahweh" or "the Lord." The body of the book contains material for more general readers, while the footnotes provide more detailed documentation and discussion. All translations of non-English sources (where no English translation exists in print) are my own. My bibliography is not exhaustive; in the interest of brevity I have chosen only selected sources. Finally, I beg the reader's understanding regarding the limitations of this book. Within the space allotted to me, I simply could not enter into a discussion of every biblical text relating to silence, much less all of the associated scholarly material written on the topic. My sincere hope, however, is that these pages will serve as an incentive for many readers to go "further up and further in" in their pursuit of silence.[48]

2
SILENCE AS ALIENATION
When Relationships Break Down

We saw in the introductory chapter that silence may be defined as a deviation from the norm—the absence of words or actions that would generally occur in a given situation. When healthy, the relationship between the Lord and the people of God is characterized by sounds and actions of various sorts—God's speech and deeds of grace and mercy to the community, and human speech to God. However, when the divine-human relationship begins to break down, God's silence in word and deed testifies to the alienation that has now entered into it.[1] While the HB places great emphasis on the mercy and forgiveness of the Lord (Ps 103), it also makes it clear that divine patience has its limits. In this chapter, we will examine several texts where, in the face of persistent human rejection, God's forbearance runs out. The people of God have refused to respond to God's voice, and as a result, the divine-human relationship is damaged. Normal relational exchanges are replaced by estrangement, alienation, and silence. We will examine three instances of such silence: the rise and demise of King Saul (1 Sam 13–31), the famine of the hearing of the word of Yahweh (Amos 8:11-12), and Yahweh's thrice-repeated command to Jeremiah that he not pray for the nation (Jer 7:16-20; 11:14-17; 14:11-16 and 15:1-4).

The Story of King Saul: The Silence of a Prison of One's Own Making

First Samuel 8–31 chronicles the rise and fall of Saul, Israel's first king. It has long been considered to be a superb example of Hebrew narrative. It is important to recognize that biblical Hebrew narratives do not present events in a neutral or objective fashion. Rather, through characterization, shifts in time and place, strategic repetitions, and the focusing or diverting of attention, the narrator leads the reader into a perception of events and persons corresponding to specific theological and ideological purposes.[2] The story of Saul is often seen as part of the Deuteronomistic History (DH), a literary corpus running from Joshua–2 Kings.[3] In it, Israel is judged according to the standards set forth in Deuteronomy. Obedience brings blessing and disobedience engenders misery (see Deut 28). Thus, we may draw upon the broader context of Deuteronomy–2 Kings to provide us with the background for the narrator's assessment of Saul's character and choices.

Silence plays a significant role in the deterioration of the relationship between Yahweh and Saul. The narrator employs various sophisticated literary techniques intended to highlight the instability of Saul's character and the folly of his decisions. We will be made to see and feel the tragedy of this person who began his career with such great promise, but died in misery and failure. Space will not permit us to trace all the contours of our narrator's skillful art. We will limit our attention to one thread that runs through the narrative of Saul's tragic career: his loss of access to the word of Yahweh, and his descent into darkness and silence. Saul's alienation from Yahweh occurs in two stages. The first stage is in evidence in 1 Samuel 13 and 15 and focuses on *divine rejection*. First Saul's dynasty is rejected, then he himself loses the divine blessing necessary for his service as Israel's king. The second stage appears in chapters 16–18. This section narrates Saul's progressive descent into alienation, silence, and ultimately death.

A bit of background information is necessary at this point. First Samuel 1–12 recounts Yahweh's rejection of the priestly house of Eli (2:27-36; 3:11-14), later to be replaced that of by Zadok, David's priest, and the Zadokite line (1 Kgs 2:26-27). First Samuel 1–12 similarly traces the emergence of the monarchy, which replaced the earlier leadership of judges and prophets (1 Sam 7:15-17). The institution of the monarchy, as presented in 1 Samuel 8–12, is depicted as comprising both positive and negative dimensions.[4] The portrait of Saul similarly contains both positive and negative elements.[5] Yet overall, he is portrayed as possessed of a flawed and ignoble character.[6] His is a tragic story.[7] His rule begins well (9:15–11:15). However, Saul's reign is soon threatened by his own inability to demonstrate dependence upon and obedience to Yahweh.

Stage One: Divine Rejection

First Samuel 13:1-14 focuses on Yahweh's rejection of Saul's dynasty. The passage understands Saul's primary failure as an *inability to wait on Yahweh in confident trust.* Saul has rallied an army of 3,000, and his son Jonathan engages the battle by attacking and defeating a Philistine garrison (v. 3). In response, the Philistines muster against Israel with greatly superior forces (v. 5). Fearful for their lives, the Israelites cower in rocks and cisterns, or desert the battlefield altogether (vv. 6-7). Saul meanwhile awaits the arrival of Samuel, who had stated that he would appear in seven days to offer sacrifices invoking Yahweh's favor on the battle. When Samuel fails to appear, and the people begin to slip away, Saul panics and offers the burnt offerings (v. 9). However, with the smoke of the offering still in the air (surely a literary trope to make the reader sense the profound tragedy of Saul's foolish action—if only he had waited just a little longer!),[8] Samuel arrives and confronts Saul, who responds by shifting the blame:

> Samuel said, "What have you done?" Saul replied, "When I saw that the people were slipping away from me, and that you did not come within the days appointed, and that the Philistines were mustering at Michmash, I said, 'Now the Philistines will come down upon me at Gilgal, and I have not entreated the favor of the LORD'; *so I forced myself*, and offered the burnt offering." (1 Sam 13:11-12)

Samuel, however, rejects such an explanation, and sees in Saul's actions a lack of trust in Yahweh, and grounds for the disqualification of his dynasty:

> Samuel said to Saul, "You have done foolishly; you have not kept the commandment of the LORD your God, which he commanded you. The LORD would have established your kingdom over Israel forever." (1 Sam 13:13)

Contrary to some interpretations of this text, Saul's essential fault is not that he is not a priest or Levite (David offers sacrifices, and he is not of priestly stock; cf. 2 Sam 24:24-25; 1 Chr 21:28),[9] or that he has usurped Samuel's role.[10] Neither is it his fault simply that he has not waited for Samuel to perform the necessary rites before the battle (although the performance of such rites may have been viewed as indispensible).[11] At the most profound level, Saul's fault lay in his inability *to see beyond the number of his soldiers, and to trust in Yahweh for the outcome of the battle.*[12]

Our narrator makes this clear by juxtaposing Saul's action here with accounts of other more praiseworthy characters in the broader context of Joshua–2 Kings. At least three other texts stand in strong intertextual relationship to this one. In Judges 7, Gideon begins with a large army of 32,000 troops. However, Yahweh declares, "The troops with you are too many for me to give the Midianites into their hand. Israel would only take the credit away from me, saying, 'My own hand has delivered me'" (v. 2). Eventually the army is whittled down to three hundred men who, with the Lord's help, put the Midianites to flight. The Midianites panic and begin to attack one another, and are defeated (7:22). Saul, by contrast, is terrified by the people's fear and flight, and panics. Where Gideon has succeeded, Saul fails.

A similar intertextual contrast occurs in 1 Samuel 14, where Jonathan attacks a Philistine garrison aided by only one soldier (vv. 6-13). Again God intervenes, resulting in complete disarray among the Philistine troops (vv. 14-15). Jonathan's statement in 14:6 is central to the narrative, and programmatic for our understanding of Saul's failure. Jonathan says: "Come, let us go over to the garrison of these uncircumcised; it may be that the LORD will act for us; for nothing can hinder the LORD from saving *by many or by few*." Whereas Jonathan sees the situation clearly, Saul, by his own words, fails to rise to the challenge.

A third illustration appears in 2 Kings 6:15-17. Here a multitude of Aramean troops has come to lay hold of Elisha. The prophet's servant is terrified, and asks Elisha what to do. The narrative underlines the importance of seeing beyond the challenging circumstances to the power of God:

> [Elisha] replied, "Do not be afraid, for there are more with us than there are with them." Then Elisha prayed: "O LORD, please open his eyes that he may see. So the LORD opened the eyes of the servant, and he saw; the mountain was full of horses and chariots of fire all around Elisha." (2 Kgs 6:16-17)

Saul is like Elisha's servant who cannot see, and dissimilar to Elisha himself, who regards the situation from the perspective of the power of Yahweh. These intertextual parallels stand in stark contrast to Saul's actions in chapter 13.

As a result of his failure in 1 Samuel 13, Saul's *dynasty* is rejected (vv. 13-14). Nevertheless, he remains Israel's king. Yahweh continues to speak to him, in a large measure through the prophet Samuel. He has not yet been engulfed by the silence of God. His downfall, however, continues in chapter 15 when the kingship is taken away from him personally. In 15:1-3, Samuel commands Saul to bring judgment upon the Amalekites, utterly destroying them. However, Saul only partially obeys Yahweh's command. He leaves the best of the livestock and the Amalekite king alive, and retains some of the valuable items (15:8-9).[13] When Yahweh speaks to Samuel and reveals to him what Saul has done, Samuel departs and confronts Saul (15:10-12), who attempts to evade his own responsibility and deflect the blame onto the people (15:17-21).[14] Samuel, however, will have none of it, and declares to Saul that Yahweh has rejected him as king (15:22-29). As the episode concludes, Samuel, in his last earthly encounter with Saul, declares Yahweh's definitive words of rejection:

> "Because you have rejected the word of the LORD, he has also rejected you from being king." Saul said to Samuel, "I have sinned; for I have transgressed the commandment of the LORD and your words, because I feared the people and obeyed their voice. Now therefore, I pray, pardon my sin, and return with me, so that I may worship the LORD." Samuel said to Saul, "I will not return with you; for you have rejected the word of the LORD, and the LORD has rejected you from being king over Israel." (1 Sam 15:23b-28)

In chapter 13, Saul has proceeded to battle without divine blessing, and loses his dynastic heritage. Here he fears the people and suffers the loss of the kingship altogether. In the following section we will discover that although he continues to serve as king, through his own choices he will lose *the one gift most needed for such undertakings—access to the word of Yahweh.*

Stage Two: Divine Silence

From this point onward, Saul descends precipitously into the darkness of God's absence and silence. The spirit of Yahweh departs from him, and an evil spirit from Yahweh torments him (16:14; 18:10).[15] Saul becomes insanely jealous of David (18:8-9), fears him (18:12, 29), makes numerous attempts to kill him (18:11, 17, 21-25; 19:2, 10, 11-15; 20:31), and suspects those around him of conspiracy (22:8, 13). However, as noted, despite being rejected by Yahweh, Saul continues to lead the Israelites in battle (17:1-58). Jonathan still refers to him as king (19:4), as does David (21:2), Ahimelech the priest (22:14), and even the narrator (22:14, 16).

At this point in the narrative, the motif of *Yahweh's silence emerges as the defining contrast between David and Saul.* In Joshua–2 Kings, one critically important role of leaders was the ability to determine the will of Yahweh, especially as it related to whether and when to embark on a battle. Such a role was common in the ANE. Kings and commanders employed various means of divination to seek the will of the gods.[16] In Israel, however, the acceptable means through which such answers could be sought were extremely limited. Such means consisted exclusively of the casting of lots, generally performed by the priests using the Urim and Thummim (likely sticks or stones, mounted on their priestly garment [the ephod]), dreams and their interpretation, and prophetic oracles.[17] In 1 Samuel 28:6, Saul attempts to discern the divine will through "dreams, Urim, and prophets," but to no avail. Earlier in his life, Saul receives several oracles from Yahweh through various means (verbally through Samuel, 9:19–10:8, and through Ahijah, by means of the casting of the Urim and Thummim, 14:41-42).[18] As his rule disintegrates, however, he descends into a place where *Yahweh's will becomes progressively inaccessible to him*. Unlike Eli, who accepts Yahweh's rejection of himself and his line with pious submission (1 Sam 3:18), Saul fights against Yahweh's decree, and loses even that which remained to him.[19]

The first intimation of Yahweh's silence toward Saul appears in 1 Samuel 21–22. In chapter 21, having fled from Saul's murderous intentions, David descends to Nob and encounters Ahimelech the priest. Unwilling to reveal the true reason for his presence, he declares to Ahimelech that he is on a special mission from Saul (v. 2). He furthermore states that he and his men require food, and that having left in haste, he has forgotten his sword (v. 3). Ahimelech then provides David with sacred bread and the sword of Goliath. Nothing, however, is said regarding Ahimelech inquiring of Yahweh on David's behalf. A certain Doeg, one of Saul's officers, is present, having been "detained before Yahweh" (21:7) at Nob.[20] In 22:9-11, Doeg reveals David's whereabouts to Saul, and narrates the details of his visit to Ahimelech, adding one critical element: "I saw the son of Jesse coming to Nob, to Ahimelech son of Ahitub; *he inquired of the LORD for him*, gave him provisions, and gave him the sword of Goliath the Philistine." Saul is livid, calls Ahimelech and his family together and retorts, "Why have you conspired against me, you and the son of Jesse, by giving him bread and a sword, *and by inquiring of God for him*, so that he has risen against me, to lie in wait, as he is doing today?" (v. 13).

The theme of Ahimelech inquiring of God for David is the key element in this dialogue. It is difficult to know whether or not Ahimelech had indeed inquired of the Lord for David. No mention is made of any such act in 1 Samuel 21. Ahimelech's response to Saul in 22:14-15 is ambiguous. The Hebrew reads, literally, "Have I begun today to seek God in his behalf?" The NRSV's translation ("Is today the first time that I have inquired of God for him? By no means!") communicates the same ambiguity. The Hebrew could mean, "Is today the first time that I have inquired of God for him? Certainly not! (I never did before and I did not do so today)."[21] Or it could be taken to affirm that Ahimelech has indeed done so for David many times in the past (likely in the context of David's role as Saul's servant), so there would have been no reason not to do so today.[22] This ambiguity leaves open numerous questions. Was Ahimelech denying having inquired of Yahweh or not? If not, why did Ahimelech not seek to refute the implications of Saul's accusation? Was it because even though he had done no wrong, he believed it was futile to argue? Or was his purpose to affirm his own innocence? The critical issue here is that in his response, Ahimelech leaves aside the matter of the bread and the spear, seizing only on the question of oracular inquiry. The reason for this is likely because this *presages the trajectory of the events soon to unfold*, where Yahweh will *no longer speak to Saul through any means*. Moreover, the narrator employs the growing silence of God here to play into Saul's deepening alienation from Yahweh, and concomitant jealousy, paranoia, mental disorientation, and disintegration.[23]

God had refused to answer Saul's inquiry once before. In 1 Samuel 14:36-37, Saul desired to join battle with the Philistines; however, the attending priest pressed Saul to first seek the will of Yahweh. Unexpectedly, Yahweh would not answer Saul. Yahweh's silence in that instance was not due to Saul's guilt, but was tied to Jonathan's inadvertent violation of an oath Saul had imposed on the people, an oath characterized by the narrator as rash and troublesome (vv. 24, 29).[24] Moreover, had the people not intervened, Saul's commitment to fulfill this ill-considered oath would have led to the execution of his son Jonathan, who had just won a great victory over the Philistines. The narrator here clearly views the oath as foolish and counterproductive. Yahweh's silence in response to Jonathan's offense is thus not likely meant to vindicate Saul's willingness to put his own son to death. Rather, the text stands *with* Jonathan and the people who ransomed him, and *against* Saul, who would do *anything* to bring back the word of Yahweh, enabling him to have success in battle. As such, Saul is much like Jephthah in Judges 11:29-40, and Mesha in 2 Kings 3:26-27, who both viewed the sacrifice of their children as a means of gaining military victory. Yahweh's silence thus enables the reader to perceive *Saul's insecurity and all-encompassing desire for success* (why put the troops under an oath if Yahweh was with them?), his *lack of wisdom* (troops on the battlefield need food), and, supremely, his inability to recognize that the *silence of Yahweh was ultimately his own fault*. He ought then to have pardoned Jonathan for his inadvertence and shown *his own willingness to take upon himself whatever consequences Yahweh might send for its violation* (as David did in 2 Sam 24:15-17).

After Ahimelech's response, Saul's action is swift and terrifying. He orders Ahimelech and the priests at Nob to be put to death (1 Sam 22:16-19). His own troops will not comply with his order, but Doeg is willing to do so, and kills not only the priests, but all the inhabitants of the village. Most importantly, Saul's action here effectively cuts him off from oracular access to Yahweh via the priestly ephod. This is highlighted in verse 18b: "on that day [Saul] killed eighty-five who wore the linen ephod." Clearly the narrator, via the words of Doeg and the response of Ahimelech, is setting Saul's point of greatest humiliation in stark relief: Yahweh is with David, and answers him, whereas Saul must lead the nation without the one thing most essential for his task: access to the counsel of Yahweh.

David's experience, meanwhile, is altogether the opposite. The Lord is with him in his battles, and he is beloved by all Israel and Judah (1 Sam 18:14-16). Both of Saul's children, Jonathan and Michal, are explicitly said to love him (18:1, 28). In 22:5, the prophet Gad warns him to flee from Saul. Most importantly, Yahweh allows himself to be inquired of by David, and responds to him. Despite Saul's attempt to destroy all the priests at Nob, Abiathar, Ahimelech's son, manages to escape and flee to David (22:20). He brings with him the priestly ephod used to discern the will of Yahweh (23:9). In 23:1-4, David inquires of Yahweh and is answered. This is repeated in 23:9-12. Thus, in contrast to David's frequent access to Yahweh, Saul, by wiping out the priests of Nob, effectively deprives himself of Yahweh's counsel.[25] He consequently descends even more deeply into a silent prison of his own making.

Saul will descend further still. Saul's experience of the silence of God reaches its nadir in 1 Kings 28.[26] David flees from Saul and hides in the wilderness (chs. 23–27). Saul continues to lead the Israelite army in the battle against the Philistines (28:1, 4-5). As the Philistine army gathers against him, Saul is terrified (28:5). He inquires of Yahweh, but to no avail.[27] The narrator explains, "When Saul inquired of the LORD, the LORD did not answer him, not by dreams, or by Urim, or by prophets" (28:6). Saul is distraught. Samuel had died (28:3), so it was not possible to ask him directly for counsel. He straightaway commands his servants to seek out a medium through whom he may inquire.[28]

The text moves very rapidly from Yahweh's silence in verse 6 to Saul's search for a medium in verse 7a. There are no entreaties, is no further seeking of divine counsel, and no prayers of earnest repentance. Saul is told that there is such a woman at Endor (v. 7b) and he immediately seeks her out. Three things are noteworthy here. First, the narrator does not reveal to the reader precisely what Saul wishes the medium to do for him. Only later do we learn that he desires to summon Samuel and seek his counsel. Second, Saul does not speak of inquiring "of God" or "of the Lord."[29] He simply says, "Seek out for me a woman who is a medium, so that I may go to her and *inquire of her*" (v. 7). The reader is left wondering to which forces, powers, or deities he wishes to make appeal.[30] Third, and most importantly, even before the Philistine threat is raised in verse 3, the narrator supplies via a subtle bit of circumstantial detail a fact that will play a pivotal role in the narrative that follows.[31] We are told that Saul had previously expelled all the mediums and wizards from the land.[32] This prepares the reader for the perilous depths to which Saul will go in his quest for counsel. This text echoes Saul's massacre of the priests of Nob in chapter 22. Having killed them, he has cut himself off from access to divine revelation. The same predicament is depicted here—in much darker hues.

Saul's quest for the word of Yahweh now takes on an even greater recklessness and desperation. Saul changes his clothes and dons a disguise. It is difficult to know whether the change of clothing constitutes the disguise, or involves other additional means. Accompanied by two men, Saul goes to Endor to seek the woman *by night*.[33] It is highly significant that everything that transpires between Saul's arrival at the woman's home and his departure takes place in darkness.[34] Essentially, the darkness that pervades the scene creates a space where the woman's house becomes, so to speak, a doorway into Sheol, the realm of the dead. Having received a promise from Saul, whom she does not yet recognize, sworn in the name of Yahweh, that she will not be put to death (vv. 9-10), the woman agrees to invoke Samuel. Samuel is said to come up "out of the ground" when called up by the medium. The verbal form used here creates the image of Samuel as a spirit or apparition emanating from Sheol below, and hovering like a mist in the house. The darkness is vitally important to the course of events narrated here. It both delays the revelation of Saul's identity to the woman (vv. 8-10), and allows her to describe Samuel only in the most general of terms (vv. 13-14). When Saul sees Samuel, he bows to the ground in respect. Samuel is irritated and demands to know why Saul has disturbed him (v. 15a). Saul recounts the dire straits in which he finds himself: "I am in great distress, for the Philistines are warring against me, and God has turned away from me and answers me no more, either by prophets or by dreams; so I have summoned you to tell me what I should do" (v. 15b). However, Samuel will not break Yahweh's silence by revealing a fresh word from God. He will only reiterate the oracle of judgment previously delivered in 15:17-29, adding to it that Saul, his sons, and the armies of Israel will die within a day (vv. 17-19).

Central to the scene is Samuel's statement that God will no longer speak to Saul because Yahweh has now *become* Saul's enemy (v. 16).[35] In point of fact, contrary to presenting Yahweh as *predisposed* to reject Saul,[36] the narrator uses various rhetorical strategies to demonstrate that Saul's choices and character were flawed.[37] He is too eager to please the people, and too fearful when they begin to flee. He reverses his earlier endeavors to rid the land of mediums (cf. Lev 20:27; 1 Chr 10:13), and, in his desperation, seeks one out to gain access to Yahweh's counsel. Above all he fails to prioritize obedience to Yahweh. Thus, his true enemy is most fundamentally *his own character*.[38] We note as well the similarity between Yahweh and Samuel's experience with reference to Saul. Both begin with high hopes and assure him of strong support (1 Sam 9:5-17; 10:3-9). Both are saddened by his failures (1 Sam 13:13-14; 15:10-11). Both refuse to reconsider their rejection of him (1 Sam 15:27-31).[39]

Saul's career has proved to be one long descent into rejection and silence. He brings divine rejection upon himself and his descendants (13:13-14; 15:26). Subsequently, in chapter 28, the "final act" of the drama, Saul becomes completely engulfed by the silence of Yahweh. As Exum states, "Moreover, to the end, he seeks Yhwh's counsel (ch. 28). But, as we have seen, *he meets ultimately with divine silence and a crushing reiteration of rejection from the ghost of Samuel.*"[40] In the midst of his quest he experiences disorientation and confusion. Exum and Whedbee appropriately comment on "the number of references to Saul's anguished state of mind [in ch. 28]: he is afraid (v. 5), his heart trembles greatly (v. 5), he is in great distress (v. 15), filled with fear (v. 20), there is no strength in him (v. 20), he is terrified (v. 21). After this journey into the abyss of divine abandonment, Saul's death can only be seen as anticlimactic."[41]

In summary, we see that silence plays a defining role in the Saul narrative. His own rejection of Yahweh's decrees leads to Yahweh's rejection of his dynasty and rule in 1 Samuel 13 and 15. Through his own folly, Saul suffers the loss of his access to divine counsel. The silence of Yahweh then drives him mad. It moves him to act in a way that is contrary to his earlier convictions. At the outset of his reign, he is Yahweh's chosen instrument for the deliverance of Israel (1 Sam 10:1). However, soon Yahweh's spirit is taken away from him (1 Sam 16:14). We are told flatly that Yahweh refuses to answer him (1 Sam 28:6, 15). Even calling up Samuel from the dead is futile. The only word he receives is the announcement of his imminent demise, and that of his sons (1 Sam 28:19). The pattern thus emerges: faithlessness and disobedience leading to Yahweh's silence, then to madness and death. Saul ends up, as it were, confined to silence in a prison of his own making.

The Book of Amos

The prophet Amos is well known for his biting critique of the social situation in the NK in the eighth century BCE.[42] He relentlessly castigates the wealthy upper classes for their heartlessness toward the poor. He accuses them of going so far as to "sell the righteous for silver, and the needy for a pair of sandals, and trample the head of the poor into the dust of the earth, and push the afflicted out of the way" (2:6b-7).[43] The wealthy meanwhile lived in luxury. They owned summer and winter homes (3:15). They lay on beds of ivory, enjoyed fine food and drink, and serenaded each other with lovely songs (6:4-6). Yet they were completely unconcerned about the "ruin of Joseph"—that is, the destruction of the poor in society (6:6b). All of this luxury was sustained by bribery, so that for the needy there was no way out of crushing poverty (5:7; 6:12). Most offensive to God was the fact that all the while religious activity abounded. Songs and sacrifice filled the air (5:21-24; 8:10). Those who perpetrated such cruel injustice also scrupulously observed the Sabbath (8:4-6). Amos, as God's prophet, called his people to turn back from their corrupt ways before it was too late.

The ideas of sound, silence and judgment play a pivotal role in Amos. The concept of a text's "soundscape" is a highly significant one for our interpretation of this passage, and one that we will employ in our study of several other passages in the HB. The term "soundscape" refers to the sounds depicted within in a text (that is, the sounds that are described in the text), as well as to those that emerge as the text is read (e.g. onomatopoeia, assonance, etc.).[44] Here the oppressors *serenaded* one another upon their beds of ivory (6:5). The *sound* of the nation's worship and festivals were offensive to God (5:21-24; cf. Isa 1:12-15). Instead of meaningless *noise* Yahweh called for righteous dealings. Amos declares: "Take away from me the *noise* of your songs; I will not *listen* to the melody of your harps. But let justice roll down like waters, and righteousness like an everflowing stream" (Amos 5:23-24). Amos consistently calls his people to "*hear* the word of Yahweh" (3:1; 4:1; 5:1; 8:4). Amos warns that if Yahweh's words go unheeded, the nation would experience massive death, destruction, and exile (2:14-15; 4:2-3, 12; 5:1-5, 16-20; 6:7-11; 7:8-9; 8:2-3, 9-14; 9:1-4).

Amos employs the terminology of silence in relationship to this overall message in three passages. One relates to the time *just before* doom falls upon Israel (8:11-12), the next *just as* it is falling (8:3), and the last *just after* it has occurred (6:9-10). In the first of these references, *divine* silence is at issue. The latter two concern *human* silence. In this chapter, I will examine the first of these three references, then in the following chapter the latter two.

Amos 8:11-12 is one of the best-known passages in the book. It is immediately preceded in verses 8-9 by the description of a day of complete disaster. The sun will go down at noon and the sky will be darkened. In yet another reference to sound, *wailing* will replace joy and festivity. Then, the text evokes an even greater disaster:

> The time is surely coming, says the Lord GOD, when I will send a famine on the land; not a famine of bread, or a thirst for water, but of hearing the words of the LORD. They shall wander from sea to sea, and from north to east; they shall run to and fro, seeking the word of the LORD, but they shall not find it. (Amos 8:11-12)

Famines were regular occurrences in ancient Israel. Agriculture was largely dependent upon rainfall and snowmelt. The idea of Yahweh "sending" a famine upon the land was a standard component of the divine judgments (often called "curses" but better labeled "maledictions") sent upon Israel when it strayed from the ways of the Lord.[45] Here, however, we find reference to a different kind of famine—one in which people are deprived of the "words" (v. 11) or "word" (v. 12) of Yahweh.[46] What does this mean? Likely the primary reference is to oracles given by the Lord to a prophet or seer to guide the people in a variety of circumstances. For example, in 1 Samuel 9, when Saul's family's donkeys go missing, his servant advises him to seek the counsel of the prophet Samuel in order to locate them (1 Sam 9:5-6). On a much larger scale, Israel's prophets served as the messengers of Yahweh, bringing words of woe or weal to the nation in various circumstances, and guiding the people as they sought to understand Yahweh's intentions for them. Both of these kinds of prophetic interventions may be termed "oracles." However, it could not be taken for granted that such oracles would be available at any given moment. First Samuel 3:1 describes such a situation: "The word of the LORD was rare in those days; visions were not widespread." Thus, the reference in Amos 8:11-12 is specifically to the *availability* of the prophetic word, which responded to both the individual and the wider community at various points of need, providing rebuke, counsel, or comfort. In this way, the prophetic word both met the community's foundational need to *know* God's will in an existential way, and also served as a *living testimony* to the relationship between Yahweh and Israel. However, the availability of Yahweh's word was not to be taken for granted. As we saw in the case of Saul in the previous section, if spurned, Yahweh's word could be held back temporarily or even completely withdrawn, indicating the termination of the relationship.[47]

Similar to Saul's experience in 1 Samuel 28, in Amos 8:11-12 loss of access to God's counsel is terrifying. Those deprived of it go staggering in search of it. While the verb used here sometimes indicates staggering due to drunkenness (Ps 107:27; Isa 24:20; 29:9), its imagery here more likely denotes trembling in abject terror (Exod 20:18; Isa 6:4; 7:2; 19:1), the panic of being deprived of that which is essential for life, and the consequent collapsing in weakness as one desperately seeks it (Gen 4:12, 14; Ps 109:10; Amos 4:8). Amos 8:11 contrasts this kind of famine with the experience of hunger and thirst, and sees it as far more devastating. The depth of the nation's despair is demonstrated by the extent it is willing to go in its search for the word of Yahweh. People will "wander from sea to sea, and from north to east; they shall run to and fro, seeking the word of the LORD." Biblical scholars debate the precise meaning of the geographical referents of the phrases "sea to sea" and "north to east."[48] They similarly question why there is no mention of the south.[49] However these matters are decided, the critical element is the qualification of their activity as "running to and fro." The NRSV's translation could give readers the impression of a confused, haphazard or erratic search (indeed, many commentators take it this way), but this is not likely the intended sense here.[50] The particular form of the verb generally implies an *extensive and exhaustive* movement. It describes the eyes of Yahweh that search throughout the earth (Zech 4:10; 2 Chr 16:9), or Yahweh's invitation to Jeremiah to look in every last corner of Jerusalem to see if anyone can be found who acts righteously (Jer 5:1).[51] The geographical dimensions in the first part of the verse, when taken together with the second, portray a people who have sought out Yahweh's word in every possible place to which they had access, and who have come to the end of their own world and their wits in so doing.[52] Thus, the last words of the verse sound the nation's death knell and seal its doom. People wander about "seeking the word of Yahweh . . . *but they will not find it*" (8:12b). Having urged his people to obey (lit. "hear") Yahweh's voice on so many prior occasions in the book (Amos 3:1; 4:1; 5:1; 7:16; 8:4), Amos now declares that the word of Yahweh will soon be withdrawn and God will speak no more.

A similar motif occurs in other prophetic passages. Hosea declares, "Israel's pride testifies against him; Ephraim stumbles in his guilt; Judah also stumbles with them. With their flocks and herds they shall go to seek the LORD, but they will not find him; *he has withdrawn from them*" (Hos 5:5-6).[53] Micah pronounces a similar condemnation on Israel's false prophets:

> Thus says the LORD concerning the prophets who lead my people astray, who cry "Peace" when they have something to eat, but declare war against those who put nothing into their mouths. Therefore it shall be night to you, without vision, and darkness to you, without revelation. The sun shall go down upon the prophets, and the day shall be black over them;

> the seers shall be disgraced, and the diviners put to shame; they shall all cover their lips, *for there is no answer from God.* (Mic 3:5-7)

At this point it is essential to set this oracle in the context of Amos' general portrait of Yahweh's judgment upon the NK. Throughout Amos 1–5, one encounters numerous calls for repentance and change. Yahweh implores Israel to return (4:6, 8-11), seek the Lord (5:4-6, 14), and fill the land with justice and righteousness (5:24). Yet beyond 5:24 there appears to be no explicit call to return, or suggestion that judgment may be averted. Instead, one finds numerous "oracles of doom"—that is, announcements of judgment and descriptions of it. Thus, it would seem that Amos' intercession and Yahweh's restraint (described in the visions of 7:1-6) were intended to give the people more time to repent (esp. 4:6-12). The famine of 8:11-12 would therefore describe a time between the closure of that window of opportunity, and the imposition of final judgment—*a time when people would desperately seek for a word from one of Yahweh's true prophets, perhaps indicating that it was not too late, and that doom could potentially be avoided.*[54] However, despite its extensive search, the community would find no prophet of Yahweh who could provide hope or instruction. It faced nothing but divine absence and silence. Thus, the NK's actions here parallel Saul's desperate search in 1 Samuel 28.[55]

In sum, Amos 8:11-12 speaks of the hearing of Yahweh's word as a privilege. Failure to heed it may lead to a silence signifying its loss. Similarly, it depicts the hearing of the word of Yahweh as *testimony to a relationship*, and conversely, Yahweh's silence as evidence of the perturbation or even loss of that relationship. Finally, this passage also implies that *access to Yahweh's word is one of the great benefits of the divine-human relationship*. To be deprived of it is to dwell in an intolerable, suffocating silence.

The Book of Jeremiah: Do Not Pray for This People

In the book of Jeremiah, the motif of silence echoes its role in 1 Samuel and Amos. In all three texts it signifies relational breakdown and alienation. However, in Jeremiah this idea is expressed somewhat differently. Instead of Yahweh *refusing to speak* out of exasperation over the people's rebelliousness, here Yahweh *refuses to hear* prayers of intercession made by Jeremiah on behalf of wayward Judah. Indeed, on three occasions Yahweh demands that Jeremiah not intercede for the nation (7:16; 11:14; 14:11-16 and 15:1-4). Three preliminary comments are necessary before we begin our examination of these passages. First, prophets not only delivered messages of judgment to their people on behalf of Yahweh, but in certain contexts also interceded for them.[56] Amos' intercession for the NK in Amos 7:1-6, and that of Abraham on behalf of Sodom and Gomorrah in Genesis 18:16-33, function in this way (cf. also Gen 20:7). The same may be said of Moses, who intercedes for the people at several critical junctures in order that disaster might be averted (Exod 32:11-14; Num 11:2; 14:13-20; cf. also Ezek 13:5; 22:30). Second, this intermediary role assumes that the prophets are God's intimate associates who can seek the Lord's favor on behalf of those who do not deserve it *on the basis of their privileged relationship with God.* As such, prophetic intercession implies an enhanced ability to influence Yahweh since it can appeal to the *affection and loyalty of God.* This is underscored by the repeated phrase, "my servants the prophets."[57] It is similarly manifested in Yahweh's reluctance to "hide from Abraham what I am about to do" (Gen 18:17). Thus, Yahweh's command to Jeremiah not to pray must be seen in light of this relational bond.[58] Third, it is not immediately apparent whether the command to Jeremiah is to be understood as prohibiting public prayer (in the context of a communal assembly) or private prayer (crying out to Yahweh, as Samuel does on behalf of Saul in 1 Sam 15:11).[59] Nor is it entirely possible to identify the specific historical situations into which these prohibitions were spoken.[60] Prophets at times led the nation in crying out to the Lord in the context of public assemblies, especially in times of national crisis (see, e.g., Joel 1:13-14, 19-20; 2:12-17). They also delivered oracles containing Yahweh's response to their cries (Joel 2:19-29). However, the precise context and scope of Yahweh's prohibitions to Jeremiah (he does later seek the will of Yahweh for the people, 42:1-22) remain unclear. What is beyond dispute, however, is that Yahweh's words to Jeremiah *effectively silence him as it relates to his intercessory role* in the years leading up to the Babylonian assaults on Jerusalem. Let us turn to examine these texts in greater detail, seeking to understand Yahweh's silence as it appears within them.

Jeremiah 7:16-20

Jeremiah has received Yahweh's command to stand at the entrance to the temple and preach his famous "Temple Sermon" (vv. 1-15). Speaking for Yahweh, Jeremiah denounces the community's erroneous belief that punishment for violations of the Sinai covenant will never overtake them as long as the temple stands in their midst (esp. vv. 4, 10). Likely the people's conviction, based in part upon the declarations of the prophets who opposed Jeremiah (14:13-15), was rooted in concepts of the "inviolability of Zion," expressed in texts such as Psalms 46 and 48, Micah 4:1-5, and Isaiah 2:1-4. But these "false prophets" had taken such ideas and pressed them far beyond their original intent and purpose. These texts were meant to reassure a faithful people, cowering in the shadow of threats and danger. They were not intended to embolden a defiant people and enable them to continue in their disobedience. In verse 16 a major turning point is reached. Yahweh turns from addressing the people and now addresses Jeremiah personally. Yahweh commands him not to intercede for the people, using several closely related terms in succession. Jeremiah is not to "pray" (*ʾal-titpallel* from the root **pillel*) for the people, nor is he to "raise a cry (*rinna*) or a prayer (*tepilla*)" for them. There is likely little appreciable difference between these terms, except perhaps that the latter two appear to express a greater degree of intensity and volume.[61] Yahweh does not wish to hear loud crying or wailing. Jeremiah is similarly commanded not to "intercede with me" (*al-tiphgaʿ* from the root **pagaʿ*). Here we move from the sound Jeremiah might make in the course of his petition to matters of *emotional intensity and the persuasive abilities of Jeremiah as intercessor*, and their *consequent effect* on Yahweh. The root **pagaʿ* occurs elsewhere in contexts where one person pleads with another in the context of an existing relationship, bringing strong emotional dynamics to bear (Gen 23:8; Jer 27:18; 26:25). Perhaps the most poignant illustration of this occurs when Naomi encourages Ruth to leave her and return to Moab. Ruth, however, steadfastly refuses, and in the well-known passage declares to her mother-in-law:

> Do not *press me* (**pagaʿ*) to leave you or to turn back from following you! Where you go, I will go; Where you lodge, I will lodge; your people shall be my people, and your God my God. Where you die, I will die—there will I be buried. May the LORD do thus and so to me, and more as well, if even death parts me from you! (Ruth 1:16-17)

Here Yahweh demands that Jeremiah neither bring forward the sounds of pleading and intercession, nor seek to engage Yahweh on *an emotional level* to secure reprieve for the community. The reason for this refusal to hear intercession is given in verses 17-18. The community is engaging in wholesale infidelity to Yahweh. Men, women, and children are involved in the worship of the Queen of Heaven and other gods (v. 18b).[62] As a result, Yahweh is "provoked to anger." This is a significant phrase, frequently used in instances of covenant infidelity (Deut 4:25; 9:18; 32:16; Judg 2:12). It especially denotes the pain of betrayal (2 Kgs 22:17; 2 Chr 34:25; Ps 78:58; Jer 8:19; Ezek 16:26). As such, Yahweh will not endure emotional pleas on the people's behalf. Things have simply gone too far. Unlike the situation in Exodus 32:10 where Yahweh tells Moses not to interfere with God's plans to destroy the nation, but Moses intercedes and is heard, here no amount of prayer will be efficacious.[63]

Jeremiah 11:15-17

In Jeremiah 11:1-17, Yahweh continues to excoriate the people for their violations of the Sinai covenant (esp. v. 10). The reference to the people crying to Yahweh (11:11, 14) may imply a public setting. However, their cries will be in vain since disaster has already been decreed (v. 12). Paralleling the shift in address we saw in 7:16, in 11:14 Yahweh turns to Jeremiah and reiterates the earlier command that Jeremiah not intercede for the people. Several features here call for attention. First, the more emotionally loaded term **pagaʿ*, present in 7:16, has been omitted here. Jeremiah is simply commanded not to "pray . . . or lift up a cry, or prayer." The reason for the omission is unclear. It might be that the term is to be implied despite its omission. However, the context in 11:1-17 is significantly different from that of 7:1-20 in two ways. First, in Jeremiah 11 there is no mention of possible reprieve should Israel repent, as there was in 7:5-7. Second, in Jeremiah 11 the reader discovers the existence of a conspiracy against Jeremiah. The conspirators seek to destroy him, and liken him to a *tree* that they will cut down and be rid of (11:19b). However, Yahweh responds by promising certain judgment. In the oracle immediately following Jeremiah's discovery of the conspiracy, Yahweh's judgment is announced via the imagery of devastating fire burning up the *branches* of an olive tree (11:16-17). As a result, the nation will be left without a remnant (11:22-23). Thus, the atmosphere in Jeremiah 11 has degenerated from that of Jeremiah 7. There is no possibility that tragedy might be averted if Israel amends its ways. What is more, the community's obduracy has increased to the extent that it wishes *to silence Yahweh's own messenger*. It may be suggested, therefore, that Yahweh does not need to prohibit Jeremiah from prayer using emotionally charged pleas because, on the one hand, it is clear that Jeremiah would not be so inclined, nor would Yahweh be likely to be moved by them, on the other hand.

As was the case in Jeremiah 7, we see here references to the nation's infidelity to Yahweh's covenant (11:1-8) and the worship of other gods (11:9-13). And just as in Jeremiah 7 the people erroneously viewed the temple as some kind of talisman, guaranteeing their protection (7:4, 10), so here Yahweh asserts that crying out in prayer (11:11), presenting choice sacrifices in the temple (11:14), or even sacrifice to Baal will not bring deliverance (11:13, 17).[64] Once again, Yahweh asserts that Jeremiah must not pray for the people in their situation. Their rebellion has gone too far.

Jeremiah 14:11-16 and 15:1-4

These passages form a part of a longer, complex section running from 14:1–15:9, and oscillating between the people's prayers for forgiveness (14:7-9, 19-22) and Yahweh's rejection of their words (14:10-11; 15:1). It also contains an additional reminder to Jeremiah that he is not to intercede for the welfare of the nation (14:11). Doom and destruction are inevitable (14:1-6; 15:1-9). Several elements of this section call for comment. First, in this third prohibition of prayer, the distance between the people and their God is even greater than in the previous two. As the book progresses, the formulations forbidding prayer become noticeably shorter: "As for you, do not pray for this people, do not raise a cry or prayer on their behalf, and do not intercede with me" (7:16); "As for you, do not pray for this people, or lift up a cry or prayer on their behalf" (11:14); "Do not pray for the welfare of this people" (14:11). This reflects a sense of the *growing distance and coldness* between Yahweh and the people. The futility of intercession is underscored in 15:1 where Moses and Samuel, two of the nation's greatest intercessors, are evoked as examples—even *their* prayers would have no effect on Yahweh.

Second, the inclusion of the penitential prayers of the people in 14:7-10 and 19-22 reinforces and echoes the instructions to Jeremiah not to pray. At first glance, these prayers seem to be in line with other scriptural prayers of lament, repentance, and hope. Like many of the psalms of lament and penitence they express acknowledgement of "our sins (*'avonenu*), apostasies (*meshuvotenu*), and wickedness (*rish'enu*)" (vv. 7, 20), express confidence in Yahweh alone as savior (14:8; 15:22), hope in Yahweh's covenantal relationship (14:9b; 21b), and appeal to the honor of Yahweh's name (14:21). Surprisingly, these prayers are rejected.[65] In response to the people's words Yahweh declares:

> Thus says the LORD concerning this people: "Truly they have loved to wander, they have not restrained their feet; therefore the LORD does not accept them, now he will remember their iniquity, and punish their sins. Although they fast, I do not hear their cry, and although they offer burnt offering and grain offering, I do not accept them; but by the sword, by famine, and by pestilence I consume them." (Jer 14:10, 12)

Why were these prayers rejected, given that their content was so similar to other prayers recorded in Scripture? Scholars generally propose three lines of explanation. (1) The people were insincere in their words (14:10).[66] A very similar expression of repentance followed by divine rejection occurs in Hosea 6:1-4, where it is clear that despite their words of contrition, there is no real loyalty to Yahweh. (2) Although the people's words were sincere and heartfelt, it was simply too late for them to reverse the judgment that had been decreed.[67] (3) Although they reflected some movement toward true repentance, the people's words were still too filled with complaint and self-interest to avert the coming destruction.[68] My personal preference is for the first explanation, although the latter two cannot be excluded.

Third, the futility of Jeremiah's praying for the people is highlighted by the fact that *even if the people themselves* repented and prayed, it would be to no avail. In the HB, intercessors generally represented those who due to weakness, sickness, ignorance, or moral failure did not have the strength or standing to represent themselves. Confessions of sin and prayers of penitence, however, could be offered for them in hope that Yahweh might forgive. Jeremiah 14:12 thus represents an *a fortiori* argument: it is futile for you, Jeremiah, to intercede for the people, for even if *they themselves* repented and sought forgiveness, I would not hear them.

Thus, in Jeremiah, the silence of divine abandonment is expressed as Yahweh's *refusal to hear* intercessory prayer. One might nevertheless question why Yahweh commands Jeremiah not to pray, rather than simply not answering his prayer. Several considerations help answer this question. First, by reporting Yahweh's request that Jeremiah not pray, the text brings the interplay of forces at work in the situation down to an existential plane. At times, Yahweh's decisions are not presented as absolute and immutable, but rather as involving *process* and *alternative possibilities*. We have noted that in other instances Yahweh's decisions can be contested and are not necessarily final (Exod 32:10; Jer 18:1-11). However, Yahweh's repeated instructions to Jeremiah here indicate that *in this situation* no further discussion of the matter is possible. Moreover, Yahweh's interdiction of prayer in 7:16, 11:14, and 14:11 uses a Hebrew construction that implies that the command is to be carried out in a specific context.[69] Indeed, as noted above, the people seek Jeremiah's prayers and counsel in Jeremiah 42:1-17, Jeremiah prays, and Yahweh answers. Here the text stresses that in this moment, Yahweh has resolved not to hear the people's prayer, and no amount of pleading by the prophet will alter that decision. Second, Yahweh's refusal *personalizes* the dynamics involved in the silence that has settled in the divine-human relationship. As noted above, intercessory prayer is frequently made on the basis of the prophet's status before Yahweh, and the latter's esteem and affection for the intercessor (Gen 18:17).[70] At times Yahweh's own affections and feeling for Israel may sway divine decisions toward more merciful treatment (Hos 11:8-9). But at this moment, no matter who the intercessor might be (cf. Jer 15:1-2), and no matter what feelings of compassion Yahweh might harbor for the people, with sorrow and reluctance the Lord withdraws from them and will hear no more prayers on their behalf. Third, the forbidding of prayer means that Yahweh's refusal to relent *cannot be put down to any failure on Jeremiah's part*. It is not that Jeremiah did not pray hard or long enough.[71] It is simply that, as noted above, the point had been passed where *anyone's* prayers would have been efficacious.

Summary

In this chapter we have seen how, as the divine-human relationship deteriorates, silence emerges as a manifestation of the alienation that now exists between the two parties. In contrast to the more regular contexts in which the community offers prayer, praise, and confession, and the Lord responds in counsel, grace, forgiveness, and salvation, now a silent chill fills the air. Human obstinacy has produced a self-inflicted silence. When it is most needed, Yahweh's voice is no longer accessible. This is precisely the situation that is bemoaned in a lament over the destruction of Judah at the hands of the Babylonians: "guidance is no more, and her prophets obtain no vision from the LORD" (Lam 2:9b).

In chapter 3, we will turn to the silence that occurs when the relational alienation we have traced in this chapter has reached its fullest extent, and Yahweh's judgment is enacted. Yet, as we will see in chapter 4, this need not be the end. If the people of God wait on God in silence and repentance, a future and a hope may yet be theirs.

3
SILENCE AS CATASTROPHE

When Everything Falls Apart

In the previous chapter, we studied several texts in which silence served as evidence of a deteriorating divine-human relationship. In this chapter, we will see that, should this situation continue, catastrophe ultimately ensues. And just as silence was closely identified with alienation, so too is it associated with catastrophe—specifically the catastrophic judgment of God.

Our discussion will be divided into three sections. In the first, we will observe the silence that is called for *at the moment of God's judgment*. Then, in the second, we will examine the motif of silence that attends *the expressions of grief and mourning* of those who are touched by it. Finally, we will investigate the role of silence in descriptions of *the aftermath of God's judgment*.

Silence and the Enactment of Divine Judgment: Zephaniah 1:7, Habakkuk 2:20, and Zechariah 2:13

Preliminary Considerations

Three important texts call for silence before Yahweh. In each instance the call to silence appears in connection both with Yahweh's judgment of evil and oppression, and the deliverance of the people of God:[1]

> Be silent before the Lord God! For the day of the Lord is at hand; the Lord has prepared a sacrifice, he has consecrated his guests. (Zeph 1:7)

> But the Lord is in his holy temple; let all the earth keep silence before him! (Hab 2:20)

> Be silent, all people, before the LORD; for he has roused himself from his holy dwelling. (Zech 2:13)

The first step toward understanding these texts is to recognize that these calls to silence likely reflect quasi-fixed expressions frequently used in specific life situations in ancient Israel. Biblical scholars generally designate such expressions as *forms*. These forms are often incorporated into prophetic speech and used as rhetorical devices to drive the prophet's words home. Many scholars speculate that the "call to silence" form (Ger. *Aufruf zu Stille*) may have originated in a liturgical setting in ancient Israel, such as a priest calling for silence prior to or immediately following the offering of a sacrifice.[2] Others see it as arising out of a liturgical but non-sacrificial setting.[3] Sweeney rightly affirms that no one specific origin can be identified for the form, but that it was "apparently used commonly in Hebrew for situations in which one might call for silence."[4] Three quasi-fixed elements unite these three passages: (1) the interjection "silence!" (*has*) in the first position, followed by (2) an indication that silence is to be kept "before (*miphne*) the Lord," then (3) an additional clause explaining the manner in which God is present.[5] The readers/hearers are likely intended to understand the call to silence as emanating from the prophet, who occupies the role of a herald or official, calling others to attention.[6]

Two specific aspects of these calls have puzzled interpreters: to whom are they addressed, and why, exactly, is silence called for? Zephaniah 1:7 supplies no indication concerning the addressees of the call. In Habakkuk 2:20 the call to silence is directed to "all the earth." This phrase may refer to all creation (as in Num 14:21; Josh 3:11, 13; 1 Chr 16:30; Ps 66:1, 4), to humans and animals combined (Josh 23:14; 1 Kgs 2:2; Ps 66:4), or specifically to human beings (Gen 18:25; Exod 9:16; Ps 33:8; Jer 51:7). Likely Habakkuk 2:20 envisages the call as directed to the entirety of the human realm, although silence in the heavenly sphere cannot be excluded (cf. Isa 6:1-6; Rev 8:1). In Zech 2:13 the call is sent out to "all flesh." This is a customary designation for both humans and animals (Gen 6:12, 17, 19; Num 18:15; Jer 45:5, among many others). However, here it is clearly humans who are in view. Most important for our purposes is the fact that the identity of the addressees of these calls is either absent or deliberately vague. Yet an understanding of *who* is being addressed in these calls and *why* is essential if one is to ascertain their meaning and significance.

Silence "because of" the Lord

The traditional interpretation of these three calls to silence views them as set within the context of sacred worship, underlining the need for a respectful and reverential demeanor in the presence of Yahweh. While reverence is certainly not foreign to these passages, limiting their sense to such an idea does not, I believe, capture the essence of their meaning. To do so, we must dig a bit deeper into the exegetical details of the three texts.

The Hebrew word usually translated "be silent" or "keep silent" is *has*, an onomatopoetic interjection, very much like the English "shh!"[7] However, as noted, this word does not always connote a worship or temple setting. Amos 6:10 and 8:3 are clear examples of a non-religious context. Furthermore, the reference to sacrifice in Zephaniah 1:7-8, to Yahweh's temple in Habakkuk 2:20, or to the Lord's habitation in Zechariah 2:13 do not imply a worship setting, as is often suggested. Rather, read carefully, in each of these contexts the references to sacrifice, the temple, and Yahweh's dwelling are part of the *implied narrative, unfolding within the world of the text* in which God's mighty acts are being revealed—acts of judgment and deliverance.[8] We will return to this important consideration shortly.

Furthermore, it is essential to recognize the distinctive nuance carried by the term translated "before the Lord" in these texts. The Hebrew word used here is *miphne*, not *liphne*. Whereas *liphne* is commonly used to describe ritual or sacred acts performed "before the Lord" (i.e., in the presence of Yahweh; Gen 18:22; 27:7; 2 Sam 5:3), often in the tabernacle or temple (Exod 16:33; 27:21; 28:35; and extensively in Exod, Lev, and Num), *miphne* generally conveys a distinctly *causal* flavor.[9] If the intent of the phrase were merely to enjoin a reverential, worshipful silence, *liphne* would likely have been used. The preposition *miphne* is frequently used to denote subjective fear either in advance of an imminent and terrifying event or because of a threatening person or thing (Gen 7:7; Judg 9:21). It rarely occurs outside of contexts of hostility and fear, and frequently with notions of flight or movement away from a threatening entity (Gen 35:1; Josh 10:11; 1 Sam 17:24; Ps 68:2; Amos 5:19). Quite frequently *miphne* is used together with the verb "to fear" (**yara'*) followed by the person or thing that generates the fear (see, e.g., Hag 1:12).[10] By the use of *miphne* in the call to silence, the speaker is certainly affirming that the Lord is present, but additionally that silence is imperative *because* of Yahweh. But why should this be the case? Why are the addressees called to silence *because* of Yahweh? And why call for silence at all? The response to these questions centers on the *judgment motif in the three passages*. Silence is called for not merely out of worshipful reverence, but because of the awesome acts of judgment that Yahweh will undertake.[11] It is essential to observe that judgment is a key theme in the broader context of all three passages. Each one depicts Yahweh as acting (or just about to act) *in opposition to certain foes and in favor of the people of God.*

Zephaniah 1:7

The book of Zephaniah is set in the late seventh century. Its central message is that the day of Yahweh is at hand. Both Judah and the nations will be judged (1:2–2:15). Yet, beyond this cataclysmic event, Yahweh will renew and purify both Israel and the nations (3:8-20).[12] The structure of Zephaniah has been the subject of ongoing debate, with little consensus.[13] Zephaniah 1:4-9 focuses especially upon Yahweh's judgment of Judah and the Jerusalemite élite. In 1:4b-6, the priests are excoriated for their apostasy. In 1:8-9, the royal officials are attacked for their assimilation to foreign practices. 1:10–2:4 continues the theme of judgment. Verses 10, 14, and 16 are rich in soundscape. Horrendous sounds are heard: cries, crashing, and wailing (v. 10), bitter sounds and cries (v. 14), hostile trumpet blast and battle cries (v. 16). Judah is rebuked concerning its attitudes and practices (1:12b, 17-18), and called to repent and return to Yahweh (2:1–4).

Zephaniah 1:7 provides a specific reason for the call to silence: "Be silent before the Lord God! For the day of the Lord is at hand." The concept of the day of the Lord was well known in ancient Israel and occupies an important place in the prophetic corpus[14] It may refer both to various moments in which the Lord intervenes in history in acts of judgment and salvation (Isa 9:4; Ezek 13:5; Hos 1:11; Ps 137:7; Lam 2:22) as well as to a final, eschatological day when the Lord appears as judge of all the earth and ushers in a new era of history (Isa 2:10-18; 24–27; Zeph 3:9-13).[15] In popular religion, the day of the Lord was frequently understood in a blindly partisan way. Many of Amos' hearers longed for the day of the Lord, believing it to be a time when they would be exalted and their enemies vanquished. But Amos, having denounced them for their corrupt behavior, informed them that the day of the Lord was not a blunt instrument, sparing all in Israel and destroying all those outside. Rather, those Israelites who refused to repent and act justly would be swept away by it as well. He states,

> Alas for you who desire the day of the Lord! Why do you want the day of the Lord? It is darkness, not light; as if someone fled from a lion, and was met by a bear; or went into the house and rested a hand against the wall, and was bitten by a snake. Is not the day of the Lord darkness, not light, and gloom with no brightness in it? (Amos 5:18-20)

Zephaniah's thought in 1:7 replicates that of Amos.

The call to silence in Zephaniah 1:7 is thus rooted in the imminence of the day of Yahweh. In 1:7b that day is depicted via the imagery of a sacrificial feast. Zephaniah declares that Yahweh has "prepared a sacrifice and consecrated his guests." Much debate surrounds the identity of the guests, and of what is meant by Yahweh's having consecrated them.[16] One view sees the invitees as those who, contrary to custom and expectation, will themselves be sacrificed.[17] Another sees the guests as the nations who will attack Israel as instruments of Yahweh's anger.[18] Either way, the call to silence is grounded in the context of a terrifying time of judgment.[19]

Habakkuk 2:20

In Habakkuk 2:20, the theme of Yahweh's judgment is less explicit, but nonetheless present. The Book of Habakkuk chronicles the prophet's struggle to understand the ways of Yahweh, specifically with regard to the presence of evil in the world, and how such evil is dealt with. It divides into three main sections. In 1:2-17, the prophet challenges Yahweh regarding the absence of divine intervention in the face of social evil. Following Habakkuk's complaint regarding the evils prevalent in Judean society (1:2-4), Yahweh asserts that the Babylonians were being raised up and sent to judge Judah (1:5-11).[20] Habakkuk then questions the justice of this, given that the idolatrous Babylonians themselves were vicious exploiters of humanity (1:12-17). Subsequently, in 2:1-20, the prophet waits upon Yahweh's response and learns that the Babylonians would themselves be destroyed due to their excesses (see the similar motif in Isa 10:5-11). The third section (3:1-19) takes the form of a psalm and asserts that just as in creation and in days of old, Yahweh will defeat the forces of chaos and bring deliverance. Habakkuk 2:20 thus serves as a transition between the series of woes called down upon idolaters and evildoers in the second section (2:6-19), and Habakkuk's "prayer" in chapter 3.[21] Verses 18-19 underline the futility of idolatry, since such gods cannot breathe, speak, or rouse themselves (v. 19).[22] Then, to highlight the great contrast between such idols and the living God, 2:20 calls attention to Yahweh's presence in his holy temple, and demands that all the earth keep silence before him. This verse marks the turning point in the book: debate and dispute in chapters 1–2 give way to the psalm of praise in 3:2-19.

One critical element here is not to be missed. Habakkuk 2:5-17 consists of five woe sayings in which the subject nations voice their disgust at the Babylonians and their practices, and, by implication, call out for vindication from Yahweh.[23] Habakkuk 2:20 therefore should be understood as a *critical element of the means by which the nations' cries for judgment will be fulfilled.*

Yahweh resides in his temple, and all the nations of the earth must be silent *because* of him—most specifically because of the imminent judgment on the Babylonians, announced in Habakkuk 2:5-17. Here we are in a similar world to that of Isaiah 13–14, 40–55, and Jeremiah 25:12-14, 26; 50–51.

Zechariah 2:13

A similar situation is found in Zechariah 2. The Book of Zechariah is generally divided into two major sections, chapters 1–8 and 9–14. The first section is usually seen as consisting of two parts, a sermonic frame (1:1-6; 7:1–8:23) and a series of visions and oracles, woven together (1:7–6:15). The call to silence in 2:13 comes at the climax of the series of oracles in 2:5-13 that are attached to the third of Zechariah's "night visions" in 2:1-4. Our passage here contains elements of both salvation and judgment. Yahweh's coming vindication of Israel and return to Jerusalem provide the basis for the call to rejoice in 2:10. Yet that call is set against the backdrop of judgment upon Israel's oppressors, who will become "plunder for their own slaves" (2:9). Most significantly, the Lord's might and fury are underlined in Zechariah 2:13, where Yahweh is described as having been "roused up" (cf. Hab 2:19) from his holy habitation. The verb used here (**'our*) generally denotes the transition from rest, sleep, or inactivity to movement or action. It sometimes describes awakening from sleep (Zech 4:1), or from inactivity or lethargy (Hag 1:14), or the awakening of internal motivation to perform a task (Joel 4:7; Hag 1:14). Most relevant to Zech 2:13, however, is its use in militaristic contexts. Some of these occur where Yahweh rouses nations for war.[24] It is frequently in contexts where Yahweh arises to execute judgment (see below).

Zechariah 2:13 asserts that Yahweh is about to be roused "from his holy dwelling" (*mimme'on qodsho*).[25] The imagery here combines three motifs found in the HB, all of which deal with a transition from *a place of stillness to one of movement or action*. The first image is that of a lion that rises up (**qoum*) and goes forth to hunt and destroy (Gen 49:9; Num 23:24; 24:9; Isa 31:4; Jer 4:7; 25:38; 49:19; Hos 5:14; 13:7-8; Mic 5:8; cf. also Nah 2:10-12). The second is that of God being "roused up" (**'our*) to execute judgment and deliverance on behalf of the people of God (Job 8:6; Pss 7:6; 35:23; 44:23; 59:4; Isa 42:13). The third is expressed through Yahweh's "rising up" (again **qoum*) on behalf of those in need of vindication (Num 10:35; Pss 10:12; 17:13; 35:2; 74:22; 82:8). A clear example of this occurs in Psalm 12:5. Following the psalmist's complaint about the persecution of the righteous by evildoers, Yahweh declares:

"Because the poor are despoiled, because the needy groan,
I will now rise up," says the LORD;
"I will place them in the safety for which they long."

The imagery in this last text moves beyond that of an animal exiting its lair to devour its prey. It evokes the actions of a king, judge, or warrior who will not allow an aberrant situation to continue any longer, but who will arise to set things right.

Silence and Yahweh's Awesome Judgment

Divine judgment thus forms a significant element in the three calls to silence we are considering here. This clearly explains why the prophet can call for silence *because of Yahweh*. God's might is overpowering and God's judgment is terrifying. That which unites these texts is the concept that moments when Yahweh moves forth in judgment are times of *extreme danger*—even for those who are not specifically the objects of the divine wrath. As such, all mention of the divine name or of any inopportune sound must be avoided lest the divine anger flare up and consume the "bystanders." Numerous passages depict Yahweh's power as explosive and dangerous. This may be seen in texts where care must be taken not to approach sacred objects or places without due preparation or consecration lest Yahweh "break out" (**peretz*, Exod 19:22, 24; 2 Sam 6:8; 1 Chr 13:11) against offenders or his wrath (*qetzeph*) "break forth" (**yatza'*, Num 17:11).

Recognition of this motif can now assist us in addressing the questions posed earlier: to whom is the call to silence addressed, and what does it mean? I would suggest that its addressees are specific characters, either explicitly mentioned or implicitly assumed to be present within the horizon of the text. Moreover, the call to silence will have different meanings for each one, depending on each one's status vis-à-vis Yahweh. Essentially, there are five *obvious* characters within the purview of text (in literary analysis these are called *dramatis personae*): the Lord, the prophet, those on whose behalf God acts, and those who stand in opposition to the Lord and who will be the objects of divine judgment.[26] Additionally, other less obvious characters may also be implied. The first of these are those who *witness* Yahweh's deeds of power. Such witnesses may include those in the *unseen world*. Israelite thought conceived of Yahweh as seated on a throne surrounded by a "heavenly council" consisting of various unseen beings. God's purposes and plans were discussed there, often with prophetic involvement, and the council appears to have witnessed the enactment of these purposes (cf. Job 1–2; Isa 6:1-13; 1 Kgs 22:5-40).[27] Turning to the *seen world*, the *nations* are at times summoned as witnesses to Yahweh's deeds of judgment and blessing. I will elaborate on their role in a moment. Finally, our list of *dramatis personae* must include the readers/hearers of the text. From the perspective of the text's framer(s) they too are addressed by the call to silence.

Remembering that the call to silence in these three texts is rooted in the fearsome presence of Yahweh, we may now ask why these various *dramatis personae* are called to silence and what that silence means for each of them. Clearly, neither the Lord nor the prophet is being called to silence, since the prophet utters the call in the name of the Lord. However, it is likely that silence is called for on the part of the other personages just mentioned for various reasons. First, silence is fitting for those who are the *objects* of judgment. Such silence may imply the acceptance of the divine verdict.[28] This is the case in Isaiah 53:7 and Lamentations 2:10; 3:28.[29] Similarly, Achan is silent after he confesses his sin, and accepts the consequence of his actions (Josh 7:19-23). Eli's acquiescence to Yahweh's rejection of him and his house suggests a similar attitude (1 Sam 3:18). If such an idea is seen here, the call to silence is a demand to those whose time has come to resign themselves to it, and accept their fate (cf. Ps 46:10, which will be discussed in chapter 5).

Similarly, the *beneficiaries* of Yahweh's deeds are likely called to silence. At times, Yahweh acts on behalf of the people of God who are called to watch in silence. Exodus 14:13-14 declares:

> But Moses said to the people, "Do not be afraid, stand firm, and see the deliverance that the LORD will accomplish for you today; for the Egyptians whom you see today you shall never see again. The LORD will fight for you, and you have only to keep still."[30]

Psalm 37 contains various exhortations to wait for the Lord (vv. 1-8) knowing that oppressors and evildoers will soon be cut off (vv. 2, 9, 10, 20, 36, 38). Especially noteworthy is the command in verse 7 to be still (or silent, **damam*-1), and the promise that those who have patiently waited for the Lord's deliverance will *look upon* (**ra'ah*) the destruction of the wicked (v. 34; cf. Pss 64:8; 73:18). A similar motif appears in Isaiah 26:20-21, where Israel is the beneficiary of Yahweh's vindication:

> Come, my people, enter your chambers, and shut your doors behind you; hide yourselves for a little while until the wrath is past. For the LORD comes out from his place to punish the inhabitants of the earth for their iniquity; the earth will disclose the blood shed on it, and will no longer cover its slain.

Silence also befits those who are the *witnesses* (either heavenly or earthly) of Yahweh's acts of judgment, especially due to the awesome and sacred nature of such deeds.[31] The role of the witness is a highly important one in the HB.[32] Witnesses could be called upon to provide evidence of legal transactions (Jer 32, esp. v. 44) or attest to other important events or agreements (Deut 17:6; Prov 12:17). Yahweh is invoked as a witness to dealings between persons (1 Sam 12:5-6; 20:23; Jer 42:5). Elements of the natural world could be called upon to serve as witnesses (Gen 31:44; Deut 30:19). Frequently they are called upon to testify against Israel for its waywardness (Deut 4:26; 30:19, 28; Josh 24:27). A similar motif appears in Amos 3:13-15, where certain unnamed individuals are called to act as witnesses to Yahweh's acts of judgment against the NK.[33]

On numerous occasions in the HB the *nations* are seen as witnesses. In Isaiah 40–55, frequent reference is made to the nations (*goyim*) who witness (lit. "see," **ra'ah*) the deeds of Yahweh (Isa 49:7; 52:10, 15; 61:9; 62:2; 66:18).[34] In Isaiah 52:10, Yahweh's vindication of the people of God is performed in the plain sight of all the nations (cf. Ezek 39:21; Mic 7:16; Nah 3:5). In Ezekiel, Yahweh's saving deeds are executed "before the eyes of the nations."[35] The role of the nations as witnesses is especially relevant to Habakkuk 2:20. As we have seen, the five woes in Habakkuk 2 express the laments of the nations who have been the victims of the Babylonians' abuse, and the call to silence in 2:20 comes as the response to and resolution of the nations' complaint.

The call to silence, then, has special relevance for *those nations who are not the objects of Yahweh's judgment*. They are the earthly witnesses of Yahweh's judgments and stand in something of an *intermediate* position—Yahweh's judgment is not directed against them, neither are they its *direct* beneficiaries. What is the significance of the call to silence for them? It would seem that caution is urged upon them due to the *furious and untamed aspect* of Yahweh's manifestations (cf. the lion imagery in Zech 2:13, and the idea of Yahweh's breaking forth [**peretz*] in Exod 19:22, 24; cf. also Isa 26:20-21, noted above). As such it is imperative that uncalled for sound or action be silenced, lest disastrous consequences ensue. As we shall see, this is likely the reason behind the command not to mention Yahweh's name in Amos 6:10 where, in the midst of divine judgment upon a city, unnamed individuals are urged to refrain from uttering the divine name lest such an action *attract the attention of Yahweh, and thus bring down judgment upon themselves*.[36]

Finally, it is likely that *the readers and hearers of the text* are also being called to silence. Moreover, the nature of that silence will be determined by the character within the world of the text that most closely reflects their own position vis-à-vis the Lord. With whom they are most closely to be identified? Are they evildoers, who must repent or silently face God's anger? Or are they those waiting patiently for the Lord's redemption? Or do they perhaps stand in an intermediate position, silently observing the Lord's mighty deeds and benefiting from them? And, having seen them, will they perhaps move into a closer relationship with the Lord and the people of God (Isa 19:25; Zech 2:11)?

The Silence of Desolation, Grief, and Mourning

Various texts in the HB employ the motif of silence as an expression of the interrelated ideas of desolation, grief, and mourning. Lamentations 2:10 and Amos 6:9-10; 8:3 are such cases.[37] In this section we will examine the concept of silence as it appears in these texts, and seek to understand why it is used in relationship to these powerful human experiences.

Lamentations 2:10

The book of Lamentations consists of five poems bemoaning the Babylonian destruction of Jerusalem in 587 BCE. The first four poems are acrostics—each verse (generally consisting of three poetic lines) begins with a successive letter of the Hebrew alphabet.[38] The final poem, chapter 5, although not itself an acrostic, does bear a similarity to the acrostic form in that it contains 22 verses, corresponding to the number of letters in the Hebrew alphabet. This acrostic structure lends itself to a cyclical and thematic expression of a series of motifs rather than a more linear, step-by-step presentation.[39] Furthermore, by means of the vehicle of several different personae, the poet (or poets) give voice to various emotions and theological issues arising from the conquest of Judah and the destruction of Jerusalem.[40] It is noteworthy that while the text repeatedly speaks *about* Yahweh, addresses laments *to* Yahweh, and even *accuses* Yahweh, nowhere in the book does Yahweh speak. On the contrary, *divine silence pervades the book*. Yahweh's purposes of judgment against Jerusalem have been carried out (2:17). Divine speech has been replaced by a wall of silence. As 2:9 expresses it: "guidance is no more, and her prophets obtain no vision from the Lord." In Lamentations 3, however, we may detect a movement from despair to hope as repentance and renewal emerge out of grief.[41] We will examine this transition in chapter 4.

Silence is explicitly evoked in Lamentations 2:10. Scholars have offered various proposals regarding the structure of Lamentations 2.[42] However such matters are decided, it is clear that verses 9-10, the center of our interest here, fall just after the description of Yahweh's judgments on Jerusalem and before the expression of the personal grief of the weeping poet. Moreover, verse 10a, with its emphasis on silence, is central to the chapter as a whole. Verses 9-10 are structured as follows. Verse 9 describes the results of Yahweh's devastation. The city's gates have been destroyed (9a), the king and nobility have been taken into exile (9b), and Judah's prophets receive no instruction or vision from Yahweh (9c).[43] The subsequent verse turns to the grief and mourning of the city's elders (10a) and young women (10b).[44] They sit or lie on the ground, place dirt upon their heads, and wear sackcloth. These acts (along with others, including weeping, tearing one's garments, and fasting) occur in numerous contexts and convey the interrelated themes of grief, defeat, humiliation, and loss.[45]

At this point we must pause and take note of an important phenomenon relating to various Hebrew verbs, many of which concern the concept of silence. The phenomenon in question is called polysemy (or sometimes homonymy). It refers to those instances where the consonants of a Hebrew root appear to designate differing concepts. When this occurs, Hebrew lexicographers usually add a supplementary numeral to the root to indicate these differences in meaning and that these consonants may reflect roots of differing origins. One of the key roots denoting silence, **damam*, is an important case in point. It can be translated "to be still or silent" (usually classified as **damam*-1), or "to wail, cry, or moan" (**damam*-2), or "to be destroyed, to perish, to be devastated" (**damam*-3). While most commentators translate Lamentations 2:10 as "the elders of daughter Zion sit on the ground in silence" (NRSV, LXX, and most ancient versions), others argue that it is preferable to render it, "They sat on the ground, moaning, the elders of Zion."[46] I prefer the rendering "sitting on the ground in silence" (thus **damam*-1) for several reasons. First, the same verb occurs just a few verses later in Lamentations 2:18, where it clearly means "to be silent."[47] Second, in Joshua 7:6; 2 Samuel 13:19; and Ezekiel 9:8; 11:13; 27:30-31, where wailing or crying does occur in connection with the nonverbal indications of mourning mentioned in Lamentations 2:10, verbs other than **damam*-1 are used to express it.[48] Furthermore, none of the other instances where the meaning "to mourn" has been proposed for the verbal root **damam* (esp. Lev 10:3; Amos 5:13) contain these allusions to traditional mourning practices. Third, while the ritualized actions may be the same, there is a *qualitative difference* between their use to express the grief involving the loss of a loved one (Deut 34:8; Num 20:29; Gen 37:34-35; Ezek 24:16-17), a personal tragedy (Judg 11:37-38), supplication (Esth 4:3) or sorrow over sin and wrongdoing (Isa 22:12;

Joel 2:12) on the one hand, and utter disaster, defeat, and devastation, on the other. Mourning behaviors expressing the latter motif appear in Joshua 7:6; 1 Samuel 4:12; 2 Samuel 1:2; Isaiah 47:1; and Ezekiel 27:28-31. The experience of being "appalled" (with reference to humans) or being "desolate" (with reference to lands or territories) frequently appears in connection with such disastrous events.[49] And most significantly, *silence appears in many of these situations*. When humans are "appalled" by something they may be unable to speak (Ezra 9:3-4; Isa 52:13-14). Nonverbal expressions of such speechlessness include placing one's hand over one's mouth (Job 21:5)[50] or simply staring at one another in dismay (Ezek 4:17) with faces convulsed (Ezek 27:35). Frequently, notions of weakness (Ps 143:4) or trembling (Ezek 32:10) accompany such a state. Similarly, when lands are made desolate there is an absence of sound (Zeph 3:6; Zech 7:14). Thus, in Lamentations 2:10 sitting in silence is a more profound and fitting response to the complete destruction of Jerusalem than weeping would have been. Fourth, it has been well documented that mourning rituals from several surrounding cultures could involve *both* weeping *and* silence.[51] In Job 2:12-13, Job's comforters arrive and weep, then sit in prolonged silence. Finally, sitting in silence seems more suited to the place of Lamentations 2:10 in the overall structure of the chapter than does weeping. Verses 1-8 describe Yahweh's relentless devastation of Jerusalem, quoted here in full, with emphasis added:

> How the Lord in his anger has *humiliated* daughter Zion! He has *thrown down* from heaven to earth the splendor of Israel; he has *not remembered* his footstool in the day of his anger. The Lord has *destroyed without mercy* all the dwellings of Jacob; in his wrath he has *broken down* the strongholds of daughter Judah; he has *brought down to the ground* in dishonor the kingdom and its rulers. He has *cut down* in fierce anger all the might of Israel; he has *withdrawn his right hand* from them in the face of the enemy; he *has burned like a flaming fire* in Jacob, *consuming* all around. He has *bent his bow* like an enemy, with his right hand *set like a foe*; he has *killed* all in whom we took pride in the tent of daughter Zion; he has *poured out his fury* like fire. The Lord has *become like an enemy*; he has *destroyed* Israel; He has *destroyed* all its palaces, *laid in ruins* its strongholds, and *multiplied in daughter Judah mourning and lamentation*. He has *broken down* his booth like a garden, he has *destroyed* his tabernacle; the LORD has *abolished* in Zion festival and sabbath, and in his fierce indignation has *spurned* king and priest. The Lord has *scorned* his altar, *disowned* his sanctuary; he has *delivered into the hand of the enemy* the walls of her palaces; a clamor was raised in the house of the LORD

> as on a day of festival. The Lord *determined to lay in ruins* the wall of daughter Zion; he *stretched the line*; he did *not withhold his hand from destroying*; he *caused rampart and wall to lament*; they languish together. (Lam 2:1-8)

Perhaps at the outset of Yahweh's judgment a response of wailing could be envisaged, expressing a plea for mercy or clemency. However, given the unrelenting manifestations of Yahweh's anger described here, the poet is more likely referring to a sustained period of silence on the part of the nation's elders. Put another way, the wailing associated with mourning, lament, or repentance has a *purposeful* element associated with it: the expression of grief over one no longer present, of sorrow over the course of events, or of the desire to implore the deity to relent. By contrast, the sustained description of Yahweh's devastation of Jerusalem would suggest that no avenue is left open to the elders of Daughter Zion. Yahweh's judgment was enacted with fury and finality. All that remained to the nation were the rituals of mourning, and the silent acceptance of the judgments decreed against it. Sitting on the ground (Josh 7:6; 2 Sam 13:31; Ezek 26:16; Job 2:13) and placing dust upon one's head (Gen 3:19; Isa 26:19; Pss 7:6; 22:16; 103:14; Job 7:21) likely signifies proximity to death.[52] Furthermore, silence (as we shall see in chapter 6) is a defining characteristic of Sheol, the realm of the dead.

Amos 6:9-10 and 8:1-3

The theme of grief and desolation continues in Amos 6:9-10 and 8:1-3. These verses call for utter silence using the interjection *has*. The rationale for this demand is grounded in the fear that any sound might bring forth further expressions of Yahweh's anger (cf. Zeph 1:7; Hab 2:20; Zech 2:13). Amos 6:9-10 are a prose insertion into the poetic oracles concerning judgment of the NK in Amos 6:1-14. More specifically, they form an addendum to verses 8 and 11 that describe the destruction of a city (v. 8) and its houses, great and small (v. 11):

> If ten people remain in one house, they shall die. And if a relative, one who burns the dead, shall take up the body to bring it out of the house, and shall say to someone in the innermost parts of the house, "Is anyone else with you?" the answer will come, "No." Then the relative shall say, "Hush! We must not mention the name of the Lord." (Amos 6:9-10)

This section illustrates how extensive the destruction will be. The cause of the destruction in this section is not direct action by hostile armies, but rather death by pestilence or starvation—both of which commonly occurred in connection with siege warfare. Verse 9 asserts that even if ten people from one house managed to survive, they would nevertheless die. Verse 10 describes a scenario in which other survivors must deal with the corpses of their dead relatives. The relationship of verse 10 to 9 is somewhat complicated, as are the specific details concerning the speakers and events described in it. At least two persons appear to be involved. The first is the relative who "burns the dead."[53] There are various suggestions regarding this person's role. The first is that this person is a relative of the deceased who is bringing the cadaver out to be burned.[54] Advocates of this position admit that although human bodies were only incinerated in severe circumstances in ancient Israel (1 Sam 31:12), we are dealing here with a time of starvation or plague, and the situation is therefore exceptional. The second position affirms that the burning alluded to here was the burning of incense as a funerary ritual for the dead.[55] A third approach asserts that there is no reference to cremation here, but rather to the anointing of the bodies with fragrant oils.[56] Due to the text's complexity, conclusions can only be tentative. Similar difficulties surround the question of who participates in the dialogue. At least two persons are involved. Many suggest that one (generally seen to be the kinsman) stands near the exterior of the house and calls to a second individual further inside. This might be a second kinsman who has gone into the building to look for bodies,[57] or another survivor lurking in its inner recesses.[58] Alternatively, the dialogue might take place between two people involved in bringing out the cadaver—the kinsman, who carries it, and another who smears the body with aromatic spices in preparation for burial.[59] However the matter is decided, the dialogue is simple, and serves to establish the fact that the house is empty ("Is anyone else with you?" The answer will come, "No."). All of these details prepare the reader for the main point, expressed in 6:10b: "Hush! We must not mention the name of the LORD."

Two questions emerge here: Why must Yahweh's name not be mentioned? And why must there be utter silence? The expression "to mention the name of Yahweh" may denote two distinct ideas. Used in oaths, it issues a command *in Yahweh's name* that some activity cease or be performed. The speaker would be enjoining total silence, but the emphasis would not fall upon refraining from mentioning the name of Yahweh. Rather, the sense would be, "In the name of the Lord, do not continue to speak!" Alternatively, the phrase *in Yahweh's name* may refer to the invocation of Yahweh (1 Chr 16:4; Isa 26:13; 48:1). It has therefore been suggested that the speaker here fears that his interlocutor may follow traditional mourning rites, which involved invoking the name of Yahweh.[60] A third possibility is that the speaker demands that great pains be taken to avoid any mention of the name of Yahweh *at all*. While different in detail, the latter two alternatives (which in my opinion are the more likely) are rooted in the same concern—the desire to avoid drawing attention to the speaker, and thus calling down further judgment from Yahweh.[61] In Amos 6:10 the call for silence (*has*) and the avoidance of mentioning Yahweh's name occur in a context of desperation and dread. The speakers tremble in the darkness amidst rotting corpses. Yahweh's destruction of the once prosperous and mighty city has been so extensive that those who may have survived it can only cower in fear.[62] As such, keeping silence here is a *prudential and self-protecting* undertaking. Perhaps too we see here echoes of the invectives against the hypocritical worship and sound decried in Amos 5:23-24 and 6:5. The speaker recognizes that Yahweh's anger may still break forth (as in Amos 5:6), and in a way similar to Lamentations 2:10, every effort is made to avoid any negative consequences that might be unleashed through any use of Yahweh's name.[63]

Amos 8:1-3 recounts Amos' fourth vision.[64] In it, Yahweh shows the prophet a basket of ripe summer fruit.[65] The Lord then declares that the end has come—no further reprieve is possible.[66] The imagery of the ripe summer fruit likely indicates that the nation's sins have gone beyond measure, and the people are now ripe for judgment. Here we see a motif we will develop in chapter 4, that of Yahweh's patience providing a window of opportunity for reform to those under threat of judgment (thus Pss 50:21-22; 2 Kgs 17:7-18). Yet, as intimated here, that moment is not of unlimited duration. Verse 3 contains a reference to silence.[67] It announces that subsequent to Yahweh's judgment on Samaria, the songs of the temple shall be turned into wailing, and corpses will be strewn everywhere. Leaving bodies unburied was a profound disgrace both in the ANE more broadly, and in ancient Israel in particular.[68] The depiction of corpses scattered everywhere evokes profound devastation, disarray, and, most importantly, ignominy[69] and accursedness.[70] The imagery here suggests that either there was no one to bury the dead, or no place left to put the corpses. The scene then closes with the interjection, "Silence!" (*has*). Although the Hebrew form here is not an imperative, it functions as one; silence is demanded. Moreover, this demand for silence falls at the end of several short phrases, fired off in a staccato-like sequence: "many corpses," "strewn everywhere," and "silence."[71] Thus the silence that is called for is integrally related to the horror of the scene.

Two leading explanations are proposed for the demand for silence here. The first is that, as in Amos 6:10, the speaker wants to avoid any possibility that Yahweh's attention may be drawn to the situation, resulting in even further destruction. Yet this explanation is difficult to accept. It is unclear whether the speaker here is Amos or Yahweh.[72] Some suggest that these are Yahweh's words, and place the closing quotation marks after the call to silence at the end of verse 3. Others see verse 3 as a separate prophetic oracle, spoken by the prophet himself.[73] The matter is too complex to be discussed in detail here.[74] Either way, it is difficult to see why, in this description of the aftermath of Yahweh's judgment, a call for silence in order to avoid further destruction at the hand of God would be addressed to those who had survived by either Yahweh or Amos.[75] Others opine that these words constitute a kind of "preventative magic" akin to the interjection "God forbid," spoken upon hearing of some potential disaster or misfortune.[76] Yet again, it is incongruous that our prophet should interject such a sentiment into a context where Yahweh's purposes of judgment have just been enacted.

I would suggest that here Amos' editor has inserted this interjection, primarily addressing the later readers/hearers of these words. Thus, the call to silence here would rhetorically serve to heighten the power of the oracle as it was read or heard in later contexts.[77] Upon hearing the interjection, "Hush!" the readers/hearers would be transported into a situation of stark darkness, death, and terror, and be called themselves to silence in the face of such horror.

Silence as the Aftermath of Catastrophe

In this final section, we turn our attention to several texts where silence *follows* the catastrophic effects of Yahweh's judgment. In such passages *silence serves as evidence of that which once was, but which is no longer*. As we saw in our introductory chapter, silence is not the absence of all sound, but a deviation from that which is normally expected in a given situation. Nowhere is this more apparent than in the expressions of the silences that follow Yahweh's judgments. In such instances the normal sounds of life are absent, and are replaced by a deathlike and terrifying emptiness. The parade paradigm of this movement from sound to silence is the Babylonian destruction of Judah and Jerusalem in the sixth century BCE. However, this descent into silence occurs in the context of divine judgment upon other nations as well (Egypt in Ezek 29:11; Babylon in Isa 13:22; 34:14; Jer 50:13; 51:43).

The HB employs several common images to describe this movement from life to silence. One of the most common is the reduction of thriving, inhabited regions to places of total desolation. In the hill country of Judea, and the ANE in general, life was extremely tenuous. Human settlements could easily disappear due to war, famine, drought, disease, or pestilence. Movement from habitation to desolation (*shemamah*) appears in numerous texts. Warning the nation of the consequences of disobedience, Moses states, "And you I will scatter among the nations, and I will unsheathe the sword against you; your land shall be a desolation, and your cities a waste" (Lev 26:33). Isaiah laments, "Your country lies desolate, your cities are burned with fire; in your very presence aliens devour your land; it is desolate, as overthrown by foreigners" (Isa 1:7; cf. 6:11).[78] The concept of the land's desolation is a common one in Jeremiah and Ezekiel.[79] Jeremiah cautions the nation, "Take warning, O Jerusalem, or I shall . . . make you a desolation, an uninhabited land" (Jer 6:8; cf. 12:10-11). Ezekiel similarly declares, "I will stretch out my hand against them, and make the land desolate and waste, throughout all their settlements, from the wilderness to Riblah. Then they shall know that I am the LORD" (Ezek 6:14).

Two images appear frequently in descriptions of these desolate places. The first is the presence of two kinds of animal life, greatly feared and viewed with extreme distaste. The first is the jackal.[80] Oded Borowski describes these as "dog-like omnivorous scavengers . . . smaller than wolves [that] look much like foxes . . . nocturnal pack hunters that sleep in holes during the day [and] interbreed with domestic dogs and wolves . . . and make a distinct wailing sound . . . that announces their presence."[81] In the ANE, jackals were believed to have magical powers and sometimes associated with evil spirits.[82] The second animal, closely associated with the jackal, is the hyena.[83] These animals, still common in the region today, feed on carrion, and may at times disinter human remains. They drag their prey into their lairs and devour it there.[84] Other wild animals and birds are listed as the inhabitants of ruined Nineveh in Zephaniah 2:13-14.

The sounds of these animals replace the normal sounds of human life. Hyenas are described as "answering" one another in the deserted towers of a city (Isa 13:22).[85] Their cries are cries of lamentations (Mic 1:8). They take possession of places formerly inhabited by humans.[86] Human dwellings are thus replaced by the dens of animals in a land that has become a wasteland (Jer 49:17-18). In addition to the devastation of urban life, agricultural activities as well as trade and commerce have ceased. As stated in Zechariah 7:14, "Thus the land they left was desolate, so that no one went to and fro, and a pleasant land was made desolate."[87]

Along with the loss of human dwellings, the sounds of everyday life disappear. The joyous voices of the bride and bridegroom are gone (Jer 7:34; 16:9; 25:10; 33:11). Sounds of gladness are replaced by sorrow and sighing

(Isa 35:10). Ordinary sounds and activities of daily life vanish. In Jeremiah 25:10, Yahweh states that he will banish (a forceful expression, *weha'abadti*) not only the mirth of bride and bridegroom, but also the sound of the millstone grinding flour at daybreak. Yahweh's judgment puts an end both to the exceptional, exuberant sounds of joy, as well as to those of everyday life.[88] Music, once a highly significant part of life, is now absent.[89] Isaiah declares Yahweh's coming judgment upon Israel's festive celebrations and luxuriant lifestyle, in which musical instruments play a significant role. The following texts vividly illustrate the changes in "soundscape" that will occur on the day of Yahweh's intervention:

> Ah, you who rise early in the morning in pursuit of strong drink, who linger in the evening to be inflamed by wine, whose feasts consist of *lyre and harp, tambourine and flute* and wine, but who do not regard the deeds of the LORD, or see the work of his hands! Therefore my people go into exile without knowledge; their nobles are dying of hunger, and their multitude is parched with thirst. (Isa 5:11-13)

Amos expresses similar sentiments:

> Alas for those who lie on beds of ivory, and lounge on their couches, and eat lambs from the flock, and calves from the stall; who *sing idle songs to the sound of the harp, and like David improvise on instruments of music*; who drink wine from bowls, and anoint themselves with the finest oils, but are not grieved over the ruin of Joseph! Therefore they shall now be the first to go into exile, and the revelry of the loungers shall pass away. (Amos 6:4-7)[90]

Similarly, in Isaiah 24:7-8 we read:

> The wine dries up, the vine languishes, all the merry-hearted sigh. The mirth of the *timbrels* is stilled, the noise of the jubilant has ceased, the mirth of the *lyre* is stilled. (Isa 24:7-8)

Psalm 137 describes the aftermath of Yahweh's judgment in terms of the impossibility of song:

> By the rivers of Babylon—there we sat down and there we wept when we remembered Zion. On the willows there we hung up our harps. For there our captors asked us for songs, and our tormentors asked for mirth, saying, "Sing us one of the songs of Zion!" How could we sing the LORD's song in a foreign land? (Ps 137:1-4)

It is impossible to ascertain with absolute certainty exactly which songs are intended in the captors' taunts here. Traditionally, Psalms 46 and 48 (among others) are identified as "Songs of Zion," but the reference here may be more general that.[91] More importantly, these "Songs of Zion" (v. 3) are identified as the "Songs of Yahweh" in verse 4. However the case may be, the exiles here cannot bring themselves to intone any such songs—they can only hang up their harps and weep. Weeping is similarly seen as characteristic of Judah under Babylonian rule. Jeremiah cries, "For a sound of wailing is heard from Zion: 'How we are ruined! We are utterly shamed, because we have left the land, because they have cast down our dwellings'" (Jer 9:19).

One further dimension of the silence of judgment involves the loss of the sounds of worship. Lamentations pays special attention to this aspect of the destruction of Jerusalem and its temple. Hosea foresees a day when such ugliness will be silenced:

> I will put an end to all her mirth,
> her festivals, her new moons, her sabbaths,
> and all her appointed festivals. . . .
> What will you do on the day of appointed festival,
> and on the day of the festival of the LORD? (Hos 2:11; 9:5)

In Lamentations 1:4, the poet laments the absence of pilgrims in attendance at Jerusalem's festivals; the sounds of festal worship are no more:

> The roads to Zion mourn,
> for no one comes to the festivals;
> all her gates are desolate,
> her priests groan.

Lamentations 2:6-7 bemoans a similar loss of worship:

> He has broken down his booth like a garden,
> he has destroyed his tabernacle;
> the LORD has abolished in Zion *festival and sabbath*,
> and in his fierce indignation has spurned king and priest.
> The Lord has *scorned his altar, disowned his sanctuary*;
> he has delivered into the hand of the enemy
> the walls of her palaces;
> a clamor was raised in the house of the LORD
> *as on a day of festival*.

The clamor of destruction replaces the sounds of Sabbath and festivals (see also Lam 2:22).

As the preceding texts demonstrate, under Yahweh's judgment the sounds of life have been removed, or, as expressed in Jeremiah 25:10, "banished." The sounds that have taken their place are sounds of emptiness and loss—wailing, lamentations, and the howling of jackals. Thus, to speak of silence is to speak of *the loss of that which once was, and the miserable remains that have been left behind.* The personified Jerusalem mourns, "He has made my teeth grind on gravel, and made me cower in ashes; my soul is bereft of peace; I have forgotten what happiness is" (Lam 3:16-17).

We noted above that the situation in Judah following the Babylonian conquests constitutes the HB's archetypal portrait of the disappearance of sounds of life, and their replacement by sounds of destruction and death. This depiction is reinforced by numerous texts that give the impression that the land was *totally empty*, and therefore silent. One might think, for example, of Jeremiah 52:3a: "Indeed, Jerusalem and Judah so angered the LORD that he expelled them from his presence." Similarly, in 2 Kings 25:21b we read, "So Judah went into exile out of its land." Second Chronicles 36:20-21 is even more explicit:

> [The King of Babylon] took into exile in Babylon those who had escaped from the sword, and they became servants to him and to his sons until the establishment of the kingdom of Persia, to fulfill the word of the LORD by the mouth of Jeremiah, until the land had made up for its sabbaths. All the days that it lay desolate it kept sabbath, to fulfill seventy years.

Three points are of particular importance here. First, these representations of the land as totally empty employ the literary device of hyperbole—conscious exaggeration for effect. Other biblical texts bear witness to a remnant left in the land, such as 2 Kings 25:11 and Jeremiah 52:16. Moreover, a number of biblical texts were clearly produced by those Judeans left in the land. These include Lamentations and several of the Psalms (Pss 44, 74, 79, 89, 102, and 106).[92] Moreover, archaeological research has consistently shown that while massive destruction occurred in parts of Judah, especially Jerusalem and its environs, other areas, such as the Benjaminite territory, were spared. Indeed, Mizpah became the new capital of Judea (the former SK, called by its new name "Yehud"), likely until the time of Nehemiah.[93] Thus, just as silence is not the total absence of sound, these descriptions of the land are not to be taken as statements of total depopulation. Rather, images of total depopulation are employed in order to emphasize the fulfillment of the prophetic word and the great extent of Yahweh's judgment. That said, however, the image of total depopulation carries with it overtones of silence and death.

Second, the exilic period in Judah is conceived as a *Sabbath for the land.* Just as Israel was commanded to observe the weekly Sabbath, and the seventh and forty-ninth years were decreed to be Sabbaths of rest for the land (Exod 23:10-11; Lev 25:2-7), so the exilic period is here understood as a compensation for those Sabbaths that were denied to it. This cessation of agricultural activities evokes silence in that the normal activities of life are brought to a halt, and calm settles over the land. We will examine the relationship between Sabbath and silence in chapter 6.

Third, and most critically, the image of the empty land, with its haunting, sorrowful "soundscape," powerfully mirrors the alienation and silence that came to characterize *the relationship between Yahweh and Israel.* Numerous texts assert that a time of separation and estrangement must intervene between the enactment of Yahweh's judgment and the restoration of the nation (Hos 3:4-5; Isa 40:1-2). This is exemplified in those texts which speak of the "seventy years" of exile which must intervene between Jerusalem's destruction and ultimate restoration (Jer 25:11-12; Dan 9:2; Zech 1:12). One further point is of the greatest importance here: this seemingly silent, empty space is also a space for *relational healing.* It demarcates a time between catastrophe and renewal. And it is in this space that the disposition of both alienated parties can turn from rejection to renewed love. Isaiah 54:7 describes this time as a brief moment: "For a brief moment I abandoned you, but with great compassion I will gather you." Speaking from the perspective of the nation, Hosea 3:5 declares: "Afterward the Israelites shall return and seek the LORD their God, and David their king; they shall come in awe to the LORD and to his goodness in the latter days." Isaiah 19:22 similarly speaks of God's purposes of healing beyond judgment: "the LORD will strike Egypt, striking and healing; they will return to the LORD, and he will listen to their supplications and heal them."

Summary

In this chapter, then, we have seen how silence accompanies catastrophe. We have noted how Zephaniah 1:7, Habakkuk 2:20, and Zechariah 2:13 call for silence as Yahweh moves to enact the divine purposes of judgment and redemption. Those within the world of the text, as well as its readers/hearers, are called to stop and to reflect on the One whose might is all surpassing and whose purposes are sure. In the second part of the chapter, we examined the use of silence in relationship to grief and mourning. Through the analysis of a series of texts, Lamentations 2:10, Amos 6:9-10, and 8:1-3, we discovered that silence can be used to convey the profoundest expressions of despair and the desire to avoid any further calamity. Silence is thus expressed in the light of Yahweh's holiness and humankind's darkest hour. In the final section we saw how warnings of judgment and descriptions of the exilic period focused on the loss of the joyous sounds of life, and the hollow echoes of despair and loss that took their place.

At this point, the reader may feel a sense of despair or frustration since the expressions of silence we have been studying thus far are closely related to brokenness and death. Many readers may have come to this book seeking to find God in silence, and not to dwell on expressions of silence connected with divine judgment or silence as a manifestation of the "absence of God." I would urge such readers not to despair. As just intimated, the silence following judgment can open up a space for healing and restoration. We will indeed move beyond the darkness of the silence seen in these opening chapters. However, it would have been impossible simply to pass over this material in silence, since the HB devotes such great attention to it. Furthermore, many who have personally journeyed through the practice of silence have testified to the reality that a time of darkness often precedes the emergence into light. However, in the following chapter we mark a change of direction. We will turn to the new hope and restoration which can emerge out of the ashes of alienation and catastrophe, and to the very different role that silence can play in the renewal of the divine-human relationship.

4
SILENCE AS REPENTANCE AND RENEWAL
Dwelling in the Space between Loss and Restoration

In this chapter, we move beyond the silence associated with alienation and catastrophe and turn to another kind of silence, one closely connected to the renewal and restoration of the divine-human relationship. We will begin by examining two psalms, Psalms 32 and 51, where silence is an *enemy* of the restoration of that relationship. We will then move on to a poem, Lamentations 3, where silence is a *significant stage* in its restoration. Finally, we will consider the soundscape depicted in Zechariah 7–8, where repentance and change issues forth in the movement from silence to joyous sound. In Psalms 32 and 51 the focus is on the experience of the *individual*, whereas Lamentations 3 and Zechariah 7–8 emphasize Israel's *collective* journey.

The broader biblical conceptions of repentance, confession of sin, and divine forgiveness are central to our discussion here. Modern readers frequently conceive of the idea of new hope after judgment in terms of repentance. Indeed, the restoration of the divine-human relationship through repentance is a significant one in the HB.[1] What is not so clearly understood is that there is a canonical and historical development to this concept. In many of the narrative materials describing Israel's early history, repentance does not play any significant role in attaining forgiveness.[2] Divine pardon is generally granted only on the basis of the intercession of a mediator (Exod 32:11-13, 31-34; 34:9; Num 12:11-13; 14:13-19; Deut 9:16-29), and primarily consists of the attenuation of punishment (as in the case of David in 2 Sam 11–12). Furthermore, in these narratives, forgiveness secures the *continuance* of the relationship between Yahweh and Israel (see esp. Exod 32:10-14), not the total removal of punishment (Exod 32:25-29; Num 14:26-35). In none of the contexts just mentioned is repentance explicitly demanded of Israel.[3] Calls to repentance begin to appear in the eighth century prophets. Israel is called to turn (**shouv*) from sin and rebellion and return to Yahweh (Hos 14:1-2; Joel 2:12-14; Amos 4:6, 8-11, among many others). Yet, generally speaking, these calls to repentance are demands for renewed obedience. Israel is called to abandon wrongdoing, most significantly social injustice (especially in Amos) and the worship of other gods (especially in Hosea); many prophets enjoin both (Isaiah; Jeremiah). A different emphasis begins to emerge in the period of the exile (597–539 BCE) and flowers in the time of Ezra and Nehemiah (ca. 450 BCE; see Ezra 9; Neh 9; Dan 9). Here greater emphasis is placed upon additional elements that must accompany a return to Yahweh. These are frequently more "internal" in nature. They include contrition for sin, accompanied by a vision of its offensiveness to God, and are expressed in a more "liturgical" way, often through formal rites of confession, and prayer. The term "penitential prayer" is frequently used to describe this new emphasis on confession of sin and appeal for divine mercy. Penitential prayer focuses the magnitude of the nation's sin, past and present (Ezra 9:6-7, 15), the need for relief from present misery (Ezra 9:7), the justness of God's punishment (indeed Ezra exclaims, "You have punished us less than our iniquities deserved"; Ezra 9:13), and the great and merciful character of God (Neh 9:32; Dan 9:4). Moreover, it is characterized by a distinctive vocabulary. Key terms include the various Hebrew terms relating to sin (*ḥaṭa'*, *'awon*, the root **rasha'*), and the verb to confess sin (hithpael of **yadah*).[4] The relevance of the emergence of penitential prayer to our discussion will become clear as we examine the role of silence in movement from death to life, both on the national and individual level.

Sin, Silence, Repentance, and Renewal in the Experience of the Individual

Psalms 32 and 51 are well-known expressions of penitence, confession, and repentance. In both cases the titles of these psalms connect them with David. These titles, however, are secondary, and added after the original composition of the material. They are likely the work of later scribes, who identified a known liturgical song with a well-known biblical figure, and, at times, placed it in a specific context in the life of that person.[5] I will take up this issue in greater detail just below in our discussion of Psalm 51.

Psalm 32

Psalm 32 records the psalmist's journey from guilt to forgiveness. Verses 1-2 describe the joy of the individual whose misdeeds have been entirely removed and covered (32:1),[6] against whom Yahweh holds no charge of iniquity,[7] and who has been freed from living a life of deceit (32:2).[8] Having stated this happy outcome, in verses 3-4 the psalmist describes the situation that existed before this forgiveness was granted. He begins with the words "when I kept silent" (3a).[9] It is most noteworthy that at this point, the psalmist does not specify what he was silent *about*. This is divulged in verse 5. The unqualified mention of silence in verse 3 draws attention *away* from whatever wrongdoing the psalmist might have committed. Silence was a common way of dealing with embarrassment over missteps both in Israel and the ANE.[10] However, here the lack of specificity regarding the precise nature of the psalmist's sin serves to focus attention upon *deleterious effects* that such silence can have upon an individual. These effects are then enumerated one after another. The psalmist describes the wasting away of the body—literally the "wearing out" of the bones (cf. Lam 3:2, where the same two terms appear together, and nowhere else within the HB). He sees this as coming from Yahweh's hand, which has been "laid heavily" upon him—a common expression of God's opposition or judgment (Exod 9:3; Num 20:20; 1 Sam 5:6, 11; Job 23:2). As a result, he groaned constantly (as in Ps 22:1 and Job 3:24). The Hebrew in the following phrase is extremely difficult, and most ancient and modern versions do their best to make sense of it. Kraus' proposed translation, "changed was my tongue as in the heat of summer," would seem the most reasonable solution.[11] All of this is put down to the psalmist's *silence regarding his sin*.

In verse 5, however, the situation takes a radical turn for the better. The terminology of this verse is replete with words used in prayers of repentance. Sin (*ḥaṭat*) is confessed (**yadah* hithpael), and iniquity (*ʿawon*) is no longer hidden (**kasah*). Most significantly, this verse underlines the reality that the cause of the grievous outcomes described in verse 3 was not the psalmist's sin itself, *but the silence surrounding it*. In the parallelism of verse 5, keeping silence is the equivalent of hiding. So, contrary to Lamentations 2:10, where silence reflects the agony resulting from Yahweh's judgment, or Lamentations 3:26 and 28, where it signals the readiness to accept and endure the suffering sent from Yahweh's hand, here silence is an entirely negative response—one of denial, deception, and dissimulation. However, verse 5b, reiterating the words of verse 1, relates the happy outcome that ensues once silence is abandoned: "you forgave [lit. bore away] the guilt of my sin." Human silence as a means of dealing with sin has been altogether counterproductive. It has blocked any possibility of forward movement, and mired the psalmist in distress.[12]

A very similar movement away from destructive silence through confession and prayer appears in Psalm 38, a text whose soundscape mirrors that of Psalm 32. The psalmist groans (v. 8) and sighs (v. 9), yet somehow cannot hear or speak (vv. 13-14). However, movement toward resolution comes when the psalmist feels remorse for his sin and confesses it (v. 18).

Psalm 51

As in Psalm 32, this psalm deals with the experiences of sin, silence, and forgiveness. However, here silence is alluded to only indirectly: through a somewhat cryptic reference in verse 14, and by the references to joyous sound which accompany the resolution of the psalmist's guilt in verses 8, 14, and 15. Most commentators divide Psalm 51 into two portions: verses 1-17, dealing with the psalmist's sin and its resolution, and verses 18-19, dealing with the rebuilding of the walls of Jerusalem. Unlike Psalm 32, which begins with the happy outcome of divine forgiveness, this psalm commences with a desperate plea (vv. 1-2). Confession of sin and pleas for forgiveness and renewal are then repeated in various forms throughout verses 3-17. These frequently employ the concepts, vocabulary, and logic of penitential prayer, noted above.[13]

The oscillation between joyous sound and deathly silence, found in verses 8-15, is particularly striking. In verse 8, the psalmist pleads that Yahweh might make him hear joy and gladness. Clearly, joy and gladness are sentiments that cannot, in themselves, be heard. By contrast, expressions of joy and gladness are indeed audible. In the present context, these would be the joyous cries and songs given voice by the one who has been forgiven. This theme of joyous sound is carried further in verses 14-15 through a reference to the praise that the forgiven one promises to offer to the Lord:

> Deliver me from bloodshed, O God,
> O God of my salvation,
> and my tongue will sing aloud of your deliverance.
> O Lord, open my lips,
> and my mouth will declare your praise. (Ps 51:14-15)

Yet it is exactly here that the great contrast between the psalmist's hope for a time for joyful praise and the potential experience of deathly silence emerges. The issue centers around the phrase commonly translated "deliver me from bloodshed" in verse 14a. What is meant by this? Three preliminary considerations are important here. First, the word translated "bloodshed" is literally "bloods" in Hebrew. The Hebrew plural can at times designate natural objects in an unnatural state. Thus, when applied to "blood," the reference is frequently to spilt blood or murder, or to responsibility for the death of another, especially through negligence.[14] Regarding the latter possibility, Deuteronomy 22:8 warns: "When you build a new house, you shall make a parapet for your roof; otherwise you might have bloodguilt [lit. bloods] on your house, if anyone should fall from it."

Second, we note that the psalmist prays that he might be "delivered" (**natzal*) from such "bloodguilt." Some assume that this constitutes a request for forgiveness for the murder of Uriah. But is this indeed the case? The verb in question here does not generally refer to forgiveness (see below). Moreover, many other verbs in the psalm do refer to forgiveness ("blot out," vv. 1, 9; "wash," vv. 2, 7; "cleanse," vv. 2, 7; "cast me not away from your presence," v. 9), but not this one. The verb "to deliver someone from something" generally denotes the idea of *rescue from a deadly and powerful threat.* Such threats may come from enemies (Gen 37:21; Exod 2:19; 3:8; 18:4, 9; Ps 59:1), a hostile deity (1 Sam 4:8), misfortune (Hab 2:9), or in a few circumstances, from the physical effects of sin (see below). However, "deliverance" is not presented as forgiveness *per se.* It is frequently used when speaking of Yahweh's deliverance of Israel (Exod 6:6; 18:10), or of the deliverance of the righteous or innocent from the power of the wicked (Gen 37:22; Jer 22:3; Ps 59:2). Moreover, the expression "deliverance from bloods" frequently refers to "rescue from having one's own blood shed."[15] In Psalm 39:8, it would seem to refer to "deliverance from sin and its physical effects."[16] Some have suggested that Psalm 51:14 should be taken in this way.[17] However, as we shall see, this is far from certain.

Third, the way in which one reads the plea for "deliverance from bloodguilt" in verse 14 will greatly depend upon how one understands the psalm's superscription: "To the leader. A psalm of David, when the prophet Nathan came to him, after he had gone in to Bathsheba." As noted above, the titles given to the various psalms are later scribal additions. Moreover, the term translated "of David" need not imply authorship. Thus, it is quite likely that a song of repentance *already in existence* (whether or not David was ultimately its author) is being given a specific setting in David's life. As such, *not every detail of the psalm need correspond perfectly with the particular setting to which it is attached.*[18] In the case of Psalm 51, this is evident in that the superscription makes no mention of the murder of Uriah, and only David's adultery with Bathsheba. This is surprising given that in 2 Samuel 12:7-14 the murder of Uriah and the consequences that will accrue to David's house are given extensive attention (vv. 9-12).

Let us return now to the petition for "deliverance from blood(s)" in verse 14a. What precisely is the psalmist seeking from Yahweh? One might suggest that David is being portrayed as praying for forgiveness from the guilt of Uriah's murder. However, as we have seen, Uriah's death is not mentioned in the title of the psalm. More importantly, in ancient Israel, except in cases of unintentional killing, only the death of the guilty could cleanse the land from the pollution caused by the murder (Num 35:25, 31-32). Moreover, it would seem completely aberrant to understand the king of Israel, one responsible for maintaining justice in the land, as praying for release from the just consequences of his own murderous deed.[19] This is all the more so, since in verse 4 Yahweh's own justice is praised. What is more, blame is heaped upon King Jehoiakim for having filled Jerusalem with "innocent blood" (2 Kgs 24:3-4). It is therefore difficult to envisage this psalm as portraying a penitential David praying for escape, normally denied to others, from the consequences of his own actions.

In light of these considerations, the meaning of this prayer must be sought elsewhere. It could potentially lie in one of three directions. First, some have suggested that the psalmist's supplication here is evocative of Ezekiel's role as a watchman, and linked to the idea of declaring God's faithfulness in verses 13b, 14b, and 17. Thus, "[t]he suppliant is acknowledging the obligation to pass on this message [of divine forgiveness] and asks to be preserved from the consequences of not doing so."[20] A second alternative views the psalmist as appealing to Yahweh to relieve him of some life-threatening illness imposed due to his sin.[21] If, as we have suggested, the sin here is not specifically murder, this would make good sense. As in Psalm 39, where sickness resulting from sin is in view and the danger of death is real, the psalmist could pray for forgiveness and thus for healing, so that his praise might not cease (see Pss 6:6; 30:9; 88:11-13). Various scholars take this view.[22] Third, others arrive at a similar conclusion, but upon a different exegetical basis. The reference in verse 14a is translated not as "deliver me from blood(s)" but "deliver me from *silence*." The consonants for the term translated "from bloods" (*middamım*) could be read as "from silence" (*middumam*) with only a slight emendation. The reference would thus be to *the silence of death*.[23]

As we have seen, the phrase commonly translated "deliver me from bloodshed, O God" is problematic in the context of the psalm. Moreover, unlike Psalm 39, where deliverance from the effects of sin is in view and clearly means healing, in Psalm 51 such a nuance is faint at best. By contrast, movement from the silence of the grave to shouts of praise is entirely apposite (Ps 51:8, 12, 14b, 15). Silence at times is very simply an alternate word for death or the grave (Jer 48:2). The psalmist would thus be praying for deliverance from descent into the realm of silence, an image of imminent death, so that he might praise God in the land of the living.[24] Of these three options, I see the third (or possibly the second) as most probable. While different in formulation, they make the same point: the psalmist is praying for deliverance from the silence of death. To summarize, in Psalm 51 the psalmist is contrasting the joyful songs of the forgiven with the mournful silence of death, and the complete absence of praise. We will discuss the silence of the realm of the dead, or Sheol, in greater detail in chapter 6.

To conclude our discussion of Psalms 32 and 51, it is most important to observe that, in terms of their "soundscape," both of these penitential texts manifest a movement *from* silence *to* sound. Psalm 32 depicts movement from the death-producing silence of refusal to acknowledge one's sin (vv. 3-4) to the joyous cries that arise from the experience of the Lord's forgiveness (vv. 7, 11). In Psalm 51, the psalmist prays for deliverance from certain death and the silence that surrounds it (v. 14a), hopes for times of renewed joy and gladness (v. 8a), and longs for the ability to sing God's praise (v. 15). Relief and joy come about only when destructive and deceptive silence is renounced.

Excursus: Toxic Silence

It is highly important to note that not all expressions of silence are beneficial or salutary. Silence can be weaponized or highly deleterious. As just noted, the silence in Psalm 32 is self-destructive. Leviticus 5:1 speaks of the guilt of one who has heard an appeal for witnesses regarding a crime but fails to testify, thereby hindering the course of justice. Twice a *paterfamilias* remains silent, refusing to act on behalf of a daughter who has been sexually violated: Judah with reference to Dinah in Genesis 34:5, 25-31, and David, concerning Tamar in 2 Samuel 13:21.[25] A similar culpable silence is alluded to in Proverbs 24:10-12, where a stern warning is issued to those who could have intervened on behalf of the victims of oppression, but did not. Numerous recent studies on silence have decried the reprehensible silence of the people of God regarding evils and injustices of various sorts, especially when such silence arises out of their own self-interest and manifests a cold indifference to the sufferings of others. Such studies rightly point out that in such instances it is the *people of God* who must break the *silence of God* by arising and *speaking and acting for God*.[26]

Silence, Mourning, and Repentance in Israel's Collective Experience

We now turn to a related, yet different facet of the relationship between sin, silence, and repentance. We shall see that, in the context of sin and wrongdoing, silence may take on a more positive dimension. In fact, it may pave the way toward the restoration of the divine-human relationship.

In chapter 3, we observed that several of the prophets declared irreverent and unwelcome noise to be highly offensive to Yahweh. Frequently, the kind of noise most offensive to God's ears is the hypocritical sound of religious praise shouted out by a community completely unconcerned with the values of justice and mercy. Isaiah decries such sound as follows:

> Hear the word of the Lord, you rulers of Sodom! Listen to the teaching of our God, you people of Gomorrah! What to me is the multitude of your sacrifices? says the Lord; I have had enough of burnt offerings of rams and the fat of fed beasts; *I do not delight in the blood of bulls, or of lambs, or of goats.*
>
> When you come to appear before me, who asked this from your hand? *Trample my courts no more*; bringing offerings is futile; incense is an *abomination* to me. New moon and sabbath and calling of convocation—*I cannot endure solemn assemblies with iniquity*. Your new moons and your appointed festivals my soul *hates*; they have become a burden to me, I am *weary* of bearing them. When you stretch out your hands, I will hide my eyes from you; *even though you make many prayers, I will not listen*; your hands are full of blood. Wash yourselves; make yourselves clean; *remove the evil of your doings* from before my eyes; cease to do evil, learn to do good; seek justice, rescue the oppressed, defend the orphan, plead for the widow. (Isa 1:10-17)

The following passage in Amos expresses similar sentiments:

> I *hate*, I *despise* your festivals, and I take no delight in your solemn assemblies. Even though you offer me your burnt offerings and grain offerings, I will not accept them; and the offerings of well-being of your fatted animals I will not look upon. *Take away from me the noise of your songs; I will not listen to the melody of your harps*. But let *justice* roll down like waters, and righteousness like an everflowing stream. (Amos 5:21-24)

Moreover, as we saw in the previous chapter, Yahweh's judgment upon both the NK and SK, enacted through the destructions and deportations inflicted upon them by the Assyrians (722 BCE) and Babylonians (597 and 587 BCE), effectively silenced such offensive sound. These catastrophic events cast the land into the depths of silence. However, as we shall now see, new hope may emerge out of the darkness and ashes of the past. In contrast to the role of silence observed in the previous chapters, a different kind of silence can play an essential part in the pathway forward.

At the beginning of this chapter, we discussed the emergence of a theology of repentance and penitential prayer in the late seventh century BCE and beyond. We noted its underlying theological foundations and key vocabulary. We will now go on to observe several texts where, in addition to penitential words, silence holds an important place in repentance and renewal.

Lamentations 3:19-33

In Lamentations 3, silence is a critical element in the movement from destruction to new hope.[27] In each major section of Lamentations,[28] a "turning point" frequently appears near the center of each poem. Such is the case in Lamentations 3:19-33.[29] As in Lamentations 1 and 2, the poet speaks in the first person. But whereas in Lamentations 1 and 2 the speaker is feminine, and likely represents personified Jerusalem, in Lamentations 3 a different voice appears—that of a "man of valor" who has suffered ignominious defeat. Numerous suggestions have been made as to how to translate the Hebrew term used here.[30] I will simply refer to the him as "the poet." The poet's despair reaches its nadir in verses 17-18: "my soul is bereft of peace; I have forgotten what happiness is; and so I say, 'Gone is my glory, and all that I had hoped for from the Lord.'" It is noteworthy that it is here that the name Yahweh is first mentioned in the chapter. This descent into darkness prepares the way for verses 19-33 where the sentiment of the poet turns, and glimmers of hope appear:

> The thought of my affliction and my homelessness is wormwood and gall! My soul continually thinks of it and is bowed down within me. But this I call to mind, and therefore I have hope: The steadfast love of the Lord never ceases, his mercies never come to an end; they are new every morning; great is your faithfulness. "The Lord is my portion," says my soul, "therefore I will hope in him."
>
> The Lord is good to those who wait for him, to the soul that seeks him. It is good that one should wait quietly for the salvation of the Lord. It is good for one to bear the yoke in youth, *to sit alone in silence* when the Lord has imposed it, to put one's mouth to the dust (there may yet be hope), to give one's cheek to the smiter, and be filled with insults.

> For the Lord will not reject forever. Although he causes grief, he will have compassion according to the abundance of his steadfast love; for he does not willingly afflict or grieve anyone. (Lam 3:19-33)

Some see more than one speaker in the chapter, and have asserted that the voice in verses 19-33 represents a "safe" or "pious" outlook that affirms Yahweh's goodness despite suffering, as opposed to the more brutally honest and unorthodox voice(s) in chapters 1–2, 3:1-18, and chapters 4–5, which view Yahweh's punishment as cruel and unjust.[31] However, such a position is unwarranted. The chapter manifests a clear structural unity through its acrostic form. Moreover, it employs the concepts and vocabulary evident in many of the psalms of individual or corporate lament. These psalms include expressions of both protest and despair (even, as we shall see in chapter 7, at times blaming God for the distress) as well as sentiments of trust and hope (see Pss 3:1-8; 27:1-3; 31:3, 5), and at times requests for forgiveness of sins (25:18).[32] Finally, these verses (esp. vv. 25-39) draw heavily upon Israelite wisdom texts and traditions, which reflect deeply upon matters of suffering and divine justice.[33] As such, verses 19-42, with their references to silence in verses 26 and 28, need not presuppose a change of speaker holding a differing theological outlook. Complaint (3:1-18) is thus linked to hope (3:25-33) by the "bi-fold hinge" of 3:19-24.[34]

Verses 19-42 then lay out what has been called a "liturgical template" for the community's path to restoration.[35] What is involved? The poet begins this upward path in 3:19-24 by speaking of "remembering" and "taking to heart" certain realities. The first of these is the deep suffering that the community, including the speaker, has experienced (vv. 19-20). It is noteworthy that suffering plays a very important role in the biblical psalms of lament (cf. Pss 6:6-7; 25:16-19). This suffering is real and cannot be denied—in fact it is only via its recognition that restoration can begin (Lev 26:40-45; Deut 4:25-31; 30:1-5). Next, and in line with the theology of penitential prayer, attention is directed to the character of Yahweh, whose mercies and compassion never cease (v. 22) and whose faithfulness (v. 23) is great. These words call to mind the great description of the divine character found in Exodus 34:6-7:

> "The Lord, the Lord,
> a God merciful and gracious,
> slow to anger,
> and abounding in steadfast love and faithfulness,
> keeping steadfast love for the thousandth generation."

This passage is sometimes called the "character credo" as it becomes a quasi-fixed confession regarding the person of Yahweh.[36] It is said to be the most often cited text in the HB by the HB. It is frequently invoked in contexts of sin and forgiveness (see Joel 2:13; Jonah 4:2; Isa 54:8; Pss 25:6; 51:1; 86:15; 103:4, 8; 145:8; Neh 9:17).

The "steadfast love" (*ḥesed*) referred to in Lamentations 3:22 and Exodus 34:6 is one of the most commented upon words of the HB.[37] It refers to the gracious character of someone who, out of loyalty and commitment to a relationship, is willing to show kindness and extend forgiveness beyond that which might normally be expected. In the context of the divine-human relationship, it signifies Yahweh's faithfulness to Israel and willingness to forgive time and time again. The text goes on to speak of Yahweh as a God of mercy (*raḥum*, Lam 3:22; cf. Exod 34:6). This term refers to the tenderness and compassion of the Lord. Finally, the poet recalls Yahweh's great faithfulness (*ʾemunah*), alluding to the unfailing loyalty of God (Pss 36:5; 89:1-2). In light of these qualities, and despite the present distress, the poet urges the community to wait upon the Lord and hope in God's unfailing love (24b, 25, 26), knowing that the divine anger will ultimately abate, and that the desperate situation in which the people of God now find themselves will someday come to an end.

The text goes on to specify *how* such waiting on God must be done. Verses 26-29 utilize two terms derived from the Hebrew root **damam*-1,[38] which can denote either silence or stillness. The NRSV translates these verses: "The LORD is good to those who wait for him, to the soul that seeks him. It is good that one should wait *quietly* for the salvation of the LORD. It is good for one to bear the yoke in youth, to sit alone *in silence* when the Lord has imposed it." Most translations follow a similar approach, rendering the term in verse 26 (*dumam*) as the adverb "quietly," modifying the verb "to wait," and the conjugated verb in verse 28 (*weyiddom*) as modifying the one just preceding it ("he shall sit alone") and describing how one should "sit alone."

The translations "quietly" and "silently" are both deemed possible by the major Hebrew lexicons.[39] However, it is important to note that these lexicographers are using the term "quietly" (*dumam*) as a synonym for "silently" rather than in the sense of "in serenity" or "calmly." In his insightful study, Göran Eidevall has argued that the primary signification of **damam*-1 is that of stillness, or motionlessness, with silence emerging as a secondary sense. Eidevall then goes on to suggest that the term in Lamentations 3:26 (*dumam*) is best translated "in stillness."[40] It is certainly accurate to say that the concepts of stillness and silence are closely linked, and often indistinguishable. Thus, either translation would be admissible.

However for simplicity's sake, in the discussion that follows I will continue to use the English "silence" for this Hebrew term, recognizing that such silence implies more than the absence of sound, but includes the notion of stillness or cessation.[41]

However, the precise sense of "stillness" or "silence" in Lamentations 3:26 still requires further clarification. This specific term used here (*dumam*) occurs elsewhere in the HB only in Isaiah 47:5 and Habakkuk 2:19. In Habakkuk 2:19, the reference is to silent idols who cannot speak; thus, the idea of silence is clearly preferable there. In Isaiah 47:5, the sense of "quietly" or "in stillness" is inappropriate given that the reference there is to Babylon, who has been destroyed and descended into darkness. Silence, conversely, is entirely apposite, since silence is a defining characteristic of the realm of the dead (Sheol).

The situation in Lamentations 3:26 is much different than either Isaiah 47:5 or Habakkuk 2:19 in that the reference is to a *human attitude or posture* that the speaker urges upon his hearers as "good" and one to be adopted while waiting for God's "salvation" or "deliverance." It appears to me, then, that *dumam* in 3:26 may be translated either as "silently" or "in stillness," whereas the rendering "quietly" is misleading. In English, doing something "quietly" generally evokes the idea of doing it discretely, without attracting attention or causing undue disruption. For example, patrons may be requested to "speak quietly in the library." In Hebrew such an idea is often conveyed by the roots **shaqaṭ* or **nouaḥ* in some form.[42] However, given the painful emotions the poet has just expressed, what sort of "quietness" would be intended here? Would the speaker be enjoining the cessation of the lamentations expressed thus far in the book? This seems most improbable. Moreover, as we have seen, pitting 3:19-33 against the rest of the book seems highly problematic.

In order to achieve a proper understanding of this text, we must begin with an accurate appreciation of the nature of the "stillness" or "silence" of 3:26 and 28, the "hoping" of verse 24, and of the "waiting" and "seeking" of verses 25-30.[43] The silence or stillness of 3:26 and 28 is not the peaceful waiting for Yahweh's deliverance, resting on God's promises, and certain of the outcome as expressed in Psalms 37:7; 38:15; 39:7; 62:5 and 130:7. Rather, it is a silence that displays the *willing acceptance of God's judgment and penitent hope for possible reprieve*. This is evident in two aspects of the text. First, the key terms and concepts in the passage are drawn from Israel's wisdom teachings, and evoke the idea that the suffering God may send is designed to purify (cf. Job 5:17-18; Ps 39:11; Prov 3:11; 5:12; 13:24). The "yoke" borne in the passage is one that the Lord has "imposed" (vv. 26-27), and it is "good" to bear it.[44] It is similarly good to accept the indignities and insults sent by God, giving one's cheek to the smiter (cf. 1 Kgs 22:24; Isa 50:6; Mic 5:1; Ps 3:7; Job 16:10; 2 Chr 18:23) and suffering social shame (1 Sam 17:26; 2 Sam 13:13; Isa 4:1; 47:3; Jer 51:51).

The second aspect is drawn from Leviticus 26:40-45 and Israel's prophets.[45] As noted at the conclusion of the previous chapter, following expressions of Yahweh's judgment a period of time was needed before the former relationship could be fully restored. A similar attitude is described here. Thus, the counsel to "sit alone" and "wait in silence" indicates an inner disposition that recognizes that Yahweh's judgment has come and is justly deserved but will not endure forever. Moreover, such silence does not exclude the expression of mourning and lamentation, but rather implicitly expresses it. In the interim, our poet here counsels silence before the Lord until he *chooses to act in restoration*.

An excellent parallel to the thought in Lamentations 3:22-33 is found in Psalm 39:7-11:

> "And now, O Lord, what do I *wait* for?
>   My *hope* is in you.
> Deliver me from all my transgressions.
>   Do not make me the scorn of the fool.
> I am *silent*; I do not *open my mouth*,
>   for it is *you who have done it*.
> Remove *your stroke* from me;
>   I am worn down by the *blows of your hand*.
>
> "You chastise mortals in punishment for sin,
> consuming like a moth what is dear to them;
>   surely everyone is a mere breath."
>   *Selah*.

Numerous intertextual elements unite these two passages: hoping in Yahweh (Lam 3:21, 24, 29; Ps 39:7b); waiting on Yahweh (Lam 3:25-26; Ps 39:7a), suffering reproach (Lam 3:30; Ps 39:8); awaiting deliverance or the cessation of Yahweh's blows (Lam 3:26; Ps 39:10); and the keeping of silence (Lam 3:26, 28; Ps 39:9). Both texts include self-examination and the admission of sin (Lam 3:40-42; Ps 39:8, 11). Most importantly, in both texts *lament begins to give way to confession and penitence*. Silence may thus be the most fitting way to express both the acceptance of Yahweh's judgment and repentance toward God. It is thus entirely possible to lament the devastating results of judgment sent by God, while at the same time waiting in silence for them to subside.[46]

It is noteworthy that the significance of silence here in 3:26-28 moves beyond that of 2:10. There, the reference to silence comes at the culmination of a long recitation of the painful blows the nation has suffered at Yahweh's hand. The silence of the elders is like that of a person brought dangerously near to death—nothing more can be said, and there seems to be no purpose or hope. However, in Lamentations 3:25-30 the silence enjoined reflects a faith in the unfailing nature of Yahweh's love and compassion (vv. 22, 32) and the belief that God will not reject forever (v. 31) or capriciously afflict the people of God (v. 33). Therefore, they are encouraged to wait in silence (vv. 26, 28) until the day of God's anger has passed (cf. Isa 26:20; 54:6-7), and, above all else, place their hope in the gracious character of God.

Zechariah 7–8

I conclude this chapter by examining this final text that describes a movement from disaster and death (with its consequent silence) to a return to the joyful sounds of life. In many ways, Zechariah 7–8 parallels the depiction of the psalmist's journey from silence to joy in Psalm 51. Chapters 7–8 focus on the prophet's message to his contemporaries as they begin to reconstruct life in Judah, now known as the Persian province of Yehud, in the years following the end of Babylonian rule. Some of those exiled to Babylon had returned to Yehud and rejoined those who had remained in the land, and the restoration of the temple was underway. Zechariah 7 begins with a question to the priests about mourning and fasting. A group had been sent from the sanctuary at Bethel to Jerusalem to entreat the favor of Yahweh. The petitioners ask: "Should I mourn and practice abstinence in the fifth month, as I have done for so many years?" (Zech 7:3). It is unclear what kind of abstinence is being referred to. The verb here is reasonably rare (cf. Lev 15:31; Num 6:1-5). However, verse 5 gives some additional information in two regards: first, the abstinence involved "fasting and mourning" (practices typically associated with grief, death and loss); and second, these practices had been observed for "seventy years." As we have seen, the reference here is to the set time of abandonment between Yahweh's judgment for the sins of the past, and the possibility of a new beginning (Lev 26:40-45; Isa 40:1-2; Jer 25:11; 29:10; Hos 3:4-5). During this period, the various Israelite communities distributed throughout the region had added four ongoing fast days to the annual Day of Atonement observance (Zech 7:3, 5; 8:19). These additional fasts commemorated various tragic events surrounding the Babylonian conquest of

Judah, and especially the destruction of the temple.[47] Much of the content of Zechariah 7–8 constitutes a critique of the *motivation* behind such self-denial (7:5-6), and demands that the community amend its ways and stop the exploitation of the poor and weak in society (7:8-10; 8:16-17).

It is here that we encounter the theme of the movement from deathly silence to joyous sound. At several points, Zechariah emphasizes that Yahweh's judgment upon the nation brought its normal "soundscape" to a halt. Our prophet remembers the time when "Jerusalem was inhabited and in prosperity, along with the towns around it, and . . . the Negeb and the Shephelah were inhabited" (Zech 7:7). However, due to its corrupt practices, Yahweh's wrath came upon the nation and habitation and prosperity were lost: "I scattered them with a whirlwind among all the nations that they had not known. Thus, the land they left was desolate, so that no one went to and fro, and a pleasant land was made desolate" (Zech 7:14). Everyday life was disrupted and dangerous (8:10). The desolation of the land mentioned here not only evokes its radical depopulation (cf. Lev 26:31, 34, 43; Amos 9:14), but also implies the impossibility of agricultural (Ezek 36:34-35) or economic activities (cf. Isa 33:8; Zeph 3:6). All the sounds associated with such activities are gone. Zechariah 1–6 have been replete with motifs of "new beginnings"—the restoration of Jerusalem, the rebuilding of the temple and the renewal of the priesthood. However, full restoration has not yet arrived.[48] Thus, in answer to the question regarding fasting, the prophet reminds the people that before the sounds of life can really be restored, ethical change must come: "Render true judgments, show kindness and mercy to one another; do not oppress the widow, the orphan, the alien, or the poor; and do not devise evil in your hearts against one another. . . . Speak the truth to one another, render in your gates judgments that are true and make for peace" (Zech 7:10; 8:16). However, should this occur, the situation will be radically reversed. The prophet then sets forth a series of images of the "everyday life" that burst with sound. Two themes are especially significant here.

The first is repopulation. Jerusalem will be filled with many people, young and old, and the sounds of daily life will return. Note that the text's soundscape mirrors the joys of restoration:

> Thus says the LORD of hosts: Old men and old women shall again sit in the streets of Jerusalem, each with staff in hand because of their great age. And the streets of the city shall be full of boys and girls playing in its streets. Thus says the LORD of hosts: Even though it seems impossible to the remnant of this people in these days, should it also seem impossible to me, says the LORD of hosts? Thus says the LORD of hosts: I will save my

> people from the east country and from the west country; and I will bring them to live in Jerusalem. They shall be my people and I will be their God, in faithfulness and in righteousness. (Zech 8:4-8)

The second motif relates to the question of fasting, with which the section began. The sounds of mourning—lamenting the departure of the dead into the silence of the grave—that have attended the fasts observed over the previous "seventy years" will be no more. In their place new sounds will come, sounds to accompany "seasons of joy and gladness, and cheerful festivals for the house of Judah" (Zech 8:19). This echoes the thought of Isaiah 65:11: "I will rejoice in Jerusalem, and delight in my people; no more shall the sound of weeping be heard in it, or the cry of distress."

Summary

To summarize, in this chapter we have examined matters of silence and sound and their relationship to sin and forgiveness in the experience of the individual and of the people of God collectively. We have seen that silence can be a negative response to personal wrongdoing. Thus, in Psalm 32 the psalmist looks back upon the silence with which he sought to hide his sin from God. However, this silence only worsened his predicament. His body and mind suffered horrendously. Relief came only through breaking the silence, as the psalmist expresses confession of sin and trust in Yahweh's forgiveness. We have also seen that silence can foreshadow one's destiny should wrongdoing not be properly resolved. In Psalm 51, the psalmist pleads for divine forgiveness, lest he descend into the grave, the realm of silence. However, cleansing from sin and renewal of the heart lead the psalmist out of silence into joyous sound. In contrast to the destructive silence mentioned in Psalms 32 and 51, in Lamentations 3 silence is a key station on the way to restoration. This kind of silence represents profound repentance and gives evidence of the willingness, following significant wrongdoing and judgment, to wait in silence for God's mercy and restoration, to amend one's ways, and to allow time for the broader divine-human relationship to heal. Finally, Zechariah 7–8 affirms that after such a time, the joyous sounds of life and worship may return.

5
SILENCE AS SECURITY

God Our Rock

In the previous chapters, we have seen how the downward spiral set in motion by wrongdoing and rebellion can lead to alienation and catastrophe, both of which are closely associated with silence. However, we also discovered that, rightly expressed, silence can mark an important step away from catastrophe and toward restoration and renewal. In this chapter, we will examine yet another side of silence—one that expresses the deep security that the people of God, either individually or collectively, may experience through trusting in God as their "rock."[1] As such, a community of faith may be called to silence and stillness, even in the direst of circumstances, awaiting God's sure and certain deliverance.[2] The focus of the present chapter, then, is the close connection between silence or stillness, God as a mighty rock, and the call for the people of God to wait on the Lord in stillness, quietness, and confident hope, even in times of extreme danger or need.

This dynamic is evident in Exodus 14:14, a text that might be aptly described as a paradigm of Yahweh as protector and deliverer. The people of Israel have departed from Egypt with great hope of reaching a new land of safety, freedom, and prosperity. However, very soon they find themselves in a seemingly impossible situation. The Red Sea is before them, and the Egyptian armies are closing in behind. The people are terrified and fear annihilation. What possible hope could there be? To their amazement, as well as to that of all subsequent readers of this narrative, Moses is not dismayed:

> As Pharaoh drew near, the Israelites looked back, and there were the Egyptians advancing on them. In great fear the Israelites cried out to the

> LORD. They said to Moses, "Was it because there were no graves in Egypt that you have taken us away to die in the wilderness? What have you done to us, bringing us out of Egypt? Is this not the very thing we told you in Egypt, 'Let us alone and let us serve the Egyptians'? For it would have been better for us to serve the Egyptians than to die in the wilderness." (Exod 14:10-12)

Moses, however, will have none of it, and counsels the people to look in an entirely different direction:

> But Moses said to the people, "Do not be afraid, stand firm, and see the deliverance that the LORD will accomplish for you today; for the Egyptians whom you see today you shall never see again. The LORD will fight for you, and you have only to keep still." (Exod 14:13-14)

Moses' words echo a formula frequently referred to by scholars as a "formula of encouragement or reassurance."[3] This formula calls the people of God (collectively or individually) to reject fear and to embrace courage and strength, because Yahweh is the one who leads them and who will fight for them. The paradigm for a foundational attitude of trust is the portrait of Yahweh as Israel's defender in Deuteronomy 20:1-4:

> When you go out to war against your enemies, and see horses and chariots, an army larger than your own, you shall not be afraid of them; for the LORD your God is with you, who brought you up from the land of Egypt. Before you engage in battle, the priest shall come forward and speak to the troops, and shall say to them: "Hear, O Israel! Today you are drawing near to do battle against your enemies. Do not lose heart, or be afraid, or panic, or be in dread of them; for it is the LORD your God who goes with you, to fight for you against your enemies, to give you victory."

Frequently these calls to encouragement are given in situations of grave threat in warfare.[4] Importantly, in most of these instances the Israelites are *active participants in battle* and these words encourage them as they go forth.[5] Here, on the contrary, we encounter a very different picture. Israel is passive and is commanded to "stand firm, and see the deliverance that the LORD will accomplish for you today." Then, to underline that which is being demanded, Moses adds, "The LORD will fight for you, and you have only to *keep still*."[6]

This explicit call to stillness or silence in the context of a "formula of encouragement" is unique in the HB.[7] Moreover here we find an excellent example of both the depth and complexity of biblical narrative, and especially its ability to play on words with more than a single meaning; as noted in our discussion of **damam* in chapter 3, this phenomenon is technically known as polysemy. The verb translated here as "keep still" (**ḥarash*) often refers to refraining from speech.[8] In only two contexts, here and Zephaniah 3:17, does it appear to convey the idea of calm or quiet.[9] The silence or stillness in Exodus 14:14 may be clearly understood by looking at its opposite, "fearing" (**yara'*), in v. 13 and at the verb parallel to it in verse 14, "taking one's stand" (**yatzav* hithpael; see Num 11:16; Deut 7:24; 1 Sam 12:16; 2 Sam 21:5). Israel may "keep still" because Yahweh will fight on its behalf. The Egyptian armies they now "see" they will "see no more." Thus, Israel can stand firm and "fear not" (14:13). The verbs to see (**ra'ah*) and to fear (**yara'*) are very similar in Hebrew, and it is easy to play upon the relationship between them, as is being done here. Furthermore, the stillness or silence enjoined in Exodus 14:13-15 goes beyond the mere cessation of crying out to God in panic. The use of the encouragement formula here, and the juxtaposition of Israel's stillness and Yahweh's activity on its behalf, clearly indicate that the silence called for is an attitude of *internal calm, arising out of trust that Yahweh is present and will not allow the people of faith to come to grief.* As such, the summative command in verse 14 is *both* a call to silence *and* a call to calm and trust. Israel is called to *silence* in contrast to its earlier crying out to Yahweh in fear, and it is also called to calm in light of the fact that Yahweh will do battle on behalf of the people.[10] Moreover, we note that the silence or stillness called for here is not a total cessation of movement or activity. In verse 15, Israel is called to journey on (**nasa'*; Exod 15:22; 16:1; 17:1)[11] and proceed across the water.[12] Furthermore, Yahweh's call for silence here, and his defeat of the Egyptians without Israel's active intervention, has a specific purpose: that "the Egyptians shall know that I am the Lord, when I have gained glory for myself over Pharaoh, his chariots, and his chariot drivers" (Exod 14:18-19). The magnificent poem in Exodus 15 then celebrates the great deliverance that Yahweh has wrought for his people.

Exodus 14, therefore, makes a significant contribution to our understanding of silence, and one that will be developed in the course of this chapter. Silence frequently indicates a series of interrelated ideas: confident expectation, waiting in peace and stillness for God's intervention, and deep security. Let us now examine how this motif is developed in a series of texts, using a variety of words and images.

Silence and Security in the Psalms

The Psalms are replete with expressions of the majesty and power of Yahweh, and focus especially upon the peace and security these divine attributes can bring. At times, personal or interpersonal challenges arise from *within* the individual psalmist or the community. At other times, they are political or military, coming from *without*. Our first example is of the latter type.

Psalm 46: God Rules over All

This psalm is typically classified as a "song of Zion" because it contains the key elements of what scholars call "Zion theology." The name Zion refers specifically to Jerusalem's eastern hill, where the temple was constructed. Zion theology emphasizes Yahweh's choice of Zion and its temple as God's dwelling place, the life-giving streams that flow forth from it, and the stability and security that this brings to the temple and the inhabitants of Jerusalem.[13] The psalm opens with the declaration that God is a *refuge* (*maḥaseh*), a place of shelter from storm or attack. This term is frequently used as an image for Yahweh's protection (Pss 14:6; 62:7; 91:2; Prov 14:26; Isa 4:6; 25:4; Jer 17:17). The Lord is also their *strength* (*ʿoz*, here in the sense of protection and defense; cf. Pss 28:8; 29:11). As a result, the psalmist declares that God's people can live without fear (v. 2) even if the world seems to disintegrate. Because God is in Zion's midst, the city will never be overturned, even if assaulted by a multitude of nations. Indeed, says the psalmist: "The LORD of hosts is with us; the God of Jacob is our refuge" (vv. 5-7). Verses 8-9 then turn to God's power over all the nations, and his ability to bring wars and hostility to an end. Then, at the psalm's climactic moment, God himself speaks. Direct address by God is relatively rare in the Psalms.[14] In verse 10, God exclaims:

> Be still, and know that I am God!
> I am exalted among the nations,
> I am exalted in the earth.

A prophet or priest in attendance at the temple may have delivered God's words to those present. The psalmist then replies in verse 11:

> The LORD of hosts is with us;
> the God of Jacob is our refuge. *Selah*

The term "be still" (**raphah*) is different from any of the words for stillness or silence that we have encountered thus far. It is most frequently used in a negative sense, and conveys the idea of becoming weak or discouraged,[15] of discouraging others,[16] of letting someone or something go or drop,[17] or showing one's self to be lax or without courage.[18] It may also be used to command someone to cease speaking (1 Sam 15:16), or in an exhortation to hold fast to a quality or characteristic (Prov 4:13).

A significant interpretive question confronts us here at this point: to whom are these words addressed, and in what sense are they to be taken? One could view them as spoken to those rebellious nations who reject Yahweh's reign and seek to dethrone Yahweh from his rule in Zion (cf. Pss 2; 110). If this approach is chosen, the verb is best translated, "Desist!"[19] A majority of commentators hold this view. Its strength lies in its reading of the verb **raphah* in its usual sense of "drop" or "let go." It also fits well into the context of the verse, which goes on to declare that Yahweh will be exalted among the nations. However, while it is clear that the nations are the primary *addressees* of these words, it is unlikely that they were its principal *audience*. The nations were not present in the Jerusalem temple to overhear this declaration, nor were they the likely readers of the biblical text. Thus, these words (like many of the so-called "oracles against the nations" in the HB) are spoken *to* the nations but are meant to serve as a means of encouragement *for* the Israelite hearers.[20] Taken this way, the call to "be still" is something of a *double entendre*. The imagery of body language frequently connected with this verb (the dropping of the hands) is still involved, but now in a positive sense. This becomes evident when our verse here is set in contrast to the numerous assertions that Israel can be secure because Yahweh will not fail the people of God (Deut 4:31; 31:6-8; Josh 1:5; 1 Chr 28:20). Thus, through these words spoken to the nations (who are not present), through them God's people are being exhorted to be silent or still and to release their fear of the nations into the hands of Yahweh, who is more than adequate to defeat any hostile forces arrayed against them.

Psalm 62: Waiting in Confident Silence

This psalm may be classified as a psalm of personal trust,[21] or as a "prayer song."[22] Either way, as is the case in Psalms 4; 16; 23; 27:1-6; 91; 121; and 131, it expresses the psalmist's unshakeable confidence in Yahweh.[23] It is important to note that the psalmist's troubles are ongoing.[24] This is not a retrospective gaze, looking back and praising God for answered prayer and blessings received, as in Psalms 30 and 116. Rather, the psalmist here is in the hard place between difficulty and deliverance—the place of waiting. The verb "to wait" is not specifically used in verses 1 and 5, although it appears in most translations. The verse reads literally, "In silence my inner being" (v. 1) and "be silent toward God, my inner being" (v. 5).[25] However, the idea of waiting is likely suggested by the use of the noun "hope" (*tiqwah*) in verse 5.

The psalmist has been the victim of some sort of assault from personal enemies, and perhaps faced moments of spiritual crisis. In verse 3, she speaks of being battered (only here in the HB) and struck, as if she were a crumbling wall.[26] Her enemies seek to push her down with their lies and cursing (v. 4). Yet, the psalmist is not reduced to fear or discouragement. She exhorts herself to wait for God's deliverance (v. 5). She is certain that God is a rock and a stronghold who will not allow her to be shaken, and that her wellbeing depends ultimately on God (vv. 6-7). In verses 8-10 she exhorts the members of her community to follow her example, looking to the Lord to whom all judgment belongs (vv. 11-12). The critical element, around which much else turns, is the "silence" that lies close to the center of the psalmist's being (vv. 1, 5).

Given the confines of the present study, we cannot enter into a detailed analysis of the many significant aspects of this psalm. The center of our interest here is the role of silence in verse 1, where the psalmist declares that her inner being is in silence, and in verse 5, where she exhorts herself to silence. Two questions face us at this point. The first concerns the most appropriate translation of the Hebrew terms here. Should they be rendered as silence, quietness, or peacefulness? The second concerns that which the psalmist implies by her statement that she waits "in silence" or by her self-exhortation to "be silent" before God.

Regarding our first question, we begin by noting that two different but related Hebrew words are used: the noun *dumia* in verse 1 and the imperative *dommi* in verse 5.[27] The standard Hebrew lexicons associate both of these terms with silence ("in silence" [v. 1] and "be silent" [v. 5]),[28] and as we have seen the relationship between silence and stillness is a close one.[29] Movement implies sound, and stillness implies silence. Furthermore, attempting to make a hard separation between "silence," on the one hand, or "stillness," on the other, when speaking of the psalmist's inner being may be attempting to impose distinctions that are simply too fine. Thus, I would accept either silence or stillness as legitimate translations of these terms.

However, as noted in the previous chapter, contemporary ideas connected with the terms "quiet" or "quietly" create a false impression. Thus, one might refer to someone "speaking quietly" in a library or children "working quietly" at their desks. The idea in such instances involves not making *undue* noise or drawing attention to oneself through *disturbing* behavior. This is entirely different from the meaning of these terms here. One *may* use the term "quiet" in Psalm 62 if one makes it clear that it designates an absence of agitation or a state of stillness or rest.[30]

Let us turn now to the second question: what is meant by "waiting in silence/stillness"? Goldingay suggests that the psalmist means waiting in the sure and certain hope of God's deliverance (as stated in vv. 11-12), yet all the while crying out in lament and frustration:

> Any fool can trust when there is no pressure. . . . The implication of vv. 1-7 is that trust implies silence, though the eight lines that say so rather contradict themselves. Arguably they have constituted a pouring out of the psalmist's heart before God (though not to God) and this is what the psalm now commends as an expression of trust. . . . The psalm is encouraging the community to an act of faith that pours out its resentment, grief and fear before God, the act the psalms are often modeling.[31]

Yet this approach may go too far. It does take into account the psalmist's exhortation to "pour one's heart" out to God in verse 8, which may denote fervent prayer (1 Sam 1:15; Ps 42:4; Lam 2:19).[32] It similarly reckons with the words "how long" in verse 3, which are frequently used in laments (Pss 13:1-2; 90:13, etc.). Yet these features of our psalm should not be overstated. To be sure, in times of personal crisis, one will pray fervently. However, this need not in itself indicate a spirit of "resentment, grief and fear." Similarly, the words "how long" in verse 3 are *not addressed to God* (as they are in the psalms of lament), but to *the psalmist's enemies*. In light of verses 11-12, the spirit of these words may well be to caution evildoers that, despite all appearances to the contrary, their end will come.[33] Thus, rather than pouring out one's grief and resentment to the Lord while trusting in God's goodness, as suggested by some, what we find here is a motif of *inner* silence (or stillness) despite *external* chaos. This can be seen in the contrast between the interior and exterior "soundscape" of the psalm. The silence of the psalmist's inner being (vv. 1, 5) stands in stark contrast to the cacophony that surrounds her. The "attacks" and "murderous assaults" of verse 4 are likened to the blows used to level a tottering wall—a noisy undertaking to be sure.[34] Words of insincere blessing abound (v. 4). Yet despite this disturbing noise, the psalmist begins with an affirmation of her inner silence in verse 1 and then returns to it in verse 5. Indeed, the psalmist's inner silence *frames* the chaos outside. Nevertheless, that inner silence is not unshakeable, either for the psalmist herself, or for those for whom and to whom she speaks. This accounts for the transformation of the assertion of verse 1 into the self-exhortation of verse 5. To reinforce this call, verses 6-7 give the basis for such hope: God is the psalmist's rock, fortress, and refuge (three images of protection and defense) and will bring about deliverance and restoration of honor. In sum, silence lies close to the heart of Psalm 62. The psalm asserts that it is possible to dwell in silence (inner quiet and peace) even in the midst of personal assaults and more general oppression and injustice. However, *this state of the heart must constantly be refreshed and renewed.* If not, it may be lost. This is the clear implication of the expressions of self-exhortation in the psalm. The key to maintaining it is a clear grasp of the basis upon which it rests. It is a silence that comes from knowing in the depths of one's being that one's ultimate security lies in God, and that, all appearances to the contrary, the Lord's ultimate justice and goodness will prevail.

Psalm 37: The Certainty of God's Justice

A very similar perspective appears in Psalm 37, which has certain intertextual and thematic links with Psalms 46 and 62. Like Psalm 62, the psalmist is troubled by evil in the world (vv. 1-4, 7-8) and is being affected by it (vv. 5-6, 12, 14, 28, 32). Most specifically, the psalmist provides wise counsel on coping with it. This counsel centers on the certainty that the Lord will ultimately vindicate the righteous and cut off the wicked (vv. 2, 5-6, 9-10, 14-15, 20, 22, 28, 34-40). In the meantime, those faithful to the Lord must trust in Yahweh and do good (vv. 3, 5, 27), take delight in Yahweh (v. 4), commit their way to Yahweh and live in a spirit of dependent trust (v. 5), and refrain from anger and wrath (v. 8). *Central to the ability to manifest these qualities is the ability to maintain a sense of inner calm or silence.* Thus, the psalmist declares in verse 7: "Be still before the Lord, and wait patiently for him; do not fret over those who prosper in their way, over those who carry out evil devices." The command to be still employs the Hebrew root **damam*-1, which denotes either silence or stillness, and was used in connection with the motif of waiting hopefully in Psalm 62:1, 5. The command in 37:8 to "refrain from anger" uses the same verb, **haraph*, that also appears in Psalm 46:10 in the command to "be still" and know that God is Yahweh. Thus, just as the nations are commanded to let go of their opposition to Yahweh's rule, so the psalmist encourages the hearers to abandon their anger and wrath over the success and machinations of those who do wrong, and to rest in the certainty of God's ultimate victory.

Psalm 131: The Security of a Nurtured Child

Apart from Psalm 117, this is the briefest psalm in the Psalter. It forms a part of the so-called "Psalms of Ascents."[35] With its central motifs of the silencing or quieting of the inner being (*nephesh*) it takes up several of the ideas we have just observed in Psalm 62. However, here these concepts are configured quite differently. According to numerous scholars, the psalmist here is a woman reflecting upon the divine-human relationship, portraying it in terms of the relationship between mother and child.[36] It does seem highly probable that the speaker in verses 1-2 knows the maternal experience quite intimately, especially as it relates to nurture and feeding. The psalmist begins by refuting any accusation that she has been arrogant or presumptuous.[37] In contrast to the haughtiness of which she has been accused, in verse 2 the psalmist declares what her heart attitude has been:

> But I have calmed and quieted my soul,
> like a weaned child with its mother;
> my soul is like the weaned child that is with me.

The first verb ("calmed") carries a wide variety of meanings, and can be used in the sense of leveling off or smoothing someone or something (Isa 28:25).[38] Its meaning is further clarified by the following verb ("quieted," *domamti*) derived from the root **damam*-1, which we have encountered numerous times. Thus, the psalmist has soothed and silenced her inner being.

The following two lines of the psalm constitute a simile giving further depth to this statement, and have occasioned extensive discussion of their translation and the meaning of this figure of speech. Several aspects of this simile call for special attention, and involve complexities of translation. First, is the child *weaned* (no longer breastfeeding) or *sated* (no longer hungry)? Second, should verse 2 be translated "my soul is like the weaned child *that is with me*" (NRSV, Hossfeld and Zenger),[39] or "my soul *within me* is like a weaned child" (NRSV margin)? The former translation emphasizes the parallel between the child on or with its mother and the psalmist's inner being on or with her/him, while the second does not.[40] Third, why mention the idea of weaned or sated at all, and not simply draw upon the image of a child with its mother? What is being suggested by this simile? Does it imply movement from a state of extreme need to one of relief (hunger to satiety) or from anxiety to comfort (the weaned child finds comfort on the mother's lap)? Put another way, the image clearly implies a transition from one state to another, but to what *reality in life* does the simile correspond? Fourth, where does Yahweh figure in this image?[41]

These complex issues have generated much scholarly discussion. I would offer the following observations and conclusions. First, although the idea of the infant's calm following hunger could fit the context, the verb in question clearly signifies "weaned" (see Gen 21:8; 1 Sam 1:22-24; 1 Kgs 11:20; Isa 11:8; Hos 1:8) rather than satiated.[42] Second, this in turn implies that what is being emphasized here is the *state of calm* the psalmist has brought to her inner being (a weaned child who sits calmly in the mother's lap) rather than the sense of relief following acute disturbance or need (a hungry child who sleeps peacefully following the discomfort of hunger). This would then speak against readings of the psalm that imply a moment of severe crisis that has been resolved.[43] *Rather, it portrays a person who is able to maintain a sense of inner stability in the midst of the storms of life.* Most importantly, the psalmist declares that it is *she* who has smoothed/soothed and "silenced" her own inner being. I will return to this important point below.

Although both Psalms 62 and 131 deal with stillness/silence in the inner being, several key differences emerge. First, in contrast to Psalm 62:1, 5, where the emphasis is upon patient waiting upon God, here the psalmist has *already succeeded* in bringing stillness or calm to her inner being. Second, whereas in Psalm 62 much attention is given to God's ability to rescue the speaker from grave threat and harm, here greater emphasis is placed upon the speaker's *own ability* to bring calm and peace to her own inner being (as in Pss 42:5, 11; 43:5). Third, whereas Psalm 62 underlines the *external threats* that the psalmist has had to confront, in Psalm 131 the critical element is the speaker's capacity to recognize and live within the limits of her own abilities of comprehension. She denies that she has attempted to pronounce judgments on matters "too great and too marvelous for me." Notably, the same attitude, using similar vocabulary, is adopted by Job after Yahweh speaks to him out of the whirlwind (Job 42:3-6). Moreover, the psalmist may imply that her inner quiet moves outward from the internal to the external world. Báez makes the intriguing suggestion that the unique verbal form used to depict this *inner* silencing may also imply the ability to *restrain one's speech*.[44] Fourth, the simile of mother and child conveys a far greater intimacy than the language in Psalm 62, where no particular portrait of the divine-human relationship is evoked. The imagery of the weaned child leaning upon the mother's breast, not for nourishment but for solace, is one of the most tender and evocative in Scripture. And here, most surprisingly, the psalmist depicts her inner being as *reposing upon herself!* The idea here is thus peace and stillness through self-nurture. But how is this possible? Clearly there is no suggestion that this was found through some kind of "self-help" technique. This would be entirely foreign to Israelite thought and to the ethos of the Psalms. The primary answer comes in verse 3, where Israel is exhorted to hope (**yaḥal*) in Yahweh.[45] A further consideration comes when one recognizes that Psalms 130 and 131 are likely set together in this collection of psalms, and that the emphasis on waiting on God in Psalm 130:5-7 is meant to carry over into the reading of Psalm 131.[46] But most importantly, the foundational means of attaining stillness/silence comes through the recognition of an "unspoken gap" in the imagery and logic of the psalm.[47] The comments of Hossfeld and Zenger merit a full citation here:

> Psalm 131:2cd . . . has left a space open that the one reciting the psalm must fill or augment in such a way that one must in fact formulate it: "Like a nursed child with its mother, like a nursed child with me—so is my soul with you, YHWH, as my mother who nurses, protects, and consoles me."[48]

This psalm asserts, then, that as the people of God, we may successfully bring silence and stillness to our inner beings. And we can ultimately do so as we lie, peacefully and silently, in the comforting and nurturing lap of God.

Silence in Times of Crisis and Threat: Peace and Security in the Assyrian Crisis

Several passages in the books of Isaiah and 1 Kings highlight the interrelated concepts of inner stillness and silence, and waiting for Yahweh's deliverance in the midst of severe threat and crisis. In the mid- to late-eighth century BCE, the Assyrian rulers began to march westward, sweeping away all the smaller kingdoms in their path.[49] In 722, they conquered the NK and its capital at Samaria. Subsequently, under Sennacherib they marched southwards, threatening Judah and Jerusalem in the waning years of the eighth century. This threat caused King Hezekiah and the people of Judah to panic. In the minds of some, Egypt could provide the needed protection from the Assyrian threat.[50] The prophet Isaiah served as Yahweh's instrument to address the situation. His message was simple: seeking deliverance through Egypt would only bring disaster, but waiting on Yahweh and trusting in his promises to Zion (see Pss 2; 46; 48; 110; 132) would bring salvation and blessing.[51] The oracles in Isaiah 28:9–33:24 speak particularly to this situation, and silence or stillness plays a key role in several of them.

Silence appears in a woe-oracle addressed to Judah in Isaiah 30:1-18. As noted, Israel had sought deliverance from the Assyrian threat through an alliance with Egypt (Isa 30:1-4). However, such aid would be worthless (vv. 6-7). Moreover, the nation's appeal to Egypt has flown in the face of the counsel given by the true prophets of Yahweh, and would therefore yield disastrous consequences (vv. 8-14). In verse 15, Yahweh declares what the nation should have done: "For thus said the Lord God, the Holy One of Israel: In returning and rest you shall be saved; in quietness and in trust shall be your strength. But you refused."

The message here is a simple one. Israel ought to have returned (**shouv*) to Yahweh and rested (**shaqaṭ*) and trusted (**bataḥ*) in him. The return to

Yahweh counseled here is different from the one called for in passages such as Deuteronomy 4:30; 30:1; Amos 4:6, 8-11; and Joel 2:13-14, where the demand is a return to obedience to Yahweh's statutes. Isaiah 30:15 refers to a state of trust and dependence. This is made clear by the noun "rest" that denotes the broader concept of silence, calm, and peace.[52] Since the nation had refused the stance of quiet dependence upon Yahweh, only chaos and destruction would follow:

> But you refused and said,
> "No! We will flee upon horses"—
>   therefore you shall flee!
> and, "We will ride upon swift steeds"—
>   therefore your pursuers shall be swift!
> A thousand shall flee at the threat of one,
>   at the threat of five you shall flee,
> until you are left
>   like a flagstaff on the top of a mountain,
>   like a signal on a hill. (Isa 30:15-17)

The final line of the oracle sums up Yahweh's gracious attitude and desire for his people:

> Therefore the LORD waits to be gracious to you;
>   therefore he will rise up to show mercy to you.
> For the LORD is a God of justice;
>   blessed are all those who wait for him. (Isa 30:18)

As we saw in our examination of silence in the Psalms, waiting for God's ultimate salvation and deliverance in times of crisis is a foundational element in numerous contexts.

In Isaiah 32, we move from an oracle of woe to one of hope. The prophet looks beyond the present corruption of the nation and the imminent Assyrian invasion (32:6-14). He sees a time when the king and nobles will deal righteously (32:1) and be like a shelter in the desert heat, bringing needed relief to the land (32:2-5). The turning point will come when

> . . . a spirit from on high is poured out on us,
>   and the wilderness becomes a fruitful field,
>   and the fruitful field is deemed a forest.
> Then justice will dwell in the wilderness,
>   and righteousness abide in the fruitful field.
> The effect of righteousness will be peace,

and the result of righteousness, quietness and trust forever.
My people will abide in a peaceful habitation,
in secure dwellings, and in quiet resting places. (Isa 32:15-18)

Several points are noteworthy here. First, the spirit here is Yahweh's spirit, for it comes down from on high.[53] The spirit's activity first touches the natural realm—the desert is transformed into a place of fruitfulness, dense as a forest (v. 15), with justice and righteousness present in every corner of the nation's life. The reference to the righteous rule of the king and princes makes clear that here the prophet is not speaking of purely personal, individual actions. Societal matters are to be included as well (esp. vv. 6-7). Then, verse 17 describes the effects of such justice. These will include peace (*shalom*, a very general term denoting wellbeing or the absence of strife and conflict), then quietness (*hashqeṭ*, from **shaqaṭ*, one of the terms closely related to silence), and trust or security (*beṭaḥ*).[54] It is important to note that the first of these three terms, *shalom*, appears in the first half of the verse, while the latter two (*hashqeṭ* and *beṭaḥ*) occur in the second half. Thus, it would seem that the latter two terms give more precise definition to the former. The Hebrew root **shaqaṭ* generally denotes a state of stillness or calm (1 Chr 4:40; Isa 7:4; 14:7; 18:4; 57:20; Jer 30:10; 46:27; Ezek 16:42; Zech 1:11). Moreover, the verb **shaqaṭ* (already encountered in Isa 30:15, above) frequently stands in close proximity to Hebrew terms denoting silence or stillness (Ps 83:1; Isa 62:1; Jer 47:6). The final term, either the verb **baṭaḥ* or the corresponding noun *beṭaḥ*, may denote the expression of human trust, either toward God[55] or toward improper objects.[56] Alternatively, it may be used in phrases that denote dwelling peacefully or in security.[57] The most likely referent for *beṭaḥ* here would be the latter—the outcome of justice will be security in the land.

In sum, quiet or calm stands alongside well-being, and security as the outworking of Yahweh's spirit enabling the leaders of the people to judge and rule with justice.[58] What is more, this state of affairs will never come to an end. Especially important for our purposes is the inclusion of the concept of stillness and quietness, which occupies a central position in this text. The importance of such quietness can be seen in the "soundscape" of the text. Yahweh's judgment and the agricultural ruin resulting from it had led to the "beating of the breast" (lit. "wailing," 32:12). The sounds of life had been replaced by the cries of wild beasts (v. 14). However, now destructive sounds are *eliminated*: fools and villains will no longer be *called* noble (32:5); fools will no longer *speak* folly, *utter error* (32:6), or put forth *lying words* (v. 7). Stillness and peace will fill the land once again. Note as well that such stillness and peace testify to a renewal of Yahweh's presence in the land. Yet here, as opposed to Zechariah 7–8 and Isaiah 51:3 and 65:19, that testimony is seen not through the soundscape of increased population, renewal of economic activity or songs of joy. Rather, it is discernable through the *silence* that attends the land and people.

One final instance of silence as reflecting confidence in Yahweh's deliverance merits consideration here. It occurs in 2 Kings 18:28-36, another text concerning the Assyrian assault on Judah. The narrator begins by underlining Hezekiah's devotion to the worship of Yahweh alone and deep trust in him (2 Kgs 18:1-6). Near the outset of his reign, Hezekiah had rebelled against the Assyrian king, withholding tribute from him (18:7). At this point the Assyrian armies were sweeping across the Levant. The NK collapsed under siege (18:9-12) and the SK was threated. Hezekiah had urged the Jerusalemite population to resist the siege and to trust in Yahweh's protection. The Assyrian general (the Rabshakeh), however, mocked such an idea, and argued that Assyrian might was insuperable:

> Then the Rabshakeh stood and called out in a loud voice in the language of Judah, "Hear the word of the great king, the king of Assyria! Thus says the king: 'Do not let Hezekiah deceive you, for he will not be able to deliver you out of my hand. Do not let Hezekiah make you rely on the LORD by saying, The LORD will surely deliver us, and this city will not be given into the hand of the king of Assyria.' Do not listen to Hezekiah; for thus says the king of Assyria: 'Make your peace with me and come out to me; then every one of you will eat from your own vine and your own fig tree, and drink water from your own cistern, until I come and take you away to a land like your own land, a land of grain and wine, a land of bread and vineyards, a land of olive oil and honey, that you may live and not die. Do not listen to Hezekiah when he misleads you by saying, The LORD will deliver us. Has any of the gods of the nations ever delivered its land out of the hand of the king of Assyria? Where are the gods of Hamath and Arpad? Where are the gods of Sepharvaim, Hena, and Ivvah? Have they delivered Samaria out of my hand? Who among all the gods of the countries have delivered their countries out of my hand, that the LORD should deliver Jerusalem out of my hand?'" (2 Kgs 18:28-35)

Hezekiah, however, had directed the people as to how best to handle the situation—he called them to total silence: "But the people were *silent* and answered him not a word, for the king's command was, '*Do not answer him*'" (2 Kgs 18:36). Silence here is clearly an *act of defiance* in the face of the propaganda of an oppressor.

It is highly interesting that the Rabshakeh has "excellent theology"! His words give expression to one of the central ideas in Isaiah and this section of 2 Kings: the necessity of trust in the promises of Yahweh and in his power, even in the face of deadly threat. Hezekiah's call to silence forms a key pivot point in the narrative. It demonstrates his determination not to be swayed by Assyrian propaganda, and the people's commitment to follow his lead. It furthermore demonstrates Hezekiah's determination not to capitulate to Assyrian aggression, but to trust in Yahweh. In the narrative progression of the text the people's silence marks a significant break. It provides time for Hezekiah's prayer and Yahweh's words of assurance delivered through Isaiah (2 Kgs 19:1-7). Most importantly, silence here serves as an expression of faith in the power and in Yahweh's trustworthiness and ability to deliver.[59]

Summary

Summing up, in this chapter we have examined numerous texts in which the concepts of silence or stillness are closely connected with trust in the Lord's care for the people of God and power to come to their aid. We have seen that in the midst of chaos or threat God's people are called to embrace silence and calm. And we have also discovered that ultimately silence and calm become the stable reality in which God's people will dwell and flourish.

6
THE TWO SILENCES

The Silence of the Grave and the Silence of the Sacred

In this chapter we will examine two further aspects of silence in the HB. Our study thus far has focused upon the divine-human relationship, and the various meanings of silence within it. We will now examine the place of silence in two realms that stand just beyond everyday human experience—death and the realm of the dead, on the one hand, and the realm of the sacred (that is, God and those things closely associated with the divine), on the other. Surprisingly, we will find that silence occupies a significant place in each one.

The Silence of Death

The HB's understanding of the afterlife has generated a great amount of scholarly literature in recent years.[1] Generally speaking, at the time of the production of most of the biblical literature, Israel's conceptualization of life beyond death displayed both remarkable similarities to and significant differences from other contemporaneous ANE cultures.[2] In the HB, death is often seen as consisting of three aspects: (1) biological death; (2) death as a metaphor for those things that diminish life as God intended it; and (3) death as a power standing in opposition to the created order.[3] Our focus here will be upon the first of these three.

Ancient Israel's view of death and the afterlife involved two important and related concepts: first, Sheol (sometimes referred to as the grave), and second, the constitution of the human person and that which transpires at death. Most significantly for our purposes, in certain texts Sheol is described as a place of silence:

If the LORD had not been my help,
my soul would soon have lived in the *land of silence.* (Ps 94:17)

and similarly

The heavens are the LORD's heavens,
but the earth he has given to human beings.
The dead do not praise the LORD,
nor do any that go down *into silence.*
But we will bless the LORD from
this time on and forevermore.
Praise the LORD! (Ps 115:16-18)

Upon closer investigation, various questions arise regarding these two passages. The Hebrew word in both is *dumah*, but its translation is uncertain. In Psalm 115:17, the idea of "going down" into *dumah* is paralleled in other texts by the idea of descent to a specific *place*; that is, going down to the pit (Ps 30:3), to destruction (Ps 30:9), or to dust (Ps 22:29).[4] Similarly, in Psalm 94:17 *dumah* is seen as a *place* where the psalmist seemed destined to *dwell*.[5] So should *dumah* be seen as a place, and thus an alternative name of Sheol? Debate also surrounds the question of whether or not *dumah* should be derived from the Hebrew roots relating to silence, and whether it ought to be understood as relating to cessation, or to destruction.[6]

That said, if the correct translation of *dumah* in these two texts is related to silence (as seems most probable), does the imagery of Sheol as a silent realm persist throughout the HB? Some texts depict the inhabitants of Sheol as engaging in sarcastic speech (Isa 14:16-20). Other texts insist that in Sheol there is no praise of God (Pss 6:5; 30:9; 22:2; 88:10-12; Isa 38:18). Is this what is meant by silence? All this would seem to indicate that the relationship between silence and Sheol requires more careful investigation. However, before we are able to address this important issue, a few preliminary considerations are in order.

Death and the Human Person

A detailed discussion of the HB's view of the constitution of the human person is not possible here.[7] However, put briefly, humans are seen as comprised of a physical body, formed from the dust of the earth, and subsequently animated by the breath of God (Gen 2:7). Death is marked by the cessation of breath (*gawa'*, Gen 25:17; 35:29; 49:33; Num 20:29; Eccl 3:19; 11:5; 12:7). When respiration ceased, the body was buried (in normal circumstances), the flesh decayed, and the bones remained in the family tomb. The bones of the deceased are highly significant in Israelite thought, in that although the flesh rotted away, one's bones were collected and preserved (but almost never burned; cf. the outrage mentioned in Amos 2:1). An individual's bones were seen, in some sense, as the repository of his or her "self" (see the repeated allusions to the transport of Joseph's bones from Egypt to Canaan in Gen 50:25; Exod 13:19; Josh 24:32), and as such demanded proper burial and respectful treatment (1 Sam 31:11-13; 2 Sam 21:11-14).[8]

Many of the images of Sheol are built upon Israelite burial practices. The two most common tomb forms were the bench tomb, generally dug into the surface of the ground or the side of a cliff (Isa 22:16), and the cave tomb, making use of an existing cave (Gen 23:4, 6, 9, 20; 49:30; 50:5, 13).[9] In burial sites where bench tombs were utilized, the entrance to the tomb gave access to a small area surrounded by slabs of hewn rock, upon which the corpses were laid. These slabs could be stacked in several tiers, similar to the sleeping berths in the trains of an earlier era. The side of the slab was slightly raised, forming a kind of bed rail, and in some cases headrests were present. Frequently there was a pit behind the benches. Once the flesh had rotted away, the bones would be cleared from the bench, and placed in the pit, providing space for further burials. Alternatively, the dead could be buried in caves. Slabs within the cave served the same function as the benches, and a repository for bones was also present. Cave tombs were often larger, sometimes able to contain the remains of nearly three hundred persons. Isaiah 65:4 alludes to those who "sit inside tombs overnight." Importantly, many descriptions of the netherworld in the HB appear to draw upon conditions in a burial site, especially a cave tomb. Indeed, it has been suggested that the netherworld consisted of one large realm to which all individual graves were connected.[10]

Sheol

Broadly speaking, in the HB and ANE the dead were seen as having a conscious existence and dwelling in the netherworld (e.g., Ezek 26:20). This region is called by various names in the HB. The most common of these is Sheol, a term found some 65 times.[11] Other designations for this realm include the pit (*shaḥat*, Isa 38:17; 51:14; Pss 16:10; 30:9), the grave (*qever*, 2 Kgs 13:21; 22:20; or *qevurah*, Gen 47:30; Isa 14:20), the depths of the earth (*taḥtiyoth 'eretz*, Isa 44:23; or *tehomoth 'eretz*, Ps 71:20), the dust (*'aphar*) of the earth (Isa 26:19), or of death (Ps 22:15), or simply death (*maweth*, Ps 89:48). The inhabitants of this realm are known as "shades" (*repha'im*, Job 26:5; Ps 88:10; Prov 2:18; Isa 14:9; 26:14).[12] Descent to the underworld is sometimes depicted as "being gathered (**'asaph*) to one's people."[13] Some texts speak of "being gathered to one's fathers" (Judg 2:10; 2 Kgs 22:20) or "sleeping (**shakan*) with one's fathers" (Deut 31:16; 2 Sam 7:12; 1 Kgs 1:21; 11:21; 14:20; 15:24; 2 Kgs 13:13).[14] At times the dead are seen as dwelling in an assembly (*qahal*, Prov 21:16). The netherworld is seen as realm of weakness (Isa 14:10) and of gloomy twilight (Job 10:21-22; 17:13; Ps 143:3; Lam 3:6). One descends (**yarad*) into it, goes past its gates (*she'arim*), and barring divine intervention, never returns (Job 7:9; 2 Sam 12:23; Isa 26:13-14). Frequently, descent to Sheol is described as going down into the depths of the earth or sea (Pss 63:9; 68:22; 71:20; 130:1), leading to speculation that at a certain point Sheol was seen as located beneath the cosmic sea upon which the earth floated.[15] As we have noted, the netherworld is characterized by the absence of any praise of God (Pss 6:5; 30:9; 22:2; 88:10-12; Isa 38:18).[16]

Sheol and Its Inhabitants

One further aspect of Sheol concerns the question of its inhabitants and their fate. Do all the dead go there, or just some? And what is experienced by those who descend to it? Interpreters have taken four broad approaches to such questions. First, appealing to Genesis 37:35; 1 Samuel 28:13, 19; Ecclesiastes 9:10; and Psalm 89:48, many view Sheol as the destiny of all humanity, both the righteous and the unjust.[17] This remains the majority position in modern scholarship; however, significant reconsideration of it has emerged in recent years (see below). A second approach suggests that there were "zones" within Sheol. Thus, varying degrees of comfort or discomfort could be experienced there. Certain references to the more remote parts of Sheol imply being thrust away from kith and kin (Deut 32:22; Ps 86:13; Prov 9:18; Isa 14:15).[18] Olyan avers that burial in peace in the family tomb reflects a better fate than other alternatives.[19] The concept of Sheol as comprising various regions also appears in 1 Enoch 21–22 (ca. fourth–to-first centuries BCE). Some twentieth-century scholars affirmed this position, but with only a few exceptions (see below), it is rarely maintained today.[20] A third view insists that, although all who die initially enter Sheol, not all remain there. God ultimately brings the righteous out of Sheol and unto himself.[21] In Christian theology, Sheol (sometimes seen as "Abraham's bosom") was frequently seen as the resting place of the OT saints (and possibly righteous gentiles) until the death and resurrection of Christ, at which time they were admitted into Christ's presence. It was also understood to be the abode of the unrighteous until their final condemnation.[22]

A final view, supported by a growing minority of scholars, holds that Sheol designates the lot of the ungodly, while the specific fate of the righteous is either left indeterminate or is implicitly positive through their ongoing connectedness to the broader kinship group. This line of interpretation sees the HB's references to "going down" or being "brought down" to Sheol (**yarad*) as generally indicating a violent or untimely death, one to be feared and avoided, and one that is generally associated with the unrighteous. Thus, James Barr suggests that Sheol is spoken of "mainly in connection with the persons disapproved, the evildoers."[23] R. S. Johnston similarly notes, "of the thirty-four times that Sheol refers to human destiny, twenty-five are linked directly with the fate of the ungodly."[24] J. Levenson and S. Cook take a similar line of approach.[25] Levenson stresses the concept of the solidarity between the individual and the group. Thus, for the righteous, there is hope in the ongoing unity that the individual has with those who have gone before.[26] Cook, using comparative data from African tribal societies, asserts that the essential issue is the ongoing connection between the living and the dead. He affirms that the deceased become the "living dead" who go on to conscious existence in the world beyond, and benefit from an "umbilical" connection to their living kinsfolk. Moreover, he asserts that Sheol is only the destiny of those who, through evildoing, have damaged their ties with the larger kinship group. Those in good standing with God and the community do not end up there.[27] Thus the dead may remain connected to the living and are spared from the darkness and terrors of Sheol. Some key aspects of maintaining such a link include burial in family tombs in proximity to familial land, or the memorializing of the deceased by the living in various ways.[28]

Sheol and Silence

It is beyond the scope of our study to engage in a detailed evaluation of these aforementioned positions and to suggest a definitive understanding of silence and Sheol on the basis of one or another.[29] It would seem, however, that the HB does not present a single and consistent perspective on Sheol. Various texts emphasize different motifs, sometimes difficult to harmonize one with the other. As seen above, some texts describe Sheol as silent, other texts concerning the dead do not mention silence at all, while yet others depict speech in Sheol. Most scholars would admit that, within the HB and beyond, there is significant development of the concept of Sheol. The later parts of the HB (esp. Isa 26:19; Dan 12:1-2),[30] and potentially certain psalms,[31] clearly move beyond an understanding of Sheol as the lot of all to a perspective that looks for some kind of ongoing life beyond the grave.[32] Moreover, in all but the last position discussed above, all the dead go to Sheol—at least for a while—and where silence is assumed, experience its silence.

It appears to me that a constructive way of approaching the question of silence and Sheol is one that seeks not so much to provide a fully coherent and self-consistent understanding of all the biblical materials relating to Sheol, silence, and the fate of the dead, but rather one that seeks to discern *why* the motif of silence served as an apt image with which to speak of Sheol and death. I would suggest that the HB manifests three *major motifs* related directly or indirectly to silence and Sheol, especially when one examines the "soundscape" of the various texts involved.

Sheol as a Place of Rest

Sheol is at times depicted as a *place of rest* where Yahweh's servants may sleep peacefully after a lifetime of tiring service. Samuel's sleep, from which he resents being disturbed, is a classic example of this (1 Sam 28, esp. v. 15). The silence here would thus be neutral, and its soundscape that of a room characterized by stillness, where sleepers may rest undisturbed. It is not difficult to see the cave tomb as the background of such imagery. This kind of silence lacks some of the negative associations with Sheol observable elsewhere. Samuel's desire for restful sleep appears to stand in continuity with various texts where individuals are depicted as "sleeping with their ancestors" (Deut 31:16; 2 Sam 7:12; 1 Kgs 1:21; 11:21; 14:20; 15:24; 2 Kgs 13:13).[33]

One further observation should be added here. According to those theological streams within the HB focusing on matters of ritual purity, human bones, corpses, and places of interment constitute the most virulent form of contamination. Human bones are seen as highly impure (see Lev 21:11; Num 6:7; 19:11, 13-14, 16; 2 Kgs 23:16; Ezek 44:25). In the rituals of corpse purification (Num 19) and the Day of Atonement (Lev 16; Num 29:7-11), sin and death are placed at the greatest degree of separation from Yahweh. However, surprisingly, while in a few instances a connection is made between the realm of the dead and uncleanness (Isa 65:4),[34] the dead are generally not designated as themselves unclean.[35] Contact with a *corpse* indeed rendered an individual ineligible for participation in ritual activities or the consumption of holy foods until rites of purification could be performed. The dead were not to be consulted (Lev 19:31).[36] To do so constituted an act of defilement. However, being gathered to one's ancestors does not appear to imply any defilement. By contrast, it resonates with aspirations of longing for communal rest.

Sheol as Separation

A second motif is that of Sheol as departure from the "land of the living" (Ps 52:5; Isa 38:11; 53:8; Jer 11:19; Ezek 32:25). In contrast to the restful silence noted above, silence here carries overtones of loss and despondency. It evokes the experience of being shut away in the cold darkness of a tomb, where the sounds of everyday life are distant and muffled. For the living, the loss of the loved one evokes grief and mourning, and is expressed in many ways, both spoken and silent.[37] As we saw in the previous chapter, death involves the loss of the sounds of life, including the sounds of praise and worship. Similar to the loss of sound at those times when Yahweh's judgment overtook the nation, death marks a total separation of the departed from the "soundscape" of this world, and an entrance into a place where the sounds of this life are lost and a deep and abiding silence encompasses all. Thus, although the dead continue to have a conscious existence, they are set apart from the living. In most depictions of the netherworld, there is little sound or movement on the part of the dead (but see below). Indeed, as noted above, death is occasionally associated with sleep (1 Sam 28:15; Job 14:12; Ps 13:3; Dan 12:2). Most importantly, strictures were placed around the consultation of the dead (Deut 18:11; Isa 8:19; 19:3). Furthermore, whereas in some texts the dead may speak to each other (Isa 14:9-11; Ezek 32:21), in the HB, in contrast to much of ANE culture, except on rare occasions, as in 1 Sam 28, *they do not speak to the living*. Apart from Yahweh and certain divine agents, no unsolicited voices from the world beyond address humans. Even in cases when justice could not be attained through human witnesses, no consultation of the dead was permitted. Instead, God's knowledge was brought to bear through the consultation of the Urim and Thummim (Exod 28:30; Lev 8:5-9). Thus, contact between the dead and the living was effectively ended by death.

The key to understanding why silence is so closely associated with death is therefore the very real human experience of *separation*. This is likely the basis of the image of "going down to dwell in silence" (*dumah*) that we encountered in Psalms 94:17 and 115:17-18. Life in the world is replete with sound. Generally speaking, the HB views death as a departure from the world of sound and an entrance into a dark, cave-like place. Human interactions are assumed to be weak or absent. The dead are depicted as sleepers. In Sheol (leaving aside for a moment the debates regarding whether all or some go there, and what it is like), one is engulfed in silence. Furthermore, in certain texts, Sheol may be portrayed as a place where even Yahweh's person and deeds are absent or forgotten.[38] The depiction of Sheol as silent likely emerges out of the very real human experience of *separation and loss brought about by death*. The dead are truly gone from everyday interaction. Even when later theological reflection resulted in more fully developed hopes for the afterlife, those affected by death nevertheless grieved (cf. 1 Thess 4:13). Death *is* loss, and the silence of the grave speaks to this reality.

This separation also implies that the silence alluded here includes distance from the joyous worship in the temple (Jonah 2:4, 7). Worship frequently involved psalms of individual or corporate thanksgiving, many of which involved thanksgiving for deliverance from death (Pss 30; 116). However, once departed from this life, there was no hope for healing (Ps 49:10-14), and therefore no hope of praising God for rescue from the pit (Ps 115:17; Isa 38:18). This perspective corresponds well with those texts that view Sheol as a place where the praise of God is absent (Pss 6:5; 30:9; 88:10-12; Isa 38:18) and see the grave as the inevitable lot of all.[39]

Sheol as the Silencing and Recompense of the Wicked

Several texts associate descent to Sheol with the recompense of the wicked. The emphasis falls not so much upon silence as a characteristic of Sheol *per se*, but upon the final *silencing* that death brings to the machinations of the evildoers. Psalm 28 is a prime example. The psalmist prays that the Lord might not be *silent* to his prayer (28:1), and that he might not be dragged away to Sheol with the evildoers (vv. 1, 3). Death and Sheol are the just recompense for their deeds (vv. 4-5). Escape from the pit comes as recompense to the righteous and needy (vv. 6-9). A similar pattern is in evidence in Psalm 145, where Yahweh's judgment is associated with death (v. 12), but forgiveness with life (v. 7). Similarly, the phrase "those who go down to the pit" is frequently used to describe the destiny of those who stood opposed to the people of God (Ezek 26:20; 31:16-30).

Significantly, certain texts appear to emphasize how the quality of the life of an individual while in this world impacts a person's experience at death (cf. Num 23:10). As noted above, the idea of "descending to Sheol" is frequently connected to a violent or untimely death, or death under divine judgment. Moreover, such inopportune death is frequently described by the addition of some further qualifying terms, such as being brought down to Sheol "in sorrow" (Gen 42:38; 44:31). Similarly, suffering a violent death means descending to Sheol, *but not in peace*. David commands Solomon to execute Joab (due to the latter's bloodguilt), saying, "do not let his gray head *go down to Sheol in peace*" (1 Kgs 2:6). By contrast, when death comes at the end of a long and fulfilled life, other expressions are used, such as being "gathered to one's fathers *in peace*" (Gen 15:15; 2 Kgs 22:20; 2 Chr 34:28), or dying at an old age, "*full of days*" (2 Sam 7:12; Isa 65:20; 1 Chr 17:11). Viewed from this perspective, one might say that while all the dead go to Sheol, not all go in the same way and not all experience death in the same manner. Some descend in peace, are gathered to their families, and rest there, as noted above (1 Sam 28:15). Others go down violently or prematurely, with "blood on their belts and sandals" (1 Kgs 2:5), or "on their heads" (1 Kgs 2:9, 32-33; Ezek 3:18, 20; 23:37, 45; 33:6, 8). The deaths of others serve to reveal them to be the fools they really are (Jer 17:11).

Other texts echo the view that the circumstances at the end of one's life are highly significant. Thus, Psalms 34:21; 37:2, 9, 20, 35-38; and 73:17-20 reassure troubled, righteous sufferers that the last days of the evildoer *in this world* will give evidence of God's judgment upon that person's life. The inter-testamental book of Ben Sira states this idea quite explicitly:

> In the day of prosperity, adversity is forgotten,
> and in the day of adversity, prosperity is not remembered.
> For it is easy for the Lord on the day of death
> to reward individuals according to their conduct.
> An hour's misery makes one forget past delights,
> and at the close of one's life one's deeds are revealed.
> Call no one happy before his death;
> by how he ends, a person becomes known. (Sir 11:25-28)

Furthermore, in certain texts the way in which one departs this world and enters the world below appears to be indicative of one's *experience after death*. This is exemplified by Isaiah's satirical taunt against the king of Babylon as his prestige is stripped away and he descends to Sheol. All the departed "shades" who dwell there mock him (Isa 14:9-11, 15-20). Ezekiel 32:24-29 also speaks of the effect of deeds above on life below: "Elam is there, and all its hordes around its grave; all of them killed, fallen by the sword, who went down uncircumcised into the world below, who spread terror in the land of the living. *They bear their shame* with those who go down to the Pit."

Sheol as a Place of Gathering and Sound

Surprisingly, some texts depict Sheol as a place of speech or gathering. Texts that speak of "being gathered to one's ancestors" (see above) likely speak to this idea and contain a note of optimism, as do those texts which speak of death and silent rest.[40] In Proverbs 21:16 the dead are seen as constituting an "assembly" (*qahal*), a term designating a collective entity and not merely a series of individuals.[41] Most striking, however, is Isaiah's satirical taunt against the king of Babylon as his prestige is stripped away and he descends to Sheol. All the departed "shades" who dwell there mock him:

> Sheol beneath is stirred up to meet you when you come; it rouses the shades to greet you, all who were leaders of the earth; it raises from their thrones all who were kings of the nations. All of them will speak and say to you: "You too have become as weak as we! You have become like us!" Your pomp is brought down to Sheol, and the sound of your harps; maggots are the bed beneath you, and worms are your covering.
>
> How you are fallen from heaven, O Day Star, son of Dawn! How you are cut down to the ground, you who laid the nations low! You said in your heart, "I will ascend to heaven; I will raise my throne above the stars of God; I will sit on the mount of assembly on the heights of Zaphon; I will ascend to the tops of the clouds, I will make myself like the Most High." But you are brought down to Sheol, to the depths of the Pit. Those who see you will stare at you, and ponder over you: "Is this the man who made the earth tremble, who shook kingdoms, who made the world like a desert and overthrew its cities, who would not let his prisoners go home?" All the kings of the nations lie in glory, each in his own tomb; but you are cast out, away from your grave, like loathsome carrion, clothed with the dead, those pierced by the sword, who go down to the stones of the Pit, like a corpse trampled underfoot. You will not be joined with them in burial, because you have destroyed your land, you have killed your people. (Isa 14:9-20)

Clearly, although some texts refer to Sheol as a place of silence, not all texts do so. In the preceding passage, the mockery of the nations serves as the recompense of the formerly arrogant king.

Conclusions

In sum, the relationship between silence and Sheol is multifaceted. To varying degrees and in diverse ways, silence forms a significant part of the imagery of death, Sheol, and the grave. Sheol could be seen as a place of repose and reunion, or of dishonor and recompense. Moreover, though its silence represented separation from the living and the impossibility of praise and worship, such silence was not seen as an absolute absence of sound or speech. The dead could at times be roused by the living or engage in mockery of those who descended to join them.

The Silence of Sacredness

We have observed that silence is closely associated with death and Sheol, both of which are frequently understood as situated at great distance from

Yahweh, the source of light and life. Yet very surprisingly, we shall now see that silence is also closely associated with Yahweh and with holiness. We will examine this collocation in relationship to two specific areas: to the Sabbath and to sacred space (the tabernacle and the temple).

Silence and Sabbath

Genesis 1:1–2:4 narrates the creation of the cosmos, culminating in God's rest on the seventh day. The text begins with the spirit of God (or alternately, a mighty wind) hovering over the face of the waters.[42] In contrast to the later intertestamental ideology reflected in 2 Esdras 6:38 and 7:30, where the pre-creation world was characterized by a perfect orderly silence (see below), here the text assumes a submerged formless mass kept in check by God's breath or wind. The Genesis account then moves forward through six days of creative activity involving divine speech and culminating in God's rest. It is essential to observe that Genesis 1:1–2:4 prepares the way for Israel's "sacred calendar" encountered in Exodus–Numbers, that is, for those special times of the year when the normal routines of life stop and Israel is called to special reflection on the person and deeds of Yahweh. Thus, Genesis 1:14 speaks of God placing lights in the sky "for signs and for seasons, and for days and for years." The word translated "seasons" (*moʿadim*) also designates times of high significance in Israel's year (Exod 23:15; 34:18; Lev 23:2, 4, 37; Num 9:2-3, 13; 10:10; 28:2; 29:39). At the conclusion of the sixth day of creation, all is complete and God sees that it is good (Gen 1:31–2:1). God then rests on the seventh day (Gen 2:2-3). One important feature of the text here can be easily overlooked: God's *work* has consisted primarily of *speaking*, and God's *rest* on the seventh consists primarily of *silence*.[43] All is well. All is secure. God's work of creation is complete; rest can ensue.[44] One further aspect deserves attention here. This pattern of speech followed by silence creates an interesting contrast with Exodus 24:15-16, where Moses ascends Sinai and waits in *silence* until Yahweh speaks to him on the seventh day.[45] Thus, biblically speaking, *this first canonical encounter with the silence of God is profoundly positive in nature.* God is silent because all is complete and harmonious.

God sets the seventh day apart, or consecrates it (**qiddesh*), rendering it sacred and holy. When something is consecrated, it is removed from the sphere of common, everyday use, and set apart for special use with reference to the Divine. In the HB various entities were set apart on the basis of God's decree. Thus, the priests (Exod 28:41), the tabernacle and its equipment (Exod 40:9), and special spaces (Exod 26:33-34) were consecrated. The incense burned in the tabernacle (Exod 30:33, 38) and the meat of the sacrifices offered on the altar (Lev 21:22; Ezra 2:63) were also held sacred. This was also true of certain special *times* such as the Sabbath and sacred feasts of the Israelite calendar (Gen 2:3; Lev 23:3, 7).

The consecration of the Sabbath anchors it in the foundational structure of the cosmos. The terms used for "resting" in 2:2-3 are derived from the root **shabat*, a verb that designates the act of ceasing, desisting, or resting. This root has given rise to the English nouns Sabbath or sabbatical. Thinking again in terms of soundscape, it becomes clear that the concepts of Sabbath and silence are closely linked. In Exodus 20:8-10 and Deuteronomy 5:12-15, Israel is called to observe the Sabbath by ceasing from all labor. Similar commands are given in Exodus 23:12; 31:12-15; 34:21; 35:2; and Leviticus 23:3, 32. In these texts, the call to abstain from work is set in contrast to the expectation that on the remaining six days Israel will be engaged in active labor. This is clear in Exodus 34:21, where Sabbath observance must continue even in times of ploughing and harvest. Read in terms of the soundscape of Israel's experience, in comparison to the other days of the week that should be characterized by the sounds of various industrious undertakings, the Sabbath was be a time of *relative silence*. This is vividly illustrated by the implied soundscape in Nehemiah's observation of offenses against the Sabbath regulations taking place in Jerusalem:

> In those days I saw in Judah people *treading wine presses* on the sabbath, and *bringing in* heaps of grain and *loading them on donkeys*; and also wine, grapes, figs, and all kinds of burdens, which they brought into Jerusalem on the sabbath day; and I warned them at that time against selling food. Tyrians also, who lived in the city, brought in fish and all kinds of merchandise and *sold them on the sabbath* to the people of Judah, and in Jerusalem. (Neh 13:15-16)

Numerous sounds would have been attached to such activities: the creaking of the wine presses, the groaning of those who placed loads upon the backs of the beasts of burden, the braying of the animals, the calls of the merchants soliciting customers, and the loud exchanges as buyer and seller bartered in the marketplace. By contrast, the Sabbath, properly observed, would have been profoundly silent.

Amos castigates the inward desires of his contemporaries who see the Sabbath as a burden, and long for its end. He satirically cites them, declaring:

> When will the new moon be over
>   so that we may *sell* grain;

and the sabbath,
so that we may *offer* wheat for sale?
We will make the ephah small and the shekel great,
and practice deceit with false balances. (Amos 8:5)

Once again, the soundscape of the passage highlights the quietness of the Sabbath in contrast to the sounds of regular business days—the calling out to offer wheat for sale, negotiations, haggling over prices, vociferous arguments over whether the containers for the grain truly reflected the quantity they ought to (a smaller ephah rather than a legitimate one) or whether the weights used on the scales (the shekel) were legitimate or falsified.

Furthermore, the verb **shabat*, when used in its more general sense of stopping or ceasing, frequently means reducing the volume of noisy activities or silencing certain activities normally involving sound (Isa 16:10; 24:8; Jer 16:9; Ezek 26:13; Hos 2:11; Neh 4:11; 2 Chr 16:5). Thus, the concepts of rest, Sabbath, and silence are closely linked. The silence of the Sabbath becomes a rest for humans and animals (Exod 20:8-11), a sign of Yahweh's covenant (Exod 31:16-17), and a way in which sacred time punctuates routines of mundane existence. This was intended to serve as a reminder that the Lord is the giver of all things, and that Israel is fully dependent upon God's sustaining goodness. This latter point is most vividly reflected in the command that Israel allow the land to lay fallow on a cyclical basis (Exod 23:10-11; Lev 25:2-7).[46]

Excursus: Toward a Positive Understanding of Sabbath

The view of the Israelite Sabbath just presented stands in sharp contrast to the negative light with which many Christian readers view it, in part due to the numerous instances of conflict over the Sabbath between Jesus and his enemies recorded in the NT. Legalistic approaches to religious practice are rife in all religious systems, and the concept of the Sabbath (whether observed on Saturday or Sunday) has certainly been taken in such a way both in Judaism, and in some strains of Christianity. However, the true nature of the biblical Sabbath is very different. Perhaps the most eloquent expression of its meaning is that of Rabbi Abraham Heschel in his book on the Sabbath.[47] This short monograph is filled with deep insight into the true significance of Sabbath observance. The introductory chapter, written by Heschel's daughter Susannah, is especially moving in its description of how their household, as observant Jews living in New York City, celebrated the Sabbath. Her description is marked by the profound sense of peace and silence that pervaded the day. More recently, Christian writers have sought to demonstrate the relevance of traditional Jewish observance to Christian thought and practice.[48] The matter of *how* to integrate the concept and spirit of Sabbath in the modern world is far from evident and requires careful reflection. That said, however conceived or observed, many of the negative conceptions of the Sabbath need to be reconsidered.

The Silence of Israel's Sacred Spaces

Just as silence is bound up with the Sabbath, it is also closely connected to the concept of sacred space. As we have noted, those things that God has set apart for ritual use are seen as sacred or holy, and in many cases, specific places or zones are set apart as sacred and must be treated in a special way. Thus, when Moses' attention is drawn to the burning bush and he seeks to approach it, the Lord warns him, "Come no closer! Remove the sandals from your feet, for the place on which you are standing is holy ground" (Exod 3:5). To treat this ground as if it were ordinary soil would be to disrespect its sacred status. The two most significant loci of sacred space in Israel were the tabernacle and the temple. Each one had three zones of ever-increasing sacredness as one moved toward the center.[49]

The silence of the tabernacle is plainly perceived when we examine the activities of the priests in its various zones, and the soundscape relating to each one. The tabernacle is depicted as a moveable shrine that accompanied Israel on its journey from Egypt to Canaan, and which remained a worship center at various locations until the construction of the temple (1 Sam 1:3; 4:3; 2 Sam 7:1-13). The ark of the covenant was placed at its physical center in the "holy of holies" or "most holy place," where the presence of Yahweh resided (Exod 25:22; Num 7:89). The high priest entered there only once per year and sprinkled the blood of the sin offering in front of the ark and on its golden cover to make atonement for the sins of the people, and to purify the tabernacle (Lev 16:15-17).[50] A second zone of lesser holiness stood next to it containing various sacred objects, including the altar of sacred incense, lampstand, and table of the showbread (Exod 26:35). The blood of certain sacrifices, offered at various times during the year, was sprinkled upon the altar of incense or on the curtain dividing this zone from the holy of holies (Lev 4:6-7, 17). As well, priests entered this area twice per day to tend to the table and lamps (Exod 27:21; Num 3:31; 4:7). Finally, a large washing basin and a large bronze altar for burnt offerings stood in the outer courtyard (Exod 30:18). Here animals were sacrificed, the fat removed, and their corpses washed. Then the dead animals were handed over to the priests who offered them upon the altar (Lev 4:32-35).

Several elements are essential to understanding the concept of silence as it relates to the tabernacle. First, the architecture of the tabernacle manifests a progressive and incremental movement in value and rarity from periphery to center.[51] In his superb analysis, Jenson demonstrates this progression in terms of materials and spaces. He notes the progression of copper > silver > gold, observing, "copper is absent from the holy of holies, and there is no gold in the court."[52] He furthermore points out that the materials used in the fabrics for the priestly garments manifest the same progression, with the high priest's vestments consisting of the most rare and precious materials (breastplate, Exod 28:14; 28:22, 29; bells, Exod 39:25; diadem, Exod 28:36). A similar progression is evident in the weave and cloth used for the tabernacle furnishings, the veil, and the priestly garments (Exod 26:1, 31, 36; 28:6, 15, 39; 35:35; 39:27), and the colors and materials used when the ark was wrapped for transport (Num 4:5-14).[53]

It is less often observed that this increment in value parallels a *movement from sound to silence*. Most pertinently, a *progressive diminution of sound* is evident as one moves from periphery to center. We advance from the outer area where animals are slaughtered (surely a tumultuous soundscape) and where speech occurs (e.g., the priestly words of Num 5:19-22; Lev 9:22; or Num 6:23-26; or the farmer's words of thanksgiving and the consequent celebration, Deut 26:3-11), to the holy place where priests enter twice per day bringing a certain level of sound with them (but where no speech is required or recorded), to the most holy place, accessed only once per year, at which time only words of confession are spoken (Lev 16:21). Thus, the movement toward the most sacred zone appears to be accompanied by a series of steps: the first is the move out of the common space of the camp, with its sounds of routine human activities, into the sacred realm of the tabernacle complex. This transition point is frequently described as the "doorway of the tent of meeting" (Lev 8:33, 35; 10:7; 12:6; 14:11, 23). The next step appears in the movement from the sacred courtyard, filled with the sounds of the slaughter of animals and the words of priest and worshipper, to the holy place accessible only to the priests and characterized by the silent burning of incense. The final transition is to the most sacred place, where only the most sacred words are uttered by Israel's most sacred representative before God, and only once per year.[54]

In addition to this movement from sound to silence, one further issue must be noted—that of silence and the priestly role in the tabernacle.[55] In 1938, in his monumental work on the development of Israelite religion, Yehezkel Kaufmann of the Hebrew University of Jerusalem suggested that, in contrast to the priests of the surrounding cultures whose role consisted in the repetition of numerous spells and incantations, Israel's priests ministered in almost complete silence:

> The priestly temple is the kingdom of silence. In Egypt, Babylonia and in the pagan world in general, word and incantation were integral parts of the cult; act was accompanied by speech. The spell expressed the magical essence of cultic activity. . . . Speech thus articulated the magical mythological sense of the rite. . . . [Leviticus–Numbers make] no reference to the spoken word in describing temple rites. All the various acts of the priest are performed in silence. . . . Not only have spells and psalms no place in the priestly cult, even prayer is absent. . . . The rite of bringing first fruits, described in Deuteronomy 26:1ff is typical. It is the farmer who recites a thanksgiving formula at the temple; the priest merely takes the basket of fruit and places it before the altar. Priestly speech is found only outside the temple or apart from the essential cultic act. . . . This silence is an intuitive expression of the priestly desire to fashion a non-pagan cult. . . . Therewith the Israelite cult became *a domain of silence. The silence of the temple cult served to heighten the awe of holiness.*[56]

Israel Knohl takes up Kaufmann's basic thesis, expressing agreement with aspects of it while disagreeing with others.[57] It is beyond the scope of this study to present a detailed analysis of Kaufmann's assertions, and of Knohl's objections and alternative proposals.[58] However, as Knohl and others aver, Kaufmann's point still stands: the priests engage in very little speech in the course of their ritual duties; by contrast, silence prevailed. Thus, silence and the sacred stood in close proximity.

In many respects, the sacredness and silence of the tabernacle are paralleled in the temple. The temple's structure closely resembled that of the tabernacle, with increasing zones of holiness as one proceeds toward the most holy place (1 Kgs 6:1-36; 1 Chr 28:1-19).[59] An increment in value and rarity of materials, design, and skill in construction emerges as one moves from the periphery to the center. First Chronicles highlights the immense quantity of precious material used for the temple's furnishings and vessels (1 Chr 28:14-18; 29:1-5, 6-9). A movement from the sound of the outer courtyard area to the silence of the most sacred space at the temple's innermost part seems also to be implied, not only by the general structure of the building, but most especially through a specific reference to *the absence of any work of stone masonry on the temple site*. In 1 Kings 6:7, the narrator observes: "The house was built with stone finished at the quarry, *so that neither hammer nor ax nor any tool of iron was heard in the temple while it was being built*."

Several comments are necessary here. First, the NRSV's translation obscures an important point. These were likely not finished stones, but rough, unfinished ones, appearing just as they emerged from the quarry or cliffside.[60] Second, absence of sound during the temple's construction evokes several earlier laws and narratives regarding the use of stones in the construction of Israelite altars. Deuteronomy 27:6 states, "You must build the altar of the LORD your God of *unhewn* stones." Similarly, in Joshua 8:30-31 we read:

> Then Joshua built on Mount Ebal an altar to the LORD, the God of Israel, just as Moses the servant of the LORD had commanded the Israelites, as it is written in the book of the law of Moses, "an altar of *unhewn* stones, on which no iron tool has been used"; and they offered on it burnt offerings to the LORD, and sacrificed offerings of well-being.

The law alluded to here is found in Exodus 20:25: "But if you make for me an altar of stone, do not build it of hewn stones; for if you use a chisel upon it you profane it." The demand is not so much for unfinished quarried stones, but for uncut field stones, gathered up from the ground.

This insistence upon field stones is sometimes seen as hearkening back to an earlier period of Israelite history when the fashioning of metal tools for use on stone was the exclusive domain of the Philistines, or the secretive province of smiths.[61] It is difficult to evaluate the validity of this suggestion, since no such connection to it is formally made in the text itself. The suggestion that the issue concerns the profanation (**ḥillel*, Exod 20:25) of the stone is far more persuasive. The central idea is that the altar must be composed of untouched or virgin stones—stones that have not been altered from their original, created state.[62] While in many instances the verb "to profane" may denote a violation of laws of sanctity (e.g., profaning the Sabbath by treating it as any other day; Exod 31:14; Isa 56:2, 6) or the placing of something under judgment (Yahweh may choose to "profane" the land by bringing disaster upon it; Isa 47:6; Ezek 7:21), at times it also means to tarnish or diminish someone or something by treating it without proper respect (see Gen 49:4; Lev 19:29; 1 Chr 5:1).[63] The case in Exodus 20:25 is peculiar in that the act of chiseling *in itself* is explicitly seen as tarnishing the stone, defiling it, and rendering it unfit for ritual service. Thus, the concern in Exodus 20:25 is the sanctity of the stones; they must be just as they emerged from the creator's hand.[64]

In 1 Kings 6:7-8, the laws of Exodus 20:25, Deuteronomy 27:6, and Joshua 8:30-31 are recontextualized, applied to the temple construction, and given an added dimension. They are *recontextualized* in that the demand for the exclusive use of uncut stones is now broadened to include the stones used not only for the altar, *but for the temple as a whole*. However, the restriction on the exclusive use of fieldstones is also *relaxed* so as to permit the use of *stones quarried elsewhere*. Indeed, our narrator does not invite us to imagine that the construction of so great a structure as the temple took place using only fieldstones! Thus some of the materials clearly involved excavation and modification using iron implements.[65] However, in order to maintain the spirit of the altar laws, our narrator stresses that the rocks were quarried *off-site* then subsequently transported to the temple. Most importantly for our purposes, in 1 Kings 6:8 sanctity is not expressed in terms of the absence of defilement through the act of hammering metal upon stone (as in Exod 20:25), *but in terms of silence*, expressed by the *absence of any profane (i.e., not specifically holy) sound on the temple site during its construction*. Put another way, while some sounds and human acts of intervention may have been involved in the preparation of the materials for the temple's construction, these occurred elsewhere. By contrast, *the unbroken silence that prevailed over the temple's site throughout its construction testifies to the sanctity of the space*. As Graeme Auld observes, "on-site dressing of the blocks . . . would have represented a noisy profanation of the place."[66] Thus, in this report of the temple's construction, silence and the sacred coalesce.

Silence as Praise in Yahweh's Presence

This association between silence and sacredness also appears in Psalm 65:1. This is obscured in certain translations, such as the NRSV, that render the verse, "Praise is due to you, O God, in Zion." However, the Hebrew MT literally reads, "To you silence [is] praise in Zion." The differences in translation rest on several rather technical matters that cannot be discussed here. It seems to me most judicious, for various reasons, to retain a reference to silence in this verse.[67] The setting is the sacredness of Yahweh's temple in Zion. It may be that the worshippers are silently awaiting a manifestation of the presence of Yahweh in some form, or the moment when they will fulfill their vows.[68] However the case may be, Goldingay is certainly correct in his observation that "silence can be a novel way of recognizing God, insofar as it implies a restful trust in God. . . . Restful silence is possible in connection with God, in whose presence the worshippers stand."[69]

In the intertestamental period, this close connection between silence and sanctity became far more pronounced. In the Letter of Aristeas (ca. mid-second to late-first centuries BCE), the totality of the worship at the Jerusalemite temple was depicted as taking place in total silence:

> The Service of the priests is in every respect unsurpassed in the physical strength (required of them) and in its orderly and silent arrangement. For they all labour spontaneously, even though the exertion is great, and each one takes care of an appointed task. And they minister without a break, some offering the wood, some the oil, some the fine flour, some the incense, others the sacrificial portions of flesh, using their strength in different degrees for the different tasks. . . . And a complete silence reigns, with the result that one might suppose that there was not a single person present in the place, even though there are around 700 ministering priests present and a great number of men bringing up the sacrifices; but everything is discharged with awe and in a manner worthy of the great Godhead. (Let. Aris. 92, 95)[70]

As Hayward notes, this text is unique in its insistence that all took place in silence.[71] Nevertheless, it presupposes that its readers would have been profoundly impressed by the silence of the proceedings, and thus it dramatically highlights the close association between silence and sanctity held in some circles. Commenting on the references to silence in Aristeas, Hayward suggests the utter silence pervading the entire proceedings is necessary because of "the great awe and reverence attending the rite."[72] In the Qumran materials there is further evidence of a close association between sanctity and silence. In the Songs of the Sabbath Sacrifice, a series of fixed prayers employed in place of animal sacrifice, there are various allusions to silence.[73] 4Q405.11–13 reads:

> The spirits of the living God [or: divine beings] walk to and fro continually with the glory of the chariots of wonder. And there is a sound of silence of blessing in the tumult of their walking. And they praise the Holy One as they return on their journey. When they exalt, they exalt marvelously, and when they tabernacle [*wbšwkn*] they stand. The sound of ringing gladness *becomes silent, and a silence* of the blessing of God is in all the camps of God, and the sound of praises.[74]

Thus, the concepts of sanctity and silence were closely associated both in the biblical text, and beyond.

What then is the significance of this association? It appears that, in certain instances, silence is depicted as that which distinguishes the holy from the ordinary, the sacred from the profane. Just as treading upon sacred ground in sandals would demonstrate a failure to honor its holiness and profane it, so too in certain places and in certain instances, only total silence is befitting to the sacredness of the time or place. This emphasis on silence as a most appropriate response to the sacred would appear to be designed to underline our relative unimportance and insignificance as humans, the inadequacy of our words, and our need to simply gaze in silence upon the majesty of the living God.

Summary

To summarize, in this chapter we have seen how silence is a characteristic element both in Sheol, the realm of the dead and frequently associated with defilement, as well as in certain places of extreme holiness. This is perhaps the most striking example of the polyvalent nature of silence in all of the HB. We now turn, in the following chapter, to address that which many consider the most problematic expression of silence in human experience: the silence of God in the face of human suffering, and God's apparent failure to answer prayer.

7
HOW LONG O LORD?
God's Silence and Human Suffering

In chapter 2, we explored the depiction of the Lord's silence as a reaction to the persistent human refusal to walk in God's ways. In this chapter we will explore a very different aspect of the silence of God—that of the Lord's apparent indifference to the cries arising from human suffering, especially the suffering of the weak, poor, and needy. However, before we can address this issue, two preliminary considerations are of prime importance. First, we must note that the silence of God we will be considering here is different from more general questions of theodicy in theology and philosophy. Second, when considering this aspect of the silence of God, we must differentiate between instances of God's *delayed* judgment, on the one hand, and God's seeming *callous indifference* to human suffering, on the other. Let us therefore briefly examine these two considerations.

Preliminary Considerations

Silence and Theodicy

My purpose in this chapter is not to engage in the broader theoretical or theological discussion of theodicy, but more specifically to examine various texts reflecting Israel's wrestling with the silence of God. Moreover, as we shall see, such texts are focused primarily on present, existential realities affecting the individual or community, and concern the need for divine intervention. Theodicy, by contrast, generally deals with more theoretical questions regarding divine justice and providence.[1] Moreover, as M. Sarot points out, theodicy is an ill-defined term, and one that at a certain level relates primarily to post-Enlightenment concerns, despite having analogous but distinct pre-Enlightenment antecedents.[2] Some approaches to theodicy may be characterized as rationalistic, theoretical, and quite often apologetic. This is, of course, not to deny that numerous biblical texts touch upon issues related to the broader concept of theodicy.[3] Abraham's question to Yahweh, "Shall not the judge of all the earth do what is right?" (Gen 18:25) clearly evokes such issues, as do other texts including Psalms 10; 17; 26; 59; 62; 64; 73; Judges 6:13; and Job.[4] However, in contrast to more abstract aspects of theodicy, the primary focus in biblical texts where God is seen to be silent is highly *personal.* Why is God unresponsive to *my* needs, or the needs of *my* community? Why is God acting "out of character" when compared to other promises and assertions found within the biblical text, Israel's confessions of faith, or memories of past experience?[5]

Silence as Judgment Delayed

Second, it is important to distinguish instances of God's *intentional delay* of judgment and recompense for evil deeds, from God's seeming *indifference* to human misery and failure to answer prayer. The fact that in the HB, God's silence is associated with both of these phenomena renders the situation potentially confusing. However, close attention to the relevant passages makes it possible to distinguish between the two. In numerous passages (especially in the Psalms), the biblical writers regard God's silence in the face of their suffering and prayers as incomprehensible, and do not hesitate to complain to the Lord about their plight. The psalmists' response to silence of this type will constitute the major emphasis of this chapter. By contrast, in other texts, fewer in number, God's silence as manifested in the form of non-intervention against evildoers represents judgment *delayed.* Let us examine some texts where silence carries this latter sense.

Psalm 50 divides into two distinct sections and addresses two categories of hearers. In verses 7-15, Yahweh's faithful ones are rebuked not for any lack of sacrificial offerings—indeed there was no shortage of these (vv. 8-13). Rather, God's people lacked thankfulness of heart (v. 14a) and commitment to fulfill their promises (v. 14b). They regularly failed to call upon the Lord in times of need (v. 15). Subsequently, in verses 16-22 the wicked are addressed. Their many evil deeds and attitudes are enumerated (vv. 17-20). Yet Yahweh has not intervened either in word or action against them, *but rather has kept silent* (v. 21a).[6] As a result of such divine restraint, these evildoers came to the erroneous conclusion that Yahweh was just like them (v. 21b).

These individuals had taken divine silence as acquiescence. It is important to understand why they may have done so. As we noted in chapter 1, silence is not the complete absence of sound, but the absence of sounds or actions that would normally be expected in a given circumstance. Given that Yahweh is frequently depicted as punishing evildoers and rewarding the righteous, such individuals had perhaps concluded that Yahweh did not truly disapprove of their deeds, and had taken God's silence as acquiescence. Their attitude seems to have been like that of the sceptics whose words are cited in Zephaniah 1:12b: "The Lord will not do good, nor will he do any harm." Such a sentiment is also in evidence in Malachi 3:14-15. However, here in Psalm 50 Yahweh declares that those who understand the divine silence in such a way are hopelessly deluded. God's silence has not been an indication of assent, but a manifestation of grace, affording time for repentance and remediation (v. 21). However, now Yahweh declares that this time of restraint is over. Such persons must amend their ways or destruction will soon follow (v. 22). So, in contrast to Numbers 30:1-15, where silence does indicate assent, here in Psalm 50 silence denotes *delayed divine judgment*.

This pattern of judgment graciously delayed is one that is deeply rooted in the HB. A *locus classicus* for this theme is 2 Kings 17:7-18. That text describes how, after many years of God's patience in the face of human recalcitrance, judgment finally falls upon the NK. This text merits quoting in full here:

> This [destruction] occurred because the people of Israel had sinned against the Lord their God, who had brought them up out of the land of Egypt from under the hand of Pharaoh king of Egypt. They had worshiped other gods and walked in the customs of the nations whom the Lord drove out before the people of Israel, and in the customs that the kings of Israel had introduced. . . . They did wicked things, provoking the Lord to anger; they served idols, of which the Lord had said to them, "You shall not do this." Yet the Lord warned Israel and Judah by every prophet and every seer, saying, "Turn from your evil ways and keep my commandments and my statutes, in accordance with all the law that I commanded your ancestors and that I sent to you by my servants the prophets." They would not listen but were stubborn, as their ancestors had been, who did not believe in the Lord their God. . . . Therefore the Lord was very angry with Israel and removed them out of his sight; none was left but the tribe of Judah alone. (2 Kgs 17:7-18)

The NT takes up the theme of divine silence (in the sense of withholding judgment) in a similar way. In Romans 2:4-5, Paul sees such restraint as evidence of divine kindness, meant to lead to repentance. The same idea appears in 2 Peter 3:9 with reference to the parousia.[7]

Understanding this aspect of God's silence or perceived inactivity can help make sense of certain texts where God appears to act unfairly. The HB takes great pains to balance the twin concepts of Yahweh's willingness to forestall judgment and to forgive, on the one hand, and God's exalted and righteous character, on the other. Thus, the biblical writers underline both the grace and mercy of Yahweh (Exod 33:19; 34:6-7; Num 14:18-19; Deut 5:10; 30:3; Pss 103:2-4; 130:3-4; Isa 30:18; 54:8; Mic 7:18-20), but also insist that divine grace does not mean complicity with human sinfulness. God in forbearance may *choose* not to enact immediate judgment in response to evil, but mankind must never abuse this grace, hoping that last-minute repentance will bring reprieve. As the narrative of the hardening of Pharaoh's heart (Exod 4:21; 7:3; 14:4, 17) dramatically illustrates, the door of divine grace may close.

In other texts manifesting the pattern of delayed judgment, the concepts of grace and repentance do not appear, and the silence of delayed judgment serves other purposes. Psalms 12; 37; and 73 contain the motif of delayed judgment, but this lack of immediate consequences in understood in a different way.[8] These passages view the *provisional impunity* of evildoers as an unavoidable aspect of life in this world. The righteous suffer (Pss 12:5; 37:7, 12, 14; 73:5, 14, 16, 32), while evildoers enjoy ease of life (Ps 37:7, 35-36). Yet the faithful are assured that this situation will not go on forever. Yahweh will rise up (Ps 12:5) and bring the wicked to their deserved end (Ps 37:9, 10, 13, 17, 20, 28b, 34, 36, 38). The emphasis in these texts is Yahweh's call to the faithful to wait patiently for deliverance, and not turn aside to wrongdoing (see esp. Ps 37:1, 7, 8, 27-28). Moreover, patient waiting during times of God's silence is seen to be profoundly beneficial (Ps 37:3, 7, 34, 37).[9] The prophet Habakkuk similarly protests against divine silence and seeming refusal to answer prayer: "O LORD, how long shall I cry for help, and you will not listen? Or cry to you 'Violence!' and you will not save? Your eyes are too pure to behold evil, and you cannot look on wrongdoing; why do you look on the treacherous, and are *silent* when the wicked swallow those more righteous than they?" (Hab 1:2, 13). Although the prophet's complaint regarding God's silence in Habakkuk 1:13 concerns God's management of national and international affairs (not merely life's injustices as experienced by individuals),[10] the same dynamic is at play as in the psalms just cited: there may be horrendous injustice in the present, but the faithful are called to wait for Yahweh's ultimate purposes and deliverance to be revealed (Hab 2:1-4).

The Silence of God and Human Suffering

We may now proceed to our discussion of the "silence of God" as most commonly understood: those instances where God seems completely oblivious to horrendous suffering and evil, and indifferent to cries for deliverance. The concept of the silence of God has received extensive attention in recent literature.[11] It emerged with great poignancy in the years following World War II as the horrors of the Nazi extermination camps came to light. Subsequently, attention also turned to other instances of manifest inhumanity: the rape of Nanking (or Massacre of Nanjing), the Rwandan genocide, and ethnic cleansing in the Balkans, to name but a few. Concern was also focused upon such historical atrocities as the enslavement of the African peoples, the massacre of indigenous populations in Australia and the Americas and their displacement and mistreatment in residential schools. Where was God in all this? Artists, philosophers, and theologians have wrestled with the seemingly irresolvable paradox of an omnipotent God, described in scripture as the God of justice and righteousness and the defender of the poor and needy, who somehow stood aloof as unspeakable suffering was perpetrated by the strong on those weaker than themselves. Furthermore, such questions became especially poignant in instances when the perpetrators of such suffering were those who would self-identify with the God of the Bible.[12] Even more problematic is the fact that texts within the canon of Scripture itself seem either to have given justification to the oppressors, or worse still, to have portrayed God as unethical in character, and one who was responsible for the suffering of the innocent.[13]

Apologists and theologians frequently offer "standard" responses for God's seeming silence. These include the following: it is inadmissible to call God to account; since all are sinners, God owes humanity nothing and thus cannot be accused of wrongdoing; there is a hidden plan in all that God does; all will work out for the best, etc. There are profound weaknesses to each of these solutions.[14] However, as noted, it is not my purpose in these pages to attempt a theological analysis of or explanation for these vexing and largely irresolvable problems, nor do I feel competent to do so. Moreover, the biblical writers themselves seem to have addressed them only in a very limited sense (e.g., Habakkuk and Ecclesiastes). My task here is primarily exegetical. Thus, within the confines of the present study, I will limit myself to the examination of specific biblical texts that depict God as *deaf or indifferent to the cries of the faithful and downtrodden in their most extreme situations of distress*, and hence *silent* toward them. In doing so I will attempt to discover the biblical writers' understanding of how and why such situations emerged, how they responded to the God who had permitted them to arise, and how they were able to cope with their distress and move forward. I would suggest that a profitable way of viewing these matters is in terms of a "three-act drama."[15]

Divine Silence in the Face of Suffering: A Drama in Three Acts

Several preliminary considerations must be noted before we move to our "three-act drama." The first concerns the depiction of God's indifference to human suffering as *silence*. In numerous passages Yahweh is portrayed as deaf to the cries of those who suffer, unresponsive to their needs, and most especially for our purposes, *silent*.[16] Such a situation is summed up in the startling words of Psalm 35:22: "You have seen, O Lord; do not be silent! O Lord, do not be far from me!"

Similar appeals are made to God elsewhere in the Psalms:

> To you, O Lord, I call;
> my rock, do not refuse to hear me,
> for if you are silent to me,
> I shall be like those who go down to the Pit. (28:1)

> Hear my prayer, O Lord,
> and give ear to my cry;
> do not hold your peace [lit. be silent] at my tears.
> For I am your passing guest,
> an alien, like all my forebears. (39:12)

> O God, do not keep silence;
> do not hold your peace or be still, O God! (83:1)

> Do not be silent, O God of my praise. (109:1)

Habakkuk likewise exclaims:

> O Lord, how long shall I cry for help,
> and you will not listen?
> Or cry to you "Violence!"
> and you will not save?
> Why do you make me see wrong-doing
> and look at trouble?
> Destruction and violence are before me;
> strife and contention arise. . . .
> Your eyes are too pure to behold evil,
> and you cannot look on wrongdoing;
> why do you look on the treacherous,

> and are silent when the wicked swallow
> those more righteous than they? (Hab 1:2-3, 13)

Whereas the psalmists and Habakkuk *decry* God's silence toward them, the Book of Jeremiah *depicts* God's silence. Yahweh is seen as having abandoned the prophet by refusing to answer his prayers or to come to his aid, thereby causing intense agony of soul to Jeremiah, Yahweh's faithful servant.[17] In 15:18 Jeremiah both addresses and accuses Yahweh: "Why is my pain unceasing, my wound incurable, refusing to be healed? Truly, you are to me like a deceitful brook, like waters that fail." Jeremiah 18:19-20 contains similar sentiments: "Give heed to me, O Lord, and listen to what my adversaries say! Is evil a recompense for good? Yet they have dug a pit for my life. Remember how I stood before you to speak good for them, to turn away your wrath from them." Thus, despite the Lord's earlier promise to be present with Jeremiah, to deliver him (1:8), to make him a "fortified city, an iron pillar, and bronze walls," and to fight against his enemies (1:18), Jeremiah's subsequent experiences appear to have shown God to have been silent and unwilling to stand by the promises once given.[18] Jeremiah finds himself betrayed by his family (12:6), opposed by the general populace (18:20), imprisoned and thrown down a cistern (38:6-13), and ultimately forced into exile in Egypt (ch. 43).

As noted earlier, in the HB silence is the absence of words or actions that *would normally be expected in a given situation*. In the passages cited above, the speakers had clearly expected that the Lord, having seen their sufferings and heard their cries, would intervene and bring deliverance. However, none was forthcoming. Put simply, for the biblical writers "the silence of God" describes the Lord's choice to remain inactive in a situation of desperate need, and at moments when it would seem that God should, by rights, intervene, bringing vindication and deliverance.

Second, it is important to set these references to the silence of God in the broader theology of disputation with God and protest against God within the HB. Such protest is a key element of the *existential drama of faith* in God, and frequently emerges at moments when the Lord has seemingly acted incomprehensibly, in light of all God's self-declarations in Scripture, of Israel's memory of God's saving deeds in the past, and of all that was proclaimed and celebrated in Israel's worship. Furthermore, protest against God's silence was most acute in relationship to the Lord's seeming indifference to those sufferers who were "in good standing" with the Almighty and called out for deliverance, yet received none (e.g. Pss 22; 26; Jer). However, similar complaints could also be expressed when Israel believed that punishment for sin had gone on for too long, or appeared disproportionate to the offense committed (as in Ps 74).[19]

For the psalmists, and for Jeremiah and Habakkuk, God's response made no sense. Most importantly, in these texts God's silence was not met with pious resignation, simply assuming that it was improper to question the Deity, or that God must have a hidden design or purpose. Rather, the biblical writers chose *to protest God's silence*, and did so most vehemently.

Human protest against God, most specifically against God's silence or inaction, constitutes an important part of ongoing theological reflection both within the HB and in Judaism.[20] In the HB such protest is frequently expressed through words of complaint addressed to God. Such speech is often labelled as lament, argumentative prayer, God-complaint or protest-prayer. In the present context I will follow William Morrow and employ the term "protest" for such address to God.[21] Protest may be expressed either indirectly (God has allowed the predicament to arise) or directly (God actually causes the predicament).[22] Furthermore, expressions of protest are related to, but not identical to the genre of lament. Laments—that is, expressions of personal distress or need—may not include elements of protest or complaint.[23] Moreover, with Broyles and Morrow, I will distinguish speech to God expressing "plea" or "supplication," on the one hand, from words of "protest" on the other.[24] The former communicates needs and concerns to God, but without accusation. Protest, by contrast, indirectly or directly blames God for the plight of the sufferer, often accusing the Lord of *indifference or carelessness*.[25] Admittedly, a strict demarcation between plea and protest is not without problems.[26] Nevertheless, for the purposes of this study I will differentiate between them, and focus on the latter.

Third, before proceeding to our drama, it is essential to, as it were, set the stage. In considering the silence of God as a drama in three acts, we must identify the principal characters (or *dramatis personae*) in the text, and the core relational dynamics between them. In the Psalms, the dynamics of protest generally involve the Lord, the sufferer, the sufferer's community, and, at times, the sufferer's enemies. Yahweh is seemingly silent to the cries of the afflicted one(s). What does this mean? Is this an indication that the individual is guilty of some hidden iniquity, known to God but hidden from view, and threatening the wellbeing of the community as a whole? Would extending comfort to the sufferer then be siding against the Lord?

Morrow has demonstrated that one of the primary functions of the complaint psalms was "to rehabilitate the individual to the larger group . . . by affirming the undeserved suffering of the petitioner and . . . [arresting] both his social exclusion and also the justification of group violence against him."[27] He points to the *public* dimension of such expressions of protest, often articulated with the assistance of specialized priests or poets. Thus, whether performed in individual homes or in the temple, such expressions of lament and protest were intended to affirm *the solidarity between the sufferer and the broader community*. The community served to embody God's care for the individual, despite the fact that such care seemed somehow to have been obscured. Moreover, the taunting of the psalmist's enemies served to magnify the isolation of the afflicted person. Emptiness, alienation, and profound silence now stand at the deepest place of the psalmist's being. Similar dynamics are in evidence in Jeremiah. The prophet sees himself as alienated both from Yahweh and from his broader family and community (see esp. 12:1-6; 15:15-18; 20:7-10). For the purposes of the present chapter, I will focus on these dynamics as seen in the Psalms.

The core relational interplay between the psalmist(s) and Yahweh can best be understood if one views them as characters sharing the same stage.[28] In the "stage directions," the director would call for expressive body language on the part of both, thereby heightening the audience's perception of the relational dynamics between them. The human sufferer would constantly move *toward* Yahweh, crying out, pleading, perhaps shaking his or her fist, kneeling, trembling with anger, and weeping. Yahweh, by contrast, would be silent, turn away, stand at a distance, and avoid all eye contact. All this would be seen as occurring despite the fact that the two had previously shared a relationship of intimacy and trust. The analogy of a dramatic presentation is especially apt in that the biblical protest texts frequently present Yahweh's actions in highly anthropomorphic terms: Yahweh may move far away (Pss 10:1; 22:1) or the divine countenance may be hidden (Pss 13:1, 30:7; 44:24; 88:14; 102:2; 143:7). The psalmists may implore Yahweh to hear, but any response rests entirely on the divine willingness to do so (10:17; 31:2; 71:2; 86:1 88:2; 102:2; 130:2).

Our drama develops as follows: in Act 1, a situation of need arises, driving the psalmists to seek God's aid, either as individuals or as a community. This sets the stage for the encounter with the silence of God that emerges in Act 2. There the psalmists cry for help, but these cries go unheeded, and there seems to be no reason for this to be so. God is incomprehensibly silent—despite the fact that the speakers are in right relationship with the Lord or have suffered long enough for any wrongdoing. All the while, the enemies engage in wholesale mockery. In certain texts it is the sufferer who is mocked; in others it is God or the people of God as a whole. The sufferers, however, will not acquiesce to their fate. Rather, they "storm the gates" and *refuse to accept silence for an answer*. In the most vehement of terms, they demand that God relent and heed their cries. In the context of our "drama," it is essential to note that the intended function of these expressions of protest was *persuasive*. The psalmists sought to move the Lord *away* from silence and *toward* intervention and rescue. In doing so they used various means and engaged the Lord at every level. In Act 3, the drama moves toward resolution. In something of a surprise and somewhat enigmatic ending, the psalmists look beyond the present crisis to a brighter day. The same may be said for the Book of Habakkuk, especially as evidenced in Habakkuk 3. The case of Jeremiah is more complex, and perhaps less optimistic.[29] Let us now examine these three acts in detail.

Act 1: The Drama Emerges

Life in ancient Israel was fraught with loss. Disease was rife, death in childbirth was frequent, and famine and drought were common. Life expectancy was limited. It is likely that less than 10 percent of the population lived beyond 50. In the Hellenistic period (ca. 332–63 BCE), the average life expectancy has been estimated at 44.2 for men and 34.7 for women.[30] Both the biblical record (Gen 11:30; 25:21; 29:31; Judg 13:2; Ps 113:9; Prov 30:16) and various biblical and extra-biblical Hebrew names suggest that infertility was a significant problem, and that pregnancy and childbirth were seen as times of grave danger.[31] Economic exploitation of the poor was common, as were bribery and corruption (Isa 5:7, 23; 33:15; Jer 5:28; Amos 5:7, 12; Mic 3:9, 11; 7:3). Moreover, the nation as a whole experienced disasters of various sorts: drought, plagues, agricultural blights, military incursions, and in 722 BCE and 587 BCE, invasion, annexation, and deportation (see 2 Kgs 17; 24:1-7; Joel 1–2; Amos 4:6-12). Thus, the need for divine intervention arose with great frequency.

In the Psalms (and elsewhere), such suffering and disorder were seen as an inevitable part of life. From Israel's perspective, Yahweh's rule was constantly under threat from evil and chaos, and opposition from such sources could emerge at any moment and challenge the stability of the created order, most especially, the peace and wellbeing of the people of God.[32] Morrow notes that the perspective of the psalmists is not one in which "God is in charge of everything all of the time . . . [rather,] God is always regarded as having the power to defeat the forces of chaos; . . . omnipotence is always potential . . . but not always actual."[33] Thus, there was no assumption that Yahweh's rule *precluded* outbreaks of chaos and evil, but only that Yahweh's aid could be called upon in times of distress.

According to traditional orthodoxy, at critical moments such as these, Israel could cry out (**za'aq*, Exod 2:23; Judg 3:9, 15; 1 Sam 7:8-9; 12:8) to the Lord for relief. God could be called (**qara'*, Ps 118:5) into a situation, and implored to hear (**shama'*, Ps 17:1, 6; 34:6), or to give ear (hiphil of **'azin*, Ps 39:12), to look down (hiphil of **nabaṭ*, Ps 80:14) or behold (**ra'ah*, Pss 10:11; 113:6; 142:4) and to arise (**quom*, Pss 3:7; 7:6; 9:19; 10:12; 12:5; 17:13) and set things to rights. And while not all suffering was alleviated, very often such deliverance did indeed arrive. The Israelites cried to Yahweh out of their sufferings in Egypt (Exod 2:23) and deliverance came (Exod 6:6; 18:8). Individuals called out to Yahweh out of times of sickness and suffering, and returned to give thanks for answers to their cries (Pss 30; 116). Yahweh had self-identified as one who came to the aid of the helpless and oppressed (Exod 22:22-24) and who was the deliverer of the people of God (Deut 23:14). Yet here, incomprehensibly, God was silent.

Act 2: The Drama Intensifies

In Act 2, the movement of the drama intensifies. The psalmists' cries for assistance become increasingly shrill and the emotions beneath them more acute. The Lord continues to disregard prayers for help, and to allow situations of grave danger or injustice to persist. Faced with such circumstances, the biblical writers express not only plea but *protest*.[34] Thus the "discourse of protest" in the HB frequently stands in close relationship to the theme of the *silence of God*.

But why did the Israelites believe they could challenge God's silence? Two important assumptions undergirded their response. The first was the belief that the Lord was a God of justice and defender of the poor and needy. Such a conviction is evident in those psalms that cry out to Yahweh for vindication from false accusations (Pss 26:1; 35:24; 43:1; cf. 58:11; 75:7). Such cries do not indicate a gloating vindictiveness, but rather call for Yahweh to bring the truth to light, unmasking lies and falsehood (Pss 27:12; 69:4; 109:4).[35] Such calls also ask the Lord to see to it that the psalmist's integrity is made evident to all (Pss 7:8; 25:21; 26:1, 11; 41:12; 101:2). This language evokes the setting of a law court, and the appearance of an innocent plaintiff, falsely accused, before a magistrate.[36] Psalm 17:1-2 encapsulates the various aspects of this general framework: "Hear a just cause, O Lord; attend to my cry; give ear to my prayer from lips free of deceit." Such imagery has sometimes been referred to as a "legal fiction" that serves as the foundation for the expressions of protest in the Psalms.[37] The basis for these appeals is that Yahweh is a God who loves and practices justice (*mishpaṭ*, Gen 18:19; Lev 19:15a; Deut 1:17; 10:18; 16:19; 27:19) and righteousness (*tzedeq* or *tzedaqah*, Gen 18:19; Lev 19:15; 19:36; Deut 16:20) but hates their opposites (Exod 23:6; Lev 19:15, 35; Deut 1:17; 16:19;

24:17). The language here also evokes the concept of the "hue and cry" within the legal structure in ancient Israel. Individuals who were the victims of violence could cry out, and it was the duty of those who heard the cry to come to the aid of the victim (Deut 22:24, 27; cf. Gen 4:8-10; Hab 1:2).[38]

However, Israel's complaints and protests go beyond the purely legal realm of plaintiff and judge, and engage the relational dimension as well.[39] This is the second of the two foundations of protest, noted above. Israel (both individually and collectively) saw itself as bound to Yahweh in an intimate and personal relationship. Yahweh was Israel's progenitor (Exod 4:22; Isa 43:6; Jer 31:9; Hos 11:1; Mal 1:6) and its deliverer (Exod 6:6; 14:30; Deut 33:29; Isa 63:7-9). Israel lived its life "before" Yahweh (Gen 15:1-2; 24:40; Ps 116:9), and frequently came "before the Lord" in contexts of ritual worship (cf. Lev 1:3; 15:30; Deut 12:12; etc.). On the more personal level, Yahweh was intimately involved in the conception, the in-utero formation, birth, and lifespan of the individual (Ps 139:13-18). As such it was assumed that Yahweh would *desire* to show loyalty to the faithful and heed their cry for deliverance from lies and oppression (Ps 145:19). Such a belief was rooted in Yahweh's declaration, "I will take you as my people, and I will be your God" (Exod 6:7; cf. Gen 17:7; Exod 29:45). Thus it would be natural to assume that Yahweh would willingly come to Israel's aid both out of a commitment to justice, and due to a relational bond. Conversely, protest would be a highly understandable response on the part of the people when extreme suffering was met with cold silence.

It would be erroneous, however, to suppose that protest against God was undertaken lightly, and without appropriate deference to Yahweh as exalted King, Judge, and Parent. This especially so when such protest was expressed within the liturgical setting of the Jerusalem temple.[40] Part of the inner logic of protest is that it was to be undertaken *in extremis*, when all persistent seeking of the Lord had failed, when the situation was desperate, and when no explanation could be found for God's silence. Westermann has suggested that the appearance of texts involving plea without protest reflects the progressive suppression of protest within ancient Israel.[41] However, such a claim is difficult to substantiate and involves numerous assumptions regarding the dating of specific texts. What is more certain is that the gravity of the situation, God's delay in response, the incomprehensibility of Yahweh's failure to intervene, or the disproportionate relationship between the punishment and any crime committed prompted the biblical writers to use protest rather than plea to express their needs to God. Morrow, following Broyles, aptly states (with reference to Ps 13), "[G]rounds for protest arise from the extreme nature of the distress and the undue delay in deliverance. . . . Explicit protest was probably only permitted to sufferers who had used up other avenues for healing and who faced a situation of prolonged hardship due to chronic disease and unanswered prayer."[42] Moving back to the analogy of a dramatic presentation, at this point in the drama, speech in calm, reserved tones would not do. Only heightened emotions, expressed through intense and extreme means, were able to communicate the pathos experienced by the sufferers as they encountered the radical dissonance between the assertions of Israel's creeds and most pivotal texts, its memory of Yahweh's goodness in the past, and their present lived experience.[43]

Certain situations are frequently associated with expressions of protest.[44] This might involve the sickness and suffering of an individual in the prime of life, especially when premature death seemed imminent (Pss 28:1; 30:3; 88:1-18; 102:3-5, 23-24; 143:7). Protest also appears when the enemies of the psalmist engaged in persistent false accusations, threatening the individual's broader connection to the community (Pss 35:12-15; 41:5-9; 55:12-14). In such situations, the psalmists frequently respond with "declarations of innocence" (e.g. Pss 7:8; 18:20, 24; 26:1-4, 6, 11-12; 73:13) and with pleas to the Lord for vindication. As well, protest was also expressed when the punishment did not fit the crime—when it seemed be too severe or extensive (Pss 13:1, 2; 6:3; 35:17; 74:10; 79:5; 80:4; 89:46; 90:13).[45] Moreover, the psalmists often described themselves as "poor and needy." This collocation is found frequently in Psalms 2–89 (Pss 9:18; 12:5; 37:14; 40:17; 70:5; 72:4, 12; 74:21; 86:1; 109:16, 22; 113:7; 140:12), and alludes to the many sufferings experienced by Yahweh's faithful ones.[46] A. Groenewald cites contempt, persecution, sickness, material oppression, injustice, and near-death experience as examples of such experiences.[47] On the collective level, protest emerged when the existence of the nation as a whole was threatened, as in the case of the 587 destructions and exile (Isa 63:7–64:11; Pss 44; 60; 74; 79; 80; 83; 89; 137).[48]

The various verbal and rhetorical means used to express protest against God reveal much about the speakers' intense psychological and emotional reaction to their situations of crisis, and to God's incomprehensible silence. Protest is frequently registered in various ways: questions addressed to God, "negative imperatives" (such as "do not forsake me" or "do not be silent"), statements of direct criticism or blame, and most surprisingly statements of confidence and praise.[49] Let us examine these in greater detail.

Questions

Various questions are commonly used to communicate complaint or protest, often indicating reproach on the part of the speaker.[50] Frequently, protest is conveyed by asking "how long?" (usually *'ad-matai*, *'ad-mah*, or *'ad-'anah*, Pss 4:2; 6:3; 13:1-2; 35:17; 74:9-10, 22; 79:5; 80:4; 89:46; 90:13; 94:3; 119:84). In asking "how long," the speaker may imply that too long a time has elapsed between a legitimate request and its answer, or that the suffering imposed due to wrongdoing has become excessive (Pss 13:1-2; 44:23; 89:46; 90:13).[51] At times the same ideas are communicated through the question "when" (*matay*, Ps 42:2). Frequently, one encounters the fear that, given God's previous failure to hear such cries, the aberrant situation might go on "forever" (*netzaḥ*, Pss 13:1; 44:23; 89:46). Such a question thus implies reproach expressed to God for various failings: negligence, tardiness, lack of awareness, or distraction. The interrogative "why?" (usually *mah*, *lamah*, or *'al-mah*; cf. Gen 4:6; Pss 22:1; 42:5, 9, 11; 43:2, 5; 44:23-24; 74:1, 11; 79:10; 80:12; 88:14; 115:2) may also communicate protest.[52] Such a question may suggest that the Deity's behavior is inconsistent, incomprehensible, or absurd (Pss 10:1; 42:9; 43:2; 44:23).[53] At times "where?" (*'aey*, Pss 42:3, 10; 79:10; 89:49) may communicate reproach suggesting that that which would normally be expected has failed to appear, and that Yahweh bears responsibility for such failure.[54]

Negative Imperatives

Attentive readers will have noticed that in the texts cited at the beginning of our discussion of the silence of God, the psalmist implores the Lord *not to be silent*. In Hebrew this is expressed through what is commonly called a "negative imperative"—the use of the imperative, prefaced by a negation (such as "do not" or "be not")—calling upon the one to whom the words are addressed not to do something or not to permit a certain event to occur. Such negative imperatives are common in the Psalms.[55] It is essential to stress that, when employed in the context of protest against God's action (or lack thereof), the negative imperative does not express a mere theoretical possibility, or even a psychological fear on the part of the psalmist. Rather, it is a plea to God *not to allow a present situation to continue, or a clearly imminent event to occur*. As such, it is a cry to God in moments of great distress to move from a stance of inaction to one of help and deliverance. Put another way, in such texts the silence of God is not raised as a theoretical matter to be discussed, or much less a "problem of apologetics" to be "solved." It is evoked as an existential reality, and one that *threatens the very life of the individual or nation*.

These negative imperatives thus express critiques of divine inactivity in the midst of desperate situations (Pss 22:19; 27:9; 28:3; 37:1; 39:8; 49:16; 70:5; 71:12; 102:2).[56] This is evident when these negative imperatives are compared to other passages conveying the same ideas, but involving the reproachful questions we have just noted.[57] For example, several of these negative petitions are paralleled in other texts where the same idea is formulated using the question "why?" Thus, the petition that Yahweh "be not far off" (Pss 22:11, 19; 35:22; 38:2; 71:12) can also be expressed through the interrogative "why do you stand afar off?" (10:1). The request that Yahweh's face not be hidden (27:9; 69:17; 102:2; 143:7) mirrors the question "why do you hide your face?" (44:24). The plea "do not forsake me" (27:9; 71:9, 18; 119:8) echoes the question "why have you forsaken me?" (22:1). The cry, "do not cast me off" (27:9; 51:11; 71:9) evokes the question "why have you cast me off?" (43:2; 74:1; 88:14). And the plea to Yahweh not to forget the psalmist (74:19, 23) corresponds to the despairing question "why have you forgotten me?" (Ps 42:9). As just noted, these cries arise out of situations that are either actually present (and thus the prayer requests the cessation of these circumstances) or are seen as inevitable, apart from timely divine intervention. Examples of the former are the following:

> As for me, I am poor and needy, but the Lord takes thought for me. You are my help and my deliverer; do not [continue to] delay, O my God. (Ps 40:17)

> But my eyes are turned toward you, O God, my Lord; in you I seek refuge; do not [continue to] leave me defenseless. (Ps 141:8)

The following citations provide examples of the latter:

> Do not sweep me away with sinners, nor my life with the bloodthirsty. (Ps 26:9)

> Do not drag me away with the wicked, with those who are workers of evil, who speak peace with their neighbors, while mischief is in their hearts. (Ps 28:3)

> Do not enter into judgment with your servant, for no one living is righteous before you. (Ps 143:2)

Statements of Blame

At times the psalmists did not hesitate to direct statements of criticism or blame toward God. The Lord is seen as the source of the Psalmist's woes in various passages. Psalm 88 contains several such statements:

> You have caused my companions to shun me; you have made me a thing of horror to them. I am shut in so that I cannot escape; my eye grows dim

> through sorrow. Every day I call on you, O LORD; I spread out my hands to you. Your wrath has swept over me; your dread assaults destroy me. They surround me like a flood all day long; from all sides they close in on me. You have caused friend and neighbor to shun me; my companions are in darkness. (Ps 88:8-9, 16-18)[58]

Similar emotionally laden expressions appear in Psalms 39:11-12 and 102:11, 24 (among others).[59] Statements of blame were also conveyed by repeating the mocking words of the enemies as the psalmists pleaded for relief before the Lord (Pss 13:4; 35:21; 42:10).

Expressions of Trust and Confidence

Careful readers of the Psalms observe that protests over God's failure to intervene are frequently expressed in close proximity to recollections of the Lord's *past* saving interventions (e.g., Pss 44:1-3; 74:1b-2, 12; 80:8-11; 89:19-37; 106:8-11, 43-46), and to expressions of *present* confidence (Pss 60:4-5a; 74:12; 85:6; 106:43-47; 115:9-11). Why is this so? Surprisingly, such declarations constitute an additional argument put forward as a motivation for God to act.[60] Yahweh has been good and faithful in the past. Why has this benevolence now seemingly ended? Moreover, the people of God continue to express their confidence and trust. As such, the psalmists (individually) or the nation (collectively) do not merit their present suffering. They were either innocent of the charges, or the sentence seemed excessively harsh.[61] These too become arguments for God to act.

It is important to underline that these expressions of protest were *cries for help* rooted both in rational argument as well as in personal distress. Their goal was to *persuade Yahweh to intervene and deliver*. The psalmists speak at length of their shame before their enemies, the inconsistency of the present situation with Yahweh's self-descriptions and past dealings with the people of God, and the great potential loss of praise that Yahweh would experience should relief not come.

At the very core of the drama in Act 2, then, is the psalmists' protest at the silence of God. And most especially significant for our purposes in this study is *the profound contrast in "soundscape" between the various expressions of the psalmists' anguish, on the one hand, and the silence with which such expressions are met by the Lord, on the other*. In the Psalms of Protest, the psalmists describe their plight by means of numerous sound-laden terms, evocative of deep emotional pathos, anguish, and need. By contrast, for a protracted period of time (the significance of this seemingly interminable delay will be explored just below), God says and does nothing that would bring relief but rather *remains silent* (see Pss 22:2; 28:1; 35:22; 39:12; 83:1; 109:1).[62]

The overall tone of the psalmist's sufferings is set by the imperative, especially when used with verbs such as "to call" (**qara'*) or "to cry" (**sheva'*), or the nouns derived from them (Pss 4:1; 17:1, 6; 22:2; 28:1,2; 31:17; 39:12; 57:2; 72:12; 86:3, 5-7; 88:1-2, 9, 13; 102:1-2; 142:1). The imperatives here express the urgency of the psalmists' needs.[63] The psalmists' pleas were not spoken in a whisper of resignation. They speak of their sighing (*hagig*, Pss 5:1; 39:3) and their moaning (*'anaḥah*, Pss 6:6; 31:10; 38:9; 102:5; cf. Isa 35:10; 51:11; Jer. 45:3; Job 3:24; 23:2; Lam. 1:22). They engage in weeping (*beki*, Pss 6:8; 30:5; 102:9; cf. Isa 16:9; 22:4, 12; 38:3; Jer 3:21; 9:10; 31:9; and many other times in Jer), they roar in agitation (**hamah*, Pss 55:17, 77:3; cf. Isa 59:11; Jer 4:19; 48:36; Ezek 7:16) and groan (*she'agah*, Ps 22:1; cf. Job 3:24). The psalmists' inner experience of pain (*ma'kov*, Ps 38:17) results in crying out for aid (**tza'aq*, Pss 34:17, 88:1).

This soundscape mirrors the psalmists' inner *emotional landscape*. The psalmists' cries "do not forsake (**'azav*) me" (Pss 27:9; 38:21; 71:9, 18) or "how long will you forget (**shakaḥ*) me" evoke the image of the searing pain and distress of a child who is abandoned by a parent (cf. Ps 27:10; Isa 49:15). The plea that Yahweh not "be far away" (**raḥaq*, Pss 22:11, 19; 35:22; 38:21; 71:12) recalls the image of a friend or loved one who suddenly becomes distant and inaccessible, and the doubt and confusion such distancing can bring. Such a background is evident in the various occurrences of this verb with reference to relational distancing, and to its effects (Isa 29:13; Jer 2:5; Ezek 8:6; 44:10; Ps 88:18; Job 19:13; 30:10; Prov 19:7; Lam 1:16). It is especially notable that this verb appears in Psalm 71:9 with reference to being abandoned in one's old age—a time of growing weakness and vulnerability. Similarly, the appeal to God not to "be silent to the psalmists' cries" (**ḥarash*, Pss 28:1; 35:22) calls forth painful instances wherein one person becomes estranged from another and is unaffected by their needs or requests (Pss 22:1; 81:11; cf. the reverse in 66:20; 69:33; 81:11). Psalm 39:12 is especially poignant in this regard. The psalmist asks the Lord not to be silent despite the psalmists' tears, conjuring up the imagery of one person weeping sorrowfully, while another sits by, dispassionately. This also evokes the callousness of Joseph's brothers who, by their own admission, refused to hear Joseph's entreaties: "They said to one another, 'Alas, we are paying the penalty for what we did to our brother; we saw his anguish when he pleaded with us, but we would not listen. That is why this anguish has come upon us.'" Importantly, this is the first time in the narrative that the reader learns of Joseph's pleading, and the brothers' heartlessness.[64]

The psalmists' words "do not hide your face" (**satar paneka*, Pss 13:1; 27:9; 44:24; 55:1; 69:17; 88:14; 102:2; 143:7) similarly recall the painful experience of rejection by friends or loved ones. The psalmists' urgent request to Yahweh that s/he, as Yahweh's servant, not be turned away in anger (**natah be'aph*, Pss 27:9; 69:15) conjures up images of a servant summarily cast off by a master who had become angry (Gen 39:19; 44:18; cf. also Jer 17:4; Job 42:7).[65] The plea that the psalmist not be surrendered "to the desire of his or her enemies" (Ps 27:12) or be made the "scorn of fools" (Ps 39:8) draws out the pain of the public humiliation of one falsely accused and condemned (Pss 22:5; 25:2-3, 20; 31:1, 17; 35:26; 40:14-15; 44:13-16; 74:21; 89:45). The psalmist fears being "dragged away (**mashak*) with the wicked" (Ps 28:3), calling up the sentiments of one who is forcibly taken away, such as Joseph in Genesis 37:28, the poor who are caught in the traps set for them and dragged away (Ps 10:9), or Leviathan caught by a fishhook (Job 41:1).[66] The cry "do not delay" (**'eḥar*) expresses the terror of one desperately waiting for needed rescue (Pss 40:17; 70:5; Dan 9:19). The note of desperation is especially evident in Psalm 70:5, where the verbs "hasten" (**ḥoush*) and "delay" (**'eḥar*) are closely associated with help (*'ezer*) and deliverance (piel of **palaṭ*), terms commonly associated with situations of desperate need.

Incomprehensibly, then, the Lord seems oblivious to the pain of the psalmists, and to their broader relationship and history together; a state of extreme incongruity now exists. A full demonstration of this incongruity would exceed the confines of this study; thus a few examples must suffice. Protest over God's *silence* (Pss 22:2; 28:1; 35:22; 39:12; 83:1; 109:1) stands in sharp opposition to assertions that Israel need but "call upon Yahweh in the day of trouble" in order to be heard and delivered (Ps 50:15). As such, in the Exodus narrative Israel cries out to Yahweh, and is heard and delivered (Exod 3:7-8). The plea that Yahweh not be *distant* (Ps 22:11, 19) flatly contradicts Moses' declaration in Deuteronomy 4:7, "For what other great nation has a god so near to it as the Lord our God is whenever we call to him?" The cry "*do not hide your face*" inverts the Aaronic benediction (Num 6:24-26), where the Yahweh's blessing is described as follows: "The Lord bless you and keep you; the Lord make his face to shine upon you, and be gracious to you; the Lord lift up his countenance [lit. face] upon you, and give you peace."[67] Indeed, the notion of the Lord as distant runs afoul of the notion that the community is exhorted to come before God continually (Ps 105:4): "seek my face" (Ps 27:7).[68] The psalmist's plea that s/he not be "dragged away with the wicked" (Ps 28:3) is the antithesis of Yahweh's purposes of upholding the righteous but "by no means clearing the guilty" (Exod 34:7). It similarly reverses Abraham's cry that it would be unthinkable for Yahweh to "sweep away the righteous with the wicked" (Gen

18:23), an assertion borne out by Yahweh's rescue of Lot and his family (Gen 19; cf. the similar motif in Hab 1:2–2:4). The request that Yahweh not *forsake* the psalmist (Ps 27:9), contrasts strongly with the promise that Yahweh will never fail or forsake the servants of God (Josh 1:5; Ps 37:28; Isa 41:17), and the reality that this had been borne out in the experience of the Persian period community in Yehud (Neh 9:19, 31). Examples such as these could be given for most all of the negative imperatives we have noted above.

In sum, in Scene 2 the dramatic tension of the drama of Yahweh's silence rises to the breaking point. Despite the psalmists' commitment to walk in integrity of heart, and of their declarations of innocence in the face of false accusations, their fervent cries to Yahweh for succor from various situations of critical need, God was now suddenly and incomprehensibly silent. There was seemingly no exit from this dilemma. Yahweh, it would appear had become "the God that failed." But then, when all hope appears to be lost, a radical turn occurs, and the drama moves in a very unexpected direction.

Act 3: From Despair to Deliverance

In the so-called Psalms of Thanksgiving, the psalmists refer back to earlier situations of distress, to their pleas for help directed Godward, and to the great relief that the Lord's response brought to them. Psalms 30 and 116 are typical examples:

> I will extol you, O Lord, for you have drawn me up,
> and did not let my foes rejoice over me.
> O Lord my God, I cried to you for help,
> and you have healed me.
> O Lord, you brought up my soul from Sheol,
> restored me to life from among those gone down to the Pit. (Ps 30:1-3)

> I love the Lord, because he has heard
> my voice and my supplications.
> Because he inclined his ear to me,
> therefore I will call on him as long as I live.
> The snares of death encompassed me;
> the pangs of Sheol laid hold on me;
> I suffered distress and anguish.
> Then I called on the name of the Lord:
> "O Lord, I pray, save my life!"
>
> Gracious is the Lord, and righteous;
> our God is merciful.

The LORD protects the simple;
when I was brought low, he saved me.
Return, O my soul, to your rest,
for the LORD has dealt bountifully with you.

For you have delivered my soul from death,
my eyes from tears,
my feet from stumbling.
I walk before the LORD
in the land of the living. (Ps 116:1-9)

Often, these Psalms of Thanksgiving allude to prayers *previously* uttered in the midst of distress (e.g., Ps 30:8-10). These earlier prayers were likely the psalms of plea, lament, and expressions of protest we have been studying. However, at other times, there is a movement from plea or protest to thanksgiving and praise within a psalm *which arises in the very moment of anxiety and despair.* As we have seen, remembrances of God's past saving deeds, or expressions of present trust and hope for future assistance frequently appear in the Psalms of Lament. These served, in part, as motivations for the Lord to act. However, it is highly important to distinguish expressions of confidence that God *will hear and act* (e.g., Ps 38:15, where God's acts are clearly seen as future)[69] from those instances where the psalmists are convinced, while still in the midst of their struggles, that the needed help is *as good as accomplished.* Suddenly, and seemingly inexplicably, the psalmists' neediness, pain, and desperation give way to the expression of praise and thanksgiving. Psalms such as 3; 6; 10; 13; 22; 27; 28; 31; 54; 56; 64; and Isaiah 38:10-20 contain examples of this.[70] Central to this conviction is the psalmists' certainty that God has *already heard* their cries (Pss 6:8; 10:17; 28:6), *seen* their plight (31:7), and *received* their prayers (22:24).[71] As such, the conviction of being heard is construed as a *past* event, using the Hebrew perfect tense.[72] In some texts the psalmists' certainty is followed by anticipatory descriptions of Yahweh's *future* acts of deliverance, described using the Hebrew imperfect (Ps 6:9b). In other passages Yahweh's attentiveness to the psalmists' prayer becomes the basis for their praise (13:5; 10:14; 22:22-25). In still others, such as Psalm 54, Yahweh's acts of deliverance appear to be portrayed as both past (v. 7) and future (v. 5). The critical element here is that the conviction of being heard forms the basis of a *volte face* on the part of the psalmist. Plea and protest give way to confidence and praise.[73] This radical change in tone has been described as an "acknowledgement of divine response."[74]

The critical question for our purposes here is what has brought about this transformed perspective? Two responses are commonly offered. Some assert that these expressions come in response to a priestly or a prophetic "oracle of salvation."[75] In some kind of ceremonial setting, either in a private home or a worship site, a priest or prophet has arisen and declared to the petitioners that Yahweh has heard their pleas and will act on their behalf. As a result, the petitioners praise God, having trusted in these words of promise. However, surprisingly, few such "oracles of salvation" are actually cited in the Psalms.[76] As a consequence, while certainly possible, such an approach is somewhat speculative.

A second response approaches the matter from the perspective of the psalmists' *inner* convictions regarding the Lord's trustworthiness. Viewed this way, the critical dimension is not the presence or absence of an "oracle of salvation," but the psalmists' ability to see beyond the present situation and find ultimate hope and assurance in his or her God. Most importantly, the specific reason for such a change in perspective is *left unexplained in the text*. As such, whether in response to an oracle of salvation or not, the sea change in the psalmists' outlook seems to have arisen out of the conviction that it would be ultimately unthinkable for Yahweh to abandon them completely. Such an assurance may have been rooted in deep reflection on the Lord's past deeds on behalf of the nation, the individual's family, and the individual him or herself (cf. Ps 22:3-5, 9-11). Or perhaps it was, in part, due to their certainty of being in right relationship with God. This is eloquently expressed in Psalm 66:17-19: "I cried aloud to him, and he was extolled with my tongue. If I had cherished iniquity in my heart, the Lord would not have listened. But truly God has listened; he has given heed to the words of my prayer." However such a conviction may have arisen, the psalmists were giving expression to a sense of *inward assurance* that their cries had reached the heart of God, and that they would not be abandoned or forsaken. Believing individuals through the ages have expressed similar moments of conviction, even though no proof or evidence formed its basis. Such a conviction may best be described as the expression of a relational connectedness, an existential faith.

The critical element here is that the psalmists' conviction in such texts must *not be read as an expression of gratefulness for deliverance received*. As we have noted, in the Psalms of Thanksgiving speakers commonly cite earlier, urgent pleas, and God's subsequent response as the basis for their ultimate praise. However, the expressions of confidence in Psalms 6:8-9; 13:6; and 22:22-24 (and elsewhere) do not depict a *retrospective* gaze.[77] Rather, they are the expression of *anticipatory* faith. Goldingay insightfully comments, "Like Ps 6, [Ps 22] now takes an extraordinary turn. . . . These statements [i.e. acknowledgements of divine response] are then made by faith. The suppliant has not yet received any sign of Yhwh's responding."[78] Westermann similarly comments,

> [T]he grief over which the suppliant is lamenting, and for the removal of which he pleads with God still remains. During the praying of these Psalms no miracle has occurred, but something else has occurred. God has heard and . . . has had mercy. . . . And in this the decisive event has taken place. . . . That which is yet to come . . . must of necessity follow.[79]

Similarly, Craigie and Tate comment, with reference to Psalm 13:6:

> The past experience of the psalmist has been one of trust in God's "lovingkindness," namely the faithful covenant love of God which characterized all his dealings with his chosen people. The present reality was of such a nature as to undermine that past experience of trust, but it is in the nature of confidence to transform the present on the basis of past experience and thus to create hope for the future; and so the psalmist can affirm that he will "rejoice" in God's deliverance, even though it has not yet come. The actual song of praise would burst forth once deliverance had been accomplished, but the knowledge that deliverance was coming created an anticipatory calm and sense of confidence.[80]

Even before any tangible outcomes of their prayers can be seen, the psalmists have thus found certainty and peace through a deep and inward connection with Israel's God. Generally speaking, we are given no insight into precisely how these psalmists believed the Lord would intervene on their behalf. Central to their expressions of assurance, however, was the conviction that relief would surely come, and one could wait for it in confident hope (Pss 27:14; 31:24; 37:7, 9, 34; 38:15; 39:7; 130:5).

Samuel Balentine rightly reminds us that these transitions from despair to assurance must not be read in a superficial, *pro forma* way, as if they were simply part of the lament genre, and a prelude to the praise to follow. Rather, we must grasp the very real anguish and anxiety that is reflected in the psalmists' words in Act 2 of the drama. To reduce them to anything less would be to minimize the very real and raw sense of divine abandonment they convey.[81] For the psalmists, God's silence was terrifying. Furthermore, these moments of despair were anything but short lived. The cry "how long . . . forever?" reflects an extended period of anxiety and despair. The sufferers had brought their plight before the Lord, yet had again and again come away empty handed. Hope deferred had, in the end, made the heart sick (Prov 13:12). Yet somehow these psalmists were able to see beyond the sickness of their hearts and lay hold of hope in Yahweh's goodness once again. Indeed, in one sense, it would seem that the joy of emerging into the light of the certainty of God's response was somehow predicated upon passing through this "dark night of the soul" where those in deep despair felt that any hope was impossible. And the descriptions of such a transition from darkness to hope were no charade, but emerged out of deep personal experience.

Conclusion: The Silence of God

Summing up, the ultimate resolution of the drama of divine silence occurs in that deep, internal place where those in pain encounter the Lord. However, and most surprisingly, *the details of this encounter are left unexplained in the drama of the silence of God reflected in these texts.* No reason is provided as to why Yahweh allowed these painful situations to arise, or for why they lasted so long, leaving the psalmists in suffering and despair. Nor do the psalmists disclose the precise reason for the change in their perspective. No words of Yahweh are recorded, and, apart from the conviction that the Lord has heard their prayer, no reasons are provided for their new outlook. Why is this so? It would seem that the effect of this enigmatic presentation is to invite us, as readers and hearers, to view this profoundly transformative encounter with God as shrouded in *silence*. Put another way, in the HB the incomprehensible silence of God as manifested by divine inactivity is ultimately *resolved in the believer's ability to wait upon God in silence, and in that silence to receive assurance and peace*. As such, whereas God's silence was once met with shrill and vociferous protest, it is now received into the inner experience of the psalmists, and surrounds them as they wait upon God:

> For God alone my soul waits in silence;
> from him comes my salvation.
> He alone is my rock and my salvation,
> my fortress; I shall never be shaken. (Ps 62:1-2)

> I wait for the LORD, my soul waits,
> and in his word I hope;
> my soul waits for the Lord
> more than those who watch for the morning,
> more than those who watch for the morning.

O Israel, hope in the LORD!
For with the LORD there is steadfast love,
and with him is great power to redeem.
It is he who will redeem Israel
from all its iniquities. (Ps 130:5-8)

It is important to note that, at times, such confident waiting on God involved the ability to cling to the Lord despite all evidence to the contrary. Habakkuk 3:17-19 expresses this poignantly:

> Though the fig tree does not blossom, and no fruit is on the vines; though the produce of the olive fails and the fields yield no food; though the flock is cut off from the fold and there is no herd in the stalls, yet I will rejoice in the LORD; I will exult in the God of my salvation. GOD, the Lord, is my strength; he makes my feet like the feet of a deer, and makes me tread upon the heights.

Thus, the drama of the silence of God involves the ability to deal with the profound "gaps" or "silences" with which the people of God must ultimately come to grips. And just as the holiness of the priests could take in and neutralize the uncleanness embodied in the purgation offerings by consuming them (Lev 10:16-20),[82] so too here the psalmists are able to neutralize the distress arising from the silence of God by means of an inner attitude of silent waiting and expectation.

The Jewish exegete and theologian André Neher comments insightfully on the interface between speech and silence, and the dynamic of faith. He states: "The believer will not be afraid for he knows, with the strength of his subjective recognition, that [God's] 'hiding of face' contains the face in its dramatic reality—that there is a mask, a curtain or a screen which will one day be removed."[83]

In sum, our treatment of the silence of God here has not dealt with the larger questions of theodicy, the suffering of the innocent, or the imponderables of divine inaction in the face of monstrous evil. However, we have seen how, within the HB, the people of God have wrestled with the challenges of faith posed by the seeming silence of God in their moments of deepest need. And we have observed how they emerged from these challenges still hoping and trusting in the Lord.

8
FINDING GOD BETWEEN SOUND AND SILENCE

In this chapter we will examine three texts where silence plays a pivotal role in the interface between God and humanity: Genesis 22, 1 Kings 19, and Job. In each one, the human actors come into a deeper understanding of the Lord's character and purposes. Most importantly, this knowledge emerges neither out of speech alone, nor out of silence alone. Rather, it is the fruit of a *journey through both words and silence*. In our analysis we will trace this journey, with an eye on its starting point, the various instances of speech and silence along the way, and its final outcome.

The psalms studied in the "three-act drama" in the previous chapter were rooted in oral expressions used in rituals of healing and restoration and in worship. The silence of God was essentially the silence of non-intervention, God's refusal to *act*. Resolution was seen either as already present, or imminent and certain, through confident hope in the goodness of God. These three texts, by contrast, are strongly *literary* in character. The first two are prose narratives, and the latter a complex blend of genres, involving both prose and poetry. The silence of God spoken of in these texts relates *not to God's inaction, but to human wrestling with the incomprehensibility of the purposes of God*. All three texts present the reader with an individual caught up in a confusing wasteland. Divine speech is neither entirely absent nor fully accessible or comprehensible. Abraham, Elijah, and Job are called to inhabit *a space between speech and silence*. God is not absent, but inscrutable. The reader knows something of what God is doing, but only partially. Nevertheless, the characters within the text, and we as its readers, are called upon to persevere in faithfulness to the Lord. And even when these texts move toward resolution, many questions are still left unanswered. These passages are among the most extensively discussed texts in the HB. As such, I will only be able to focus on those aspects of them that directly relate to speech and silence. I will deal with these texts in the order in which they appear in the HB: Genesis 22, 1 Kings 19, and Job. The reason for this choice will become evident as the chapter concludes.

Genesis 22: Speech, Silence, and Isolation

Genesis 22 stands at the apex of the so-called Abraham Cycle (Gen 12:1–25:11). God has called Abraham and given him great promises: he will become the father of a great multitude, his seed is promised a land, kings will come forth from him. Most significantly, he will be blessed and protected by God, and become the one through whom God's blessing will flow to all the earth (Gen 12:1-3, 7; 15:1-17; 17:1-8). Many challenges arise that threaten the promise. These include the infertility of Abraham's wife Sarah (11:30), famine in the land causing Abraham to go down to Egypt (12:10-11), Sarah's presence in the harem of a foreign ruler (12:17-20; 20:1-17), and inner-family disputes (13:6-7). Finally, after many twists and turns, Isaac is born (21:1-6). Then, incomprehensibly, God demands that Abraham sacrifice Isaac, the child of promise through whom the promises to Abraham were to be fulfilled (Gen 21:12), as a whole burnt offering (22:1-2).

God's demand here has perplexed interpreters both Jewish and Christian over the centuries.[1] Why would the God who had been guiding Abraham toward the fulfillment of these promises suddenly turn and act in this incomprehensible way? Why would the Lord ask Abraham to *incinerate* the embodiment of all God's previous promises? Whole burnt offerings involved not only the death of the victim, but the complete burning of the corpse. Generally speaking, in both Jewish and Christian traditions two major approaches are taken. Traditionally, Abraham is lionized for his heroic display of faith and obedience.[2] The ethical problems involved in God's demand are either bracketed out entirely and subsumed under the greater good of leading Abraham into more profound depths of trust and obedience, or seen as a rejection of human sacrifice and its replacement in Israel's sacrificial cult.[3] A second, more recent view sees God's demand as fundamentally immoral. The purpose of the test was to determine whether Abraham would rise to the occasion and challenge God's unethical demand.[4] Viewed from the perspective of the framer(s) of the Abraham Cycle, the former approach seems to me to be most likely.[5]

Let us turn now to matters of speech and silence in Genesis 22. Perhaps the most frequently cited remark relating to silence in this text is that of E. A. Speiser, who suggested that the repeated phrase used in reference to Abraham and Isaac, "the two walked on together" (22:6, 8), constitutes the "most poignant and eloquent silence in all literature."[6] Speiser is perhaps correct, at least with reference to the biblical literature. Moreover, the silences present in Genesis 22 can only be properly understood when set in relationship to the sounds and words in the passage. These silences are not identified by means of the standard words for silence used elsewhere in the HB. Nor are they denoted by the negation of verbs of saying, speaking, or acting. Rather, such silences are expressed subtly, through narrative description and dialogue. As we shall see, these narrative descriptions and dialogues are characterized by ambiguity and silence, resulting in a dialectic between stability and unresolved tension. Nahum Sarna, for example, senses this and suggests that "[t]here is perfect rapport between [Abraham and Isaac], encompassed as they are in mutual solitariness and enveloped in silence." Yet in the following sentence he speaks of this silence as "oppressive."[7] Indeed, both rapport and isolation infuse the ethos of the passage.

Let us examine this phenomenon in greater detail. In Genesis 22:1-2, the reader encounters the foundational event that sets up the dramatic movement of the passage: the demand that Isaac be sacrificed. The passage is entirely *unambiguous* as it relates to who utters the command ("*God* [Elohim] said . . ."), who should perform the deed ("God said to *Abraham* . . ."), who is to be sacrificed ("take your *son*, your only *son*, whom you love . . . *Isaac*"), in what manner ("*as a whole burnt offering* . . ."; *'olah*, cf. Gen 8:20; Exod 29:25; Lev 1:3, 10, 13), and where ("*on one of the mountains that I will show you* . . ."). Most specifically, the reader is informed of God's purpose (God *tested* Abraham). Despite this clarity, certain aspects of this passage remain shrouded in silence. Why is it *Elohim* and not Yahweh who makes the demand? The name Yahweh does not appear until 22:11. Why? What is the significance of the introduction of this proper name for God? Should the verb "take" be translated as a direct command, or as a request? The Hebrew form could be translated either way.[8] Why is the specific location for the sacrifice unnamed, yet couched in similar terms to the description of the land that Abraham is promised in 12:1-3?

Moreover, the God-Abraham relationship is engulfed in silence. The reader is told that God is testing Abraham (22:1), but Abraham does not know this. Moreover, why does Abraham not remonstrate with God over this outrageous demand? Abraham has shown himself ready to plead for Lot and for Sodom and Gomorrah (18:22-33) and to object to the expulsion of his son Ishmael (17:18; 21:11). He has even been told that it will be through Isaac that the promises made to his seed will be fulfilled (21:12), and there is no indication that Isaac has had a child. Why does he not object here? In 22:3-4 we read of Abraham's response to God's demand. But here, too, silence pervades the scene. Abraham acts, but says nothing, even to Sarah his wife and the mother of the child of promise. Nor is the reader given any explicit, unambiguous indications of Abraham's inner state. Does the description of his preparations (22:3) indicate determination or inner turmoil?[9] How does he feel when he looks up and sees the place from afar (22:4)? The text is silent on these critical issues, leaving the reader to fill the gaps.

Silence also characterizes the relationship between Abraham and the servants. Abraham speaks, but the servants are silent. Why does Abraham take them along?[10] Dramatically, they enable Abraham to say (and thus communicate to the reader) the words of 22:5, "We will go up, we will worship, and we will return." However, it is immediately apparent that these words are highly enigmatic, and conceal as much—if not more—than they reveal. What is Abraham thinking? What does he believe? Is he trying to hide his true purpose from Isaac and the servants? Why does he leave the servants behind? In saying "we will return," does he really think that he will return with his son? Why does he use the term "worship" for the sacrifice he must perform? What do his words imply?[11]

The dialogue between Abraham and Isaac contains the same ambiguity. Isaac speaks only after hearing himself referred to in Abraham's words to the servants in 22:5. In 22:7, walking alone with his father and out of earshot of the servants he asks, "Where is the lamb for the burnt offering?"[12] Are his words meant to denote suspicion or naïveté? His words are more appropriately those of a young child. But in the inner chronology of the narrative he would be at least an adolescent. Abraham's response is once again cloaked in ambiguity. He responds: "The Lord will provide for himself the lamb for the burnt offering, my son" (22:8). Do the latter two words hold within them a note of cruel irony—the lamb will be my son?

The text goes on to narrate Abraham's carrying out of God's demand, excruciatingly slowing down the pace of the narration and drawing out its details.[13] Abraham binds Isaac, then lays him on the wood, then takes the knife to slay his son. *All of this takes place in a soundscape of complete silence.* As readers we hold our breath. One might hear a pin drop.

Suddenly, in verse 11 the silence is broken. Whereas up to this point it was God (Elohim) who had spoken, now the angel of Yahweh commands

Abraham to desist. A voice, speaking in the first person, declares, "Now I know that you fear God." But who is "I"? And can the "I" voice be distinguished from the "God" of 22:1, 8, 9? Abraham then discovers a ram caught in a thicket and offers it up instead of his son, and names the place in honor of the momentous event (22:13-14). The angel then reiterates and expands the Lord's previous promises to Abraham (22:18-19). Those earlier promises had been based on God's faithfulness alone (although certain demands of obedience were attached to them; 12:1-3; 17:1-14). However, now they are explicitly grounded in Abraham's obedience and given even greater depth and permanence through a divine oath. Divine speech has followed silence and brought with it greater understanding. Abraham then returns to his servants and they go together to Beer-Sheba (22:19).

J.-L. Ska has demonstrated how the dramatic development of Genesis 22 places its characters into "airtight compartments" in which each one possesses differing degrees of knowledge.[14] Moreover, this isolation is *also true of the reader*. Each *dramatis persona* knows matters that cannot be communicated to the others present in the text. Abraham knows more than Isaac and the servants, but cannot (or chooses not to) reveal that knowledge to them. Similarly, the reader knows more than Abraham, but cannot communicate that knowledge to him. Most significantly, even though we as readers know that God's action here is a test, we cannot understand God's action in any ultimate sense. Why would God choose to demand such a thing?

The overall pattern of speech and silence in the passage is significant. As just noted, the passage opens with speech providing many important details relevant to the reading of it (vv. 1-2). Then, from verses 3-10 we encounter various profound silences. These silences isolate each character, and render the words of each one opaque and ambiguous. Finally, in verses 11-12 God's silence is broken. The crisis is averted, Isaac is spared. The blessing is renewed and made even more secure through a divine oath (vv. 15-18). At first glance, readers might see this as a "happy ending"—a full resolution and restoration of all that had gone before. Yet in the resolution there are profound gaps and silences. Had God no concern for the feelings of Abraham, or for Isaac's ongoing ability to trust other humans, or, more importantly, God?[15] Was Abraham lying to Isaac? What justification could be given for Abraham's failure to consult Sarah? Why is Yahweh, the proper name of God, omitted when the demand is uttered in 22:1-2, but only introduced when the angel of Yahweh intervenes to stop the deed in 22:11-12? Why is there no mention of Isaac when it is stated that Abraham and the servants returned together (22:19)?

What then can be said regarding these unresolved silences that pervade the text, broken up at times by words whose meaning is equally difficult to ascertain? If the text's purpose is, as many suggest, to reassure the people of God that their ultimate security lies in God's protection, do we have here an instance of a biblical text providing an important answer to a pressing issue but creating other problems in its wake? The biblical writers have left us unanswered and potentially unanswerable questions. Why? What are the people of God meant to make of this aspect of their Scriptures?

Ska observes that one effect of these narrative gaps and silences is to draw the reader into the dynamics of the narrative. As readers, we are forced to enter into the psyche of the various characters, wondering what we might do in their place. More poignantly, I would suggest these silences have an *isolating* effect on the reader. The various "airtight compartments" inhabited by the text's characters force the reader to grapple with those moments of life lived before and with God that may be painful and isolating. God's demand here *distances* Abraham from all those around him—even God. As such, the text may, in part, have been addressed to those times when in its journey of faith, Israel, either collectively or individually, faced difficult issues and was called to wrestle with incomprehension, doubt, intrapsychic pain, and, most significantly, experienced the desperate need to hear God's voice.[16] Jacob's solitary wrestling all night with an unknown opponent at the Jabbok (Gen 32:22-32) follows a similar pattern and depicts such a drama.

Whatever their broader theological purposes may have been, the text's framer(s) are willing to let the readers stand by in silence, wondering what Abraham will choose to do, unable to reveal to him what they know concerning the purposes of God. Indeed, this is the existential reality faced in the course of life before God—being thrust into situations where one is confronted with the need to choose, but without the absolute certainty of the outcome. Faith, by necessity, involves uncertainty, the possibility of doubt, and the reality of unanswered questions. And, as evidenced by Genesis 22, such doubt, uncertainty, and questioning *must ultimately be wrestled through in deep silence.*

In sum, Genesis 22 manifests the following pattern: a person of faith is thrust into a situation of extreme duress, and yet is called to manifest steadfast trust in God. Such trust must be demonstrated despite the extreme nature of the test, and potentially disastrous outcomes involved in obedience to the Lord. Silence engulfs the protagonist and the characters in the text. Even the reader does not know what the protagonist is thinking or feeling, what his words actually mean, or even what God's purposes are. Yet, in the end, the protagonist perseveres in faithful obedience. God speaks again, renewing earlier divine promises. Yet, all is not fully resolved. Many imponderable questions remain. As we shall see, variations on this pattern will reappear in 1 Kings 19 and Job.

Excursus: Potential Abuses of Genesis 22

Genesis 22 is, in many ways, a highly troubling text, and needs to be taught with great caution. A child, upon hearing it read for the first time, might not only have severe misgivings about Abraham's God, but become fearful that a parent might somehow come to feel that God had demanded the same act of them. Similarly, at times certain individuals for one or another reason have become persuaded that God is asking them to perform some outrageous act as a test of faith. While any number of biblical or theological responses could and should be given to this issue (most specifically that the text depicts the test itself as unique and unrepeatable, and that human sacrifice is roundly condemned elsewhere in scripture; cf. Lev 18:21; 20:2; 2 Kgs 23:10; Jer 32:35), I would like to point to a very practical one: the importance of reading the biblical text in the context of a faith community. Except in rare abusive or dysfunctional situations, most believing communities would be able to provide sufficient emotional and psychological support to children or adults so as to enable them to avoid misappropriations of this passage. By contrast, when texts are read without reference to the wisdom of the broader community, individuals may form erroneous beliefs, be thrown into panic, and make destructive choices.

1 Kings 19: Sound, Silence, and the Voice of God

First Kings 19, with its reference to the "still small voice," is one of the most commonly cited biblical texts involving silence. However, as we shall see, although a very important text on silence, 1 Kings 19 is also poorly understood. Numerous questions emerge as one examines its details. Why does Elijah, who has previously been so courageous, now run away from Jezebel who has just threatened him (19:1-2)? And why does he run south, right through the SK, where there would be no threat to his life, and into the desert (19:3-4)? Why, despite the people's resounding declarations of fidelity to Yahweh in 18:39, does he ask for death (19:4) and believe that the whole nation has forsaken the Lord, and that his own life is in jeopardy (19:10-11)? Why does he leave his servant behind (19:3; as did Abraham in Gen 22:5) and journey on to "Horeb, the mountain of God" (19:8)? Moreover, was this the destination intended by the Lord in 19:7 or has Elijah run away in disobedience? Is the Lord sympathetic to Elijah, or frustrated by his self-perception as the only remaining true worshipper of Yahweh? Furthermore, what is the significance of the "wind, earthquake, and fire" that Elijah perceives on the mountain? What is the meaning of the narrator's note that Yahweh was not "in" any of these phenomena (19:11-12)? And, most significantly, is the translation "still small voice" an accurate rendering of the Hebrew phrase *qol demamah daqqah* in 19:12? What is the relationship between 19:12, where the *qol demamah daqqah* appears to provoke Elijah's movement from the interior of the cave to its entrance, to verse 13, where the prophet is specifically addressed by the Lord's voice (*qol*)? Such questions will require us to proceed slowly through the text, lingering over many of its details.

Literary and Theological Context

Before approaching our passage, it is essential to understand its broader context. The Elijah material is found in 1 Kings 17-19; 21; and 2 Kings 1–2. It appears likely that, prior to its incorporation into 1–2 Kings, 1 Kings 17–19 constituted an independent literary unit. As a whole, 1–2 Kings bear the theological imprint of the so-called "Deuteronomistic Historian(s)" (often abbreviated Dtr) whose work we discussed in chapter 2, with reference to the narrative of Saul's demise.[17] The principal concerns of this individual or group can be seen in the Ten Commandments and the laws of Deuteronomy. The Sinai Covenant constitutes the core of the nation's relationship to Yahweh, and Moses holds pride of place as its mediator and inaugurator. Chief among the demands of the covenant is exclusive devotion to Yahweh. The worship of other gods is its most quintessential violation (Deut 5:6-10). The Book of Kings stands squarely in this theological tradition, and Elijah is depicted as a prophet firmly dedicated to its ideals (1 Kgs 19:10, 14). It would be an overstatement to describe Elijah as a "new Moses." Moses held a unique and distinct position in Deuteronomistic thought (cf. Deut 34:10-12). It would be more accurate, however, to view Elijah as a prophet standing in the direct lineage of Moses.

Two key features of the depiction of Elijah in 1–2 Kings flow from this literary and theological context. First, Elijah is portrayed as a champion of fidelity to the Sinai covenant, primarily due to his denunciation of Israel's defection from its covenantal duties, and its worship of the Tyrian storm god Baal.[18] Elijah's concern for covenant faithfulness is evident from the outset. He appears on the scene rather suddenly in 17:1, and in a direct affront to Baal and demonstration of the supremacy of Yahweh declares that dew and rain will henceforth be suspended, and only reinstated upon Yahweh's direct command. He is opposed by King Ahab, an Israelite of the Omride dynasty, and his wife Jezebel, the daughter of King Ethbaal of Tyre (1 Kgs 16:31). Jezebel is portrayed as exerting a powerful influence over Ahab and all of the NK, leading it into the worship of Baal (1 Kgs 16:31-32). In 1 Kings 18:21, Elijah asks the people: "How long will you go limping with two different opinions? If the LORD is God, follow him; but if Baal, then follow him." Strikingly, however, the people are *silent*. As the narrator observes, "The people did not answer him a word." This then leads Elijah to propose a public challenge that will resolve the matter:

> "Let two bulls be given to us; let them choose one bull for themselves, cut it in pieces, and lay it on the wood, but put no fire to it; I will prepare the other bull and lay it on the wood, but put no fire to it. Then you call on the name of your god and I will call on the name of the LORD; *the god who answers by fire is indeed God.*" (1 Kgs 18:23-24a)

The proposal pleases the people, who respond, "Well spoken!" (18:24b). In verse 39, fire falls from heaven. "When all the people saw it, they fell on their faces and said, 'The LORD indeed is God; the LORD indeed is God.'" The narrator here clearly wishes to portray Baal as a weak and ineffectual deity. Elijah had declared a drought (17:1-2) and Baal has been powerless to overcome it. This was especially humiliating since Baal was understood to be the god of fertility, whose appearance was heralded by thunder, lightning, and abundant rain.[19] Here, in an even greater display of superiority, Yahweh sends fire, whereas in spite of much pleading and self-immolation on the part of his prophets, Baal cannot (1 Kgs 18:28-29). As we shall see, Elijah's encounter with the Lord on Sinai/Horeb in 1 Kings 19 must be read in light of this foundational conflict.

The second key theme in the depiction of Elijah concerns the relationship between Moses and Elijah. As noted, it would be incorrect to maintain that Elijah is portrayed as the "new Moses." However, it seems evident that for the writer(s) of 1–2 Kings Elijah is not far behind.[20] Many of Moses' life experiences are replicated, with some modification, in Elijah's. J. Walsh notes the similarities in the geographical framework of both figures: "each prophet begins his journey with a flight eastward to escape a king's wrath; each lodges with a family. Each returns to his country to face and challenge the king, and to awaken faith among the Israelites. Each leaves the country again on a journey to Sinai/Horeb, where he experiences a theophany. Each then departs for Israel via Transjordan."[21] Other similarities abound. Both receive divine provision of food in the wilderness (Exod 16; 1 Kgs 17:1-7; 19:5). Moses spends forty years there (Deut 8:2, 4), and Elijah forty days (1 Kgs

19:8). During the theophany on Sinai/Horeb, Yahweh places Moses in a crevice in the rock and covers him, lest he be consumed by Yahweh's overwhelming glory (Exod 33:17-21). Similarly, Elijah ascends the mountain and hides himself in "*the*" cave (1 Kgs 19:9). This is likely an allusion to the place where Moses was hidden, although a different word is used. Both Moses and Elijah "stand" (**'amad*) before Yahweh (Deut 4:10-11; 5:5; 1 Kgs 19:11, 13), and Yahweh's glorious presence "passes by" (**'avar*, Exod 33:10, 22; 1 Kgs 19:11). Moses dies in Moab, beyond the Jordan, and is buried there by God (Deut 34:5). Elijah is taken directly into the presence of Yahweh from beyond the Jordan (2 Kgs 2:9-12). Both are seen as having weakened at critical moments (Deut 32:48-52; 1 Kgs 19:3-4, 10, 14) and as a result, end their careers on a bittersweet note (Deut 34:1-4; 1 Kgs 17:15-17). The significance of these two considerations is this: Elijah's encounter with the "still small voice" (I will discuss the matter of the correct translation of this phrase below) must be set in the broader context of Moses' experience at Sinai/Horeb, and of the conflict with Ahab, Jezebel, and Baal.

The Portrait of Elijah in 1 Kings 19

Many interpreters have viewed Elijah as a burned out, discouraged prophet whose perspective had become radically distorted. This is said to account for his belief that the entire nation had forsaken Yahweh and that his own life was in danger (1 Kgs 19:10, 14), his desire to abandon his prophetic calling, and his request that Yahweh take his life (19:4). First Kings 19:9-18 is then read as Yahweh's renewal and recommissioning of his discouraged prophet.[22] More recently, certain commentators have challenged this approach and depicted Elijah as intransigent and self-focused, and viewed 1 Kings 19 as a revocation of Elijah's commission.[23] Evidence of Elijah's selfish attitude is seen in his declaration in 17:1 that *his* word alone will control all dew and rainfall, *his* demand for the slaughter of all the prophets of Baal (18:40), *his* repeated references to *his* "zeal" for Yahweh (19:10, 14, with subtle allusions to Yahweh's "zeal" or "jealousy" in Exod 20:5; Deut 4:24; 6:15), *his* belief that *he alone* is the only faithful Yahwist remaining in the land (19:10, 14, this despite 18:4), and *his refusal* to exit the cave on Horeb and stand before Yahweh as commanded in 19:11 (in 19:13 the narrator depicts him as standing at the *entrance* of the cave). In a similar vein, some have suggested that the flight to Horeb itself was a rejection of Yahweh's purposes.[24] However, in line with the overall perspective on Elijah as a prophet following in Moses' footsteps and standing against apostasy, it is difficult to view the narrator as desiring to portray Elijah as possessed of such an inflated sense of self-importance and vaulting ambition.[25] Such a perspective might be drawn on the basis of a purely literary or psychological reading of the text, but it appears unlikely that it reflects the purposes of the framer(s) of the "Elijah Cycle" or that of the Deuteronomistic writers who viewed Elijah as an heroic figure and subsequently incorporated the Elijah materials into their work.[26] Most especially, such a perspective does not accord with the description of Elijah's departure into the heavens, escorted by Yahweh's fiery hosts (2 Kgs 2:11-12). Rather, the seeming indications of Elijah's character deficiencies are more likely the fruit of the process through which the text has passed *en route* to the form in which we now have it.[27] If the narrative depicts a certain degree of intransigence and frustration within Elijah, this may be accounted for inasmuch as Moses also manifested such characteristics (see below).

Elijah on the Mountain

We may now turn to the central focus of this section, the theophany on Sinai/Horeb, and the *qol demamah daqqah*, or "still small voice" of 1 Kings 19:12. Our analysis will proceed as follows. I will first discuss the translation of the phrase *qol demamah daqqah* and present my own understanding of it. Second, I will examine the complex relationship of three key aspects of the text: the wind, earthquake, and fire of 19:11, the "still small voice" of verse 12, and the voice of the Lord in verse 13. Third, we will observe how the "still small voice" in verse 12 emerges as a key turning point in the Elijah cycle as a whole, coming at a critical moment and opening up a sacred space. Fourth, we shall see how, following Elijah's encounter with the "still small voice," the text signals a change in his perspective and moves the narrative toward a resolution.

The Translation of *qol demamah daqqah*

Numerous proposals have been made regarding the translation of this phrase.[28] The LXX understood it as a "the sound of a light breeze" (NETS); the Vulgate, "a whistling of gentle air"; and the Targum "the voice of those who were praising quietly."[29] Other translations include "a still small voice" (KJV); "a sound of sheer silence" (NRSV); a "sound of faint silence"[30] and "a sound of gentle silence."[31] The phrase consists of two words relating to sound, and one whose sense is tactile.[32] The first term, *qol*, may refer to a noise or sound (of footsteps, cf. Gen 3:8, 10; of a leaf, cf. Lev 26:36; of millstones, cf. Jer 25:10) or a human or divine voice (Deut 5:25). The second term, *demamah* is one that forms a part of the core lexical field of silence, and is closely related to the verb **damam*-1 that we have encountered on numerous occasions.[33] It is generally agreed that the term can refer to either silence or stillness.[34] Taken together, these constitute something of an enigma. How can silence or stillness be described as a "sound"? A significant parallel to this phrase occurs in Job 4:16, where Eliphaz states, "I hear silence and then a sound."[35] Frequently, the stillness or silence in this text is seen as the "calm after the storm."[36] However, as we shall see, such imagery requires further clarification if it is to be of help to us in understanding 1 Kings 19:12. The final term, *daqqah*, derives from the verb **daqaq*, which designates the grinding of a substance into fine powder (Exod 30:36; 32:20; 2 Sam 22:43; Isa 28:28). It seems most likely that *qol demamah daqqah* is a phrase deliberately constructed to stand in opposition to the intensely soniferous and physical manifestations described in 19:11-12, yet describe a phenomenon *sufficiently perceptible so as to draw Elijah's attention to it*. As such, its sense is highly elusive and virtually impossible to translate with exactitude. A rendering bringing together the concepts of "sound," "stillness," and "reduction to fine particles (dust)" is likely as close as one might get.[37] I would propose "a sound of finely ground stillness" as a translation.[38] This would capture the intentional, elusive quality of the expression, since it designates an almost inaudible, *yet still perceptible sound*, at the limits of human hearing, lying just at the borderline between sound and total silence. So while either "silence" or "stillness" are potential renderings of *demamah*, I view the latter as more fitting in the context. This "fine stillness" draws Elijah into its mystery, just as the burning bush arrested Moses' attention (Exod 3:1-4). Elijah comes to the entrance of the cave. The reader is intrigued as well, and anxious to know its meaning.

The "Wind, Earthquake, and Fire" (v. 11), the "Sound of Finely Ground Stillness" (v. 12), and the Voice of Yahweh (v. 13)

Two points are of prime importance for understanding these central and interrelated concepts. First, it is essential to distinguish the *qol demamah daqqah*, "the sound of finely ground stillness," in verse 12 from the *qol* (i.e., voice) in verse 13. In verse 12, "*qol*" in the phrase *qol demamah daqqah* is best translated as "sound." There is no sense there that a *voice* speaks to Elijah in the cave and calls him out of it. In verse 13, however, a speaking voice is clearly intended.[39] Thus, in 19:12-13 the text carefully distinguishes between the *qol demamah daqqah* and the voice of God. The narrator takes great pains to inform us that the Lord was not "in" the wind, earthquake, or the fire. But neither was the Deity "in" the *qol demamah daqqah*. Rather, the *qol demamah daqqah* serves to motivate Elijah *to move to the entrance of the cave, a place where he will hear* Yahweh's *qol* (19:13).

Second, it is essential to understand the significance of the great wind (*ruaḥ gedolah*), earthquake (*ra'ash*), and devastating fire (*'esh*) of v. 12. These elements constitute key aspects of the Elijah narrative more broadly. All three phenomena commonly accompany descriptions of theophanies in the HB (cf. Judg 5:4; Pss 18:8, 10-13; 50:3; 77:17-18; 97:2; Isa 30:27) and figure prominently in the Moses story (see below). Fire plays a significant role in Elijah's conflict with Baal. The prophet famously declares, "*the god who answers by fire is indeed God*" (1 Kgs 18:24). Fire appears at the outset of Moses' encounter with Yahweh (Exod 3:1-12). Fire, generally accompanied by references to thunder, clouds, and smoke, appears at Sinai/Horeb in Exodus 19:18-24; 24:15-16; and Deuteronomy 4:11-12, 15, 33-36; 5:4-5, 22-26. Wind signals the end of the drought in 1 Kings 18:45, and is a significant element of Yahweh's deliverance of Israel in Exodus 10:13, 19; 14:21; 15:10 and Numbers 11:31. In Exodus 19:18, when the Lord descends on the mountain, Sinai/Horeb is said to shake violently. The shaking of the mountain is mirrored by the people's trembling with fear in 19:16 and 20:18. In all these texts, Yahweh's voice (*qol*) plays an important role (1 Kgs 19:12-13; cf. Exod 19:19; 24:3; Deut 4:33, 36; 5:22-26).

As noted *supra*, at this point the cacophonous and destructive perturbations of nature heralding the arrival of the Deity in verse 12 are replaced by a "sound of finely ground stillness" in verse 13. The radical *absence* of noise, motion, destruction, and the *presence* of the "sound of *finely ground stillness*" are so compelling that Elijah is drawn out of the cave in which he has sheltered. As demonstrated by his covering of his face, he is aware that he is entering into sacred space.[40] And it is only at this point that Yahweh's voice (*qol*) is heard.

The "Sound of Finely Ground Stillness" as Turning Point

The theophany of 19:11-12 and the *qol demamah daqqah* of verse 13 form the fulcrum upon which the Elijah Cycle turns. All the preceding events lead up to this moment, and those reported after it flow from it. Its role as the dramatic apex of the Elijah Cycle is underlined by its almost ethereal setting atop a high mountain. Its centrality is further emphasized by a significant change in the description of the Lord's address to Elijah immediately *preceding* and *following* the theophany and the *qol demamah daqqah*. In 19:9, it is the *word* (*dabar*) of the Lord that "comes" to Elijah.[41] The phrase used here is identical to the description of Yahweh's word to Abraham in Genesis 15:4.[42] However, following the *qol demamah daqqah*, Elijah is addressed by the voice (*qol*) of Yahweh (19:13).[43] But what is the reason for this change in terminology? While it might be possible to view this shift as entirely inadvertent, careful attention to the contours of the text reveals evidence of a more intentional design at work. Such a design becomes apparent when one observes certain parallels between Moses' experiences on Sinai-Horeb in Exodus 19–24 and 32–34, and those of Elijah in 1 Kings 19.

We have already noted that 1–2 Kings closely identifies Elijah with Moses. However, now it is essential to undertake an even closer investigation of the links between 1 Kings 19 and the Moses story, especially with reference to the theme of encountering God on Sinai/Horeb. The precise details of Israel's encounter with Yahweh as presented in Exodus and Deuteronomy involve numerous, complex matters of detail, and have challenged scholars over the centuries.[44] Here I will discuss only the broad outlines of the narrative, with special attention to the way in which the framer(s) of the Elijah Cycle have employed them.

It is essential to note that there are *two distinct textual groupings* (with several varying points of detail within each one) concerning the divine theophanies granted to Moses at Sinai/Horeb. The first grouping focuses on the terrifying majesty of Yahweh's appearance on the mountain before the nation as a whole, while the second reflects the Lord's more personal and tender dealings with Moses individually. In the three-part drama of covenant making, covenant breaking, and covenant remaking in Exodus 19:16-25; 24:12-18; 32–34 and Deuteronomy 4:9-14; 5:22-33; 9:7-10:11, only the first and third scenes are clearly located on the mountain and involve theophanies.[45] In the first scene, Moses goes up to receive the tablets and meet God (Exod 19:16-25). Terrifyingly, the mountain is covered in fire and cloud. Moses ascends the mountain while the people wait below (19:20-21; 24:14). Deuteronomy emphasizes that, at first, Yahweh speaks to the people in a loud voice "out of the fire" burning atop the mountain's summit (Deut 4:11-12, 15, 33-36; 5:4-5, 22-26). The voice of God so terrified the people that they feared for their lives and begged Moses to ascend the mountain and bring the words of Yahweh back to them (Deut 5:25-27). Deuteronomy 4:12 is a critical text in this regard: "Then the Lord spoke to you out of the fire. You heard the sound of words but saw no form; there was only a voice."[46]

Moses receives Yahweh's commandments on the mountain top, written on stone tablets (Exod 20:1–23:33; 24:12-18; 31:18). The narrative continues in Exodus 32–34.[47] Moses has been detained on the mountain for forty days (Exod 24:15; 32:1), and Israel quickly turns aside to the worship of the golden calf. Upon discovery of the people's defection, Moses smashes the tablets at the foot of the mountain (32:19), symbolizing the breaking of the covenant only just given.

The need for the restoration of Yahweh's relationship with the people requires Moses to ascend the mountain once again (Exod 33:12–34:9; cf. Deut 10:1-11). Here we encounter the *second* pattern of the motif of meeting God on the mountain—that of a more intimate and personal encounter with Yahweh (Exod 32:30–34:35). Moses' forty-day intercession referenced in Exodus 34:28 and Deuteronomy 9:9, 11, 18, 25; 10:10 (cf. Exod 24:18) secures Yahweh's ongoing presence with the people and their onward progress on the journey to Canaan. Most significantly, here *there is no mention of terrifying manifestations involving fire or smoke—only a cloud out of which Yahweh speaks.* In response to Moses' request to see Yahweh's glory (*kavod*, 33:18), God declares that the Deity's goodness (*touv*) will instead be manifested (33:19a). Yahweh then speaks to Moses of the divine mercy and grace (33:19b), patience, steadfast love, forgiveness, and justice (34:6-7). To be sure, the awesome quality of Yahweh's presence is to be implied by the necessity of Moses' being hidden by Yahweh's hand (33:21-23), but this is significantly different from Yahweh's displays of power in Exodus 19.

Thus, in Exodus and Deuteronomy there is a substantial difference between the terrifying divine manifestations accompanying the inauguration of the Sinai covenant, carried out *in the presence of the nation as a whole* (Deut 4:11-12, 15, 33-36; 5:4-5, 22-26), and Yahweh's more gentle and intimate interaction with Moses in the description of the relational reparation, effected by Moses' mediation, depicted in Exodus 32–34 and Deuteronomy 10:1-11. This greater degree of intimacy is reflected in Deuteronomy 34:10-12, and explicitly stated by Yahweh in Numbers 12:6-8:

> "When there are prophets among you,
> I the Lord make myself known to them in visions;
> I speak to them in dreams.
> Not so with my servant Moses;
> he is entrusted with all my house.
> With him I speak face to face—clearly, not in riddles;
> and he beholds the form of the Lord."

A significant point here is often missed: Elijah's encounter with Yahweh on Sinai/Horeb in 1 Kings 19:11-12 deliberately leads Elijah (and the readers of the text) *away* from the first pattern of divine human encounter mentioned above, with its terrifying and awe-inspiring phenomena and collective dimension, and *toward* the *second* pattern, with its more gentle, personal, and individual overtones.[48] It is for this reason, as Carlson rightly observes, that Yahweh chooses not to speak to Elijah through the wind, earthquake, and fire—the spectacular, terrifying manifestations in evidence at the Deity's initial appearance at Sinai, or in those that had accompanied Yahweh's demonstration of the superiority of Israel's God to Jezebel's Baal in 1 Kings 18.[49] He thus states: "Yahweh uses different means depending on whether he is addressing a person, or wishes to express his power or anger."[50]

The *qol demamah daqqah*: A Critical Moment and a Sacred Space

We have proposed the translation "a sound of finely ground stillness" for this unique Hebrew phrase and argued that in 1 Kings 19:12, it likely refers to a scarcely audible sound, especially noticeable after the turbulence that has immediately preceded it. This unusual auditory event was sufficiently striking so as to draw Elijah's attention to it, and move him to the entrance of the cave. The Lord had previously called him to come forth and stand on the mountain before the Lord as the Lord passed by (v. 11). However, Elijah will only venture as far as the entrance to the cave.[51] This is hardly surprising given the terrifying manifestations of divine power that had just occurred, and Israel's earlier experiences with God's voice at Sinai! However, most importantly, as noted above, this "sound of finely ground stillness" is *not the speaking voice of God*. Thus, although frequent in current parlance, the idea of God speaking *in* a still small voice is foreign to the sense of 1 Kings 19. As we have noted, *qol* in verse 12 should not be rendered "voice," but "sound." Rather, the *qol demamah daqqah* marks a pause *between* the crashing of the theophany and Elijah's hearing of the voice of God. It thus serves as a *precursor* to the speech of God, and creates the context for it. Carlson has plausibly suggested that the "sound of finely ground stillness" subtly evokes the allusion to the "time of the evening breeze" in Genesis 3:8 when Yahweh sought communion with the human pair, and they hear the sound (*qol*) of Yahweh walking in the garden.[52] Thus, in a sense, the *qol demamah daqqah* is analogous to the garden. Or, put another way, the "sound of finely ground stillness" creates a space into which Yahweh may speak.

Elijah's Inward Change

In 19:9-10 Elijah enters into the cave and laments over his sad lot. His words in verse 9 belie his sense of abandonment and frustration, sentiments also associated with Moses (Exod 17:1-4; 32:19-20; Num 11:10-15; 20:9-13) and Jeremiah (Jer 8:20–9:2; 11:18–12:6; 15:10-18; 18:18-23; 20:7-18). He describes the people's unfaithfulness and his own sense of rejection and persecution (19:10; cf. earlier, 19:4). It is at this point that he is called to stand before the extraordinary manifestations of Yahweh's presence described in verses 11-12.[53] As Wray Beal comments, "YHWH's answer to Elijah is his theophanic presence."[54] This response, of course, is paralleled in Job 38–41.

But what does the theophany accomplish? At first glance it appears to have achieved very little. The Lord's question and the prophet's rejoinder are essentially the same both before and after the theophany (vv. 9-10; cf. 19:13-14). However, subsequent to Elijah's encounter with the *qol demamah daqqah* there are subtle indications that some of Elijah's struggles are moving toward resolution. Most significantly, after his words in verse 14, *Elijah stops talking and is silent.* The Masoretes, it would seem, sensed an important pause here, and marked it with a *setumah*, a gap in the line of the manuscript that invites the reader to stop before reading on.

Elijah says no more. Why? It may be inferred that now he is *listening*. Yahweh can now recommission him, giving him specific instructions (vv. 15-17). Elijah is sent off to complete three tasks, the most significant of which is anointing Elisha as his successor (19:15-18).[55] Most importantly, in v. 18 the Lord reveals to Elijah something of which he was previously unaware: "Yet I will leave [alive] seven thousand in Israel, *all the knees that have not bowed to Baal, and every mouth that has not kissed him.*" As such, the *qol demamah daqqah* moves our prophet *away* from his own perceptions of the situation, as well as *away* from Yahweh's past demonstrations of power and awesome deeds (Exod 19–24; Deut 4–5; 9–10), and *toward* a place where he can hear a fresh word from the Lord regarding the true state of affairs in Israel and Yahweh's own future purposes for him. This speaks to an important theme within the Elijah-Elisha materials: the issue of *perspective*. In 2 Kings 2:12, Elisha suddenly *perceives* the chariots and horses of Yahweh taking Elijah away. Second Kings 6:15-23 stresses the need for divine enabling for an *accurate understanding* of one's situation. Moreover, as it relates to our prophet, here in 1 Kings 17–19, Elijah's belief that all Israel has turned away from Yahweh and that his life is in danger is a misrepresentation of the true situation.

Then in verse 19, a fulfillment formula immediately follows: "So he set out from there." Elijah has heard the voice of God and followed it. The wind, earthquake, and fire, although a significant aspect of Moses' experience and of Elijah's journey thus far, were not what was required in that moment. Elijah's ability not only to hear but to receive the voice of God came only subsequent to the "the sound of finely ground stillness."

Once again, however, the narrator feels under no compulsion to tie up all the loose ends. The subsequent Elijah narratives in 1–2 Kings are brief and laconic. He is certainly viewed in a positive light; however, there are gaps in the text. He is told to anoint Jehu (1 Kgs 19:16), but never does so. Elisha's servant carries out this task (2 Kgs 9:6-7). He appears as something of a marginal figure in 2 Kings 1, dwelling away from Samaria, and described as a "hairy man wearing a leather belt" (2 Kgs 1:8). There is no mention of him being welcomed back as a conquering hero.

In sum, in its broad outlines, the depiction of Elijah's experiences in 1 Kings 17–19 parallels Abraham's experience in Genesis 22. Both face a crisis. Both appear isolated, vis-à-vis God and their broader communities. Both must face the realities of their situations alone. The climax of both narratives takes place on a high mountain. In both texts an interlude of silence prepares the protagonists for a fresh word from God. And in the experience of both, while God's intervention brings both silence and stability, it also leaves behind it a sense of open-endedness. Much, but not all, has been resolved. As we shall now see, many of these themes will reappear in the Book of Job.

Sound, Speech, and Silence in Job

The Book of Job is likely the most complex text in the HB in terms of its vocabulary and syntax, its compositional history, and its purpose and meaning.[56] In many ways the most intractable questions surrounding Job are hermeneutical.[57] How should this book be read? What is its genre? Is it a single work reflecting a unified viewpoint, or is it a series of diverse voices, inviting the reader to enter into a discussion of various perspectives? How does it relate to issues of divine goodness and human suffering?

It is important to note that Job is not a text about theodicy *per se*, or even innocent suffering in itself. Rather, the text focuses on two important and interrelated issues. The first is the questioning of "self-interested" piety and religious activity. The testing of Job is, at its core, a test of whether Job will be a true friend to Yahweh (cf. Prov 17:17) or will flee when the benefits of such piety cease to arrive, and affliction takes their place.[58] A second emphasis is the nature of God's governance of the world. Does the so-called "retribution principle" (that God rewards the righteous and brings judgment on evildoers) truly function in life? Or is God a tyrant who delights in reducing his creatures to unspeakable misery? And, most importantly, can any sense be made of God's choices and purposes in history?

I will focus here on one specific and overarching aspect of the book: its depiction of sound, speech, and silence. It has been widely observed that one of the most striking characteristics of Job is its dialogical nature.[59] The prologue (1:1–2:13) and epilogue (42:7-17) stand in a conversant relationship to the dialogues and monologues at its center. Dialogue appears in most of its sections. Most importantly, the various dialogical dimensions of the book are generated by *the necessity of dealing with the experience of silence*. As was the case in Genesis 22 and 1 Kings 19, silence plays a major role in the Book of Job. However, in contrast to Genesis 22 and 1 Kings 19, relatively brief prose narratives, Job is a lengthy text consisting of narration and dialogue, moving between the unseen world above and the seen world below. Its various sections represent diverse dynamics involving sound, speech, and silence. These are depicted through a rich diversity of vocabulary for sound and silence, statements regarding the speech (or lack thereof) of the characters, and an impressive soundscape. An awareness of the overarching structure of Job is critical for our analysis here. Schmid and Oeming highlight the chiastic structure of the book:

A. The prose prologue and epilogue (1:1–2:13 and 42:7-17) with special attention to Job's loss and recovery of good fortune;

B. Job's self-declarations (in poetry); in 3:1-26, Job declares himself accursed then retracts his words in 42:1-6;

C. Three dialogues in poetry, 4:1-27:23 (Job, Eliphaz, Zophar)[60] followed by three monologues 29:1–41:34 (Job, Elihu, God), all in poetry;

D. The hymn to wisdom (poetry) in chapter 28 that stands at its center.[61]

For my discussion here, I will deal with matters of sound, speech, and silence in four major sections: (1) the prologue (1:1–2:13); (2) the dialogues between Job and his "comforters" in 3:1–27:12 and Job's concluding monologues in 29:1–31:40; (3) the speeches of Yahweh and the responses of Job in 38:1–42:6; (4) the epilogue (42:7-17).[62] I will conclude by proposing several theological conclusions regarding the interplay between sound, speech, and silence in the book.

The Prologue: 1:1–2:13

The prologue consists of narration and reported discourse. Our eyes are initially directed to the world below, to a setting that readers would clearly understand as lying outside Israel.[63] We are introduced to Job, a model of piety, integrity, and moral perfection, and to his family, wealth, and community standing (1:1-6). Then, suddenly, the scene switches to the heavenly realm, to the so-called "heavenly council" (cf. 1 Kgs 22; Jer 23:18, 21-22). Various beings present themselves before Yahweh (2:6a). Speech infuses the scene. Reports are demanded and given (1:7; 2:2-3). Dialogue takes place

(1:7-11; 2:2-6). Yet the content of the discussions and their significance are inaccessible to those below.

The "Adversary" or "Challenger" (*satan*) appears in the scene. I will use the term Adversary to refer to this being despite the frequent translation "Satan" in many Bibles.[64] The Adversary suggests to the Lord that Job will curse and thereby repudiate Yahweh should he undergo affliction (1:11; 2:5). Yahweh then permits the Adversary to put Job to the test (1:12; 2:6).[65] Job then suffers catastrophic devastation—the loss of his health, wealth, and the death of his children (1:13-19; 2:7-8).

Various aspects of speech and silence are important in this section. First, the narrator presents the heavenly and earthly realms as standing in an *unequal* relationship to one another as it relates to speech and sound. The inhabitants of the heavenly realm can see the actions and hear the words of those in the world below. The Adversary suggests to Yahweh that Job will "curse you to your face" (1:11; 2:5). Cursing is a voluble action, and has public and communicative aspects (cf. Lev 24:15; 1 Kgs 21:10, 13; Ps 10:3). The soundscape involved in cursing amplifies the emotions implicit in the Adversary's suggestion. Should Job choose to curse God, Yahweh would be audibly and publicly shamed on earth and in heaven. Interestingly, Job fears only that his children may have cursed God *in their hearts* (1:5), a more silent response lacking this public dimension.[66] Job, however, cannot hear the words of the Adversary, and is not privy (unlike the reader) to the dynamics being played out around him and to the high stakes involved.

The narrator appears to soften the seeming impermeability between the two realms. Job's wife, who suddenly appears in 2:9 (and then is mentioned no more), uses similar words to those uttered by the Adversary in the unseen world.[67] Her words contain a veiled reference to silence. She asks, "Do you still persist in your integrity? Curse God, and die" (2:9). Job's wife clearly links cursing God with death. According to some, she is urging Job to make peace with God because the end is near.[68] Others view her as suggesting that, since his integrity has brought him nothing but suffering, there is nothing left for Job to do but to "hurl one final blasphemy, so that God, in return, will obliterate him completely."[69] As we have seen in chapter 6, in ancient Israel loss of life was seen as descent to Sheol, the realm of silence. However, although Job does long for peace in death (3:11-19; 30:27), he refuses to find silence in this manner. Rather, in 3:10b he piously expresses his willingness to silently submit to whatever the Lord may appoint as his lot: "Shall we receive the good at the hand of God, and not receive the bad?"[70] The Prologue concludes with the seven-day silence through which Job's friends manifest their compassion. Whereas in his prime, Job's arrival was greeted with the silence of respect and honor (29:7-10, 21-23), now in his misery he is greeted with the silence of grief and devastation (2:11-13; cf. 30:1-15).[71]

Sound, Speech, and Silence in 3:1–37:24

The issues of soundscape, speech and silence in this section are complex and extensive. Silence here serves a variety of functions. In 13:13 (Job as speaker) and 33:31, 33 (Elihu as speaker), silence is called for so that another might speak. In 6:24; 11:3; 13:5, 19; 29:21; and 34:29, silence is viewed as the appropriate response when one has lost an argument, or when one is in the presence of a person of superior wisdom. Silence is depicted as a response of fear and weakness in 31:34. In 30:27, Job longs for stillness or peace, but finds none. He wishes that, like a stillborn child, he might "be lying down and quiet . . . asleep . . . at rest" (3:13). Whereas before his affliction reverent silence attended Job's arrival or words (29:7-10), now he is pitied and shunned (17:6; 19:3, 13-19). He previously responded to the Lord's providence with silent resignation (2:10); now he thrashes about in a torrent of arguments and bitter complaints (9:27-35; 10:1-7; 23:1-7). Peace eludes him completely. Much of the imagery in this section of the book is violent and suggests a terrifying soundscape. 16:12-14 is a prime example. Job describes God's actions in the most gruesome of terms:

> I was at ease, and he broke me in two;
> he seized me by the neck and dashed me to pieces;
> he set me up as his target;
> his archers surround me.
> He slashes open my kidneys, and shows no mercy;
> he pours out my gall on the ground.
> He bursts upon me again and again;
> he rushes at me like a warrior.

At first glance, it would seem that there is little space given to silence in the dialogues between Job and his comforters. However, as Jürgen Ebach observes, there is a silence or deadness that pervades them. He notes that while there is an *appearance* of dialogue, it is ultimately a "failed dialogue."[72] The dialogue fails because, despite some essential agreement on the validity of the retribution principle, the personal circumstances of the speakers make it impossible to move beyond their own positions. The comforting silence of 2:11-13 is lost. Words of anger and reproach take its place. And beneath these words lies the silence of incomprehension.[73]

Furthermore, in this section, beyond this silence of failed dialogue, we encounter the silence and inaccessibility of God. As in the prologue, the separation between the earthly and heavenly realms here is very great. Job cannot comprehend why he should be so sorely afflicted. He is subject to dynamics playing out around him but does not know why. Job seeks a word from God, an explanation for his plight, an indictment containing a detailed enumeration of the misdeeds for which he is being punished so severely, but receives none (9:20-23). He believes that God refuses to answer him, and instead chooses to crush him to reduce him to silence (9:14-19).[74] Seeking to propel God out of silence, Job takes upon himself several oaths, calling forth greater punishment upon himself should he be guilty (31:1-40). As Hartley notes, "The oath requires God to either activate the curses of the oath or clear the swearer. Should God remain silent, Job would be declared innocent by not being cursed."[75] Yet God remains silent. What does this mean? How does this relate to the oath and Job's innocence? Finally, Job too falls silent. An editor (or possibly the narrator) adds, "The words of Job are ended" (31:40b).[76] The situation, it would appear, stands at an impasse. In the progression of the book, the reader will have to wait until chapter 38 for the drama to move forward in the form of a response from God. Finally, it is critical to note that Job's words in 3:1–31:40 are frequently seen as irreverent and quasi-blasphemous, leading ultimately to Yahweh's censure of him in 38:2 and 40:8. Yahweh's commendation of Job in 42:7 then becomes either evidence of the ultimate inconsistency of the book as we have it, or the result of differing perspectives within its various sources.[77] However, as we shall see in our concluding section, there exists another explanation for this seeming incongruity, and one that offers a significant key to the purpose and theological import of the book.

Yahweh Speaks and Job Responds: 38:1–42:6

In contrast to the Lord's silence up to this point, Yahweh now speaks and counters Job's assertions. The dramatic movement of Job heads toward its apex. Many of the issues relating to the meaning of Yahweh's two discourses (38:1–40:2; 40:6–41:34) and Job's responses (40:3-5; 42:1-6) are too complex to be discussed in detail here.[78] More general, overarching observations regarding sound, speech, and silence must suffice. The structure of 38:1–42:6 is straightforward. Twice Yahweh "answers" (*wayya'an*) Job out of the whirlwind (38:1; 40:6). Yahweh's responses are lengthy and enigmatic, and are rich in imagery and soundscape. In them we learn that Yahweh has heard all that Job has said. Twice Job "answers" (*wayya'an*) Yahweh (40:3; 42:1).

By contrast, Job's responses are terse, and conclude with his determination henceforth to remain silent.[79]

In both 38:1 and 40:6, Yahweh responds to Job "out of the whirlwind" (*min hasse'ara*, generally referring to a storm or tempest; cf. 2 Kgs 2:1, 11; Isa 29:6; 40:24; 41:16; Jer 23:19; 30:23; Ezek 1:4; 13:11, 13; Zech 9:14; Pss 107:25, 29; 148:8). Such imagery implies intense sound, lightning, and violent wind (cf. Job 37:1-13). But what is the tone of Yahweh's words?[80] Some see in them an angry rebuke, or a desire to humble Job.[81] Others suggest that Yahweh's response is viewed as pedagogical in force.[82] Ham and Middleton are likely correct in regarding Yahweh's response as more nuanced, seeing in it a mixture of rebuke, pedagogy, mitigated anger, consolation, and comfort.[83]

Yahweh's first speech makes Job *aware of his own limitations*. These limitations are temporal (38:4-6, 18), spatial (38:16-17, 22), knowledge-related (38:6, 19, 24-25, 28-29, 33; 39:1-2), and power-related (38:8-11, 31-32; 38:39-41). The speech then goes on to stress Yahweh's tender care for all of creation, God's sense of humour, and the wisdom given to various animals. God's care for the animals is likely intended to persuade Job that it is implausible for him to perceive himself as the only being out of all the living who is unloved by the Creator.[84] Yahweh concludes by demanding that Job state his basis for finding fault (40:1-2).[85] Job then declares his awareness of his own insignificance, lays his hand on his mouth (a common indication of an unwillingness to speak further),[86] then says so in as many words. Various understandings of Job's silence have been suggested. It is seen as: (1) obstinate entrenchment in his position—Job is "sticking to his guns";[87] (2) an admission of his own fault;[88] (3) a recognition of his own limitations and an affirmation of his humility before God's wisdom;[89] (4) a stance of neutrality and a refusal to answer;[90] or (5) an inadequate response. God had desired "a vigorous conversation partner," but inadvertently overpowered Job.[91] Yahweh then speaks to Job a second time, emphasizing two areas where Yahweh's strength and wisdom are essential to the governance of the universe: God's ability to bring perfect justice, a capacity not possessed by Job (40:6-14), and God's ability to master even the most ferocious of beasts, Behemoth (likely the hippopotamus, 40:15-24) and Leviathan (41:1-34, likely the Nile crocodile, or perhaps a whale surrounded by dolphins).[92]

Various aspects of Job's response to Yahweh in 42:1-6 are hotly debated. Who is the speaker in verses 3-6 (or parts thereof), Job or Yahweh?[93] What does it mean to "hide counsel without knowledge" (v. 3). What is the sense of the contrast between "hearing" and "seeing" in verse 5?[94] Most significantly, in 42:6 Job "repents" (**niḥam*). This is clearly the capstone of Job's response to

God and central to the understanding of the book. But what does Job mean? The precise translation and sense of 42:6 have been the subject of much scholarly dispute. Clines and Martin have presented an extensive survey of the various proposals and issues involved.[95] Indeed, Morrow suggests that the narrator here has set forth an intentionally ambiguous phrase.[96] However the verse is construed, Job's statement clearly expresses his determination to be silent and say no more.[97] He recognizes Yahweh's power and wisdom (42:2) and the limits of his own understanding and experience of God (42:3-6). And given the lack of any direct response to Job, Yahweh seemingly accepts Job's decision and, as it relates to Job, returns to silence. One further detail should be mentioned at this point. Ebach points out that Yahweh's words to Job in 38–41 are the last words of God's *direct discourse* recorded in the HB.[98] Thus, in a sense Yahweh's words in Job here are the entrée into a silence that will endure for centuries. I will develop this concept just below.

The Epilogue: 42:7-17

In the epilogue that follows, the Lord speaks one last time, expressing anger toward Job's friends and demanding that they seek Job out that he might pray for them (42:7-8). The narrator then declares that the Lord accepted Job's prayer (42:10). A narrative describing the restoration of Job's fortunes then follows (42:10-17). Most significantly, in the epilogue, in contrast to the friends' mistaken words, the Lord asserts that Job, the servant of God (cf. 1:8; 2:3), has spoken "*rightly*" (42:7; *nekonah* in this form usually means "true, certain, sure, enduring, permanent"; cf. Gen 41:32; Deut 13:14; Prov 12:19). However, readers are not told in what way this is so. How does this statement relate to Yahweh's words of censure in Job 38–41 and to Job's "repentance" in 42:6?[99] How does this square with Yahweh's anger against the friends, and approbation of Job (42:7)? I would suggest that these unanswered questions hold a significant key for the meaning of the Book of Job and the significance of silence within it.

The Silence of Job and the Silence of God: Theological and Canonical Implications

The foregoing discussion has demonstrated that sound, speech, and silence occupy a central position in the Book of Job. In chapters 1–2, the drama is set in motion by words in heaven that are unheard on earth. In the dialogues and monologues of Job 3–37, the speakers appear to "speak past" one another and dwell in their own respective silences. Job longs for a word from God, but receives none. Then, in 38–42 Yahweh speaks twice to Job, and twice reduces him to silence. In the *dénouement* in 42:7-16, Yahweh directs no further speech to Job. However, the reader learns that, despite all of his vehement and violent speech toward God, Job has spoken *rightly* (42:7). The friends must seek out Job, who like Abraham in Genesis 20:7, 17 prays for them. The book concludes with the renewed blessing of Job and his house. At first this appears to be a "happy ending" forming a satisfying conclusion to the book and to the questions under debate in it.[100] However, is this truly so, given the numerous unanswered questions with which the reader is left (as in Gen 22 and 1 Kgs 19)? Job never becomes aware of the Adversary's challenge to Yahweh. Why? We are not told what happens to Job's wife. Was she the mother of the children mentioned in 42:13-16? Was Job himself traumatized by his experience? There is no mention of any healing of his skin disease (2:7). Is this intentional, and if so, what does this silence signify?[101] Most importantly, what is the reader meant to make of the apparent disconnect between Yahweh's censure of Job and Job's repentance in 38:2 and 40:8, and Yahweh's words of approval of Job in 42:7? The sense of renewed stability in the epilogue is therefore only partial, and the finale is thus one that is infused with silence. But why does silence pervade the final sections of the book?

Perhaps the answer to such questions and the explanation for these many silences may be found through a better understanding of Yahweh's words in 42:7. Previously, God has spoken either away from Job's hearing (chs. 1–2), or been silent in the face of his pleas for assistance in understanding (chs. 3–31). When indeed God has spoken, the import of his speech has been enigmatic (chs. 38–41). However, God's last words in the book clearly express approbation of Job's words—but in what sense, given the apparent censure of them in 38:2 and 40:8? In contrast to the numerous suggestions that the error of Job's friends and the approval of Job's statements is to be found in the inaccuracy of the propositional content of their words, Oeming suggests that the issue lay elsewhere than at the level of *content*. Rather, divine approbation or disapproval was rooted in the *stance of the speakers vis-à-vis God*. The friends uttered words *about God*, but their words were not directed *toward God*.[102] He suggests that this does not mean that in Job words about God are seen as of no value, and that only silence is an adequate vehicle for understanding the Divine. Rather, Oeming affirms that the knowledge of God *cannot be reduced to mere words and speech about God*. He views this as central to the message of Job as a whole, thus relativizing the gaps and silences mentioned just above. His conclusion is rooted in the conviction that the correct translation of 42:7

is: "you have not spoken rightly *to me*," as opposed to "*about* me" as in most translations.[103] He comments,

> God does not praise a specific statement made by Job (neither the patient sufferer of the beginning, the passionate rebel of the middle section, nor the individual who rebukes himself in the end). God does not justify a specific teaching about himself but rather the direction of Job's speech, his internal stance, his knowledge of the place to which and from which his thoughts proceed. God praises Job's speech as a speech to God. In contrast, the friends are not scolded for what they have said, but for their attitude toward God. It is their distant stance toward God that incurs God's wrath: Job's friends are studious and earnest theologians. They use their full cognitive competence and produce an impressive system of thought. Yet their mistake lies in the foundation of their theology: "You have not spoken well to me, not toward me, not in personal relation to me. Instead, you only spoke of me. In this, all theology is perverted, becomes sinful, and incurs God's wrath." Job may speak against God and perhaps even make mistakes, but he speaks to God and thus receives God's praise.[104]

Richard Middleton adopts the same translation as Oeming and comes to an analogous conclusion.[105] Ebach similarly sees the friends as having reduced God to an object of theoretical discussion, whereas Job, despite his violent and near blasphemous speech, spoke *to* God, holding on tightly to the Lord.[106]

However, even if the more traditional translation, "spoken rightly *about* me," is maintained, the basic point still stands. As we have seen in our discussion of silence as an expression of security and trust in God in chapter 5, and in our study of the motif of silence and sacredness in chapter 6, engagement with God lies not only in sound and speech, *but beyond sound and speech, in silence*—either the silence of peaceful trust in God, or the silence of trust despite an ultimate comprehension of God's ways. Thus, the Book of Job employs various silences to press toward the ultimate conclusion that the ability to understand who God is, and especially of how one may move beyond the imponderables of life and its sufferings, is to be found in a connectedness to God that *lies in a silence both beneath and beyond words*. Put another way, the message of Job is that the most durable element of the knowledge of God, beyond all the vicissitudes of human existence, consists in a *relational* knowledge of the Divine. Job remains faithful to the God he has come to know and trust even when his circumstances would suggest that God had abandoned him, and *even when Job's own words might appear to indicate that he felt that all hope and trust had departed*. In his superlative analysis of this aspect of the book, Jean Lévêque insightfully observes that

Job's seemingly insolent and irreverent words are not of primary importance. Rather, "a person's spiritual attitude often lies at a much deeper level than that person's words. . . . [Job's almost blasphemous] words are words of passion; but this passion in itself desires to say something, and *Job is certain that God, and God alone, can hear this other discourse*."[107]

The motif of silence in Job may therefore be summarized as follows: human words may and will fail. God's words may even appear to be inadequate or incomprehensible. God may be perceived as silent. But in spite of such incomprehension and apparent silence, somehow, in and through an even deeper silence, a way forward rooted in ongoing connectedness to God may be found.

Conclusion: The Silence of Unanswered Questions

There is, I believe, one further dimension of silence that is highly relevant to our discussion. In this chapter, we have examined three texts involving sound, speech, and silence. In these texts, readers are led on a journey: a crisis is set in motion by divine speech, divine decision, or circumstance; this crisis produces silence and isolation, specifically rooted in the inability to perceive God's purposes; finally, the silence is broken by renewed divine speech, and fuller understanding. However, we have observed that the journey's conclusion does not include a complete explanation of every aspect of the crisis. *The narrator feels no immediate need to tie up all the loose ends.* Readers are left to ponder the various silences of the text in their own personal silence. What might this signify? Why leave matters open-ended? Why were such texts not smoothed over when they were taken up into the canon? Perhaps this lack of total resolution indicates that a significant part of the HB's understanding of spirituality, or life with God, involves *silence of many kinds*—not only the silence of prayer, reflection, contemplation, but also the acceptance of unanswered, and potentially unanswerable questions. The HB says much regarding the Lord and the life of faith. However, it does not say all that one might want to know. In this way, the biblical text perhaps indicates to those who seek the voice of God within its pages that they must learn the discipline of waiting in silence before God. Waiting for the Lord is an important and deeply-rooted theme in the HB (Gen 49:18; Pss 27:14; 31:24; 33:20; 37:7, 9, 34; 38:15; 39:7; 40:1; 130:5-6; Prov 20:22; Isa 8:17; 25:9; 26:8; 33:2; 40:31; 49:23; Lam 3:25-26; Mic 7:7; Zeph 3:8). Significantly, such waiting is at times associated with silence or stillness (Job 29:21; Ps 37:7). In the words of the psalmist, "For God alone my soul waits in silence; from him comes my salvation. He alone is my rock and my salvation, my fortress; I shall never be shaken" (Ps 62:2, 5).

EPILOGUE

One of my favorite experiences is spending a week away hiking in some very quiet part of the world. I have a strong predilection for walks through mountainous forests, at times breaking out over magnificent vistas, or for coastal trails near sheer cliffs with views over the open ocean. My preferred locations include the Ariège region and Pyrenees in the south of France, the Azores Islands, and the coasts of Nova Scotia and Newfoundland. In such places, at times I walk by myself for hours without encountering another soul. Although the trail may be long, and the weather sometimes inclement, I am deeply nurtured by my silent journey. Then in the evening, I return to the comforts of my accommodations for a good meal and sleep. Quite frequently I take photos along my way. Months and years later, I can return and relive the journey through the progression of the images.

I have written the preceding pages over a period of about five years, on and off. They reflect my own journey deep into silence, much like a solitary trip into the forest or along a rocky Atlantic cliffside. My goal in this final chapter is not to return and revisit the journey step-by-step. Rather, I want to set out some of its most vivid images, vistas, and seascapes, much like one might choose various photos taken on different walks and then spread them out on a large table. Visitors could then select certain snapshots and reflect upon them, as their content caught their eyes. I would invite my readers to view these following brief paragraphs regarding sound, speech, stillness, and silence as just that—striking images of a journey into silence in the HB, set out for ongoing reflection.

I have been deeply marked by the way the HB so closely situates *silence within relationships*. Rather than being something to be discussed in a detached and abstract way, the HB views silence as something that occurs within a broader relational context, for good or for ill. On the one hand, silence might indicate that a relationship is suffering. We saw that silence is frequently the absence of (or cessation or restraint of) that which would *normally* occur in a given context. Thus, if speech, exchange, and communication are the norm, a troubled relationship may be marked by silence. I was struck by the reality that one of the greatest privileges of the divine-human relationship was the ability to communicate, to speak to God and to hear from God. But when the silence of alienation enters in, that privilege may be obscured, with potentially devastating consequences. Saul's loss of access to Yahweh's counsel in 1 Samuel 28:15, and Amos' image of a "famine of the hearing of the word of God" (Amos 8:11) underlined this in the starkest of terms.

At this point I hasten to add a qualification: the withdrawal of the divine word in these texts is related principally to God's refusal to speak through the prophets, or other oracular phenomena, due to a deliberate and ongoing refusal on the part of the people of God to live in faithfulness to their relational commitments to the Lord. Today, most religious traditions rooted in the Bible view God as speaking primarily through the biblical text, and only secondarily through inward convictions and sentiments. Such inward feelings are doubtlessly important. However, at times, due to psychological or situational factors, individuals may become convinced that the Lord has abandoned them. I would plead with my readers not to jump to such conclusions, most especially if they are in the midst of tragic or chaotic life situations, or if they have had a tendency to dwell on such feelings over the course of their lives. Rather, such sentiments need to be brought forward both to wise individuals, trained in matters of psychology and spirituality, and to fellow members of the community of faith. It is all too easy to become lost in a prison of darkness, wherein the Scriptures themselves seem to utter only words of condemnation and judgment.

Moreover, silence may be indicative of harm and brokenness arising out of *reprehensible human silence* in broader interpersonal relationships and social obligations. Such silence can occur when those who should have spoken up or intervened on behalf of others refuse to do so (Gen 34:5, 25-31; Lev 5:1; 2 Sam 13:21; Prov 24:10-12). Silence can similarly be self-destructive. Such silence appears in Psalm 32, where the psalmist rejects transparency and shelters silently in the darkness.

But the reverse can also be true. In the HB silence or stillness may denote a relationship marked by trust and security. God's silence can indicate that nothing is amiss, that there are no areas of reproach in the relationship (Zeph 3:17). Similarly, as human persons we can be invited into a silence rooted in the knowledge that the faithful Lord will be present and will act on our behalf (Exod 14:14). This is the silence of knowing that if God is at my right hand, I shall not be moved (Ps 16:8). This aspect of silence is especially meaningful at those times when, humanly speaking, there is nothing that we can do but wait on God in silent hope and trust (Ps 61:1, 5; 130:5-6; Isa 40:31).

Similarly, a true relational exchange with God can transcend words. In human relationships, deep friendship and intimacy can be experienced without speaking, simply by sitting together in silence. So also in the divine-human relationship, silence can be praise (Ps 65:1). One can enter the divine presence simply to "behold the beauty of the Lord and inquire in his temple" (Ps 27:4).

As in Elijah's experience in 1 Kings 19:11-18, silence or stillness can turn attention away from noise and confusion and serve as a precursor for a true hearing of a word from God. Similarly, at times the voice or actions of God must be awaited in silence or stillness (Ps 27:14; Lam 3:25-26, Isa 40:31; Mic 7:7; and as discussed above, Ps 61:1, 5; 130:5-6; Isa 40:31). Silence may also be closely identified with sacred places and times. Israel's most sacred spaces (tabernacle, temple) and sacred times (Sabbath) called for silence—intentional distancing from those sounds and movements of ordinary life. As in 1 Samuel 3, it is often in moments and contexts of great silence or stillness that the voice of God is heard.

However, the distressing theme of the "silence of God" also appears in the HB. God's silence is at times comprehensible, granting opportunity for repentance and change (Ps 50:21-22; Rom 2:4; 2 Pet 3:8-9). Yet, at other times God seems incomprehensibly silent in the face of suffering and anguished prayer. This silence, however, is not meant to be the final word. Rather, it invites ongoing protest and prayer (Pss 13; 22; and many others; cf. Luke 11:5-10), seeking to move the Lord to action.

Silence is also closely related to repentance and healing. Sometimes, in the HB, words are a critical element in repentance (Hos 14:1). Yet at other moments, deep contrition may best be expressed by sitting in the divine presence in silence and *not uttering a word* (Lam 3:1-30, esp. vv. 27-30). Silence may also reflect the time needed for relational repair before a wounded relationship can be restored. The seventy years of silence and alienation that intervened between the destruction of the Jerusalem temple and its restoration are a dramatic enactment of this (cf. Jer 25:11-12; Zech 1:12; 7:5). Relational healing may require silence and space, and take place over time.

Finally, we have observed the dialectic between sound and speech, on the one hand, and silence and stillness, on the other. Generally speaking, our lives do not consist exclusively of one or the other. Rather, we move back and forth between them. Although John Cage is likely correct in affirming that there is no such thing as absolute silence, the sounds and speech we experience in everyday life are broken up by times of stillness and silence. Moreover, the various silences that punctuate the more regular times of sound and speech render those silences all the more striking. And although moments of silence may at times be a welcome relief, silence itself may also become oppressive and leave us desirous of a return to the more customary sounds and exchanges of our lives. Both are needed in our experiences in the world. And thus we live, as it were, between sound and silence.

As we have seen in the preceding pages, frequently it is somewhere between sound and silence that individuals and communities of faith may humbly approach the presence of God, wrestle with the word and will of God, and seek the wisdom of God. Many who are readers of the HB as well as the NT (as noted in chapter 1, the same relational dynamics are present in both testaments) have found this to be the case in their own spiritual experience—that it is in that space between sound and silence that the Lord can indeed be found.

PLAYLIST FOR SILENCE

This list contains a number of musical compositions that I believe can meaningfully accompany reflection on the concept of silence. Some of them speak explicitly of silence. Others evoke some of the ideas reflected in the biblical texts considered in this book. In still others, silence is held within the music itself. That is to say that certain musical pieces have much "space" within them (as composer and pianist Keith Jarrett once observed). The entries on this list are drawn from a variety of musical styles and traditions. Many are available on both YouTube Music and Spotify under the title "Silence Playlist by John Kessler." My hope is that they might be meaningful to my readers and provide them with lines of pursuit for further reflection and listening.

Title	Composer	Preferred Performer or Performance (if applicable)	Preferred Album or Source
"Peace Piece"	B. Evans	Don Sebesky	*I Remember Bill*
"Some Other Time"	L. Bernstein	Bill Evans	*The Lost Sessions from the Black Forest*
"The Dharma at Big Sur," pts 1 and 2	J. Adams	John Adams	*The Dharma at Big Sur/ My Father Knew Charles Ives*
Pastoral Symphony, from *The Messiah*	G. F. Handel	Many possibilities	

Title	Composer	Preferred Performer or Performance (if applicable)	Preferred Album or Source
"I Loves You Porgy"	G. Gershwin	Keith Jarrett	*The Melody, at Night, with You*
"Elsewhere"	S. McLachlan	Sarah McLachlan	*Fumbling Toward Ecstasy*
"Silence"	K. Jarrett	K. Jarrett	*Bop-Be*
"Blue in Green"	B. Evans	Miles Davis	*Kind of Blue*
"Time Remembered"	B. Evans	Bill Evans Trio	*Time Remembered*
Spiegel im Spiegel	A. Pärt	Many possibilities	
"My Love and I"	D. Raskin	Charlie Haden Quartet West	*Always Say Goodbye*
"In My Solitude"	D. Ellington	Billie Holliday	Many versions available
Gymnopédie No. 1	E. Satie	Many possibilities	Many versions available
"Become Desert"	J. Adams	Seattle Symphony, Ludovic Morlot	*Become Desert*
"Oceania"	L. Mays	Pat Metheny Group	*Quartet*
Mad Rush	P. Glass	Philip Glass	Live in Montréal; cbc-radio-canada. Ici-musique (YouTube)
"Flamenco Sketches"	B. Evans/M. Davis	Miles Davis	*Kind of Blue*
"Love Minus Zero/No Limit"	B. Dylan	Bob Dylan	*Bringing It All Back Home*
"Nuages"	D. Reinhardt	Joe Pass	*For Django*
Cantus in Memoriam Benjamin Britten	A Pärt	Many possibilities	Many versions available

Title	Composer	Preferred Performer or Performance (if applicable)	Preferred Album or Source
On the Nature of Daylight	M. Richter	Max Richter	*The Blue Notebooks*
"Like Someone in Love"	J. Burke J. Van Heusen	John Coltrane	*Stardust (Remastered)*
"Always and Forever"	P. Metheny	Pat Metheny	Live (youtube), or *Secret Story*, or *Upojenie* with Anna Maria Jopek
Piano Etudes 9 and 20	P. Glass	Maki Namekawa	YouTube
Cinema Paradiso Main Theme	E. Morricone	Charlie Haden and Pat Metheny	*Beyond the Missouri Sky*
Gabriel's Oboe	E. Morricone	Lucia Micarelli	*An Evening with Lucia Micarelli*; PBS; YouTube; many other versions as well
"Illuminados"	I. Lins	Ivan Lins	*A Doce Presença*
Sleep (longer or shorter versions)	M. Richter	Max Richter	*Sleep*
"The Sound of Silence"	P. Simon	Simon & Garfunkel	*The Sounds of Silence*
"Wheatland"	O. Peterson	Oscar Peterson Trio	*Canadiana Suite*

NOTES

1 Understanding Silence

1 Rachel Louise Carson, *Silent Spring*, 40th anniversary ed. (Boston: Houghton Mifflin, 2002).

2 Alex Ross, "Searching for Silence: John Cage's Art of Noise," *New Yorker*, October 4, 2010, https://www.newyorker.com/magazine/2010/10/04/searching-for-silence. It is noteworthy that *4'33"* is titled in terms of its duration, not its content, i.e., its silence. The concept of duration is a critical element in Cage's work, and in *4'33"* in particular. Cage states, "If you consider that sound is characterized by its pitch, its loudness, its timbre, and its duration, and that silence, which is the opposite and, therefore, the necessary partner of sound, is characterized only by its duration, you will be drawn to the conclusion that of the four characteristics of the material of music, duration, that is, time length, is the most fundamental. Silence cannot be heard in terms of pitch or harmony: It is heard in terms of time length." Cited in Kyle Gann, *No Such Thing as Silence: John Cage's 4'33"* (New Haven: Yale University Press, 2010), 80.

3 Cited in Stuart Sim, *Manifesto for Silence: Confronting the Politics and Culture of Noise* (Edinburgh: Edinburgh University Press, 2007), 22. As I write about silence, I seek to be highly respectful of those persons whose hearing is impaired. Their experience must not be viewed simplistically. Dianne K. Brooks, who suddenly experienced a total and permanent loss of hearing at age 12, comments: "That night, I truly came to understand the phrase, 'silence can be deafening.' This profound silence, so new to me and exacerbated by the profound darkness, was more than I could tolerate." Dianne K. Brooks, "In Search of Self: Experiences of a Postlingually Deaf AfricanAmerican," in *Cultural and Language*

Diversity and the Deaf Experience, ed. Ila Parasnis (Cambridge: Cambridge University Press, 1996), 246–57.

4 An article in the *Helsinki Times* from September 4, 2014 describes efforts to promote tourism via silence: "Kristiina Hietasaari, a research and development director at the Finnish Tourist Board, believes silence to be a genuine opportunity for Finland, despite the fact that it has yet to be successfully productised."

5 Alain Corbin, *Histoire du silence: De la Renaissance à nos jours* (Paris: Albin Michel, 2016), 13–32. See also Christos Kakalis, Jeff Malpas, and Alberto Pérez Gómez, *Architecture and Silence*, Routledge Research in Architecture (London: Routledge, 2020); Mark Dorrian and Christos Kakalis, *The Place of Silence: Architecture/Media/Philosophy* (London: Bloomsbury, 2020), https://doi.org/10.5040/9781350076624.

6 Simone Weil, *Waiting for God* (New York: Harper & Row, 1973).

7 Haig Khatchadourian, *How to Do Things with Silence*, Philosophical Analysis 63 (Berlin: de Gruyter, 2015).

8 A. A. Milne, *The Complete Tales and Poems of Winnie-the-Pooh*, rev. ed. (New York: Dutton's Children's Books, 2001), 287–91.

9 See Dennis Kurzon, *Discourse of Silence* (Amsterdam: John Benjamins, 1998), 113–15; Per F. Broman, "Music, Sound, and Silence in the Films of Ingmar Bergman," in *Music, Sound, and Filmmakers: Sonic Style in Cinema*, ed. James Wierzbicki (London: Routledge, 2012), 15–31; Marjo C. A. Korpel and Johannes C. de Moor, *The Silent God* (Leiden: Brill, 2011), 279–304.

10 See the full text and discussion in https://owlcation.com/humanities/Edgar-Lee-Masters-Silence.

11 See, for example, Sim, *Manifesto for Silence*. Sim points to those who have advocated for silence, both past and present. He calls significant attention to Aldous Huxley's famous rejection of noise: "The twentieth century is, among other things, the Age of Noise. Physical noise, mental noise and noise of desire—we hold history's record for all of them. And no wonder; for all the resources of our almost miraculous technology have been thrown into the current assault against silence." Huxley, *The Perennial Philosophy*, 249–50, cited in Sim, *Manifesto for Silence*, 2–3; 40–42. Sim also highlights Thoreau's devotion to solitude (53–54) and especially Thomas Merton's dedicated pursuit of silence (71–74). See also the discussion of the influential work of Max Picard and George Steiner on silence in Colum Kenny, *The Power of Silence: Silent Communication in Daily Life* (London: Karnac, 2011), 69–76.

12 William Shakespeare, *Hamlet*, act 5, scene 2.

13 See the back cover of *Bringing It All Back Home*, Columbia, 1965.

14 Sonja Noll has documented this ever-increasing interest in silence. She observes that while in the 1980s books with "silence" in their titles averaged

about 200–300 per year, and in the 1990s 400–700 per year appeared, by 2000 that number had jumped to 700–1,000, and beyond 2010 to about 1,000 per year. See Sonja Noll, *The Semantics of Silence in Biblical Hebrew*, SSLL 100 (Leiden: Brill, 2020), 2. Significant films include *Into the Great Silence* (Gröning, 2005), *In Pursuit of Silence* (Shen, 2015), and *Silence* (Scorsese, 2016).

15 Adam Jaworski, ed., *Silence: Interdisciplinary Perspectives* (Berlin: de Gruyter, 1997); Kenny, *Power of Silence*, 67–87.

16 See Lois Wilkinson and Yumiko Olliver-Gray, "The Significance of Silence: Differences in Meaning, Learning Styles, and Teaching Strategies in Cross-Cultural Settings," *Psychologia* 49, no. 2 (2006): 74–88; Oyinkan Medubi, "A Cross-Cultural Study of Silence in Nigeria: An Ethnolinguistic Approach," *JMD* 5, no. 1 (2010): 27–44.

17 Sim, *Manifesto for Silence*.

18 See Martin Laird, *Into the Silent Land: A Guide to the Christian Practice of Contemplation* (Oxford: Oxford University Press, 2006); Sebastian Painadath, "The Transforming Power of Contemplative Silence," *Concilium* 5 (2015): 33–43, among many others.

19 Robert Sarah and Nicolas Diat, *The Power of Silence: Against the Dictatorship of Noise*, trans. Michael J. Miller (San Francisco: Ignatius, 2017).

20 Diarmaid MacCulloch, *Silence: A Christian History* (New York: Viking, 2013); Ekman P. C. Tam, "The Silence of Ch'an and the Experience of God: A Christian Reflection," *CSQ* 32, no. 4 (1997): 499–514; Susan Walker, ed., *Speaking of Silence: Christians and Buddhists on the Contemplative Way* (New York: Paulist, 1987); Frederick John Streng, "The Ontology of Silence and Comparative Mysticism," *PT* 27 (1983): 121–27; Won Yong Ji, review of *The Silence of God: The Answer of the Buddha*, by Raimundo Panikkar, *ConJ* 17, no. 1 (1991): 93–95; Frances S. Adeney, "How I, a Christian, Have Learned from Buddhist Practice, or 'The Frog Sat on the Lily Pond, Not Waiting,'" in *Gospel among Religions: Christian Ministry, Theology, and Spirituality in a Global Society*, ed. David R. Brockman and Ruben L. F. Habito (Maryknoll, N.Y.: Orbis Books, 2010), 225–28.

21 Walter Brueggemann, *Interrupting Silence: God's Command to Speak Out* (London: Hodder & Stoughton, 2019); Korpel and de Moor, *Silent God*, 279–305.

22 See esp. Paolo Torresan, "Dumah, demamah e dumiyyah: Il silenzio e l'esperienza del sacro nella Bibbia Ebraica," *BeO* 46, no. 2 (2004): 85–101. See also idem, "Silence in the Bible," *JBQ* 31, no. 3 (2003): 153–60.

23 Silvio José Báez, *Tiempo de callar y tiempo de hablar: El silencio en la Biblia Hebrea* (Rome: Teresianum, 2000); idem, *Cuando todo calla: El silencio en la Biblia* (Madrid: Editorial de Espiritualidad, 2009).

24 Korpel and de Moor, *Silent God.*

25 Göran Eidevall, "Sounds of Silence in Biblical Hebrew: A Lexical Study," *VT* 62, no. 2 (2012): 159–74.

26 Noll, *Semantics of Silence.*

27 Noll, *Semantics of Silence*, 6.

28 Noll insightfully comments on the importance and challenges of such an undertaking: "It is therefore important for the disciplines of both lexicography and textual interpretation that we attempt to re-create the 'native' semantic field (along with linguistic and cultural understandings) as much as possible without colouring it with our own imported understandings. No language exists in a vacuum, and no language speaker exists outside a specific (even if variable) cultural setting. The objective, then, is to understand the social and cultural setting of the speakers in addition to the linguistic system used by those inhabiting that world. Meaning cannot be separated from its context. . . . For a concept such as 'silence', however, which is multi-faceted and hard to pin down, and also differs greatly between ancient and modern cultures, the attempt to identify the concepts behind ancient biblical vocabulary is a difficult and slippery venture indeed." Noll, *Semantics of Silence*, 8.

29 William Shakespeare, *Macbeth*, act 5, scene 5, line 27.

30 Thus, Jürgen Ebach, *Beredtes Schweigen: Exegetisch-literarische Beobachtungen zu einer Kommunikationsform in biblischen Texten* (Gütersloh: Gütersloher Verlagshaus, 2014).

31 Aaron Schart, "Deathly Silence and Apocalyptic Noise: Observations on the Soundscape of the Book of the Twelve," *VEccl* 31, no. 1 (2010): article #383, 5 pages, https://doi.org/10.4102/ve.v31i1.383.

32 On silence as a form of politeness, see Maria Sifianou, "Silence and Politeness," in *Silence: Interdisciplinary Perspectives*, ed. Adam Jaworski (Berlin: de Gruyter, 1997), 63–84. Conversational speech is said to occur in "adjacency pairs," where the interlocutors regularly pause and anticipate the other's response. See Cynthia L. Miller, "Silence as a Response in Biblical Hebrew Narrative: Strategies of Speakers and Narrators," *JNSL* 32 (2006): 23–43.

33 Sim makes a distinction between silence as a condition and silence as a response, as well as between noise as natural versus unnatural or justified versus unjustified; see Sim, *Manifesto for Silence.* Kristine Muñoz discusses the more subtle issue of silence is a means of coping with that which cannot easily be said; see Kristine L. Muñoz, *Transcribing Silence: Culture, Relationships, and Communication* (Walnut Creek, Calif.: Left Coast Press, 2014), 15–43. Wittgenstein famously remarked, "What we cannot speak about we must pass over in silence"; cited in Sim, *Manifesto for Silence*, 12.

34 See esp. Min-Sun Kim, "Perspectives on Human Communication: Implications for Transculture Theory," in *Transcultural Realities: Interdisciplinary Perspectives on Cross-Cultural Relations*, ed. Peter Nwosu, Molefi K. Asante, and Virginia Hall Milhouse (Thousand Oaks, Calif.: Sage, 2001), 3–31; Noll, *Semantics of Silence*, 7–8. See also Muñoz, *Transcribing Silence*; and the reflections in Paul M. Sadler, "Learning to 'Read the Air': Three Ways to Improve Communication in Cultures Where Silence Is Golden," *EMQ* 51, no. 4 (2015): 388–92.

35 My study is thus similar in many regards to that of Báez, *Tiempo de callar*.

36 E. A. Speiser, *Genesis*, AB 1 (New Haven: Yale University Press, 2008), 164–65.

37 See Muñoz, *Transcribing Silence*; Michael Richardson and Kyla Allison, "Affect and the Unsaid: Silences, Impasses, and Testimonies to Trauma," in *Qualitative Studies of Silence: The Unsaid as Social Action*, ed. Amy Jo Murray and Kevin Durrheim (Cambridge: Cambridge University Press, 2019), 236–53; Alphonso Groenewald, "'Trauma Is the Suffering that Remains': The Contribution of Trauma Studies to Prophetic Studies," *AcT* 26 (2018): 88–102.

38 Some of the fuller bibliography relating to these areas is cited in the literature survey above.

39 On this, see Dale C. Allison Jr., "The Silence of Angels: Reflections on the Songs of the Sabbath Sacrifice," *RevQ* 13 (1988): 189–97; Michal Beth Dinkler, *Silent Statements: Narrative Representations of Speech and Silence in the Gospel of Luke*, BZNW 191 (Berlin: de Gruyter, 2013); Ryan Leif Hansen, *Silence and Praise: Rhetorical Cosmology and Political Theology in the Book of Revelation*, Emerging Scholars (Minneapolis: Fortress, 2014); Jean Lévêque, "Silence de Dieu, silence de l'homme," *PeP* 60 (1974): 10–18. The most relevant texts in this regard are the primeval silence alluded to in 2 Esd 7:28-34; the silence of the Jerusalem temple worship in Let. Aris. 83-99; the prudential silence called for in Sir 13:21-23; 20:1-9; 26:13-16; and the silent angelic prayer in 4QShirShabb. In the NT, the subject of silence occupies a far more limited place than in the HB. It appears most frequently in Christ's silence before Caiaphas, Herod, and Pilate (Matt 26:62-63; 27:12-14; Mark 14:60-61; 15:4; John 19:9), in connection with women and speech in Christian assemblies (1 Cor 14), and, most interestingly, in the reference to the "silence in heaven for about half an hour" in Rev 8:1. On this latter text, see esp. Hansen, *Silence and Praise*.

40 See my development of the concept of "theological streams" in John Kessler, *Old Testament Theology: Divine Call and Human Response* (Waco, Tex.: Baylor University Press, 2013).

41 Noll, *Semantics of Silence*. Noll's monograph is a revision of her Oxford dissertation completed under Professor Hugh G. M. Williamson.

42 Noll, *Semantics of Silence*, 7 (emphasis mine).

43 It should be noted, however, that this root is at times understood as meaning "to wail" or "to moan." Such a sense is likely in mind in Lev 10:3; Amos 5:13 and Ps 4:5.

44 This is presented in greater detail in Báez, *Tiempo de callar*, 71–86. This exploration of negated verbs of speech or action in a distinctive of Báez' work.

45 See further B. Couroyer, "'Mettre sa main sur sa bouche' en Égypte et dans la Bible," *RB* 67 (1960): 197–209; Mayer I. Gruber, *Aspects of Nonverbal Communication in the Ancient Near East*, StPohl 12 (Rome: Biblical Institute Press, 1980), 2:401–79.

46 See the foundational insights in Walther Eichrodt, *Theology of the Old Testament*, trans. John Baker (London: SCM Press, 1967), 2:268–315.

47 Kessler, *Old Testament Theology*. See also Rolf P. Knierim, "On the Task of Old Testament Theology," in *A Biblical Itinerary: In Search of Method, Form and Content: Essays in Honor of George W. Coats*, ed. Eugene E. Carpenter, JSOTSup 240 (Sheffield: JSOT Press, 1997), 153–66.

48 Per the refrain in C. S. Lewis, *The Last Battle* (New York: HarperCollins, 1994).

2 Silence as Alienation

1 This pattern of divine withdrawal and rejection due to human sin was widely known in the ANE; see the examples in Korpel and de Moor, *Silent God*, 238–44.

2 Narratological analysis of biblical texts is a burgeoning discipline. Early pioneering work was undertaken by Robert Alter, Meier Sternberg, and Shimeon Bar-Efrat. See Meir Sternberg, *The Poetics of Biblical Narrative: Ideological Literature and the Drama of Reading* (Bloomington: Indiana University Press, 1985); Shimeon Bar-Efrat, *Narrative Art in the Bible*, JSOTSup 70 (Sheffield: Sheffield Academic, 1997); Robert Alter, *The Art of Biblical Narrative* (New York: Basic Books, 1981). Alongside and subsequent to these studies, important contributions were made by Adele Berlin, Yairah Amit, and J. Cheryl Exum. See J. Cheryl Exum, *Tragedy and Biblical Narrative: Arrows of the Almighty* (Cambridge: Cambridge University Press, 1992); Adele Berlin, *Poetics and Interpretation of Biblical Narrative* (Winona Lake, Ind.: Eisenbrauns, 1994). For a brief introduction to narrative analysis, see Yairah Amit, "Narrative Art of Israel's Historians," *DOTHB* 708–15; Danna N. Fewell and David M. Gunn, "Narrative, Hebrew," *ABD* 4:1023–27, and Jean Louis Ska, *"Our Fathers Have Told Us": Introduction to the Analysis of Hebrew Narratives*, SubBi 13 (Roma: Pontifical Biblical Institute, 1990).

3 The proposal for reading Josh–2 Kgs in this way was first made by the German scholar Martin Noth in 1943, and has since that time generated much discussion. The majority of modern scholars still speak of the existence of such a literary corpus, but with numerous modifications vis-à-vis Noth's original proposal. For a concise discussion see Sandra L. Richter, "Deuteronomistic History," *DOTHB* 219–30, Stephen L. McKenzie, "Deuteronomistic History," *ABD* 2:160–67.

4 See the excellent discussion of the juxtaposition of these two themes in 1 Sam 8–12 in Brevard S. Childs, *Introduction to the Old Testament as Scripture*, OTL (Philadelphia: Fortress, 1979), 277–78.

5 See, for example, the positive evaluation of Saul in 1 Sam 14:47-48, versus the numerous condemnations of him elsewhere in 1 Sam 13–31. On the contradictory aspects of Saul's character, see esp. J. Cheryl Exum and J. William Whedbee, "Isaac, Samson, and Saul: Reflections on the Comic and Tragic Visions," *Semeia* 32 (1984): 5–40, here 31–32, 34. Exum rightly observes (34), "But whereas Saul is guilty, he is not really evil." Some have suggested that this diversity may stem from the various sources and traditions used by our narrator to construct the text as we have it now.

6 See the observations in Hans Wilhelm Hertzberg, *1 & 2 Samuel: A Commentary*, trans. J. S. Bowden, OTL (Philadelphia: Westminster, 1964), 106, 133–34.

7 See David M. Gunn, *The Fate of King Saul: An Interpretation of a Biblical Story*, JSOTSup 14 (Sheffield: Sheffield Academic, 1980); Exum, *Tragedy and Biblical Narrative*. Generally speaking, there are two lines of approach to understanding Saul as a tragic figure. On the one hand, several modern authors have suggested that the narrative views God as being negatively predisposed toward Saul from the outset. Yahweh's hard feelings due to the people's rejection of him as King spill over onto Saul, who becomes a scapegoat for them; see Gunn, *Fate of King Saul*, 123–31. The alternative, and in my opinion more likely approach, sees Saul as a promising figure, but one whose character deficiencies prove to be his undoing. This view is taken by the majority of more traditional interpreters and likely corresponds to the narrator's intentions. One important aspect of the presentation of the Saul and David materials in 1–2 Sam is that the promise of dynastic succession made to Saul is *conditional* (1 Sam 13:13-14), whereas David receives the *unconditional* promise of an enduring dynasty (2 Sam 7:8-17). Rather than viewing Yahweh as negatively predisposed to Saul from the outset, Fretheim views this transition to an unconditional promise as Yahweh's way of providing a more secure basis upon which to guarantee the outcome of his own purposes; see Terence E. Fretheim, "Divine Foreknowledge, Divine Constancy, and the Rejection of Saul's Kingship," *CBQ* 47 (1985): 595–602.

8 The Hebrew of v. 10 is quite emphatic; Samuel's arrival occurs immediately after the sacrifices are offered.

9 At this period, it appears likely that sacrifice was not a uniquely priestly prerogative. See Bruce C. Birch, *The Rise of the Israelite Monarchy: The Growth and Development of 1 Samuel 7–15*, SBLDS 27 (Missoula, Mont.: Society of Biblical Literature, 1976), 84, who notes that Saul himself builds an altar in 14:35 and Samuel blesses sacrifices in 1 Sam 9:13. Moreover, it is likely that when Saul says he offers the sacrifices, he may be speaking of having ordered the priests to perform them.

10 Thus Hertzberg, *1 & 2 Samuel*, 106; Ralph W. Klein, *1 Samuel*, WBC 10 (Waco, Tex.: Word, 1983), 128.

11 *Pace* Birch, *Rise of the Israelite Monarchy*, 84.

12 So David G. Firth, *1 & 2 Samuel*, ApOTC 8 (Nottingham: Apollos, 2009), 157.

13 Saul's actions here are in many ways parallel to those of Achan in Josh 7. However, there are significant differences as well. On the intertextual relationship of these two passages, see Meir Sternberg, "The Bible's Art of Persuasion: Ideology, Rhetoric, and Poetics in Saul's Fall," *HUCA* 54 (1983): 45–82, esp. 63–64. Sternberg also provides excellent insight into why Yahweh commands Israel to enact such extensive judgment upon the Amalekites.

14 Note that in v. 15, Saul says, "*They* have brought them from the Amalekites; for the people spared the best of the sheep and the cattle, to sacrifice to the LORD your God; but the rest we have utterly destroyed," whereas in v. 9 the narrator observes that "*Saul and the people* spared Agag, and the best of the sheep and of the cattle and of the fatlings, and the lambs, and all that was valuable, and would not utterly destroy them; all that was despised and worthless they utterly destroyed." Saul repeats the same idea in vv. 21-22. This raises an interesting point of contrast between chs. 13 and 15. Whereas in 13:6 it is obvious why Saul's troops fled, it is unclear why in ch. 15 the people should have desired to spare Agag (although their desire to save the best of the livestock is not difficult to explain). Saul's self-defense when confronted here is an excellent example of the complexity and genius of OT narrative art. See Amos Frisch, "'For I Feared the People, and I Yielded to Them' (1 Sam 15,24): Is Saul's Guilt Attenuated or Intensified?" *ZAW* 108, no. 1 (1996): 98–101.

15 On this see A. Jeffers, "Magic and Divination," *DOTHB* 670–74.

16 See J. A. Scurlock, "Magic, Ancient Near East," *ABD* 4:464–68.

17 Generally, when referring to non-Israelite contexts, the term "divination" is used for practices employed to determine the counsel of the gods. Scholars frequently refer to such practices as "mantic." See further, Mark A. Phelps, "Divination," *EDB* 349–50. On the role of the high priest's breastplate and the

Urim and Thummim, see Carol L. Meyers, "Breastpiece," *ABD* 1:781; idem, "Ephod," *ABD* 2:550.

18 First Samuel 14:18-19 is an interesting case in point. Here Saul commands Ahijah the priest to withdraw his hand before the lot casting gives a final result. Nevertheless, the Lord grants victory to Israel (vv. 20-23). This likely implies that the answer would have been in the affirmative, had the lot been cast.

19 As Exum and Whedbee note, the refusal to accept one's fate is the defining characteristic of the tragic hero; Exum and Whedbee, "Isaac, Samson, and Saul," 5–40, *passim*, esp. 24, 35.

20 The expression is enigmatic. Numerous suggestions have been made regarding the cause of Doeg's "detention": penance (Hertzberg, *1 & 2 Samuel*, 181); a vow, act of penance, or an incubation oracle (Klein, *1 Samuel*, 213); a ceremonial obligation (Henry P. Smith, *Samuel I and II*, ICC [Edinburgh: T&T Clark, 1898], 198).

21 Thus Keith Bodner, *1 Samuel: A Narrative Commentary*, HBM 19 (Sheffield: Sheffield Phoenix, 2008), 236; Diana V. Edelman, *King Saul in the Historiography of Judah*, JSOTSup 121 (Sheffield, UK: Sheffield Academic and JSOT Press, 1991), 178; Firth, *1 & 2 Samuel*, 243; Alter, *Art of Biblical Narrative*, 138.

22 Thus P. Kyle McCarter Jr., *1 Samuel*, AB 8 (New York: Doubleday, 1980), 364. Also see the discussion in Firth, *1 & 2 Samuel*, 239–43.

23 See Exum and Whedbee, "Isaac, Samson, and Saul," 5–40, who refer to Saul's "anguished state of mind . . . isolation and hopelessness" (23) and "disintegrated personality" (34).

24 Oaths were seen as sacred in the ancient world, and violation of them brought down consequences from the deities invoked when the vows or oaths were made. Examples of oath violation bringing such consequences (often in the form of drought, famine, or defeat in battle) occur in numerous passages in the HB, including Josh 7; 2 Sam 21:1-9; Hag 1:1-11. On this, see further John Kessler, "Curse, Covenant, and Temple in the Book of Haggai," in *Covenant in the Persian Period: From Genesis to Chronicles*, ed. Richard Bautch and Gary N. Knoppers (Winona Lake, Ind.: Eisenbrauns, 2014), 229–54; idem, "Patterns of Descriptive Curse Formulae in the Hebrew Bible, with Special Attention to Leviticus 26 and Amos 4:6-12," in *The Formation of the Pentateuch: Bridging the Academic Cultures of Europe, Israel, and North America*, ed. Jan C. Gertz, et al., FAT 111 (Tübingen: Mohr Siebeck, 2016), 943–84.

25 McCarter judiciously comments, "The story shows David acquiring a priest of Yahweh who will be associated with him throughout the remainder of his fugitive days [while at] the same time Saul is left without one. The narrative . . . depicts David as one who will have the benefit of priestly counsel in contrast to Saul who will not." McCarter, *1 Samuel*, 365–66.

26 This chapter has been the object of much research both in the commentaries and in specialized studies. Here we can only touch upon those aspects of the text directly related to the question of silence.

27 There is a strong play on words in the Hebrew here that is difficult to replicate in English. Saul's name and the verb "to seek or inquire" come from the same root, and sound very similar. One could possibly render it as "So Saul sought . . ." to catch the assonance of the Hebrew original.

28 The English translation "medium" renders the Heb *ʾesheth baʿalat ʾob*. See further, J. K. Kuemmerlin-McLean, "Magic, Old Testament," *ABD* 4:467–70.

29 Normally the full expression is used when seeking the counsel of the God of Israel; cf. Gen 25:22; Exod 18:15; Num 27:21; Judg 18:5; 1 Sam 9:9; 10:22; 1 Kgs 22:5, 7-8.

30 The concept of the unseen world in the HB is very different from the one we encounter in the intertestamental literature and in the NT. The dead were seen as shades (i.e., vapid, insubstantial beings; Heb *repha'im*, Isa 14:9; 26:14, 19; Ps 88:10; Job 26:5; Prov 2:18; 9:18; 21:16) inhabiting Sheol, a dark and shadowy realm. See the discussion in Theodore J. Lewis, "Dead, Abode of the," *ABD* 2:101–5. For an alternative view, see Philip S. Johnston, *Shades of Sheol: Death and Afterlife in the Old Testament* (Leicester: Apollos, 2002); Stephen L. Cook, "Funerary Practices and Afterlife Expectations in Ancient Israel," *RC* 6 (2007): 660–83. We will explore these issues in greater detail in ch. 6.

31 Hebrew grammarians describe these as circumstantial clauses. Their function is to provide additional details relating to the main action of the narrative. They are nonsequential; that is, they do not form a part of the chain of events making up the main narrative, but belong to the backdrop that surrounds it. The precise point at which the narrator reveals such circumstantial information to the reader is of critical importance in the unfolding of the story. It is somewhat like the placement of "clues" in a detective novel.

32 Such action is consistent with the laws in Lev 19:31; 20:6, 27; and Deut 18:10-12. It also sets Saul's previous decree in great contrast to what he is about to do here.

33 A change of clothing is highly significant in biblical narrative, frequently signifying a change in status. Joseph serves as an excellent illustration of this. See Victor H. Matthews, "The Anthropology of Clothing in the Joseph Narrative," *JSOT* 20, no. 65 (1995): 25–36; John R. Huddlestun, "Divestiture, Deception, and Demotion: The Garment Motif in Genesis 37–39," *JSOT* 26, no. 4 (2002): 47–62.

34 Exum and Whedbee comment, "For sheer starkness and terror, and in its gripping evocation of isolation and hopelessness, this scene stands out amid biblical narrative"; see Exum and Whedbee, "Isaac, Samson, and Saul," 5–40.

35 The word used here for enemy is a highly unusual one. It only appears here and in Ps 139:20. See Firth, *1 & 2 Samuel*, 289.

36 Cf. n. 7 *supra*. Note that here the text does not begin with the concept of Yahweh as Saul's enemy. Rather, Samuel states that this is something that God "becomes" (*wayehi 'areka*).

37 See Sternberg, "Bible's Art of Persuasion," 45–82.

38 Thus Firth, *1 & 2 Samuel*, 295–96; McCarter, *1 Samuel*, 243.

39 To be sure, readers are left wondering why Saul is definitively rejected while David, despite all his failures, is not. In this sense, many of the ambiguities and tensions below the surface of the text do strain against its final form, which places the weight of Saul's demise entirely upon his own shoulders.

40 Exum and Whedbee, "Isaac, Samson, and Saul," 35 (emphasis mine).

41 Exum and Whedbee, "Isaac, Samson, and Saul," 23.

42 This is the setting presented in the book's superscription in 1:1. Numerous scholars, however, see the book as having undergone a series of redactions and recontextualizations up until the fifth century BCE, resulting in its present, final configuration. For a survey and evaluation of the various hypotheses see Shalom M. Paul, *Amos* (Minneapolis: Fortress, 1991); Jörg Jeremias, *The Book of Amos: A Commentary*, trans. Douglas W. Stott, OTL (Louisville: Westminster John Knox, 1998); Tchavdar S. Hadjiev, *The Composition and Redaction of the Book of Amos*, BZAW 393 (Berlin: de Gruyter, 2009). We will not engage these important and fascinating questions here. Our study will focus on the issues of obedience and silence in the book in its finished form.

43 The Hebrew of these verses is difficult, and numerous understandings have been proposed. For an excellent survey, see Francis I. Andersen and David Noel Freedman, *Amos: A New Translation with Introduction and Commentary*, AB 24a (New York: Doubleday, 1989), 313–16. However the finer points of the discussion are construed, it is clear that oppression of the poor is being targeted.

44 See Schart, "Deathly Silence."

45 See Deut 32:24; Jer 24:10; 29:17; Ezek 5:16; 14:13, 21, where famine is described as having been "sent" (**shalach*) by Yahweh. More generally, famine is a standard element in ANE and ancient Israelite "curse formulations"—that is, the misfortunes that the Deity might send upon those who transgressed the covenantal promises and to which they had sworn allegiance. See esp. Lev 26:14-39; Deut 28:15-29:1. Such maledictions served two purposes: to lead to repentance (Deut 4:28-32; 30:1-10), and as a punishment for sin (Deut 28; Lev 26).

46 On the variation between sg. and pl. here, see *infra*, n. 55.

47 Mays insightfully summarizes the meaning here: "The intention of this text is to warn and entice. The generation of the exile should not consider itself rescued merely because it survived the destruction of Jerusalem and the land; rather it is rescued if only at least, now after God's judgment, it takes seriously Amos' word of God. For this generation too there may be a 'too late' when God himself withdraws his word. [These words] would make it quite clear to generations after 587/6 that the people of God would lose all contact with God—and thus be irrevocably lost—not just with the destruction of the Jerusalem temple, but rather with the withdrawal of the prophetic word." James Luther Mays, *Amos: A Commentary*, OTL (London: SCM Press, 1969), 151.

48 See the survey in Paul, *Amos*, 265–67.

49 The kingdom of Judah and the temple of Jerusalem lay to the south. Perhaps Amos avoids mention of the south because Jerusalem/Zion has already been called Yahweh's dwelling place and the place from which Yahweh "roars" (Amos 1:2). This also fits with the book's overall focus on Yahweh's judgment on the NK.

50 Cf. Wolff, who sees this as a reference to "agitated and aimless running to and fro in a state of distress." Hans Walter Wolff, *Joel and Amos*, trans. W. Janzen (Philadelphia: Fortress, 1977), 330. It is difficult to see how a quest with a very definite object, i.e., the word of Yahweh, can be described as aimless.

51 One exception may be Dan 12:4, where the idea of erratic movement seems to appear, but this text is somewhat unique and idiosyncratic.

52 Mays appropriately comments, "The picture is that of a people fluttering against the limits of their spatial cage in hope of transcending the prison of their situation by finding the opening to the divine." Mays, *Amos*, 149.

53 See, similarly, Hos 3:3-5. Wolff comments, "Thus Yahweh will withdraw himself from Israel, together with every means of approaching him that had become an idol." Hans Walter Wolff, *Hosea: A Commentary on the Book of the Prophet Hosea*, trans. Gary Stansell, Hermeneia (Philadelphia: Fortress, 1974), 62.

54 Cf. the role played by false prophets and their superficial declarations of peace and security in Jer 5:13-14; 14:13-14; 23:16-22; 1 Kgs 22:5-28.

55 It should be noted that while Amos 8:11-12 employs the motif of Yahweh's word as sustenance, a motif that also appears in Deut 8:1-3, the two texts are actually quite different. Deuteronomy 8 occurs in the context of a lengthy sermon exhorting Israel to obey Yahweh's word, or *torah*. It describes how Yahweh led the people for forty years in the wilderness. The need for food in the wilderness was meant to reveal whether or not the nation would walk in obedience to Yahweh's commandments (v. 2). Deuteronomy 8:1-3 stresses

that ultimately that which is necessary for life is not merely physical food, but rather obedience to Yahweh's commandments. Clearly, Amos 8:11-12 moves in a different world. People are not seeking desperately to hear the *torah* taught, but rather a specific word pertaining to their situation, one which might perhaps give counsel and hope. Numerous commentators see Deut 8 and Amos 8 as intertextually related; see, e.g., Jeremias, *Amos*, 148–50; Mays, *Amos*, 147–50; Paul, *Amos*, 266–67. Andersen and Freedman try to include both *torah* and prophecy. They suggest that the famine of the hearing of the *words* of Yahweh in 8:11b means "a failure to abide by the Decalogue," resulting in the loss of direct access to Yahweh's *word* in 12b, because Yahweh will no longer send prophets to them; Andersen and Freedman, *Amos*, 824. This, however, seems far too subtle. Despite the fact that the expression "the word(s) of Yahweh" generally refers to a written code (as Andersen and Freedman rightly affirm), the particular context here makes any idea of a "famine of [human] obedience to Yahweh's statutes" rather difficult. As noted above, I see no substantial difference between the sg. and pl. here.

56 On this general theme see Samuel E. Balentine, "Jeremiah, Prophet of Prayer," *RevExp* 78, no. 3 (1981): 331–44; idem, "The Prophet as Intercessor: A Reassessment," *JBL* 103, no. 2 (1984): 161–73. However, as Balentine observes in his reassessment, this aspect of the prophetic role ought not to be unduly stressed and viewed as normative in all instances.

57 Cf. 2 Kgs 17:13; 24:2; Ezra 9:11; Job 1:8; 2:3; Jer 7:25; 25:4; Ezek 38:17; Dan 9:6, 10; Amos 3:7; Zech 1:6.

58 Indeed, the relational bond between Yahweh and Jeremiah plays a central and critical role in the book. It forms the basis of the so-called "confessions" or "complaints" of Jeremiah (Jer 11:18-20; 12:1-6; 15:10-21, 17:14-18; 18:18-23; 20:7-13) that play an important role in the unfolding drama in the book. On these, see esp. Samuel E. Balentine, *Prayer in the Hebrew Bible: The Drama of Divine-Human Dialogue*, OBT (Minneapolis: Fortress, 1993), 150–68; A. R. Pete Diamond, *The Confessions of Jeremiah in Context: Scenes of Prophetic Drama*, JSOTSup 45 (Sheffield: JSOT Press, 1987).

59 See the detailed examination in Mark J. Boda, "From Complaint to Contrition: Peering through the Liturgical Window of Jer 14,1–15,4," *ZAW* 113 (2001): 186–97.

60 See, e.g., the suggestions in William L. Holladay, *Jeremiah 1: A Commentary on the Book of the Prophet Jeremiah, Chapters 1–25*, Hermeneia (Philadelphia: Fortress, 1986), 251–52. Holladay situates these prohibitions at a point after 601 BCE, when Jehoiakim burned the scroll containing Jeremiah's oracles (Jer 36). Many commentators, however, refrain from proposing any precise context.

61 Again, the text's soundscape comes to the fore. On the Hebrew terms for prayer, see Patrick D. Miller, *They Cried to the Lord: The Form and Theology of Biblical Prayer* (Minneapolis: Fortress, 1994), 32–54.

62 The identity of the Queen of Heaven (referenced in the HB only in Jeremiah) is a matter of significant scholarly debate. See Phillip C. Schmitz, "Queen of Heaven," *ABD* 5:586–88.

63 See Terence E. Fretheim, *Jeremiah*, SHBC (Macon, Ga.: Smith & Helwys, 2002), 183. Fretheim discusses the intriguing question of why Yahweh forbids Jeremiah to intercede, as opposed to simply ignoring his prayer. I will return to this question at the end of this section.

64 The sense of the Hebrew of this verse is notoriously difficult to reconstruct. For a fuller discussion, see Holladay, *Jeremiah 1*, 347; 354–56; William McKane, *Jeremiah 1–25*, ICC (Edinburgh: T&T Clark, 2014), 247–53. My reading here is similar to that of McKane and the NRSV.

65 See the discussion in Mark J. Boda, *A Severe Mercy: Sin and Its Remedy in the Old Testament*, Siphrut 1 (Winona Lake, Ind.: Eisenbrauns, 2010), 240–41. Scholars debate whether the peoples' words here are taken from psalms and laments already in existence and in use in Israel's liturgy, or specifically composed for use in the passage under study here. Either way, our point remains the same.

66 This is the explanation most commonly found in the commentaries.

67 Thus Fretheim, *Jeremiah*, 230–31.

68 Boda, "Complaint to Contrition," 186–97.

69 This is sometimes called a negative imperative or vetitive. We will be examining the relevance of this construction in greater detail ch. 7.

70 See further Kessler, *Old Testament Theology*.

71 See R. E. Clements, *Jeremiah*, Interpretation (Louisville: Westminster John Knox, 1988), 89–91.

3 Silence as Catastrophe

1 Other HB texts call for silence (see Num 13:30; Judg 3:19; Amos 6:10; 8:3; Neh 8:11), but only these three specifically call for silence before (*miphne*) Yahweh. See our discussion *infra*.

2 Wilhelm Rudolph, *Micha, Nahum, Habakuk, Zephanja*, KAT 13, no. 3 (Gütersloh: Gütersloher Verlagshaus, 1975), 266; Ernst Sellin, *Das Zwölfprophetenbuch*, KAT 12 (Leipzig: Deichertsche Verlagsbuchhandlung, 1922), 377.

3 J. J. M. Roberts, *Nahum, Habakkuk, and Zephaniah: A Commentary*, OTL (Louisville: Westminster John Knox, 1991), 177: "The cry . . . 'be silent!' . . . was apparently widely used as a liturgical cry to silence the gathered commu-

nity prior to the beginning of communal worship (Hab 2:20; Zech 2:17[13]), and it is that liturgical use that the prophet is imitating here."

4 Marvin A. Sweeney, *Zephaniah: A Commentary*, Hermeneia (Minneapolis: Fortress, 2003), 79.

5 Schart, "Deathly Silence." In these passages, we also find various other terms employed in addition to these three elements and certain variations of the elements themselves. Moreover, the fact that the basic form could be subject to various modifications suggests that in these passages we have a "semi-fixed" formula, capable of being shaped and adapted according to the needs of diverse contexts.

6 René Vuilleumier and Carl-Albert Keller, *Michée, Nahoum, Habacuc, Sophonie*, CAT 11b (Neuchâtel: Delachaux & Niestlé, 1971), 190.

7 See Noll, *Semantics of Silence*, 233–48.

8 On the concept of an implied narrative within a prophetic text, see John Kessler, "Diaspora and Homeland in the Early Achaemenid Period: Community, Geography and Demography in Zechariah 1–8," in *Approaching Yehud: New Approaches to the Persian Period*, ed. Jonah L. Berquist, SemeiaSt 50 (Atlanta: Society of Biblical Literature, 2007), 137–66.

9 See esp. BDB, s.v. "פנה." BDB notes that this term is "freq[uently] rendered *before* in AV [and] RV, and so confused with לפני; but the מִן retains always its full [causal] force in the Heb." As this is a citation from a Hebrew lexicon, I have chosen to retain the Hebrew characters present in the lexicon in this citation.

10 See Christo H. J. Van der Merwe, "Is There Any Difference between ירא מפני, ירא מן, and ירא את?" *JNSWSL* 18 (1992): 177–83.

11 Out of a desire to avoid unduly cumbersome English circumlocutions, I am choosing to use the masculine pronouns "him" and "his" with reference to Yahweh in this section, especially in connection with *miphne*.

12 Scholars differ as to whether the day of the Lord in Zephaniah is an eschatological (i.e., "end of time") event or a manifestation of Yahweh's intervention in the historical context in which the book is set (the late seventh century). For the latter view, see Marvin A. Sweeney, "Zephaniah: Prophet of His Time—Not the End Time!" *BRev* 20, no. 6 (2004): 34–40, 43; idem, *Zephaniah*, 10–18. For the former, see Johannes Vlaardingerbroek, *Zephaniah*, HCOT (Leuven: Peeters, 1999), 80–82. However the matter is decided, Zephaniah affirms that his own people will ultimately be exalted and at peace in the midst of a reconstituted world of nations (see esp. Zeph 3:9-20).

13 As Berlin notes, "its fifty-three verses could conceivably constitute one long chapter." Adele Berlin, *Zephaniah*, AB 25a (New York: Doubleday, 1994), 17. See Berlin's survey of the structural proposals on 17–20. See also the extensive discussion in Sweeney, *Zephaniah*, 3–10.

14 Joel D. Barker, "Day of the Lord," *DOTP* 132–43. See also the excellent discussions in Jean-Marie van Cangh, "Temps et eschatologie dans l'Ancien Testament," in *Temps et eschatologie: Données bibliques et problématiques contemporaines*, ed. Jean-Louis Leuba (Paris: Cerf, 1994), 17–38; Benjamin Uffenheimer, "From Prophetic to Apocalyptic Eschatology," in *Eschatology in the Bible and in Jewish and Christian Tradition*, ed. Henning Graf Reventlov (Sheffield: Sheffield Academic, 1997), 200–217; Rolf Rendtorff, "Alas for the Day: The 'Day of the Lord' in the Book of the Twelve," in *God in the Fray: A Tribute to Walter Brueggemann*, ed. Tod Linafelt and Timothy K. Beal (Minneapolis: Fortress, 1998), 186–97.

15 There is much controversy over the dating of these sections, and to which chronological era they refer. However, I am not able to discuss these issues here.

16 See the excellent discussion in Ehud Ben Zvi, *A Historical-Critical Study of the Book of Zephaniah*, BZAW 198 (Berlin: de Gruyter, 1991), 88.

17 Thus Sweeney, *Zephaniah*, 81.

18 So Vlaardingerbroek, *Zephaniah*, 84.

19 For a fuller discussion of this issue, see Ben Zvi, *Zephaniah*, 82–83.

20 This is the traditional approach to these verses. For a discussion of various alternative proposals, see Heath Thomas, *Habakkuk*, THOTC (Grand Rapids: Eerdmans, 2018), 22–25; Francis I. Andersen, *Habakkuk: A New Translation with Introduction and Commentary*, AB 25 (New Haven: Yale University Press, 2007), 24–27.

21 The language and forms used in Hab 3 are highly complex and differ in many respects from the rest of the book. Moreover, ch. 3 is missing in the Qumran manuscripts. For a detailed discussion of the chapter, see esp. Andersen, *Habakkuk*.

22 As we shall soon see, this stands in contrast to Zech 2:12, where Yahweh is *roused* from his resting place to go forth in judgment.

23 Following the general approach of Michael H. Floyd, *Minor Prophets, Part 2*, FOTL 22 (Grand Rapids: Eerdmans, 2000), 82–161.

24 Cf. 2 Chr 21:16; Isa 41:2, 25; 51:9; Jer 50:9; 51:1, 11; Ezek 23:22; Zech 9:13. Others describe Yahweh as being aroused for war (Isa 42:13; 51:9), or rousing one or another of his weapons of war (Isa 10:26, a whip; Hab 3:9, a bow; Zech 13:7, a sword).

25 Note the difference in terminology from Hab 2:20 which speaks of Yahweh's temple or palace using Heb *hekal*. The term "holy dwelling" can refer both to Yahweh's heavenly abode (as here, cf. Deut 26:15; 2 Chr 30:27; Ps 68:5; Jer 25:30), and to the Jerusalem temple (Ps 26:8).

26 Beyond that there is, of course, the reader, who is also an intended hearer of the words of the passage. We will take up the implications of this later.

27 Silence in the unseen world is not explicitly referred to in the HB, but becomes increasingly important in the intertestamental period and the NT. On the role of silence in the portrait of angelic worship at Qumran, see Allison, "Silence of Angels," 189–97; Israel Knohl, "Between Voice and Silence: The Relationship between Prayer and Temple Cult," *JBL* 115 (1996): 17–30; Carol A. Newsom, *Songs of the Sabbath Sacrifice: A Critical Edition* (Atlanta: Scholars Press, 1985).

28 Silence signifies agreement or acquiescence in Num 30:3, 7; Neh 5:8.

29 Leviticus 10:3b is sometimes cited in this regard; see Baruch A. Levine, *Leviticus: The Traditional Hebrew Text with the New JPS Translation*, JPSTC (Philadelphia: Jewish Publication Society, 1989), 60. However, various other interpretations of this text are possible.

30 The verb translated "be still" (**ḥarash*) frequently has the sense "be silent" (Gen 24:21; 34:5; Judg 16:2; 1 Sam 10:27; etc.)

31 See the discussion in Jonathan Klawans, *Impurity and Sin in Ancient Judaism* (New York: Oxford University Press, 2000). In the HB, the legitimate taking of human life required those involved to be in a state of ritual purity (cf. Josh 3:5). The ultimate right to enact such judgment belonged to Yahweh alone. Yahweh could, however, in certain contexts, confer the right to take life to other humans. Judgment is called Yahweh's "strange" or "alien" work (Isa 28:21), stressing both its sanctity and the reality that, while such judgment might occur in some instances, it does not reflect Yahweh's most profound desire for humankind.

32 See C. van Leeuwen, "עד," *TLOT* 2:839–46; Robert B. Chisholm, "עוד," *NIDOTTE* 3:339–40.

33 There is a broad consensus that these are non-Israelites.

34 See the excellent (although now dated) discussion in Allison A. Trites, *The New Testament Concept of Witness*, SNTSMS 31 (Cambridge: Cambridge University Press, 1977), 35–47.

35 *le'ene 'hagoyim*; Ezek 5:8; 20:9, 14, 22, 41; 22:16; 28:25; 38:23; 39:27; cf. also Lev 26:45; Ps 98:2.

36 Amos 8:3 is sometimes understood in the same way; thus, Paul, *Amos*, 255 (among many others). However, there are problems with such an interpretation, as we shall see below.

37 Leviticus 10:3 is often cited in this regard; however, significant debate surrounds its translation and meaning.

38 In chs. 1, 2, and 4, each verse begins with a successive letter of the alphabet (with some minor variations), while, for most of the poem, ch. 3 employs the same letter in three successive verses. Moreover, there is a slight irregularity in the acrostic form in chs. 2, 3, and 4, in that near the center of the poem the normal order of two of the letters (*ayin* and *pe*) is reversed. Many see this as

reflecting a stage of the Hebrew language when a certain fluidity existed in the order of these letters. The normal order is preserved in ch. 1. For a fuller discussion, see Will Soll, "Acrostic," *ABD* 1:58–60.

39 What is more, the central point within each poem may be seen as indicating a pivot or change in direction; see Bo Johnson, "Form and Message in Lamentations," *ZAW* 97, no. 1 (1985): 58–73.

40 For a general introduction to Lamentations, see F. W. Dobbs-Allsopp, "Lamentations," *EDB* 785–86; D. R. Hillers, "Lamentations," *ABD* 4:137–42. See also Mark J. Boda, "The Priceless Gain of Penitence: From Communal Lament to Penitential Prayer in the 'Exilic' Liturgy of Israel," in *Lamentations in Ancient and Contemporary Cultural Contexts*, ed. Nancy C. Lee and Carleen Mandolfo, Symposium Series (Atlanta: Society of Biblical Literature, 2008), 81–101. I will expand on my use of "the poet" for the speaker in Lamentations in ch. 4.

41 This transition is examined in detail in Boda, "Priceless Gain of Penitence," and B. Johnson, "Form and Message in Lamentations," 58–73.

42 Various proposals include: 2:1-12, narrator's speech to the reader; 2:13-19, narrator's speech to Zion; 2:21-22, Zion's address to God. See Iain Provan, *Lamentations*, NCBC (Grand Rapids: Eerdmans, 1991), 57. B. Johnson, "Form and Message in Lamentations," 58–73, suggests the description of the "facts" of Jerusalem's destruction, 2:1-12; the interpretation of the aforementioned facts, 2:13-22. For a survey of other proposed divisions, see Robert B. Salters, *A Critical and Exegetical Commentary on Lamentations*, ICC (London: T&T Clark, 2010), 106.

43 The word translated "guidance" by the NRSV is the Heb *torah*, which may carry the more specific sense of instruction or ruling (cf. Isa 2:3; Jer 18:18; Hag 2:11).

44 On Israelite mourning practices, see Gary A. Anderson, *A Time to Mourn, a Time to Dance: The Expression of Grief and Joy in Israelite Religion* (University Park: Pennsylvania State University Press, 1991); E. Jacob, "Mourning," *IDB* 3:452–54; Baruch A. Levine, "Silence, Sound, and the Phenomenology of Mourning in Biblical Israel," *JANESCU* 22 (1993): 89–106; and esp. Gruber, *Aspects of Nonverbal Communication*, 2:401–79.

45 Cf. Josh 7:6; 1 Sam 4:12; 2 Sam 1:2; 12:16, 20; 13:19; 15:32; Isa 3:6; 47:1; Ezek 27:28-31; Job 2:12-13; 16:15; Neh 9:1.

46 Thus Adele Berlin, *Lamentations: A Commentary*, OTL (Louisville: Westminster John Knox, 2002), 63; and with greater detail, Levine, "Silence, Sound, and the Phenomenology of Mourning," 89–106, 341–42.

47 See the discussion in Salters, *Lamentations*, 143–44.

48 See the examples in Gruber, *Aspects of Nonverbal Communication*, 2:402–34; 476–77.

49 The same Hebrew verb (*shamam*) is used for both senses. Cf. Lev 26:32; Ezra 9:3-4; Job 21:5; Pss 40:15; 143:4; Isa 52:14; Jer 2:12; 18:16; 49:17, 20; 50:13; Ezek 4:17; 26:16; 32:10; Zeph 3:6; Zech 7:14.

50 See Couroyer, "'Mettre sa main sur la bouche,'" 197–209.

51 Norbert Lohfink, "Enthielten die im Alten Testament bezeugten Klageriten eine Phase des Schweigens?" *VT* 12, no. 3 (1962): 260–77.

52 See Delbert R. Hillers, *Lamentations*, AB 7a (Garden City, N.Y.: Doubleday, 1972), 105–6; Báez, *Tiempo de callar*, 34.

53 The Hebrew word here is obscure, only occurring once in the HB. See J. Alberto Soggin, *The Prophet Amos: A Translation and Commentary*, trans. J. Bowden, OTL (London: SCM Press, 1987), 107.

54 Marvin A. Sweeney, *The Twelve Prophets*, Berit Olam (Collegeville, Minn.: Liturgical Press, 2000), 2:146; and many others.

55 S. R. Driver, *The Books of Joel and Amos*, CBSC (Cambridge: Cambridge University Press, 1901), 201.

56 So Paul, *Amos*, 215–16.

57 Mays, *Amos*, 119–20.

58 William Rainey Harper, *A Critical and Exegetical Commentary on Amos and Hosea*, ICC (Edinburgh: T&T Clark, 1905), 155.

59 See Paul, *Amos*, 216.

60 Thus, the desire to avoid the mention of Yahweh's name need not be seen as pious. The speakers are likely portrayed by Amos as typical citizens of the NK whose religious beliefs would be characterized by heterodoxy and superstition.

61 So Driver, *Joel and Amos*, 201; Mays, *Amos*, 119–20.

62 The setting for the narrative is likely the city of Samaria (cf. 4:1) due to the mention of "strongholds" in v. 8 and "great and small houses" in v. 11.

63 Significantly, this interpretation has the support of the LXX which translates *has* by *eulabeomai*, a verb which in many of its instances carries overtones of care or caution (see *LSJ*, s.v. "eulabeomai"). I am grateful to Professor Rob Hiebert of Trinity Western University, Langley, British Columbia for his assistance on this point. See also the examples cited in Vlaardingerbroek, *Zephaniah*, 82.

64 The first three visions appear in 7:1-3; 7:4-6; and 7:7-9.

65 Ripe summer fruit; Heb *qayitz*, 2 Sam 16:1; Jer 40:10; Mic 7:1.

66 Note the similar sounding *qetz*, "the end"; cf. Gen 6:13; Ps 39:4; Jer 51:13; Lam 4:18; Ezek 7:2, 6; 21:25; Dan 8:17, 19; Hab 2:3. Such wordplays are standard devices in prophetic literature. A similar one appears in Jer 1:11-12.

67 The verse contains one slight translational difficulty, largely inconsequential for our study here. Some suggest that 3a should be translated "the songs of the temple shall become wailing" (NRSV) while others render it "then the songstresses of the palace will wail"; see Wolff, *Joel and Amos*, 317.

68 On funerary practices more broadly, see Elizabeth Bloch-Smith, "Life in Judah from the Perspective of the Dead," *NEA* 65 (2002): 120–30; idem, "Burials, Israelite," *ABD* 1:785–89.

69 Josh 8:29; 10:27; 1 Kgs 13:24-25, 28; 2 Kgs 9:25-26; Isa 14:19; 34:3; Jer 14:16; 22:19; 36:30; Ezek 16:5; Amos 4:3. See Paul, *Amos*, 255.

70 On this see Delbert R. Hillers, *Treaty Curses and the Old Testament Prophets*, BibOr 16 (Rome: Pontifical Biblical Institute, 1964), 68–69; and the earlier F. Charles Fensham, "Malediction and Benediction in Ancient Near Eastern Vassal-Treaties and the Old Testament," *ZAW* 74, no. 1 (1962): 1–9; idem, "Common Trends in Curses of the Near Eastern Treaties and *Kudurru*-Inscriptions Compared with Maledictions of Amos and Isaiah," *ZAW* 75, no. 2 (1963): 155–75.

71 Paul, *Amos*, 255.

72 Wolff, *Joel and Amos*, 317; Jeremias, *Amos*, 143.

73 Thus Paul, *Amos*, 253–55; Andersen and Freedman, *Amos*, 794.

74 E. A. Edghill observes, "It has been conjectured that these words were the very words with which Amos was removed from Bethel: 'Throw him out! Silence.'" Ernest Arthur Edghill, *The Book of Amos*, 2nd ed., WC (London: Methuen, 1926), 82.

75 This is in contrast to Amos 6:10, where clearly some have survived and the speaker is neither the prophet nor Yahweh.

76 Susan Niditch, *The Symbolic Vision in Biblical Tradition*, HSM 30 (Chico, Calif.: Scholars Press, 1983), 40.

77 As noted above, many see the book of Amos as having been configured by the prophet's disciples and later scribes who collected and wrote down Amos' words, making them accessible for later generations. Many would suggest that this occurred in connection with the flight of a circle of Amos' followers to Judah in the late eighth century, around the time of the fall of the NK, thus giving the book the additional purpose of serving as a warning to the SK. On the role of such a process in the creation of the biblical literature and its relationship to biblical authority, see Kessler, *Old Testament Theology*, 91–94.

78 The use of the verb **ʿazab* in the Isaianic corpus carries with it a sense of great sadness—an almost melancholic yearning for that which used to be, but now is no more. Thus, the land is lost and forsaken like an egg left behind by a mother bird (10:14) or like a woman cast off or widowed (62:4). See further, Kessler, "Images of Exile: Representations of the 'Exile' and 'Empty Land' in Sixth to Fourth Century BCE Yehudite Literature," in *The Concept of Exile in Ancient Israel and Its Historical Contexts*, ed. Ehud Ben Zvi and C. Levin, BZAW 404 (Berlin: de Gruyter, 2010), 209–51, esp. 243.

79 Cf. Jer 4:27; 6:8; 9:11; 10:22; 12:10-11; 32:43; 44:6; Ezek 6:14; 7:27; 12:20; 15:8; 23:33; 33:28-29; 36:34.

80 *tan*; Job 30:29; Ps 44:19; Isa 13:22; 34:13; Jer 9:11; 10:22; Lam 4:3; Mic 1:8; Mal 1:3.

81 Oded Borowski, *Every Living Thing: Daily Use of Animals in Ancient Israel* (Walnut Creek, Calif.: AltaMira Press, 1998), 204.

82 See Borowski, *Every Living Thing*, 204; J. K. Kuemmerlin-McLean, "Demons, Old Testament," *ABD* 2:139.

83 *ʾiy*; Isa 13:22; 34:14; Jer 50:39.

84 Borowski, *Every Living Thing*, 205.

85 The NRSV's "cry out" misses the clear sense of the Hebrew here, which always implies the idea of "statement/call and response."

86 Sometimes a more neutral term for dwelling place is used for their habitations (Isa 34:13; 35:7), but at times (Jer 10:22) the term lair (*meʿon*), clearly an animal's abode, appears.

87 See also Jer 9:10.

88 Georg Fischer, *Jeremia 1-25*, HThKAT (Freiburg: Herder, 2005), 740.

89 In this section I am much indebted to the discussion of Báez, *Tiempo de callar*, 70–72.

90 It is difficult to determine with any precision the nature of these musical compositions. They seem to have some sort of religious aspect to them, but the contexts in which they are sung do not appear to indicate settings of formal worship. See the extended discussion, with bibliography, in Paul, *Amos*, 206–7.

91 See the discussion in Frank-Lothar Hossfeld and Erich Zenger, *Psalms 3: A Commentary on Psalms 101–150*, trans. Linda M. Maloney, Hermeneia (Minneapolis: Fortress, 2011), 515–16.

92 For a more complete listing of the literature of the period see Rainer Albertz, *Israel in Exile: The History and Literature of the Sixth Century BCE*, trans. David Green, SBLStBL 3 (Atlanta: Society of Biblical Literature, 2003), 139–433.

93 See esp. Ehud Ben Zvi, "Inclusion in and Exclusion from 'Israel' as Conveyed by the Term 'Israel' in Post-Monarchic Biblical Texts," in *The Pitcher Is Broken*, ed. Steven W. Holloway and Lowell K. Handy, JSOTSup 190 (Sheffield: JSOT Press, 1995), 95–149; Oded Lipschits, *The Fall and Rise of Jerusalem: Judah under Babylonian Rule* (Winona Lake, Ind.: Eisenbrauns, 2005); idem, "The Babylonian Period in Judah: In Search of the Half Full Cup," *JHebS* 7 (2007): 40–49; Oded Lipschits and Joseph Blenkinsopp, eds., *Judah and the Judeans in the Neo-Babylonian Period* (Winona Lake, Ind.: Eisenbrauns, 2003). See also Kessler, "Images of Exile," 309–51.

4 Silence as Repentance and Renewal

1 See Mark J. Boda, "Renewal in Heart, Word, and Deed: Repentance in the Torah," in *Repentance in Christian Theology*, ed. Mark J. Boda and Gordon

T. Smith (Collegeville, Minn.: Liturgical Press, 2006), 3–24; idem, "Repentance," *DOTP* 664–71; Carol J. Dempsey, "'Turn Back, O People': Repentance in the Latter Prophets," in *Repentance in Christian Theology*, ed. Boda and Smith, 47–66; Terence E. Fretheim, "Repentance in the Former Prophets," in *Repentance in Christian Theology*, ed. Boda and Smith, 36–41; Jacob Milgrom, "Repentance in the OT," *IDBSup* 736–38.

2 See Milgrom, "Repentance in the OT."

3 One possible exception might be Yahweh's demand that the people strip off their ornaments after the incident of the golden calf (Exod 33:4-6). This act was doubtlessly emblematic of mourning, which in turn could indicate repentance (see below). However, this case is an isolated one and deals primarily with punishment and national destiny; Yahweh states, "Take off your ornaments, and I will decide what to do with you" (33:5).

4 The literature on this point is immense. See Boda, "Priceless Gain of Penitence"; idem, "Confession as Theological Expression: Ideological Origins of Penitential Prayer," in *Seeking the Favor of God, Volume 1: The Origins of Penitential Prayer in Second Temple Judaism*, ed. Mark J. Boda, Daniel K. Falk, and Rodney A. Werline (Atlanta: Society of Biblical Literature, 2006), 21–50; idem, "Form Criticism in Transition: Penitential Prayer and Lament, Sitz Im Leben and Form," in *Seeking the Favor of God*, ed. Boda, Falk, and Werline, 1:181–92; William S. Morrow, "The Affirmation of Divine Righteousness in Early Penitential Prayers: A Sign of Judaism's Entry into the Axial Age," in *Seeking the Favor of God*, ed. Boda, Falk, and Werline, 1:101–17.

5 Thirteen of the Psalms are identified with specific events in the life of David. As James Limburg observes, "Since all of these events are recorded in 1–2 Samuel, these notes appear to have been provided by someone searching for an appropriate setting for the psalm in the life of David as known from the biblical account, thereby attributing authorship to him." James Limburg, "Psalms, Book of," *ABD* 5:527. James Crenshaw similarly notes, "The tendency during the postexilic period to attribute sacred writings to revered leaders . . . led to an identification of David as the author of numerous psalms. The attribution of psalms to him in 2 Sam. 1:17-27; 22:2-51 (which also appears as Ps. 18), together with the tradition that he was a musician (1 Sam. 18:10; Amos 6:5), encouraged this trend. The Septuagint carries it even beyond the point reached by the Masoretic Text, increasing the number of psalms attributed to David from seventy-three to eighty-five. Although Hebrew *lĕḏāwiḏ* (pertaining to David) does not necessarily mean Davidic authorship, its intent seems to have been that in many instances. It could also suggest that the particular psalm was written for a collection honoring David." James L. Crenshaw, *The Psalms: An Introduction* (Grand Rapids: Eerdmans, 2001), 5. See further, W. D. Tucker Jr., "Psalms 1: Book of,"

DOTWis 578–79; Brevard S. Childs, "Psalm Titles and Midrashic Exegesis," *JSS* 16, no. 2 (1971): 137–50; Tremper Longman III, *Psalms: An Introduction and Commentary*, TOTC 15–16 (Downers Grove, Ill.: IVP Academic, 2014), 23–28.

6 These terms are frequently used for descriptions of divine removal of sin; see Exod 34:7; Num 14:18; Isa 53:12; Mic 7:18; Job 7:21.

7 As in Lev 7:18; 2 Sam 19:19.

8 The word here (*remia*) is frequently used with reference to lying; see Job 27:4; Pss 101:7; 120:2; Mic 6:12.

9 The syntax of the psalm does not rule out a possible female speaker, although the psalm's title might appear to do so. The "I-voice" here is meant to represent all those in need of Yahweh's forgiveness, and a more inclusive vision is to be implied. Some of the psalms seem clearly to imply a female speaker; see Miller, *They Cried to the Lord*, 233–43. However, for the sake of simplicity, and to fit in with the psalm's title, I have chosen to use masculine personal pronouns for my discussion of this psalm. Elsewhere I will use either masc. or fem. pronouns.

10 See Korpel and de Moor, *Silent God*, 79–84.

11 Hans-Joachim Kraus, *Psalms 1–59*, trans. Hilton C. Oswald, CC (Minneapolis: Fortress, 1993), 367.

12 There are other texts that deal with culpable human silence. We will examine some of these in ch. 8.

13 See further n. 4 above, and Stanley D. Walters, "I Talk of My Sin (to God) (and to You): Psalm 51, with David Speaking," *CTJ* 50, no. 1 (2015): 91–109.

14 See Gen 4:10-11; Exod 22:2; 1 Sam 25:26; 2 Sam 1:16; Isa 1:15; Ezek 9:9; 24:6; Hos 4:2; Nah 3:1; Hab 2:8, 12.

15 John Goldingay, *Psalms*, vol. 2: *Psalms 42–89*, BCOTWP 2 (Grand Rapids: Baker Academic, 2007), 136.

16 As suggested by D. A. Hubbard, "נצל," *NIDOTTE* 3:144, who also includes Ps 51:14 in this category.

17 Hubbard, *NIDOTTE* 3:144.

18 Regarding the superscription's identification of the psalm with 2 Sam 11–12, Longman comments, "While the words of this prayer fit that occasion well, we should note that nowhere is this particular historical event mentioned specifically, indicating that the poem was written not to memorialize that moment, but to serve as a model prayer for those who find themselves in similar, though not identical, circumstances." Longman, *Psalms*, 218–19.

19 Calvin recognizes the tension here and suggests that David is praying not for release from the consequences of his sin, but from its guilt. Jean Calvin, *Psalms of David*, vol. 2 (Oxford: Talboys, 1839), https://www.ccel.org/ccel/calvin/calcom09.xvii.v.html. Kidner follows a similar approach; see Derek Kidner, *Psalms 1–72*, TOTC (Downers Grove, Ill.: InterVarsity, 1973), 193.

However, in my opinion, introducing the idea of moral guilt as distinct from judicial consequences seems strained in the context here.

20 Goldingay, *Psalms 42–89*, 137. See also the related discussion in Frank-Lothar Hossfeld and Erich Zenger, *Psalms 2: A Commentary on Psalms 51–100*, trans. Linda M. Maloney, Hermeneia (Minneapolis: Fortress, 2005), 22.

21 This involves translating the words "deliver me from bloodshed" as "deliver me from wailing" (thus *damam*-2), referring to one's own impending death. However, there are difficulties in rendering the Hebrew in this way.

22 See esp. Mitchell J. Dahood, *Psalms*, vol. 2: *51–100*, AB 17 (New York: Doubleday, 1968), 8.

23 Kraus, *Psalms 1–59*, 505. This approach goes back at least to H. Gunkel's commentary of 1926, and is also reprised in B. Renaud, "Purification et recréation, le 'miserere' (Ps 51)," *RevScRel* 62, no. 4 (1988): 201–18. Slight problems of textual transmission are not infrequent in the HB. Often a tension between a word and its context signals the presence of such cases, and a slight emendation provides a reasonable explanation and solution.

24 Cf. Pss 30:1, 9, 12; 94:17; 115:17; 116:2, 13, 14, 17; and "deliverance of a person's life from death" in Pss 56:13; 86:13.

25 See the discussion of these and other related texts in Ebach, *Beredtes Schweigen*, 59–69.

26 Brueggemann, *Interrupting Silence*; Korpel and de Moor, *Silent God*, 280–305.

27 Many of the points in this section are commonly noted in the commentaries. See esp. Berlin, *Lamentations*; F. W. Dobbs-Allsopp, *Lamentations*, Interpretation (Louisville: Westminster John Knox, 2002); Hillers, *Lamentations*; Robin A. Parry, *Lamentations*, THOTC (Grand Rapids: Eerdmans, 2010); Provan, *Lamentations*; Johan Renkema, *Lamentations*, HCOT (Leuven: Peeters, 1998); Salters, *Lamentations*; Claus Westermann, *Lamentations: Issues and Interpretation* (Minneapolis: Fortress, 1994).

28 In addition to our general introduction to the structure of Lamentations in ch. 3, see also Mark J. Boda, "Lamentations 1: Book of," *DOTWis* 399–410.

29 While this is widely affirmed (see the commentaries), certain exegetes have downplayed the significance of these verses. Thus Dobbs-Allsopp, *Lamentations*; Provan, *Lamentations*. They view the book's emphasis as falling far more on the theme of lament than hope. While it must be admitted that "hopeful" material in the book appears far less frequently than more sorrowful lamentation, the importance of this "positive turn" must not be gainsaid. Lamentations 3:19-33 lies both near the center of the poem and of the book as a whole—a position of great importance in Hebrew literary composition.

30 Parry dubs him "the Valiant Man"; O'Connor, "the strongman"; Dobbs-Allsopp "the everyman"; Renkema, "the devout man"; Berlin, "the personified voice of the exile"; Parry, *Lamentations*, 95–96; Kathleen M. O'Connor,

Lamentations and the Tears of the World (Maryknoll, N.Y.: Orbis Books, 2002), 44–45; Dobbs-Allsopp, *Lamentations*, 106–8; Renkema, *Lamentations*, 348–52; Berlin, *Lamentations*, 84–85. Parry and Renkema include a fuller survey of the other proposals of the speaker's identity.

31 See Provan, *Lamentations*, 23.

32 See the discussion in Craig C. Broyles, "Lament, Psalms of," *DOTWis* 384–99.

33 For example, Job; Ecclesiastes; Ps 73. See also Dobbs-Allsopp, *Lamentations*, 119–22. On theodicy more broadly, see James L. Crenshaw, *Defending God: Biblical Responses to the Problem of Evil* (Oxford: Oxford University Press, 2005). On wisdom and divine justice see Kessler, *Old Testament Theology*, 484–99.

34 Dobbs-Allsopp, *Lamentations*, 120.

35 Thus Boda, "Priceless Gain," 81–101, here 95.

36 See the extended discussion in Boda, *Severe Mercy*, 43–47. This "character credo" becomes a significant element in penitential prayer.

37 See esp. Katharine Doob Sakenfeld, *Faithfulness in Action: Loyalty in Biblical Perspective*, OBT 16 (Philadelphia: Fortress, 1985); idem, "Loyalty," *NIDB* 3:718.

38 That is, in v. 26, the adverbial particle *dumam* ("silently" or "in stillness"), and v. 28, the conjugated verb *weyiddom* ("he shall be silent [or still])."

39 *HALOT*; *BDB*; *DCH*.

40 Eidevall, "Sounds of Silence," 159–74, here 170.

41 Noll, *Semantics of Silence*, esp. 231–32.

42 Isaiah 14:7 uses both terms in parallel. On **shaqaṭ*, see Isa 18:4; Ps 94:13. For **nouaḥ*, see Deut 25:19; Zech 6:8; Hab 3:16. These terms generally carry strongly positive and hopeful associations.

43 On this concept see Kessler, *Old Testament Theology*, 275–315.

44 The image here is of a burden being taken up and carried. Lam 1:14 sees the nation's sins as metaphorically being bound together into a yoke which is then placed around its neck.

45 See Hos 3:5; Isa 40:1-2; 54:6-7, and the reference to the "seventy years" of exile in Jer 25:11-12; 29:10; Dan 9:2; Zech 1:12; 7:5.

46 See the excellent discussion in Renkema, *Lamentations*, 394–96. See also Boda, "Priceless Gain," 81–101.

47 For a fuller listing and description, see Carol L. Meyers and Eric M. Meyers, *Haggai, Zechariah 1–8*, AB 25b (Garden City, N.Y.: Doubleday, 1987), 433–35. See also Mark J. Boda, *The Book of Zechariah*, NICOT (Grand Rapids: Eerdmans, 2016), 438.

48 Yehud remained a weak and depopulated region until the second century BCE. See Lipschits, *Fall and Rise of Jerusalem*; idem, "Babylonian Period in Judah"; idem, "Shedding New Light on the Dark Years of the 'Exilic Period': New Stud-

ies, Further Elucidation and Some Questions Regarding the Archaeology of Judah as an Empty Land," in *Interpreting Exile: Displacement and Deportation in Biblical and Modern Contexts*, ed. Brad E. Kelle, Frank R. Ames, and Jacob L. Wright, AIL 10 (Atlanta: Society of Biblical Literature, 2011), 57–90.

5 Silence as Security

1 On this imagery, see A. S. van der Woude "צור, אבן," *TLOT* 2:1066–71, who states, "Primarily in hymns, individual songs of thanksgiving, of confidence, and of lament, the firm, unshakable rock is a stereotypical image for God's help (Pss 18:47; 62:3; 89:27; 95:1), the protection that he offers (Isa 17:10; Pss 28:1; 31:3; 62:8; 71:3), the refuge found with him (Pss 18:3, 32; 94:22; 144:1), his saving activity (Pss 19:15; 78:35), and his unshakable faithfulness (Isa 26:4; Pss 73:26; 92:16)" (1070).

2 On this see the more general treatment of "Promise Theology" in Kessler, *Old Testament Theology*, 275–318.

3 For a fuller treatment, see Edgar W. Conrad, *Fear Not Warrior: A Study of 'al tîrā' Pericopes in the Hebrew Scriptures*, BJS 75 (Chico, Calif.: Scholars Press, 1985).

4 Cf. Num 14:9; Deut 1:21; 3:2; Josh 10:8, 25; 2 Kgs 6:16; 1 Chr 28:20; Isa 7:4; 35:4; 37:6; 40:9; Jer 40:9.

5 See Num 21:34-35; Deut 1:20-21; 3:1-3; 20:2-4; 31:5-6; Josh 8:1; 10:7-8, 24-25; 11:5-7.

6 Georg Fischer and Dominik Markl, *Das Buch Exodus*, NSKAT (Stuttgart: Verlag Katholisches Bibelwerk, 2009), suggest the presence of an "anti-militaristic" perspective in vv. 13-14.

7 It must be noted, however, that in certain narrative contexts Yahweh comes to Israel's aid while Israel remains passive; e.g., 2 Kgs 7; Zech 14.

8 See Gen 24:21; Judg 18:19; 2 Sam 13:20; 2 Kgs 18:36; Job 6:24; Pss 32:3; 39:12; Prov 11:12; Isa 36:21; Jer 4:19.

9 The meaning of Zeph 3:17 is greatly debated. On **ḥarash* as not acting, see Noll, *Semantics of Silence*, 31–49; on Zeph 3:17 specifically, 38–44.

10 See William Henry Propp, *Exodus 1–18: A New Translation with Introduction and Commentary*, AB 2 (New York: Doubleday, 1999), 496–97.

11 The NRSV's "go forward" does not quite capture the idea of moving on along God's intended trajectory, implied in the Hebrew.

12 Yahweh's rebuke to Moses in 14:15 ("Why do you cry out to me? Tell the Israelites to go forward") has long puzzled interpreters, given that it had been the people, not Moses, who cried out to Yahweh, and Moses who had encouraged them to trust in the Lord. Commentators tend to resolve this issue by seeing Yahweh's words, "why do you cry out to me?" as addressed to the people, rather than to Moses; thus John I. Durham, *Exodus*, WBC 3

(Waco, Tex.: Word, 1987), 192. Alternatively, one might suggest that Moses is being addressed as the representative of the people, or that he himself has cried to God regarding the people's challenge to his authority. These suggestions have been advanced by both ancient and modern authors; cf. Propp, *Exodus 1–18*, 497.

13 See Jon D. Levenson, *Sinai and Zion: An Entry into the Jewish Bible*, NVBS (San Francisco: HarperSanFrancisco, 1987).

14 Occurring in Pss 2:6, 7-9; 12:5; 46:10; 50:7-23; 60:6-8; 75:4-5; 81:6-16; 82:2-7; 91:14-16; 95:8-11; 105:11, 15; 110:1, 4; 132:3-5, 11-12, 14-18. See further, Carl J. Bosma, "Discerning the Voices in the Psalms: A Discussion of Two Problems in Psalmic Interpretation, Part 2," *CTJ* 44 (2009): 127–70.

15 Manifested nonverbally by letting the hands droop or drop; Isa 13:7; Jer 6:24; Zeph 3:16.

16 Expressed as "making their hands drop"; Jer 38:4; Ezra 4:4.

17 Specifically in the sense of abandonment; Deut 4:31; 31:6.

18 Joshua 18:3; Prov 24:10.

19 So, for example, Kraus translates, "Stop and realize that I am Yahweh, exalted among the nations, exalted on the earth." Kraus, *Psalms 1–59*, 459. See, similarly, Goldingay, *Psalms 42–89*, 65, 72.

20 Hossfeld and Zenger note that here peace comes through the acknowledgement of the supremacy of the God of Jacob by *both* Israel *and* the nations. See Frank-Lothar Hossfeld and Erich Zenger, *Die Psalmen: Psalm 1–50*, NEchtB (Würzburg: Echter, 1993), 288–89.

21 See Hossfeld and Zenger, *Psalms 51–100*, 111–13, with full discussion and bibliography. See also Erhard Gerstenberger, *Psalms, Part 2, and Lamentations*, FOTL 15 (Grand Rapids: Eerdmans, 2001), 8.

22 Hans-Joachim Kraus, *Psalms 60–150*, trans. Hilton C. Oswald, CC (Minneapolis: Fortress, 1989), 13.

23 Tate notes that it has much in common with the confidence sections of certain psalms of lament (e.g. 22:23-32) and with several thanksgiving psalms (31:24-25; 32:6, 10-11; 34:10-23; 66:16-20). See Marvin E. Tate, *Psalms 51–100*, WBC 20 (Dallas: Word, 1990), 117–23.

24 This point is debated. Some, such as Tate, *Psalms 51–100*, and Artur Weiser, *The Psalms: A Commentary*, trans. Herbert Hartwell, OTL (Louisville: Westminster John Knox, 1962), 446–47, affirm that the expressions of confidence here have come in light of the deliverance the psalmist has already experienced. Others reject such a view; thus Goldingay, *Psalms 42–89*, 246-47, 53; and with greater detail, Hossfeld and Zenger, *Psalms 51–100*, 111–13.

25 Most translations use the English "soul" to translate Heb *nephesh* in vv. 1, 5. However, such a translation is misleading, as "soul" is frequently understood to denote a nonmaterial, ethereal part of the human person that survives

death. This is not an accurate definition of *nephesh*. The word itself may denote various aspects of the human person, such as physical life or breath (Gen 2:7; 33:40; Exod 21:23; Pss 26:9; 30:3), or one's inner being or personality (Pss 35:3, 9; 41:5; 42:5-6). See further, C. Westermann, "נפש," *TLOT* 2:743–59. In the present discussion, I will use the phrase "inner being" to translate this Hebrew noun.

26 Frequently this verb means to murder, as in Exod 20:13; here it likely indicates an assault. In this section I will use feminine personal pronouns. This corresponds to the likely intent of the psalmist, male or female, that these words be expressive of anyone in such a situation.

27 The NRSV translation obscures this somewhat by making v. 5 a word-for-word repetition of v. 1. However, in Hebrew v. 5 contains an imperative form of the verb.

28 Thus *DCH*, *HALOT*.

29 See the fuller discussion in Eidevall, "Sounds of Silence," 159–74. Eidevall prefers the translation "stillness" for *dumia* in v. 1, but avers, "one should keep in mind that there is no sharp line between stillness and silence" (170).

30 See the excellent discussion in Báez, *Tiempo de callar*, 26–36, esp. 27. The distinction between stillness or silence, on the one hand, and quiet (that is, relative diminution of sound), on the other, will become important in our discussion of the "still small voice" heard by Elijah in 1 Kgs 19. We will examine that text in ch. 8.

31 Goldingay, *Psalms 42–89*, 249.

32 In some texts, such as 1 Sam 1:15, one pours out one's "inner being" (*nephesh*) to God.

33 "[T]he reproachful question 'How long?' . . . is an expression of revolt and resistance." Hossfeld and Zenger, *Psalms 51–100*, 114.

34 Hossfeld and Zenger suggest that the imagery here is that of a battering ram being deployed against the wall of a city; idem, *Psalms 51–100*, 114.

35 See Loren D. Crow, *The Songs of Ascents (Psalms 120–134): Their Place in Israelite History and Religion*, SBLDS 148 (Atlanta: Scholars Press, 1996); John Goldingay, *Psalms*, vol. 3: *Psalms 90–150*, BCOTWP 3 (Grand Rapids: Baker Academic, 2008), 752.

36 Miller, *They Cried to the Lord*, 239, esp. n. 18; Hossfeld and Zenger, *Psalms 51–100*, 444–52. This, however, is questioned by Goldingay, *Psalms 90–150*, 534, who sees the words as those of a man in leadership. There does, however, seem to be some indication of a difference in speaker between vv. 1-2 (depicting an intimate reflection on the mother-infant relationship), and v. 3, where the speaker addresses the congregation as a whole (as suggested by Hossfeld and Zenger). On the superscription "to" or "for" David, Goldingay provocatively suggests, "There would be food for thought in the notion that

as 'David's' this might be a psalm for the king to take note of and live by." Goldingay, *Psalms 90–150*, 535.

37 Gerstenberger describes this aspect of the psalm as a "declaration of innocence"; idem, *Psalms, Part 2*, 360.

38 For a fuller discussion, see Goldingay, *Psalms 90–150*, 536, n. 13.

39 Hossfeld and Zenger, *Psalms 101–150*, 444–52.

40 As Miller points out, the second option diminishes the simile: the psalmist is not merely saying her inner being is like a weaned or sated child, but like such a child *with his or her mother*: idem, *They Cried to the Lord*, 414, n. 17. The close physical proximity between the two greatly magnifies the sense of rest and silence being underscored by the psalmist.

41 There are a number of other debated issues here, especially relating to matters of textual criticism. Given the great divergence of the Greek and Latin versions, some have suggested that the Hebrew Masoretic text requires an emendation here. On this, see Hossfeld and Zenger, *Psalms 51–100*, 444–46.

42 Dominique Barthélemy, *Critique textuelle de l'Ancien Testament: Tome 4, Psaumes*, OBO 50, no. 4 (Göttingen: Vandenhoeck & Ruprecht, 2005), 812.

43 See Goldingay, *Psalms 90–150*, 534, nn. 4, 5. Similarly, Hossfeld and Zenger may be taking matters too far when they state, "The speaker . . . is thus a feminine Job figure who speaks with YHWH about her 'life history' and above all about an experience of life and of God given her by YHWH." Hossfeld and Zenger, *Psalms 51–100*, 451. A "life history" form would likely require a longer poem; cf. Job, Ps 73.

44 Báez, *Tiempo de callar*, 30, n. 18. Báez notes the important contrast between the more internal aspects of vv. 1-2 (heart, inner being) and more externally focused ones (haughty eyes, walking in great things).

45 A different verb is used in Ps 62:5, but the meanings are largely the same.

46 Goldingay, *Psalms 90–150*, 534.

47 Hossfeld and Zenger, *Psalms 101–150*, 451.

48 Hossfeld and Zenger, *Psalms 101–150*, 451.

49 Assyria has a long history, and its strength fluctuated over the centuries. However, in the eighth–seventh centuries BCE, it experienced a resurgence under Tiglath-pileser III (r. 747–727), Shalmaneser V (r. 726–722), Sargon II (r. 721–705), Sennacherib (r. 704–681), and Esarhaddon (r. 680–669). For a brief summary of Assyrian history, see Tammi J. Schneider, "Assyria," *EDB* 119–23.

50 For a concise discussion of the political situation, and Isaiah's role in it, with annotated bibliography, see John Barton, *Isaiah 1–39*, OTG (Sheffield: Sheffield Academic, 1995), 34–44.

51 A similar crisis had occurred some 35 years earlier, when Pekah, the ruler of the NK, and Rezin, the Syrian king, plotted to depose Ahaz, the Davidic ruler, and install another dynasty (Isa 7:1-6). However, Isaiah counseled

Ahaz to remain calm and trust in the Lord (Isa 7:7-10). Ahaz unfortunately refused to heed Isaiah's advice, and sought the aid of Assyria. As a result, Isaiah proclaimed that judgment would fall upon the land (Isa 7:17-25; 8:5-22). See Bryan Beyer, *Encountering the Book of Isaiah: A Historical and Theological Survey*, EBS (Grand Rapids: Baker Academic, 2007), 69–80.

52 The term translated "rest" (*naḥat*) appears only in Isa 30:15; Job 36:16; Prov 29:9; Eccl 4:6; 6:5; 9:17.

53 See Hans Wildberger, *Isaiah 28–39*, trans. Thomas H. Trapp, CC (Minneapolis: Fortress, 2002), 260. I have refrained from capitalizing "spirit" (following the NRSV) to make a clear distinction between the meaning here and the NT's use of the term, with its broader connotations. In the HB, the "spirit" of Yahweh can refer to the mighty power of Yahweh that comes upon certain individuals for the accomplishment of certain purposes. See F. W. Horn, "Holy Spirit," *ABD* 3:260–82.

54 Thus Wildberger, *Isaiah 28–39*, 260.

55 Cf. 2 Kgs 18:30; Isa 12:2; 26:4; 50:10; Ps 4:5; Prov 3:5.

56 Oppression, Isa 30:12; foreign powers, Isa 31:1; idols, Isa 42:17; Hab 2:18; deceptive words, Jer 7:14; 17:5.

57 See Lev 25:18; 26:5; Deut 12:10; Jer 23:6; 32:37; Ezek 34:27; Ps 4:8.

58 Otto Kaiser states that in v. 17 our author turns to consider "the effects of righteousness, consisting of the free and untroubled existence and unhindered progress of men, animals and fields, in all-embracing peace and prosperity, *šālôm*, and secondly in the quiet confidence of men towards their God (cf. 30.15) and security in the relationship between men and their fellow men, men and animals and animals and other animals." Otto Kaiser, *Isaiah 13–39: A Commentary*, trans. R. A. Wilson, OTL (London: SCM Press, 1974), 335. Kaiser here perhaps reads too much into *hashqeṭ* and *beṭaḥ* in saying that these terms refer to "quiet confidence of men towards their God." Yet, he is doubtlessly correct to evoke the broader concept of stillness and security within all dimensions of life. This corresponds to the idea of relational dynamics as a means for moving beyond the HB text to the contemporary world that I alluded to in ch. 1.

59 See the insightful treatment of this text in Ehud Ben Zvi, "Who Wrote the Speech of Rabshakeh and When?" *JBL* 109 (1990): 79–92.

6 The Two Silences

1 See, among many others, T. Desmond Alexander, "The Old Testament View of Life after Death," *Them* 11 (1986): 41–46; idem, "The Psalms and the Afterlife," *IBS* 9 (1987): 2–17; Jacob Chinitz, "Death in the Bible," *JBQ* 32, no. 2 (2004): 98–103; Cook, "Funerary Practices," 660–83; John Goldingay, "Death and Afterlife in the Psalms," in *Judaism in Late Antiquity*, ed. Jacob Neusner,

Alan J. Avery-Peck, and Bruce Chilton (Leiden: Brill, 2000), 61–85; Johnston, *Shades of Sheol*; Bernhard Lang, "Afterlife: Ancient Israel's Changing Vision of the World Beyond," *BRev* 4, no. 1 (1988): 12–23; Aron Pinker, "Sheol," *JBQ* 23, no. 3 (1995): 168–79; Robin L. Routledge, "Death and Afterlife in the Old Testament," *JEBS* 9, no. 1 (2008): 22–39; Matthew Suriano, "Sheol, the Tomb, and the Problem of Postmortem Existence," *JHebS* 16 (2016): article #11, 31 pages, https://doi.org/10.5508/jhs.2016.v16.a11; Bruce Francis Vawter, "Intimations of Immortality and the Old Testament," *JBL* 91 (1972): 158–71.

2 This is a generally agreed upon assumption among scholars. See the surveys in Christopher B. Hays, *A Covenant with Death: Death in the Iron Age II and Its Rhetorical Uses in Proto-Isaiah* (Grand Rapids: Eerdmans, 2015), 11–132; Edwin M. Yamauchi, "Life, Death, and the Afterlife in the Ancient Near East," in *Life in the Face of Death: The Resurrection Message of the New Testament*, ed. Richard N. Longenecker (Grand Rapids: Eerdmans, 1998), 21–50; Klaas Spronk, *Beatific Afterlife in Ancient Israel and in the Ancient Near East*, AOAT 219 (Kevelaer: Butzon & Bercker, 1986), 86–236. Of course, the dating of the various biblical texts in question remains highly disputed, and thus any reconstructions must remain tentative. However, it is clear that far more elaborate descriptions of the afterlife and of heaven and hell developed in the Hellenistic period and later (i.e., from 333 BCE onward).

3 Kent H. Richards, "Death: Old Testament," *ABD* 2:108–10; Lloyd R. Bailey, *Biblical Perspectives on Death*, OBT (Minneapolis: Fortress, 1979), 39–40.

4 See Noll, *Semantics of Silence*, 183–88.

5 The Hebrew of Ps 94:17 is somewhat laconic. It reads, lit., "my inner being would have dwelt [in] silence." The LXX seeks to clarify the psalmist's intent by adding "the land" before silence. Similarly, the NRSV translates, "my soul would soon have lived in the land of silence."

6 See Báez, *Tiempo de callar*, 36–44; Noll, *Semantics of Silence*, 179–81.

7 The point of departure for the subject is still Hans Walter Wolff, *The Anthropology of the Old Testament*, trans. Margaret Kohl (Philadelphia: Fortress, 1973). See the more recent discussions in Michael A. Knibb, "Life and Death in the Old Testament," in *The World of Ancient Israel: Sociological, Anthropological and Political Perspectives*, ed. R. E. Clements (Cambridge: Cambridge University Press, 1989), 395–415; Robert A. Di Vito, "Old Testament Anthropology and the Construction of Personal Identity," *CBQ* 61 (1999): 217–38.

8 The bones of idolaters, however, were seen as highly unclean and defiling; cf. 2 Kgs 23:14, 20; Jer 8:1-2; Ezek 6:5; etc.

9 The literature on this subject is immense. See Cook, "Funerary Practices," 660–83; Elizabeth Bloch-Smith, "Burials, Israelite," *ABD* 1:785–89; Rachel Hachlili, "Burials, Ancient Jewish," *ABD* 1:789–94.

10 So, among others, Robert Martin-Achard, *From Death to Life: A Study of the Development of the Doctrine of the Resurrection in the Old Testament*, trans. J. P. Smith (Edinburgh: Oliver & Boyd, 1960), 38.

11 The following survey articles discuss many of the key issues related to the term: Theodore J. Lewis, "Dead, Abode of the" *ABD* 2:101–6; Eugene H. Merrill, "Sheol, netherworld," *NIDOTTE* 4:6; R. L. Harris, "*šᵉʾôl*," *TWOT* 2:892–93; L. Wächter, "*šᵉʾôl*," *TDOT* 14:239–48. See also the extended treatment in Johnston, *Shades of Sheol*. Despite numerous points of commonality, the perspectives, practices, and values surrounding death and the afterlife varied from culture to culture. See the discussion in Cook, "Funerary Practices," 660–83, esp. 662.

12 See the detailed analysis in Hedwige Rouillard, "Rephaim," *DDD* 692–700.

13 This phrase is employed with reference to Abraham (Gen 25:8), Ishmael (Gen 25:17), Isaac (Gen 35:29), Jacob (Gen 49:33), and Aaron and Moses (Num 20:24; 27:13; Deut 32:50).

14 See the important discussion of this point in Johnston, *Shades of Sheol*, 33–35; Routledge, "Death and Afterlife in the Old Testament," 22–39.

15 Kaiser suggests that the motif of "sinking down into watery depths" indicates a belief that Sheol lay "deep beneath the cosmic sea upon which the earth rested like a disc." Kaiser, *Isaiah 13–39*, 35–36. The term "depths" clearly implies water (Exod 15:5; Zech 10:11) and thus "going down into the depths" might imply passing into or through water on one's way to Sheol (Pss 30:3; 63:9; 88:4; Isa 14:15; 38:18; Ezek 31:16). The image of mud and mire is also present in certain texts (Ps 40:2). It should be noted, however, that the imagery of watery depths appears in some, but not all, texts. This might suggest that an earlier view of Sheol as far beneath the earth and less connected to individual family tombs was either a poetic construct or an earlier belief that diminished over time (as Kaiser suggests). See the broader survey of this theme in Johnston, *Shades of Sheol*, 118–24.

16 See the more detailed examination of these names and descriptors in Goldingay, "Death and Afterlife in the Psalms," 61–85.

17 It is noteworthy that, for Pedersen, descent to Sheol meant *both* the loss of the experience of life in this world *and* reunion with predeceased family members. It was therefore a mixture of sorrow and joy; Johannes Pedersen, *Israel: Its Life and Culture*, SFSHJ 28–29 (Atlanta: Scholars Press, 1991), 460–70, esp. 462. See the discussion of this point *infra* and in Suriano, "Sheol." Cf. also Routledge, "Death and Afterlife in the Old Testament," 22–39; Goldingay, "Death and Afterlife in the Psalms," 61–85.

18 Cook, "Funerary Practices," 660–83.

19 See Olyan's excellent treatment in Saul M. Olyan, "Some Neglected Aspects of Israelite Interment Ideology," *JBL* 124 (2005): 601–16. He convincingly

argues for the following typology of burials, from most to least preferred: honorable burial in the family tomb > honorable burial in a substitute for the family tomb > honorable burial in the family tomb of another > other forms of dishonorable burial > abandonment of the corpse on a field.

20 See Samuel Mercer, "The Destiny of the Righteous in Israel," *AThR* 4 (1921): 185–91. Nevertheless, the idea of regions or zones in Sheol is suggested by Cook, "Funerary Practices," 660–83.

21 So, e.g., Alexander, "Old Testament View of Life after Death," 41–46. On resurrection in the HB more broadly, see Jon D. Levenson, *Resurrection and the Restoration of Israel: The Ultimate Victory of the God of Life* (New Haven: Yale University Press, 2006); Ben C. Ollenburger, "If Mortals Die, Will They Live Again?: The Old Testament and Resurrection," *ExAud* 9 (1993): 29–44.

22 This understanding had its roots in intertestamental Judaism and became a widely held position in the early church; see Richard Baukham, "Descent to the Underworld," *ABD* 2:145–60, esp. 154–59. It continues to be held in traditional Catholicism (Catechism of the Catholic Church, pt. 1, sec. 2, art. 5). See also the discussion in J. H. Wright, "Judgment, Divine (in Theology)" *NCE* 8:30-41. The Westminster Catechism (ch. 32), by contrast, appears to view Abraham's bosom as the place where Christian believers abide between the time of their death and the resurrection, and does not relate it to the fate of the OT saints or righteous gentiles.

23 James Barr, *The Garden of Eden and the Hope of Immortality* (Minneapolis: Fortress, 1993), 29.

24 Johnston, *Shades of Sheol*, 81.

25 Cook, "Funerary Practices," 660–83; Levenson, *Resurrection*.

26 Levenson, *Resurrection*, 67–81.

27 Cook, "Funerary Practices," 660–83.

28 Cook, "Funerary Practices," 673–79. Cook is careful to distinguish such memorialization from illicit necromancy (679–80).

29 See the discussions in Alexander, "Old Testament View of Life after Death," 41–46; Ollenburger, "If Mortals Die," 29–44; Routledge, "Death and Afterlife in the Old Testament," 22–39; Suriano, "Sheol."

30 On Isa 26, see Kaiser, *Isaiah 13–39*, 215–20; J. J. M. Roberts, *First Isaiah: A Commentary*, Hermeneia (Minneapolis: Fortress, 2015), 332–33; on Dan 12:1-2, see John J. Collins, *Daniel: A Commentary on the Book of Daniel*, Hermeneia (Minneapolis: Fortress, 1993), 390–99; John E. Goldingay, *Daniel*, WBC 30 (Waco, Tex.: Word, 1989), 308–10.

31 Day suggests that Pss 49 and 73 manifest a belief in the afterlife; John Day, "The Development of Belief in Life after Death in Ancient Israel," in *After the Exile: Essays in Honour of Rex Mason* (Macon, Ga.: Mercer University Press,

1996), 23–57, esp. 53–55. Goldingay explicitly rejects this; see Goldingay, "Death and Afterlife in the Psalms," 78–83.

32 There is, however, still widespread disagreement as to the route through which this concept was arrived at and any earlier HB, Canaanite, or Persian concepts that may have been at play in its development. On this, see Day, "Development of Belief," 23–57; John J. Collins, "Death and the Afterlife," *EDEJ* 524–27.

33 Adherents of positions 3 and 4 above frequently appeal to these texts in support of their positions.

34 The fuller context reads as follows: "I held out my hands all day long to a rebellious people, who walk in a way that is not good, following their own devices; a people who provoke me to my face continually, sacrificing in gardens and offering incense on bricks; *who sit inside tombs*, and spend the night in secret places; who *eat swine's flesh*, with *broth of abominable things* in their vessels; who say, 'Keep to yourself, do not come near me, for I am too holy for you.' These are a smoke in my nostrils, a fire that burns all day long. See, it is written before me: I will not keep silent, but I will repay; I will indeed repay into their laps" (Isa 65:2-6).

35 As noted, while human bones are seen as impure (see Lev 21:11; Num 6:7; 19:11, 13-14, 16; 2 Kgs 23:16; Ezek 44:25), Sheol and its denizens are not said to be so. It would have perhaps seemed odd to view the righteous dead as having themselves become unclean during their passage through death. Thus, the association between death as a generator of uncleanness and the netherworld more broadly may have been held in tension. However, in the understanding of the Israelite community more broadly, it may have been difficult to keep them apart. On the theology of sacredness, cleanness, and uncleanness, see David P. Wright, "Unclean and Clean, Old Testament" *ABD* 6:729–41; Philip Peter Jenson, *Graded Holiness: A Key to the Priestly Conception of the World*, JSOTSup 106 (Sheffield: Sheffield University Press, 1992); Kessler, *Old Testament Theology*, 319–79.

36 Leviticus 19:31 makes a close association between defilement and mediums and wizards who call upon the dead. See Cook, "Funerary Practices," 660–83.

37 See our discussion of Lam 2:10 in ch. 4, and the bibliography there.

38 Goldingay states this in the strongest of terms: "Like the grave, Sheol is a place of silence (31:18[17]; cf., 94:17; 115:17). Among the dead there is no commemorating of God (6:6[5]), no testimony or thanksgiving for what God has done (6:6[5]; 30:10[9]; 88:11[10]), no making known or telling of God's faithfulness or commitment or just acts (30:10[9]; 88:12-13[11-12]), no praising of God (115:17). YHWH does not work wonders there (88:11, 13[10, 12]), so there is nothing to commemorate, give thanks for, make

known, or tell of. The dead are people who are put out of God's mind and are (therefore) cut off from the activity of God's hand (88:6 [5]); in context, Ps. 31:13 [12] also seems to refer to being put out of God's mind and therefore not being people for whom God acts. Death is a land that YHWH puts out of mind (88:13 [12]). It is [t]his collocation of ideas, which explains why there is no praise in Sheol, not the fact that the dead are tainted, to which idea the Psalms do not allude. The dead cannot commemorate and give praise for YHWH's deeds not because they stand outside the orbit of worship but because they stand outside the orbit in which YHWH acts; they therefore have no deeds to commemorate or give praise for." Goldingay, "Death and Afterlife in the Psalms," 64. See the similar conclusions in Routledge, "Death and Afterlife in the Old Testament," 22–39.

39 Cf. also Ecclesiastes. This perspective corresponds well both with those interpretations that view Sheol as the lot of all (position 1, above), or of the ungodly alone.

40 Alexander comments, "Significantly, in their use of the expression 'to be gathered to one's fathers' (or 'people') the biblical writers seem to convey a sense of optimism regarding death." Alexander, "Old Testament View of Life after Death," 45. Cf. also Suriano, "Sheol."

41 See E. Carpenter, "קהל," *NIDOTTE* 3:885–89.

42 Scholars both ancient and modern are divided over the best translation of this phrase. See Bill T. Arnold, *Genesis*, NCamBC (Cambridge: Cambridge University Press, 2009), 38–39; Gordon J. Wenham, *Genesis 1–15*, WBC 1 (Waco, Tex.: Word, 1987), 16–17. As in earlier chapters, spirit is written in lower case to mark the difference between the likely sense here and the fuller NT understanding of the Holy Spirit.

43 To be sure, not all of God's activity on days 1–6 involves speaking. God also "makes" the firmament (1:7), the celestial lights (1:16), the animals (1:25), and human persons (1:27). This "making" appears to be separate from that which is done through speaking. Similarly, God speaks on the seventh day and blesses the Sabbath (Gen 2:3). These, however, are only slight deviations from the more stable pattern of creation through speech followed by rest manifested in silence.

44 Divine rest is a common motif in the ANE. It signifies the full accomplishment of a task and the experience of peace on all sides. It is specifically alluded to in 2 Sam 7:1-2, with reference to David's victories. On this theme more broadly, see Bernard F. Batto, "The Sleeping God: An Ancient Near Eastern Motif of Divine Sovereignty," *Bib* 68 (1987): 153–77.

45 I am thankful to Professor Konrad Schmid of the University of Zurich for this interesting insight.

46 See Jeffrey F. Fager, *Land Tenure and the Biblical Jubilee*, JSOTSup 155 (Sheffield: JSOT Press, 1993); Christopher J. H. Wright, "Sabbatical Year," *ABD* 5:857–61; idem, "What Happened Every Seven Years in Israel: Old Testament Sabbatical Institutions for Land, Debts and Slaves," *EvQ* 56 (1984): 193–201.

47 Abraham Joshua Heschel, *The Sabbath: Its Meaning for Modern Man*, FSG Classics (New York: Farrar, Straus & Giroux, 2005).

48 See Marvin R. Wilson, *Our Father Abraham: Jewish Roots of the Christian Faith* (Grand Rapids: Eerdmans, 1989); Lauren F. Winner, *Mudhouse Sabbath: Seven Ways of Christian Formation Inspired by the Jewishness of Jesus* (Brewster, Mass.: Paraclete Press, 2009).

49 John G. Gammie, *Holiness in Israel*, OBT (Minneapolis: Fortress, 1989); Jenson, *Graded Holiness*. See also Richard E. Friedman, "Tabernacle," *ABD* 6:292–300.

50 Many aspects of the rites involved in the Day of Atonement are hotly disputed and have elicited a huge body of scholarly literature. For a fuller discussion, see Boda, *Severe Mercy*; Roy Gane, *Cult and Character: Purification Offerings, Day of Atonement, and Theodicy* (Winona Lake, Ind.: Eisenbrauns, 2005); Nobuyoshi Kiuchi, *Leviticus*, ApOTC 3 (Nottingham: Apollos, 2007); Jacob Milgrom, "The Priestly Doctrine of Repentance," *RB* 82, no. 2 (1975): 186–205; idem, *Leviticus 1–16: A New Translation with Introduction and Commentary*, AB 3 (New York: Doubleday, 1991); Jay Sklar, *Sin, Impurity, Sacrifice, Atonement: The Priestly Conceptions*, HBM 2 (Sheffield: Sheffield Phoenix, 2005).

51 See esp. Jenson's discussion of the material gradation of the tabernacle, the impact of this gradation upon the senses and its symbolism in *Graded Holiness*, 101–13.

52 Jenson, *Graded Holiness*, 101.

53 See Jenson, *Graded Holiness*, 104–6.

54 In Exod 28:33-35 bells and sound are mentioned in connection with the high priest's presence in the holy place. This, however, does not gainsay its relative silence. Moreover, it should be remembered that the description of the tabernacle found in Exodus–Numbers is highly schematized, and serves to convey theological significance. Exegetes have long noticed this "idealized" nature of the tabernacle descriptions. Thus, the question of how much sound could actually permeate the various layers of the tabernacle is beside the point.

55 There are numerous references to priests carrying out functions such as teaching or delivering rulings (2 Chr 15:3; Hag 2:10-14; Mal 2:7), but our concern here is with the role of the priests in the tabernacle rituals.

56 Yehezkel Kaufmann, *The Religion of Israel: From Its Beginnings to the Babylonian Exile*, trans. M. Greenberg (London: Allen & Unwin, 1960), 303–5 (emphasis mine).

57 See Knohl, "Between Voice and Silence," 17–30; idem, *The Sanctuary of Silence: The Priestly Torah and the Holiness School* (Minneapolis: Fortress, 1995).

58 In contrast to Kaufmann's position, Knohl argues that the silence of the priests reflects the author's desire to depict Yahweh's profound separation from humanity in every regard. See Knohl, *Sanctuary of Silence*, 149.

59 See Carol Meyers, "Temple, Jerusalem," *ABD* 6:350–69. See also Mordechai Cogan, *1 Kings: A New Translation with Commentary*, AB 10 (New York: Doubleday, 2001), 248–53.

60 See Martin J. Mulder, *1 Kings*, vol. 1: *1 Kings 1–11*, trans. John Vriend, HCOT (Leuven: Peeters, 1998), 243–45; Cogan, *1 Kings*, 239–40.

61 See for example, John Gray, *I & II Kings: A Commentary*, 2nd rev. ed., OTL (Philadelphia: Westminster, 1970), 155–56.

62 Roland de Vaux states, "things should be used for the service of God only in their natural condition before they have been interfered with in any way by man." Roland de Vaux, *Ancient Israel: Its Life and Institutions*, trans. J. McHugh (New York: McGraw-Hill, 1961), 2:408. Olyan similarly notes that anything used for sacred purposes must have no defect, and that the use of iron tools on stones would render them "defective" and thus unfit for ritual purposes; see Saul M. Olyan, "Why an Altar of Unfinished Stones? Some Thoughts on Ex 20,25 and Dtn 27,5-6," *ZAW* 108 (1996): 161–71.

63 O'Kennedy comments, "The concept 'profane' in the OT often has merely a moral significance: to offend, to insult (especially when the object is the name of Yahweh, his sanctuary, his holy things, or the Sabbath and festivals). In other instances, profane means degrading." D. F. O'Kennedy, "חלל," *NIDOTTE* 2:143.

64 See, on this point, Thomas B. Dozeman, *Exodus*, ECC (Grand Rapids: Eerdmans, 2009), 513–14, who notes that the altar of earth (Exod 20:24) and uncut stones (20:25) both "idealize nature and the land as a divine gift." He then cites Sprinkle's observation: "Those who build altars must use material from the ground as it left the hand of the creator rather than humanly manufactured material." Joe M. Sprinkle, *The Book of the Covenant: A Literary Approach* (Sheffield: JSOT Press, 1994), 41. He similarly references Olyan's observation that the altar of earth and the requirement of uncut stones serve "to preserve the holiness of the deity's space." Olyan, "Unfinished Stones," 161–71.

65 See esp. here Olyan, "Unfinished Stones," 161–71.

66 A. Graeme Auld, *I & II Kings*, DSB (Philadelphia: Westminster, 1986), 44.

67 See esp. Hossfeld and Zenger, *Psalms 51–100*, 138; Goldingay, *Psalms 42–89*, 272.

68 Tate, *Psalms 51–100*, 139.

69 Goldingay, *Psalms 42–89*, 274–75.

70 Translation by Robert Hayward, *The Jewish Temple: A Non-Biblical Sourcebook* (London: Routledge, 2002), based on the Greek text of A. Pelletier, *Lettre d'Aristée à Philocrate*, SC 89 (Paris: Cerf, 1962).

71 Hayward, *Jewish Temple*, 37.

72 Hayward, *Jewish Temple*, 33.

73 The Qumran community eschewed the Jerusalemite temple, viewing it as corrupt. See the fuller discussion in Hayward, *Jewish Temple*, 26–27. See also Allison, "Silence of Angels," 189–97; Knohl, "Between Voice and Silence," 17–30; Newsom, *Songs of the Sabbath Sacrifice*.

74 This is the translation of Hayward, *Jewish Temple*, 34 (emphasis original). Hayward's translation emphasizes the element of silence. Compare Hayward's translation with that of Newsom, *Songs of the Sabbath Sacrifice*, 306–7, who opts for "stillness" rather than "silence" where both renderings are possible.

7 How Long O Lord?

1 The bibliography on theodicy is immense. For a more general introduction and historical overview of theodicy see John Hick, "Evil, The Problem of," *EncPhil* 3:471–77; Ronald M. Green, "Theodicy," *ER* 13:9111–21. See also the bibliography and references listed by Jason Goroncy, https://jasongoroncy.com/2010/04/22/theodicy-suffering-and-faith-a-bibliography.

2 Marcel Sarot, "Theodicy and Modernity: An Inquiry into the Historicity of Theodicy," in *Theodicy in the World of the Bible*, ed. Antti Laato and Johannes C. de Moor (Leiden: Brill, 2003), 1–26.

3 For discussions of theodicy more specifically focused on the biblical text, see James L. Crenshaw, "Theodicy," *ABD* 6:444–47; idem, "Popular Questioning of the Justice of God in Ancient Israel," *ZAW* 82 (1970): 380–95; idem, *Theodicy in the Old Testament*, IRT 4 (Philadelphia: Fortress, 1983); idem, *Defending God*; Antti Laato and Johannes C. de Moor, eds., *Theodicy in the World of the Bible* (Leiden: Brill, 2003); Paul L. Redditt, "Theodicy," *OEBE*, http://www.oxfordbiblicalstudies.com/article/opr/t430/e335; Jerry L. Sumney, "Suffering," *OEBE*, http://www.oxfordbiblicalstudies.com/article/opr/t430/e330; Balentine, *Prayer in the Hebrew Bible*, 189–98.

4 See Sarot, "Theodicy and Modernity," 1–26.

5 The important concept of prayer as a call to God to act "in character" is stressed by Miller, *They Cried to the Lord*, 126. On the key statements regarding God's character in the HB, see Mark J. Boda, *The Heartbeat of Old Testament Theology: Three Creedal Expressions*, ASBT (Grand Rapids: Baker Academic, 2017).

6 The verb here is **ḥarash*, which carries connotations of refraining or restraining in many instances. See Noll, *Semantics of Silence*, 31–49.

7 See further the important observations in Rachel Muers, "Silence and the Patience of God," *MT* 17 (2001): 85–98.

8 The specific terminology of silence is not used in these texts (as it was in Ps 50:3, 21), but the concept of divine inactivity or silence is nonetheless present.

9 See further Kessler, *Old Testament Theology*, 486–89.

10 The identity of the various parties referred to in Hab 1–2 has been the object of extensive debate. The Babylonians are in view in 1:5-11, but the identity of the "treacherous" and "wicked" elsewhere in the chapter is unclear. For a concise survey, see Julia M. O'Brien, *Nahum, Habakkuk, Zephaniah, Haggai, Zechariah, Malachi*, AOTC (Nashville: Abingdon, 2004), 66–73.

11 See the numerous references and examples in Korpel and de Moor, *Silent God*, 1–54.

12 See, for example, the discussion of slavery and the American Civil War in Kevin Giles, "The Biblical Argument for Slavery: Can the Bible Mislead? A Case Study in Hermeneutics," *EvQ* 66 (1994): 3–17. Giles convincingly demonstrates that the anti-abolitionist forces in the southern United States were driven by the conviction that the Bible condoned slavery, and that any questioning of the institution of slavery was an assault upon the authority of scripture.

13 The literature on negative portrayals of God in the OT is extensive. See, among many others, James L. Crenshaw, *A Whirlpool of Torment: Israelite Traditions of God as an Oppressive Presence*, OBT 12 (Philadelphia: Fortress, 1984); Thomas Römer, *Dark God: Cruelty, Sex, and Violence in the Old Testament* (New York: Paulist, 2013); Eric A. Seibert, *Disturbing Divine Behavior: Troubling Old Testament Images of God* (Minneapolis: Fortress, 2009); Paul Copan, *Is God a Moral Monster? Making Sense of the Old Testament God* (Grand Rapids: Baker, 2011); Crenshaw, "Popular Questioning," 380–95; David Penchansky, *What Rough Beast? Images of God in the Hebrew Bible* (Louisville: Westminster John Knox, 1999). See also the extensive and balanced discussion in Michael Bergmann, Michael J. Murray, and Michael C. Rea, *Divine Evil? The Moral Character of the God of Abraham* (Oxford: Oxford University Press, 2013).

14 See the critiques in Korpel and de Moor, *Silent God*, 53–54.

15 The struggles reflected in the "Confessions of Jeremiah" (11:18-23; 12:1-6; 15:10; 18:18-23; 20:7-13, 14-18) have been understood as a "prophetic drama" rooted in dialogue between the prophet and Yahweh, and involving prophetic complaint and ultimate resolution, cf. Diamond, *Confessions of Jeremiah*. A similar "dramatic" approach was taken by Elie Wiesel, who famously addressed the silence of God in the face of horrendous evil in his three-act play; see Elie Wiesel, *The Trial of God (as It Was Held on February 25, 1649, in Shamgorod):*

A Play in Three Acts (New York: Random House, 1979). On faith as a drama, see the superb essays in Jean Lévêque, *Job ou le drame de la foi: Essais*, LD 216, ed. M. Gilbert and F. Mies (Paris: Cerf, 2007). See also the metaphor of the divine-human interchange as a drama in André Neher, "Speech and Silence in Prophecy," *DlD* 6, no. 2 (1977–1978): 61–73.

16 In order to simplify our discussion, I will not differentiate between individual and collective expressions of protest, despite the attention given to such distinctions in the broader scholarly literature.

17 Jeremiah's "confessions" (see above, n. 15) are replete with such sentiments. See further, Balentine, "Jeremiah, Prophet of Prayer," 331–44; idem, *Prayer in the Hebrew Bible*, 150–68; Diamond, *Confessions of Jeremiah*. Georg Fischer appropriately observes, "No one ought to experience that which Jeremiah went through." Georg Fischer, *Jeremia: Prophet über Völker und Königreiche*, BibG 29 (Leipzig: Evangelische Verlagsanstalt, 2015), 150.

18 See esp. Balentine, "Jeremiah, Prophet of Prayer," 331–44.

19 The traditional understanding of Israel's suffering as arising due to its sin is seen in Ezra 9:6-15 (esp. v. 13), and became a significant strain in certain streams of Jewish thought in later periods. This understanding of suffering is often designated by the term *mippenei ḥata'einu* ("because of our sins"). Significantly, more recent Jewish theological reflection has distanced itself from this explanation, especially with reference to the Holocaust. See Steven T. Katz, "Holocaust, The: Jewish Theological Responses," *ER* 6:4088–95.

20 See the more general treatments in Anson Laytner, *Arguing with God: A Jewish Tradition* (Northvale, N.J.: Aronson, 1990); Jacob B. Agus and Michael J. Graetz, "Good and Evil," *EncJud* 7:752–54.

21 See William S. Morrow, *Protest against God: The Eclipse of a Biblical Tradition*, HBM 4 (Sheffield: Sheffield Phoenix, 2007), 1–3. I am deeply grateful to Professor Morrow for his numerous suggestions regarding this chapter.

22 Morrow, *Protest against God*, 48–51.

23 Morrow, *Protest against God*, 8–11, 49.

24 Craig C. Broyles, *The Conflict of Faith and Experience in the Psalms: A Form-Critical and Theological Study*, JSOTSup 52 (Sheffield: JSOT Press, 1989), 33–53; Morrow, *Protest against God*, 51. There are, however, some differences between these two scholars as to which psalms belong to either category. More specifically, Morrow (49) objects to Broyles' limitation of the term "complaint" to refer to instances of "protest against God." By contrast, Morrow sees any reference to the psalmist's distress as an instance of complaint, but reserves the term "protest" for instances of direct or indirect accusation against God that may be established on verbal and/or form-critical grounds. These include the presence of "negative imperatives" (i.e., "do not," "let not" [49–50], and the use of accusatory questions and accusatory state-

ments [79–81]). Miller, by contrast, is skeptical of an unduly strict bifurcation between plea and protest; Miller, *They Cried to the Lord*, 69–70.

25 Morrow, *Protest against God*, 2.

26 As pointed out by Miller, *They Cried to the Lord*, 68–70. Furthermore, protest (perhaps communicated nonverbally, or by tone of voice) may exist without the explicit use of any of the formal expressions of it. For a form-critical list of such expressions, see Morrow, *Protest against God*, 9–10, 49–65, 76–81; Balentine, *Prayer in the Hebrew Bible*, 146–98.

27 Morrow, *Protest against God*, 53–54. Morrow similarly points to the motifs of ostracism and abandonment by former friends and companions in Mesopotamian parallels (personal communication).

28 For brevity's sake, I will not extend my analogy here to the roles of the community, the officiating priest or poet, or the enemies.

29 On the non-resolution of lament in Jeremiah, see Balentine, *Prayer in the Hebrew Bible*, 150–68.

30 Joseph Blenkinsopp, "Life Expectancy in Ancient Palestine," *SJOT* 11 (1997): 44-55.

31 On Hebrew names relating to infertility and its resolution, see Rainer Albertz and Rüdiger Schmitt, *Family and Household Religion in Ancient Israel and the Levant* (Winona Lake, Ind.: Eisenbrauns, 2012), 269–84.

32 See the excellent discussion in Jon D. Levenson, *Creation and the Persistence of Evil: The Jewish Drama of Divine Omnipotence* (Princeton: Princeton University Press, 1994), 14–50.

33 Morrow, *Protest against God*, 52.

34 To be sure, at times protest is expressed against God's plans (Gen 18:16-33) or that which God has permitted (1 Sam 4:3), but this is another matter.

35 Craigie and Tate comment regarding Ps 17, "The words of the psalmist are not those of a self-righteous person asserting absolute innocence; they emerge in a particular context, and the affirmation of innocence and the prayer for vindication must be interpreted specifically in the context of the unjust charges and attacks set against the psalmist." Peter C. Craigie and Marvin E. Tate, *Psalms 1–50*, 2nd ed., WBC 19 (Nashville: Nelson, 2004), 162.

36 A similar legal framework for prayer existed in Mesopotamia; cf. Shalom E. Holtz, *Praying Legally*, BJS 364 (Providence, R.I.: Brown Judaic Studies, 2019); and in later Judaism, Laytner, *Arguing with God*, xx–xxii.

37 Morrow, *Protest against God*, 47–48, following Oswald Loretz, "Der Altorientalische rechtliche Hintergrund der biblischen 'Klage des Einzelnen': 'Fortschrittsglaube' in der kanonischen Auslegung des Psalters," in *Textarbeit: Studien zu Texten und ihrer Rezeption aus dem Alten Testament und der*

Umwelt Israels, ed. Klaus Kiesow and Thomas Meurer, AOAT 294 (Münster: Ugarit-Verlag, 2002), 285–310.

38 On the "hue and cry," see H. J. Boecker, *Law and the Administration of Justice in the Old Testament and Ancient East*, trans. Jeremy Moiser (London: SPCK, 1980), 49–52.

39 See Murray Joseph Haar, "The God-Israel Relationship in the Community Lament Psalms" (Ph.D. diss., Union Theological Seminary, 1985), 129; Morrow, *Protest against God*, 92–93. Morrow (93) perceptively underlines the fact that, in the psalms of communal lament, Yahweh's responsibility toward Israel is not grounded primarily in the Sinai covenant, but in the fact that "YHWH is thought to have authored Israel's history . . . and created all of its fundamental institutions, including covenant, kingship, and temple." See also Balentine, *Prayer in the Hebrew Bible*, 260–71. Similarly, Balentine draws attention to the "fundamentally dialogical" nature of the divine-human relationship; idem, "Jeremiah, Prophet of Prayer," 331–44.

40 Formal expressions of protest may have been made at an earlier stage in family or tribal settings, perhaps with the aid of a prophet or priest. See Morrow, *Protest against God*, 60–69. On individual and family piety and religion, see esp. Albertz and Schmitt, *Family and Household Religion*.

41 Claus Westermann, *Praise and Lament in the Psalms*, trans. Keith R. Crim and Richard N. Soulen (Atlanta: John Knox, 1981), 165–213.

42 Morrow, *Protest against God*, 58, 73.

43 Broyles presents a detailed analysis of the use of earlier traditions in the understanding and expression of distress over divine unresponsiveness; see Broyles, *Conflict of Faith and Experience*, 111–31.

44 See the fuller treatment in Broyles, *Conflict of Faith and Experience*, 83–109.

45 See further, James Barr, "'Why' in Biblical Hebrew," *JTS* 36 (1985): 1–33; Leann Snow Flesher, Carol J. Dempsey, and Mark J. Boda, eds., *Why? . . . How Long? Studies on Voices of Lamentation Rooted in Biblical Hebrew Poetry*, LHBOTS 552 (London: Bloomsbury, 2015).

46 See most recently Willem A. M. Beuken, *From Servant of YHWH to Being Considerate of the Wretched: The Figure David in the Reading Perspective of Psalms 35–41 MT*, BETL 305 (Leuven: Peeters, 2020).

47 Alphonso Groenewald, "Psalms 69:33-34 in the Light of the Poor in the Psalter as a Whole," *VEccl* 28 (2007): 425–41. See also E. Gerstenberger, "אֶבְיוֹן," *THAT* 1:18–19. More positively, these terms also include connotations of poverty of spirit and dependence on God alone.

48 See the fuller discussion in Morrow, *Protest against God*, 76–105.

49 See esp. Westermann, *Praise and Lament*, 173–88; Morrow, *Protest against God*, 49–51; 79–80.

50 See esp. Barr, "'Why' in Biblical Hebrew," 1–33.

51 Westermann maintains that the questions "why" and "how long" evoke the question of the *absence* of God; Westermann, *Praise and Lament*, 177. Morrow, at times, uses similar language; Morrow, *Protest against God*, 57. However, to be precise, the problem is not divine *absence* (as if God has somehow departed), but rather God's *silence* in the form of inaction or non-intervention.

52 Barr, "'Why' in Biblical Hebrew," 19–22. Westermann also supplies a list of important "why" texts in Pss and Isa 40–55, and a comparison between these two bodies of literature; Westermann, *Praise and Lament*, 176, n. 28.

53 Barr uses the term "hypothetical deprecations" for questions challenging the logic of a certain course of action or attitude; Barr, "'Why' in Biblical Hebrew," 1–33. Westermann comments that the interrogative "why" calls into question divine rejection and depicts an "utterly unnerving and incomprehensible" experience, "like the feeble groping of one who has lost the way in the dark." Westermann, *Praise and Lament*, 176–77.

54 On the use of "where" with reference to divine absence, see Joel S. Burnett, "The Question of Divine Absence in Israelite and West Semitic Religion," *CBQ* 67 (2005): 215–35.

55 Strictly speaking, these are jussives, not imperatives. In point of fact, two different grammatical formulations are used in Hebrew to express negative injunctions. Neither use the imperative *form*. One of these uses the particle *'al* followed by the so-called jussive aspect. This is also known as the "vetitive" construction; Ronald J. Williams and John C. Beckman, *Williams' Hebrew Syntax*, 3rd ed. (Toronto: University of Toronto Press, 2007), ¶402. The second uses the particle *lo'* followed by the imperfect aspect. This is frequently labeled the "prohibitive" use; see idem, *Williams' Hebrew Syntax*, 396. It is the first formulation that is used most frequently in the "negative imperatives" in the context of protest or lament in the Psalms. The difference in meaning between the two constructions is debated. The prohibitive is generally seen as more general or wide-ranging in its scope (e.g., it is used in the Ten Commandments), while the vetitive is understood to be related more specifically to a given situation. For further discussion of this point, see *IBHS* 34.2.1b, n. 6, and the literature cited there. However, since the terminology "negative imperative" is commonly used in the literature, I will employ it in my discussion here.

56 Westermann notes that these are especially prevalent in the psalms of individual lament; Westermann, *Praise and Lament*, 181–82. Morrow suggests that the distribution of such negative imperatives in these psalms indicates the following typology: Psalms of Plea: no allusion to sin, suffering not seen as divine punishment; Psalms of Indirect Protest: recognition of sin and fear of divine punishment; Psalms of Direct Protest: little allusion to

sin, suffering seen as unjust and incomprehensible. See Morrow, *Protest against God*, 72–73.

57 Walter Brueggemann, *Theology of the Old Testament: Testimony, Dispute, Advocacy* (Minneapolis: Fortress, 2005), 375–76. See the fuller analysis in Morrow, *Protest against God*, 49–51. I am deeply indebted to Aejmelaeus for the examples and discussion in this section; see Anneli Aejmelaeus, *The Traditional Prayer in the Psalms*, BZAW 167 (Berlin: de Gruyter, 1986).

58 On the specific situation facing the psalmist, see the discussion in Hossfeld and Zenger, *Psalms 51–100*, 392–94.

59 Aejmelaeus, *Traditional Prayer in the Psalms*, 45–47.

60 See the discussion in Westermann, *Praise and Lament*, 55–64. Westermann states, "Declarative praise . . . serves as one of the motifs which should move God to intervene in the present, desperate situation" (55). Similarly, "In these sentences Israel expresses its relation to God, from whom it expects assistance" (58). The passages cited just above are those set forth by Westermann as examples.

61 Morrow remarks, "The prospect of imminent death [i.e., of those unworthy of such an extreme punishment] is presented in the Psalms of Direct Protest as a condition that God is both ultimately responsible for and yet out of keeping with the divine character. But how is it possible for the divine reality to act so contrary to its own character, to be the agent of chaos and death rather than the deliverer?" Morrow, *Protest against God*, 73.

62 In the Psalms, Yahweh's silence and indifference are most frequently depicted by means of *ḥarash* (Pss 28:1; 35:22; 39:12; 83:1; 109:1). See the full listing of these Psalms of Protest in Morrow, *Protest against God*, 51.

63 Additionally, as noted, the Hebrew jussive may be used, especially with the negative particle *ʾal*. On the use of the imperative and jussive to express urgent need, see *IBHS* 34.4. See also the fuller discussion in Aejmelaeus, *Traditional Prayer in the Psalms*, 11, 15–59.

64 See esp. G. Fischer, "Die Josefgeschichte als Modell für Versöhnung," in *Studies in the Book of Genesis: Literature, Redaction and History*, ed. André Wénin, BETL 155 (Leuven: Peeters, 2001), 243–71.

65 This expression also at times refers to instances where the innocent or righteous are turned away and oppressed in, e.g., Job 24:4; Prov 18:5; Isa 10:2; 29:21; Amos 5:12; Mal 3:5.

66 This verb it is also used to describe animals that are harnessed and forced to work, e.g. in Deut 21:3.

67 On the echoes of the Aaronic benediction in the Psalms of Lament, see Aejmelaeus, *Traditional Prayer in the Psalms*, 24–26. Aejmelaeus discusses the relationship between the petitions within the Priestly Blessing and those within the Psalms, noting especially the allusions to the phrase "make your

face to shine" in Pss 31:16; 80:3, 7, 19; and 119:135. She does not, however, reference the contrast between the Priestly Blessing and the motif of the hidden face of God.

68 Hossfeld and Zenger, *Psalms 51–100*, 196.

69 On which, see Beuken, *From Servant of YHWH to Being Considerate of the Wretched*, 52–53.

70 See Westermann, *Praise and Lament*, 80.

71 Thus Westermann, *Praise and Lament*, 79–80.

72 Hebrew grammar contains some ambiguity, and thus poses something of a challenge here. The Hebrew perfect tense generally refers to past actions but can at times refer to future ones as well. However, in the context of these passages, a past-time translation seems more contextually probable.

73 Morrow notes that this transition is "often missing in biblical texts belonging to the tradition of argumentative prayer." Morrow, *Protest against God*, 11. However, Morrow does include Pss 6, 13, and 22 in the category of Psalms of Direct Protest, thus reinforcing our assertion that such a turn may occur even in the context of protest.

74 Erhard Gerstenberger, *Psalms, Part 1: With an Introduction to Cultic Poetry*, FOTL 14 (Grand Rapids: Eerdmans, 1988), 13; Aubrey R. Johnson, *The Cultic Prophet and Israel's Psalmody* (Cardiff: University of Wales Press, 1979), 241.

75 See esp. Gerstenberger, *Psalms, Part 1*, 13.

76 As Gerstenberger himself acknowledges; idem, *Psalms, Part 1*, 13. Gerstenberger cites Pss 12:5; 35:3; and 91:3-13 as examples of such oracular responses. These examples require some qualification, however. Ps 12:5 does respond to the psalmist's cry over the destruction of the righteous, but it is noteworthy that this complaint is not directly linked to the psalmist's personal suffering. Ps 35:3 is not so much an oracle of salvation but a prayer that such an oracle might be given. Ps 91:3-13 is a generalized promise of divine protection, not an oracular response to a crisis situation.

77 A retrospective reading is proposed by Weiser, *Psalms*, 224–25.

78 John Goldingay, *Psalms*, vol. 1: *Psalms 1–41*, BCOTWP 1 (Grand Rapids: Baker Academic, 2006), 335–36.

79 Westermann, *Praise and Lament*, 79–80.

80 Craigie and Tate, *Psalms 1–50*, 143. See also the similar conclusions in Korpel and de Moor, *Silent God*, 268–72.

81 Samuel E. Balentine, *The Hidden God: The Hiding of the Face of God in the Old Testament*, OxTM (Oxford: Oxford University Press, 1983), 120–24.

82 See Milgrom, *Leviticus 1–16*, 622–25; 35–40. As Milgrom states, "holiness has swallowed impurity; life can defeat death" (638).

83 Neher, "Speech and Silence in Prophecy," 61–73. Neher goes on to affirm that even a more detached, phenomenological approach must acknowledge the place of silence, stating, "[T]he phenomenologist, commentator and historian who are outside objective observers must also not forget that biblical prophetic silence is not something frivolous, a fault in the edition or a spiritual vacuum; they must see it as a rest in a musical score without which it is impossible to understand the whole intention of the composer."

8 Finding God Between Sound and Silence

1 See esp. Edward Noort and Eibert J. C. Tigchelaar, *The Sacrifice of Isaac: The Aqedah (Genesis 22) and Its Interpretations*, TBN 4 (Leiden: Brill, 2002). See similarly the survey of Jewish interpretations in Abraham Sung-Ho Oh, "Early Jewish Understanding of the Sacrifice of Isaac," *KJCS* 93 (2014): 5–24; Jonathan Jacobs, "Willing Obedience with Doubts: Abraham at the Binding of Isaac," *VT* 60 (2010): 546–59.

2 Thus S. R. Driver, *The Book of Genesis*, 2nd ed., WC (London: Methuen, 1926), 216; Gerhard von Rad, *Genesis: A Commentary*, rev. ed., OTL (Philadelphia: Westminster, 1972), 243–45; Ellen F. Davis, "Abraham's Radical Trust," *ChrCent* 133, no. 22 (2016): 29–31; and the majority of interpreters. On the rabbinic material stressing this, see Isaac Kalimi, "'Go, I Beg You, Take Your Beloved Son and Slay Him!': The Binding of Isaac in Rabbinic Literature and Thought," *RRJ* 13, no. 1 (2010): 1–29.

3 Driver, *Book of Genesis*, 221–22.

4 Omri Boehm, *The Binding of Isaac: A Religious Model of Disobedience*, LHBOTS (New York: T&T Clark, 2007); idem, "The Binding of Isaac: An Inner-Biblical Polemic on the Question of 'Disobeying' a Manifestly Illegal Order," *VT* 52 (2002): 1–12; Lippman Bodoff, "The Real Test of the Akedah: Blind Obedience Versus Moral Choice," *Judaism* 42, no. 1 (1993): 71–92. Cf. also the nuanced observations in J. Richard Middleton, "Does God Come to Bury Job or to Praise Him? The Significance of YHWH's Second Speech from the Whirlwind," *StMR* 239 (2017): 1–27.

5 See Konrad Schmid, "Abraham's Sacrifice: Gerhard Von Rad's Interpretation of Genesis 22," *Int* 62, no. 3 (2008): 268–76. It is beyond the scope of the present study to attempt a full evaluation of these approaches.

6 Speiser, *Genesis*, 164–65.

7 Nahum M. Sarna, *Genesis: The Traditional Hebrew Text with New JPS Translation*, JPSTC (Philadelphia: Jewish Publication Society, 1989), 152. Von Rad, too, sees the silence as oppressive; von Rad, *Genesis*, 241.

8 The verbal form contains a suffixed *-na'*. This can simply be a means of designating an imperative or indicating politeness. Contrast *IBHS* 34.7 and Stephen A. Kaufman, "An Emphatic Plea for Please," *Maarav* 7 (1991): 195–98.

9 Thus Jacobs, "Willing Obedience," 546–59.

10 On this interesting question see further Jacobs, "Willing Obedience," 552–55, esp. n. 16.

11 Wenham describes the passage as enigmatically ambiguous, and suggests three major possibilities: Abraham is dissimulating to disguise his true purpose, Abraham does not intend to sacrifice Isaac, or Abraham is affirming his faith. See Gordon J. Wenham, *Genesis 16–50*, WBC 2 (Dallas: Word, 1994), 108–9.

12 Ska observes, "Isaac discovers the 'missing element'" (Fr. *l'objet manquant*); Jean Louis Ska, "Gn 22, 1-19: Essai sur les niveaux de lecture," *Bib* 69 (1988): 324–39.

13 Ska stresses the importance of "narrative speed" in the description of events (see *"Our Fathers Have Told Us,"* 7–15), noting that the slowing of the narrative speed in a text indicates heightened stress and importance.

14 Fr. *cloisons étanches*; see Ska, "Gn 22, 1-19," 324–39.

15 Cf. Middleton, "Does God Come to Bury Job or to Praise Him?" 1–27.

16 See, for example, Schmid, "Abraham's Sacrifice," 268–76, who suggests a reading of Gen 22 against the backdrop of the sociopolitical realities of the Persian period.

17 On the various approaches to the incorporation of the Elijah narratives into Kings, see James K. Mead, "Elijah," *DOTHB* 249–54. Bernard P. Robinson, "Elijah at Horeb, 1 Kings 19:1-18: A Coherent Narrative?" *RB* 98 (1991): 513–36; Marvin A. Sweeney, *I & II Kings: A Commentary*, OTL (Louisville: Westminster John Knox, 2007), 210; and contrast Baruch Halpern and David S. Vanderhooft, "The Editions of Kings in the 7th–6th Centuries B.C.E.," *HUCA* 62 (1991): 179–244; and Steven L. McKenzie, *The Trouble with Kings: The Composition of the Book of Kings in the Deuteronomistic History*, VTSup 42 (Leiden: Brill, 1991), 98. The details of the debate need not detain us here. It is sufficient to point out that the figure of Elijah stands in close conformity to the ideals of Deuteronomy–2 Kings.

18 As Carlson notes, the principal theme of 1 Kgs 17-19 is Yahweh versus Baal. See Rolf A. Carlson, "Élie à l'Horeb," *VT* 19 (1969): 416–39.

19 See further W. Hermann, "Baal," *DDD* 132–39.

20 This is certainly the understanding in traditional Jewish theological reflection. See, for example, Jerome T. Walsh, "Elijah (Person)," *ABD* 2:463–66. It is also reflected in the intertestamental literature (Sir 48:1, 4, 12; 1 Macc 2:58) and the NT (Matt 11:14; 16:14; 17:3-4, 17-27; 24:47-49; Luke 1:17; 9:8), among others.

21 Walsh, *ABD* 2:465.

22 Thus, among many others, Lissa M. Wray Beal, *1 & 2 Kings*, ApOTC 9 (Nottingham: Apollos, 2014), 256–58.

23 Robinson, "Elijah at Horeb," 513–36.

24 Tchavdar Hadjiev, "Elijah's Alleged Megalomania: Reading Strategies for Composite Texts, with 1 Kings 19 as an Example," *JSOT* 39 (2015): 433–49, provides further examples. See also Jerome T. Walsh, *1 Kings*, BeOl (Collegeville, Minn.: Liturgical Press, 1996), 264–82, for an example of this approach. For Walsh, the narrator depicts Elijah as "fanatic in his Yahwism yet focused on himself, scrupulously obedient and stubbornly resistant, heroic and heroically flawed" (282). Robinson similarly views the drift of the passage is intended to pass judgment on Elijah for his "egotism . . . [and preoccupation with] his image as a prophet of YHWH; a *propheta gloriosus*." Robinson, "Elijah at Horeb," 513–36, here p. 528. Hens-Piazza views him as "participating in religious conflict with an eye to his personal agenda" and ultimately "inflating [his] own importance" thus "confounding [his] relationship with God" and eroding "the mutuality of their cause." Gina Hens-Piazza, *1–2 Kings*, AOTC (Nashville: Abingdon, 2006), 194–95.

25 This point is made with great cogency in Hadjiev, "Elijah's Alleged Megalomania," 433–49.

26 See above, nn. 21, 22.

27 See the persuasive arguments in Hadjiev, "Elijah's Alleged Megalomania," 433–49.

28 I leave aside the suggestion of Lust that the phrase be translated "a roaring and thunderous voice"; see J. Lust, "Gentle Breeze or a Roaring Thunderous Sound: Elijah at Horeb, 1 Kings 19:12," *VT* 25, no. 1 (1975): 110–15. See the critique of Lust's view in Robinson, "Elijah at Horeb," 513–36.

29 Note the similarity to the imagery regarding the silence of the angels in the Songs of the Sabbath Sacrifice in the DSS; Allison, "Silence of Angels," 189–97.

30 Sweeney, *I & II Kings*, 219; Cogan, *1 Kings*, 449.

31 Wray Beal, *1 & 2 Kings*, 249.

32 Walsh, *1 Kings*, 276.

33 See *HALOT*, s.v. "דממה," and more broadly, Noll, *Semantics of Silence*, 117–232.

34 Eidevall, "Sounds of Silence," 159–74. As Eidevall points out, a hard distinction between silence and stillness is difficult to maintain, thus a degree of fluidity should be implied.

35 The context of a night vision seems to render the alternative proposal "a thunderous voice" less probable; cf. David J. A. Clines, *Job 1–20*, WBC 17 (Dallas: Word, 1989), 112.

36 Thus Sweeney's translation, "a sound of faint silence"; Sweeney, *I & II Kings*, 219. See also his discussion of the renderings in Targum Jonathan and the LXX. Robinson has provided an extensive survey of suggestions regarding

the significance of the *qol demamah daqqah*, both ancient and modern. He points out that the "still small voice" has been understood as the voice of conscience, a reference to meditative prayer, the prophetic word, as affirming the priority of quiet love and piety, or the ultimate inscrutability of God, to name but a few proposals. See Robinson, "Elijah at Horeb," 513–36. His own opinion is that *qol demamah daqqah* on Horeb is meant to remind Elijah of the privilege of hearing Yahweh's words and of his duty as a prophet to attend to and fulfill them.

37 Walsh suggests that "The numinous power of the image lies precisely in our inability to grasp it. . . . As climax to the theophanic procession, it puts the divine not only beyond all-natural phenomena but also beyond all human ability to comprehend it." Walsh, *1 Kings*, 276.

38 Reading *qol* as a construct, *demamah* as the fem. absolute noun "silence," and *daqqah* as the fem. adj. form of *daq* (fine, thin) from the root **daqaq* (to crush, pulverize, grind into dust).

39 This distinction is maintained by the majority of exegetes; thus Walsh, *1 Kings*, 276.

40 See Sweeney, *I and II Kings*, 232–33.

41 There is no verb in the Hebrew of this clause. It reads literally, "The word of Yahweh to Elijah."

42 Similar formulations are used for the reception of the prophetic word in numerous passages (Gen 15:1; 2 Sam 7:4; 1 Kgs 6:11; Isa 38:4; Jer 1:4; Ezek 3:16; Jonah 1:1; Hag 1:1).

43 Walsh calls attention to the parallelism between v. 9 and v. 13, and the use of *qol* in v. 13, but does not comment on the transition from *dabar* to *qol*. This transition is noted by Carmen Yebra Rovira, "Dios y Elías, su profeta, en 1 Reyes 19," *EstBib* 64, no. 3–4 (2006): 447–71, without elaboration on the significance of the change.

44 See the discussions in Joseph Blenkinsopp, "Structure and Meaning in the Sinai-Horeb Narrative (Exodus 19–34)," in *A Biblical Itinerary: In Search of Method, Form and Content*, ed. Eugene E. Carpenter, JSOTSup 240 (Sheffield: Sheffield Academic, 1997), 109–25; Mark S. Smith, "The Literary Arrangement of the Priestly Redaction of Exodus: A Preliminary Investigation," *CBQ* 58 (1996): 25–50. My discussion below follows the broad outline of the narrative in Exod and Deut without entering into points of detail.

45 See the outlines in Dozeman, *Exodus*, 697–98.

46 Interestingly, two elements of this passage contrast significantly with the theophany in 1 Kgs 19:11-12: first, the divine voice is portrayed as coming directly "out of the midst of the fire" (*mitok ha'esh*); second, the divine speech from the fire is described as a "sound of words" (*qol devarim*).

47 The events of Exod 32–34 are closely paralleled in Deut 9:7–10:11.

48 Robinson observes: "The theophany that he experiences on Horeb while having Mosaic overtones owes its climax more to the Ex 33–34 than to the Ex 19 tradition." Robinson, "Elijah at Horeb," 527.

49 Carlson, "Élie," 416–39.

50 Carlson, "Élie," 435. Carlson sees the gentler interaction with human persons as reflecting "intimacy and familiarity."

51 As noted above, certain scholars view this reticence as a failure to fulfil the divine command. This, however, reads too much into this detail.

52 Carlson, "Élie," 425, esp. n. 2.

53 See the closer discussion of the order of events presupposed in the passage in Max Rogland, "Elijah and the 'Voice' at Horeb (1 Kings 19): Narrative Sequence in the Masoretic Text and Josephus," *VT* 62, no. 1 (2012): 88–94. There is a significant translational difficulty here regarding the time when the Lord will pass by. As Robinson points out, despite the fact that many translations view 19:11b as an event already in the past (thus, NRSV: "the Lord passed by"), the Hebrew here could equally read as a prediction of that which was soon to occur ("the Lord *will* pass by"); Robinson, "Elijah at Horeb," 513–36.

54 Wray Beal, *1 & 2 Kings*, 253.

55 Some see the fact that Elijah is said to have carried out only certain aspects of his commission as an implicit critique of him. However, this is not convincing in light of the approbation of his ministry denoted in 2 Kgs 2:9-12; cf. the discussion in Hadjiev, "Elijah's Alleged Megalomania," 433–49.

56 The bibliography here is immense. See the extensive discussions and bibliographies in Manfred Oeming and Konrad Schmid, *Job's Journey: Stations of Suffering*, CSHebB 7 (Winona Lake, Ind.: Eisenbrauns, 2015); Carol A. Newsom, "Considering Job," *CurBR* 1 (1993): 87–118; idem, "Re-Considering Job," *CurBR* 5, no. 2 (2007): 155–82; idem, *The Book of Job: A Contest of Moral Imaginations* (Oxford: Oxford University Press, 2003); Clines, *Job 1–20*; idem, *Job 38–42*, WBC 18b (Nashville: Nelson, 2011), 1443–72.

57 Newsom, "Re-Considering Job," 155–82.

58 See Oeming and Schmid, *Job's Journey*, 74. Although coauthored by Schmid, only ch. 1 is attributed to him. Accordingly, I will refer to Oeming as the author of passages taken from the remaining chapters. See also Michael V. Fox, "God's Answer and Job's Response," *Bib* 94, no. 1 (2013): 1–23; John H. Walton, *Job*, NIVAC (Grand Rapids: Zondervan, 2012), 19–23.

59 Newsom, "Re-Considering Job," 157, states, "The most common approach [to Job] makes the dialogical nature of the book the fundamental hermeneutical key." Newsom traces this dialogue as it relates to the various characters in the book, the various sections of the book, and the book and its readers.

60 There is some asymmetry here. In the first two cycles, Eliphaz, Bildad, and Zophar speak in turn, and Job responds to each of them immediately afterwards (4:1–21:34). The third cycle (22:1–27:23) lacks a response from Zophar.

61 See also Clines, *Job 1–20*, xxxvi–xxxvii; Jean Lévêque, *Job et son Dieu: Essai d'exégèse et de théologie biblique* (Paris: Gabalda, 1970), 2:826. Clines provides a detailed breakdown of the speakers in the dialogues. Cf. John E. Hartley, *The Book of Job*, NICOT (Grand Rapids: Eerdmans, 1988), 36–37.

62 Space does not permit a treatment of the hymn to wisdom and the Elihu speeches.

63 Clines, *Job 1–20*, 10.

64 A careful distinction must be made between this character and the Satan of the intertestamental literature and the NT. Here the term is not a proper name. It is prefaced by the definite article, and thus more likely indicates a *role*. The role of the Adversary in Job is to place pressure on both Yahweh and Job, and thereby determine whether Job's loyalty to Yahweh arose principally out of self-interest. See Lévêque, *Job ou le drame de la foi*, 258–59. Put another way, the text introduces the Adversary as a means of revealing whether Job's fidelity to Yahweh depends on the benefits he receives. See further, Walton, *Job*, 75–86, idem, "Satan," *DOTWis* 714–17; C. Breytenbach and P. Day, "Satan," *DDD* 726–32.

65 This representation should not be termed a "wager" as no stakes are mentioned; Hartley, *Book of Job*, 74; Francis I. Andersen, *Job: An Introduction and Commentary*, TOTC (Downers Grove, Ill.: InterVarsity, 1976), 84–85.

66 On Job's fear over his children's secret misdeed, see Clines, *Job 1–20*, 15–16; Walton, *Job*, 61–62.

67 On the characterization of Job's wife and the sense of her words, see Hartley, *Book of Job*, 83–84; Clines, *Job 1–20*, 50–53; Oeming and Schmid, *Job's Journey*, 31–34.

68 Oeming and Schmid, *Job's Journey*, 32–33.

69 Lévêque, *Job ou le drame de la foi*, 260. Andersen sees in her suggestion "an indirect way of committing suicide"; Andersen, *Job*, 92.

70 Middleton views Job's silence in ch. 3 and in 40:3-5 as something that Job himself rejects in chs. 3–37 and in 42:6, and from which Yahweh himself had sought to move Job away in 40:6–41:34; see Middleton, "Does God Come to Bury Job or to Praise Him?" 1–27, esp. 19.

71 Jürgen Ebach, "Silence in the Bible: A Short Introduction and Seven Miniatures," *Concilium* 2015, no. 5 (2015): 104–13.

72 Ger. "*gescheiterte Dialogue*"; see Ebach, *Beredtes Schweigen*, 73. See the similar observations in Abigail Pelham, "Job's Crisis of Language: Power and

Powerlessness in Job's Oaths," *JSOT* 36, no. 3 (2012): 333–54. She describes the dialogues between Job and his friends as a "shouting match."

73 Compare the older Fr. idiom "*un dialogue de sourdes*." The phrase refers to an exchange where the speakers are so obstinate that they are incapable of hearing one another and consequently cannot engage in meaningful dialogue.

74 See Pelham, "Job's Crisis of Language," 333–54.

75 Hartley, *Book of Job*, 406. Cf. also idem, "From Lament to Oath: A Study of Progression in the Speeches of Job," in *The Book of Job*, ed. W. A. M. Beuken, BETL 114 (Leuven: Peeters, 1994), 79–100; Pelham, "Job's Crisis of Language," 333–54; Sheldon H. Blank, "The Curse, Blasphemy, the Spell, and the Oath," *HUCA* 23 (1951): 73–95; idem, "An Effective Literary Device in Job 31," *JJS* 2, no. 2 (1951): 105–7.

76 Commentators assess the meaning and implications of Job's silence at this point in various ways, the details of which cannot be discussed here. See Hartley, *Book of Job*, 426, for a more positive assessment. Others see 31:40 as a simple editorial comment.

77 See the extensive discussion in Oeming and Schmid, *Job's Journey*, 85–96.

78 See the surveys and discussion in Clines, *Job 38–42*, 1134–36; 1202–3; Lévêque, *Job ou le drame de la foi*, 131–55; Middleton, "Does God Come to Bury Job or to Praise Him?" 1–27; Newsom, *Book of Job*; idem, "Re-Considering Job," 155–82.

79 Most commentators view Yahweh as dissatisfied with Job's first response. This then provides the rationale for the second speech.

80 Newsom, *Book of Job*, 235; T. C. Ham, "The Gentle Voice of God in Job 38," *JBL* 132, no. 3 (2013): 527–41.

81 See the examples in Ham, "Gentle Voice of God in Job 38," 527–41.

82 Thus B. Lynne Newell, "Job: Repentant or Rebellious," *WTJ* 46, no. 2 (1984): 298–316; Hartley, *Book of Job*, 515–17.

83 Ham, "Gentle Voice of God in Job 38," 527–41; Middleton, "Does God Come to Bury Job or to Praise Him?" 1–27.

84 Lévêque, *Job ou le drame de la foi*, 149.

85 Following the summary in Lévêque, *Job ou le drame de la foi*, 139–40.

86 See Newell, "Job," 298–316; Couroyer, "'Main Sur La Bouche,'" 197–209; Gruber, *Aspects of Nonverbal Communication*, 2:289–90.

87 Andersen, *Job*, 285; Clines, *Job 38–42*, 1139–40.

88 H. H. Rowley, *Job*, NCB (London: Nelson, 1970), 254.

89 Lévêque, *Job ou le drame de la foi*, 151.

90 Walton, *Job*, 404–5.

91 Middleton, "Does God Come to Bury Job or to Praise Him?" 1–27, here p. 15.

92 See Fox, "God's Answer and Job's Response," 1–23.

93 See Edward Ho, "In the Eyes of the Beholder: Unmarked Attibuted Quotations in Job," *JBL* 128, no. 4 (2009): 703–15; Troy W. Martin, "Concluding the

Book of Job and YHWH: Reading Job from the End to the Beginning," *JBL* 137, no. 2 (2018): 299–318.

94 The meaning of the contrast between hearing and seeing in v. 5 is debated. Numerous interpreters ancient and modern see here a movement into a more direct and intimate experience of God; thus Rowley, *Job*, 266. Such an approach is rejected in Clines, *Job 38–42*, 1217–18.

95 Clines, *Job 38–42*, 1205–11. He opts for the translation: "So I submit, and accept consolation for my dust and ashes." See also Martin, "Concluding the Book of Job and YHWH," 299–318. Martin sees vv. 2-6 as entirely the words of Job, as do Édouard Dhorme, *A Commentary on the Book of Job* (London: Nelson, 1967), 645, cited in Martin, "Concluding the Book of Job and YHWH," 307, and Ho, "In the Eyes of the Beholder," 711–14.

96 William S. Morrow, "Consolation, Rejection, and Repentance in Job 42:6," *JBL* 105, no. 2 (1986): 211–25, also presents a review of potential renderings and an argument for intentional ambiguity. See also the discussion in Newsom, "Re-Considering Job," 173–82.

97 See the fuller discussion in Oeming and Schmid, *Job's Journey*, 83, n. 49; Fox, "God's Answer and Job's Response," 1–23.

98 Ebach, *Beredtes Schweigen*, 79–80. Ebach recognizes that divine speech appears in Chronicles, but maintains that such instances are citations from 1 and 2 Samuel. He concludes that not only has Yahweh reduced Job to silence, Job has done the same to God. The order of the books in the HB differs from that of the Christian OT. The Hebrew order is the older of the two, and the one that Jesus assumed when he spoke of all the martyrs from Abel to Zechariah (Matt 23:35; Luke 11:51). The Zechariah mentioned here appears in 2 Chr 24:20-21. Second Chronicles is the last book of the HB.

99 Oeming surveys the various ways scholars have sought to address this difficulty in Oeming and Schmid, *Job's Journey*, 84–96.

100 Thus Andrew Prideaux, "Job 42:7-17, and the God of the Happy Ending," *RTR* 71, no. 3 (2012): 170–84. This perspective is subjected to extensive analysis in Kenneth Numfor Ngwa, *The Hermeneutics of the "Happy" Ending in Job 42:7-17*, BZAW 354 (Berlin: de Gruyter, 2005).

101 See Jeremy Schipper, "Healing and Silence in the Epilogue of Job," *WW* 30, no. 1 (2010): 16–22.

102 Oeming and Schmid, *Job's Journey*, 96–99; Manfred Oeming, "'Ihr habt nicht recht von mir geredet wie mein Knecht Hiob': Gottes Schlusswort als Schlüssel zur Interpretation des Hiobbuchs und als kritische Anfrage an die moderne Theologie," *EvT* 60, no. 2 (2000): 103–16.

103 Oeming and Schmid, *Job's Journey*, 96–99.

104 Oeming and Schmid, *Job's Journey*, 98.

105 Middleton, "Does God Come to Bury Job or to Praise Him?" 19–20.

106 Ebach, *Beredtes Schweigen*, 79.

107 Lévêque, *Job ou le drame de la foi*, 92 (emphasis mine).

BIBLIOGRAPHY

Adeney, Frances S. "How I, a Christian, Have Learned from Buddhist Practice, or 'The Frog Sat on the Lily Pond, Not Waiting.'" In *The Gospel among Religions: Christian Ministry, Theology, and Spirituality in a Global Society*, edited by David R. Brockman and Ruben L. F. Habito, 225–28. Maryknoll, N.Y.: Orbis Books, 2010.

Aejmelaeus, Anneli. *The Traditional Prayer in the Psalms*. BZAW 167. Berlin: de Gruyter, 1986.

Albertz, Rainer. *Israel in Exile: The History and Literature of the Sixth Century BCE*. Translated by David Green. SBLStBL 3. Atlanta: Society of Biblical Literature, 2003.

Albertz, Rainer, and Rüdiger Schmitt. *Family and Household Religion in Ancient Israel and the Levant*. Winona Lake, Ind.: Eisenbrauns, 2012.

Alexander, T. Desmond. "The Old Testament View of Life after Death." *Them* 11 (1986): 41–46.

———. "The Psalms and the Afterlife." *IBS* 9 (1987): 2–17.

Allison, Dale C., Jr. "The Silence of Angels: Reflections on the Songs of the Sabbath Sacrifice." *RevQ* 13 (1988): 189–97.

Alter, Robert. *The Art of Biblical Narrative*. New York: Basic Books, 1981.

Andersen, Francis I. *Habakkuk: A New Translation with Introduction and Commentary*. AB 25. New Haven: Yale University Press, 2007.

———. *Job*. TOTC. Downers Grove, Ill.: InterVarsity, 1976.

Andersen, Francis I., and David Noel Freedman. *Amos: A New Translation with Introduction and Commentary*. AB 24a. New York: Doubleday, 1989.

Anderson, Gary A. *A Time to Mourn, a Time to Dance: The Expression of Grief and Joy in Israelite Religion*. University Park: Pennsylvania State University Press, 1991.

Arnold, Bill T. *Genesis*. NCamBC. Cambridge: Cambridge University Press, 2009.

Arnold, Bill T., and H. G. M. Williamson, eds. *Dictionary of the Old Testament: Historical Books*. Downers Grove, Ill.: InterVarsity, 2005.

Auld, A. Graeme. *I & II Kings*. DSB. Philadelphia: Westminster, 1986.

Báez, Silvio José. *Cuando todo calla: El silencio en la Biblia*. Madrid: Editorial de Espiritualidad, 2009.

———. *Tiempo de callar y tiempo de hablar: El silencio en la Biblia Hebrea*. Rome: Teresianum, 2000.

Bailey, Lloyd R. *Biblical Perspectives on Death*. OBT. Minneapolis: Fortress, 1979.

Balentine, Samuel E. *The Hidden God: The Hiding of the Face of God in the Old Testament*. OxTM. Oxford: Oxford University Press, 1983.

———. "Jeremiah, Prophet of Prayer." *RevExp* 78, no. 3 (1981): 331–44.

———. *Prayer in the Hebrew Bible: The Drama of Divine-Human Dialogue*. OBT. Minneapolis: Fortress, 1993.

———. "The Prophet as Intercessor: A Reassessment." *JBL* 103, no. 2 (1984): 161–73.

Bar-Efrat, Shimeon. *Narrative Art in the Bible*. JSOTSup 70. Sheffield: Sheffield Academic, 1997.

Barr, James. *The Garden of Eden and the Hope of Immortality*. Minneapolis: Fortress, 1993.

———. "'Why' in Biblical Hebrew." *JTS* 36 (1985): 1–33.

Barthélemy, Dominique. *Critique textuelle de l'Ancien Testament: Tome 4, Psaumes*. OBO 50, no. 4. Göttingen: Vandenhoeck & Ruprecht, 2005.

Barton, John. *Isaiah 1–39*. OTG. Sheffield: Sheffield Academic, 1995.

Batto, Bernard F. "The Sleeping God: An Ancient Near Eastern Motif of Divine Sovereignty." *Bib* 68 (1987): 153–77.

Ben Zvi, Ehud. *A Historical-Critical Study of the Book of Zephaniah*. BZAW 198. Berlin: de Gruyter, 1991.

———. "Inclusion in and Exclusion from 'Israel' as Conveyed by the Term 'Israel' in Post-Monarchic Biblical Texts." In *The Pitcher Is Broken*, edited by Steven W. Holloway and Lowell K. Handy, 95–149. JSOTSup 190. Sheffield: JSOT Press, 1995.

———. "Who Wrote the Speech of Rabshakeh and When?" *JBL* 109 (1990): 79–92.

Bergmann, Michael, Michael J. Murray, and Michael C. Rea. *Divine Evil? The Moral Character of the God of Abraham*. Oxford: Oxford University Press, 2013.

Berlin, Adele. *Lamentations: A Commentary*. OTL. Louisville: Westminster John Knox, 2002.

———. *Poetics and Interpretation of Biblical Narrative*. Winona Lake, Ind.: Eisenbrauns, 1994.

———. *Zephaniah*. AB 25a. New York: Doubleday, 1994.

Beuken, Willem A. M. *From Servant of YHWH to Being Considerate of the Wretched: The Figure David in the Reading Perspective of Psalms 35–41 MT*. BETL 305. Leuven: Peeters, 2020.

Beyer, Bryan. *Encountering the Book of Isaiah: A Historical and Theological Survey*. EBS. Grand Rapids: Baker Academic, 2007.

Birch, Bruce C. *The Rise of the Israelite Monarchy: The Growth and Development of 1 Samuel 7–15*. SBLDS 27. Missoula, Mont.: Society of Biblical Literature, 1976.

Blank, Sheldon H. "The Curse, Blasphemy, the Spell, and the Oath." *HUCA* 23 (1951): 73–95.

———. "An Effective Literary Device in Job 31." *JJS* 2, no. 2 (1951): 105–7.

Blenkinsopp, Joseph. "Life Expectancy in Ancient Palestine." *SJOT* 11 (1997): 44–55.

———. "Structure and Meaning in the Sinai-Horeb Narrative (Exodus 19–34)." In *A Biblical Itinerary: In Search of Method, Form and Content*, edited by Eugene E. Carpenter, 109–25. JSOTSup 240. Sheffield: Sheffield Academic, 1997.

Bloch-Smith, Elizabeth. "Life in Judah from the Perspective of the Dead." *NEA* 65 (2002): 120–30.

Boda, Mark J. *The Book of Zechariah*. NICOT. Grand Rapids: Eerdmans, 2016.

———. "Confession as Theological Expression: Ideological Origins of Penitential Prayer." In *Seeking the Favor of God, Volume 1: The Origins of Penitential Prayer in Second Temple Judaism*, edited by Mark J. Boda, Daniel K. Falk, and Rodney A. Werline, 21–50. Atlanta: Society of Biblical Literature, 2006.

———. "Form Criticism in Transition: Penitential Prayer and Lament, Sitz Im Leben and Form." In *Seeking the Favor of God, Volume 1: The Origins of Penitential Prayer in Second Temple Judaism*, edited by Mark J. Boda, Daniel K. Falk, and Rodney A. Werline, 181–92. Atlanta: Society of Biblical Literature, 2006.

———. "From Complaint to Contrition: Peering through the Liturgical Window of Jer 14,1–15,4." *ZAW* 113 (2001): 186–97.

———. *The Heartbeat of Old Testament Theology: Three Creedal Expressions*. ASBT. Grand Rapids: Baker Academic, 2017.

———. "The Priceless Gain of Penitence: From Communal Lament to Penitential Prayer in the 'Exilic' Liturgy of Israel." In *Lamentations in Ancient and Contemporary Cultural Contexts*, edited by Nancy C. Lee and Carleen Mandolfo, 81–101. Symposium Series. Atlanta: Society of Biblical Literature, 2008.

———. "Renewal in Heart, Word, and Deed: Repentance in the Torah." In *Repentance in Christian Theology*, edited by Mark J. Boda and Gordon T. Smith, 3–24. Collegeville, Minn.: Liturgical Press, 2006.

———. *A Severe Mercy: Sin and Its Remedy in the Old Testament*. Siphrut 1. Winona Lake, Ind.: Eisenbrauns, 2010.

Boda, Mark J., and J. Gordon McConville, eds. *Dictionary of the Old Testament: Prophets*. Downers Grove, Ill.: IVP Academic, 2012.

Bodner, Keith. *1 Samuel: A Narrative Commentary*. HBM 19. Sheffield: Sheffield Phoenix, 2008.

Bodoff, Lippman. "The Real Test of the Akedah: Blind Obedience Versus Moral Choice." *Judaism* 42, no. 1 (1993): 71–92.

Boecker, H. J. *Law and the Administration of Justice in the Old Testament and Ancient East*. Translated by Jeremy Moiser. London: SPCK, 1980.

Boehm, Omri. *The Binding of Isaac: A Religious Model of Disobedience*. LHBOTS. New York: T&T Clark, 2007.

———. "The Binding of Isaac: An Inner-Biblical Polemic on the Question of 'Disobeying' a Manifestly Illegal Order." *VT* 52 (2002): 1–12.

Borchert, Donald M., ed. *Encyclopedia of Philosophy*. 2nd ed. 10 vols. Detroit: Macmillan Reference, 2006.

Borowski, Oded. *Every Living Thing: Daily Use of Animals in Ancient Israel*. Walnut Creek, Calif.: AltaMira Press, 1998.

Bosma, Carl J. "Discerning the Voices in the Psalms: A Discussion of Two Problems in Psalmic Interpretation, Part 2." *CTJ* 44 (2009): 127–70.

Botterweck, G. Johannes, and Helmer Ringgren, eds. *Theological Dictionary of the Old Testament*. Translated by John T. Willis, et. al. 8 vols. Grand Rapids: Eerdmans, 1974–2006.

Brawley, Robert L., ed. *The Oxford Encyclopedia of the Bible and Ethics*. Oxford: Oxford University Press, 2014.

Broman, Per F. "Music, Sound, and Silence in the Films of Ingmar Bergman." In *Music, Sound, and Filmmakers: Sonic Style in Cinema*, edited by James Wierzbicki, 15–31. London: Routledge, 2012.

Brown, Francis, S. R. Driver, and Charles A. Briggs. *A Hebrew and English Lexicon of the Old Testament*. Oxford: Clarendon, 1907.

Brooks, Dianne K. "In Search of Self: Experiences of a Postlingually Deaf African-American." In *Cultural and Language Diversity and the Deaf Experience*, edited by Ila Parasnis, 246–57. Cambridge: Cambridge University Press, 1996.

Broyles, Craig C. *The Conflict of Faith and Experience in the Psalms: A Form-Critical and Theological Study*. JSOTSup 52. Sheffield: JSOT Press, 1989.

Brueggemann, Walter. *Interrupting Silence: God's Command to Speak Out*. London: Hodder & Stoughton, 2019.

———. *Theology of the Old Testament: Testimony, Dispute, Advocacy*. Minneapolis: Fortress, 2005.

Burnett, Joel S. "The Question of Divine Absence in Israelite and West Semitic Religion." *CBQ* 67 (2005): 215–35.

Buttrick, George A., ed. *The Interpreter's Dictionary of the Bible*. 4 vols. New York: Abingdon, 1962.

Calvin, Jean. *Psalms of David*, vol 2. Oxford: Talboys, 1839. https://ccel.org/ccel/calvin/calcom09/calcom09.i.html.

Cangh, Jean-Marie van. "Temps et eschatologie dans l'Ancien Testament." In *Temps et eschatologie: Données bibliques et problématiques contemporaines*, edited by Jean-Louis Leuba, 17–38. Paris: Cerf, 1994.

Carlson, Rolf A. "Élie à l'Horeb." *VT* 19 (1969): 416–39.

Carson, Rachel Louise. *Silent Spring*. 40th anniversary ed. Boston: Houghton Mifflin, 2002.

Childs, Brevard S. *Introduction to the Old Testament as Scripture*. OTL. Philadelphia: Fortress, 1979.

———. "Psalm Titles and Midrashic Exegesis." *JSS* 16, no. 2 (1971): 137–50.

Chinitz, Jacob. "Death in the Bible." *JBQ* 32, no. 2 (2004): 98–103.

Clements, R. E. *Jeremiah*. Interpretation. Louisville: Westminster John Knox, 1988.

Clines, David J. A. *Job 1–20*. WBC 17. Dallas: Word, 1989.

———. *Job 38–42*. WBC 18b. Nashville: Nelson, 2011.

———, ed. *Dictionary of Classical Hebrew*. 9 vols. Sheffield: Sheffield Phoenix, 1993–2014.

Cogan, Mordechai. *1 Kings: A New Translation with Commentary*. AB 10. New York: Doubleday, 2001.

Collins, John J. *Daniel: A Commentary on the Book of Daniel*. Hermeneia. Minneapolis: Fortress, 1993.

Collins, John J., and Daniel C. Harlow, eds. *The Eerdmans Dictionary of Early Judaism*. Grand Rapids: Eerdmans, 2010.

Conrad, Edgar W. *Fear Not Warrior: A Study of ʾal tîrāʾ Pericopes in the Hebrew Scriptures*. BJS 75. Chico, Calif.: Scholars Press, 1985.

Cook, Stephen L. "Funerary Practices and Afterlife Expectations in Ancient Israel." *RC* 6 (2007): 660–83.

Copan, Paul. *Is God a Moral Monster? Making Sense of the Old Testament God*. Grand Rapids: Baker, 2011.

Corbin, Alain. *Histoire du silence: De la Renaissance à nos jours*. Paris: Albin Michel, 2016.

Couroyer, B. "'Mettre sa main sur sa bouche' en Égypte et dans la Bible." *RB* 67 (1960): 197–209.

Craigie, Peter C., and Marvin E. Tate. *Psalms 1–50*. 2nd ed. WBC 19. Nashville: Nelson, 2004.

Crenshaw, James L. *Defending God: Biblical Responses to the Problem of Evil*. Oxford: Oxford University Press, 2005.

———. "Popular Questioning of the Justice of God in Ancient Israel." *ZAW* 82 (1970): 380–95.

———. *The Psalms: An Introduction*. Grand Rapids: Eerdmans, 2001.

———. *Theodicy in the Old Testament*. IRT 4. Philadelphia: Fortress, 1983.

———. *A Whirlpool of Torment: Israelite Traditions of God as an Oppressive Presence*. OBT 12. Philadelphia: Fortress, 1984.

Crim, Keith, ed. *Interpreter's Dictionary of the Bible: Supplementary Volume*. Nashville: Abingdon, 1976.

Crow, Loren D. *The Songs of Ascents (Psalms 120–134): Their Place in Israelite History and Religion*. SBLDS 148. Atlanta: Scholars Press, 1996.

Dahood, Mitchell J. *Psalms*, vol. 2: *51–100*. AB 17. New York: Doubleday, 1968.

Davis, Ellen F. "Abraham's Radical Trust." *ChrCent* 133, no. 22 (2016): 29–31.

Day, John. "The Development of Belief in Life after Death in Ancient Israel." In *After the Exile: Essays in Honour of Rex Mason*, 23–57. Macon, Ga.: Mercer University Press, 1996.

Dempsey, Carol J. "'Turn Back, O People': Repentance in the Latter Prophets." In *Repentance in Christian Theology*, edited by Mark J. Boda and Gordon T. Smith, 47–66. Collegeville, Minn.: Liturgical Press, 2006.

Dhorme, Édouard. *A Commentary on the Book of Job*. Translated by Harold Knight. London: Nelson, 1967.

Diamond, A. R. Pete. *The Confessions of Jeremiah in Context: Scenes of Prophetic Drama*. JSOTSup 45. Sheffield: JSOT Press, 1987.

Dinkler, Michal Beth. *Silent Statements: Narrative Representations of Speech and Silence in the Gospel of Luke*. BZNW 191. Berlin: de Gruyter, 2013.

Di Vito, Robert A. "Old Testament Anthropology and the Construction of Personal Identity." *CBQ* 61 (1999): 217–38.

Dobbs-Allsopp, F. W. *Lamentations*. Interpretation. Louisville: Westminster John Knox, 2002.

Dorrian, Mark, and Christos Kakalis. *The Place of Silence: Architecture/Media/Philosophy*. London: Bloomsbury, 2020. https://doi.org/10.5040/9781350076624.

Dozeman, Thomas B. *Exodus*. ECC. Grand Rapids: Eerdmans, 2009.

Driver, S. R. *The Book of Genesis*. WC. 2nd ed. London: Methuen, 1926.

———. *The Books of Joel and Amos*. CBSC. Cambridge: Cambridge University Press, 1901.

Durham, John I. *Exodus*. WBC 3. Waco, Tex.: Word, 1987.

Ebach, Jürgen. *Beredtes Schweigen: Exegetisch-literarische Beobachtungen zu einer Kommunikationsform in biblischen Texten*. Gütersloh: Gütersloher Verlagshaus, 2014.

———. "Silence in the Bible: A Short Introduction and Seven Miniatures." *Concilium* 2015, no. 5 (2015): 104–13.

Edelman, Diana V. *King Saul in the Historiography of Judah*. JSOTSup 121. Sheffield, UK: Sheffield Academic and JSOT Press, 1991.

Edghill, Ernest Arthur. *The Book of Amos*. 2nd ed. WC. London: Methuen, 1926.

Eichrodt, Walther. *Theology of the Old Testament*. Translated by John Baker. 2 vols. London: SCM Press, 1961–1967.

Eidevall, Göran. "Sounds of Silence in Biblical Hebrew: A Lexical Study." *VT* 62, no. 2 (2012): 159–74.

Exum, J. Cheryl. *Tragedy and Biblical Narrative: Arrows of the Almighty*. Cambridge: Cambridge University Press, 1992.

Exum, J. Cheryl, and J. William Whedbee. "Isaac, Samson, and Saul: Reflections on the Comic and Tragic Visions." *Semeia* 32 (1984): 5–40.

Fager, Jeffrey F. *Land Tenure and the Biblical Jubilee*. JSOTSup 155. Sheffield: JSOT Press, 1993.

Fensham, F. Charles. "Common Trends in Curses of the Near Eastern Treaties and *Kudurru*-Inscriptions Compared with Maledictions of Amos and Isaiah." *ZAW* 75, no. 2 (1963): 155–75.

———. "Malediction and Benediction in Ancient Near Eastern Vassal-Treaties and the Old Testament." *ZAW* 74, no. 1 (1962): 1–9.

Firth, David G. *1 & 2 Samuel*. ApOTC 8. Nottingham: Apollos, 2009.

Fischer, Georg. *Jeremia 1–25*. HThKAT. Freiburg: Herder, 2005.

———. *Jeremia: Prophet über Völker und Königreiche*. BibG 29. Leipzig: Evangelische Verlagsanstalt, 2015.

———. "Die Josefgeschichte als Modell für Versöhnung." In *Studies in the Book of Genesis: Literature, Redaction and History*, edited by André Wénin, 243–71. BETL 155. Leuven: Peeters, 2001.

Fischer, Georg, and Dominik Markl. *Das Buch Exodus*. NSKAT. Stuttgart: Verlag Katholisches Bibelwerk, 2009.

Floyd, Michael H. *Minor Prophets, Part 2*. FOTL 22. Grand Rapids: Eerdmans, 2000.

Fox, Michael V. "God's Answer and Job's Response." *Bib* 94, no. 1 (2013): 1–23.

Freedman, David Noel, ed. *Anchor Bible Dictionary*. 6 vols. New York: Doubleday, 1992.

———. *Eerdmans Dictionary of the Bible*. Grand Rapids: Eerdmans, 2000.

Fretheim, Terence E. "Divine Foreknowledge, Divine Constancy, and the Rejection of Saul's Kingship." *CBQ* 47 (1985): 595–602.

———. *Jeremiah*. SHBC. Macon, Ga.: Smith & Helwys, 2002.

———. "Repentance in the Former Prophets." In *Repentance in Christian Theology*, edited by Mark J. Boda and Gordon T. Smith, 25–46. Collegeville, Minn.: Liturgical Press, 2006.

Frisch, Amos. "'For I Feared the People, and I Yielded to Them' (1 Sam 15,24): Is Saul's Guilt Attenuated or Intensified?" *ZAW* 108, no. 1 (1996): 98–101.

Gammie, John G. *Holiness in Israel*. OBT. Minneapolis: Fortress, 1989.

Gane, Roy. *Cult and Character: Purification Offerings, Day of Atonement, and Theodicy*. Winona Lake, Ind.: Eisenbrauns, 2005.

Gann, Kyle. *No Such Thing as Silence: John Cage's 4'33"*. New Haven: Yale University Press, 2010.

Gerstenberger, Erhard. *Psalms, Part 1: With an Introduction to Cultic Poetry*. FOTL 14. Grand Rapids: Eerdmans, 1988.

———. *Psalms, Part 2, and Lamentations*. FOTL 15. Grand Rapids: Eerdmans, 2001.

Giles, Kevin. "The Biblical Argument for Slavery: Can the Bible Mislead? A Case Study in Hermeneutics." *EvQ* 66 (1994): 3–17.

Goldingay, John. *Daniel*. WBC 30. Waco, Tex.: Word, 1989.

———. "Death and Afterlife in the Psalms." In *Judaism in Late Antiquity*, edited by Jacob Neusner, Alan J. Avery-Peck, and Bruce Chilton, 61–85. Leiden: Brill, 2000.

———. *Psalms*, vol. 1: *Psalms 1–41*. BCOTWP 1. Grand Rapids: Baker Academic, 2006.

———. *Psalms*, vol. 2: *Psalms 42–89*. BCOTWP 2. Grand Rapids: Baker Academic, 2007.

———. *Psalms*, vol. 3: *Psalms 90–150*. BCOTWP 3. Grand Rapids: Baker Academic, 2008.

Gray, John. *I & II Kings: A Commentary*. OTL. 2nd rev. ed. Philadelphia: Westminster, 1970.

Groenewald, Alphonso. "Psalms 69:33-34 in the Light of the Poor in the Psalter as a Whole." *VEccl* 28 (2007): 425–41.

———. "'Trauma Is the Suffering That Remains': The Contribution of Trauma Studies to Prophetic Studies." *AcT* 26 (2018): 88–102.

Gruber, Mayer I. *Aspects of Nonverbal Communication in the Ancient Near East*. StPohl 12. 2 vols. Rome: Biblical Institute Press, 1980.

Gunn, David M. *The Fate of King Saul: An Interpretation of a Biblical Story*. JSOTSup 14. Sheffield: Sheffield Academic, 1980.

Haar, Murray Joseph. "The God-Israel Relationship in the Community Lament Psalms." Ph.D. diss., Union Theological Seminary, 1985.

Hadjiev, Tchavdar S. *The Composition and Redaction of the Book of Amos*. BZAW 393. Berlin: de Gruyter, 2009.

———. "Elijah's Alleged Megalomania: Reading Strategies for Composite Texts, with 1 Kings 19 as an Example." *JSOT* 39, no. 4 (2015): 433–49.

Halpern, Baruch, and David S. Vanderhooft. "The Editions of Kings in the 7th–6th Centuries B.C.E." *HUCA* 62 (1991): 179–244.

Ham, T. C. "The Gentle Voice of God in Job 38." *JBL* 132, no. 3 (2013): 527–41.

Hansen, Ryan Leif. *Silence and Praise: Rhetorical Cosmology and Political Theology in the Book of Revelation*. Emerging Scholars. Minneapolis: Fortress, 2014.

Harper, William Rainey. *A Critical and Exegetical Commentary on Amos and Hosea*. ICC. Edinburgh: T&T Clark, 1905.

Harris, R. Laird, Gleason L. Archer Jr., and Bruce K. Waltke, eds. *Theological Wordbook of the Old Testament*. 2 vols. Chicago: Moody Press, 1980.

Hartley, John E. *The Book of Job*. NICOT. Grand Rapids: Eerdmans, 1988.

———. "From Lament to Oath: A Study of Progression in the Speeches of Job." In *The Book of Job*, edited by W. A. M. Beuken, 79–100. BETL 114. Leuven: Peeters, 1994.

Hays, Christopher B. *A Covenant with Death: Death in the Iron Age II and Its Rhetorical Uses in Proto-Isaiah*. Grand Rapids: Eerdmans, 2015.

Hayward, Robert. *The Jewish Temple: A Non-Biblical Sourcebook*. London: Routledge, 2002.

Hens-Piazza, Gina. *1–2 Kings*. AOTC. Nashville: Abingdon, 2006.

Hertzberg, Hans Wilhelm. *1 & 2 Samuel: A Commentary*. Translated by J. S. Bowden. OTL. Philadelphia: Westminster, 1964.

Heschel, Abraham Joshua. *The Sabbath: Its Meaning for Modern Man*. FSG Classics. New York: Farrar, Straus & Giroux, 2005.

Hillers, Delbert R. *Lamentations*. AB 7a. Garden City, N.Y.: Doubleday, 1972.

———. *Treaty Curses and the Old Testament Prophets*. BibOr 16. Rome: Pontifical Biblical Institute, 1964.

Ho, Edward. "In the Eyes of the Beholder: Unmarked Attibuted Quotations in Job." *JBL* 128, no. 4 (2009): 703–15.

Holladay, William L. *Jeremiah 1: A Commentary on the Book of the Prophet Jeremiah, Chapters 1–25*. Hermeneia. Philadelphia: Fortress, 1986.

Holtz, Shalom E. *Praying Legally*. BJS 364. Providence, R.I.: Brown Judaic Studies, 2019.

Hossfeld, Frank-Lothar, and Erich Zenger. *Die Psalmen: Psalm 1-50*. NEchtB. Würzburg: Echter, 1993.

———. *Psalms 2: A Commentary on Psalms 51–100*. Translated by Linda M. Maloney. Hermeneia. Minneapolis: Fortress, 2005.

———. *Psalms 3: A Commentary on Psalms 101–150*. Translated by Linda M. Maloney. Hermeneia. Minneapolis: Fortress, 2011.

Huddlestun, John R. "Divestiture, Deception, and Demotion: The Garment Motif in Genesis 37–39." *JSOT* 26, no. 4 (2002): 47–62.

Jacobs, Jonathan. "Willing Obedience with Doubts: Abraham at the Binding of Isaac." *VT* 60 (2010): 546–59.

Jaworski, Adam, ed. *Silence: Interdisciplinary Perspectives*. Berlin: de Gruyter, 1997.

Jenni, Ernst, ed., with Claus Westermann. *Theological Lexicon of the Old Testament*. Translated by Mark E. Biddle. 3 vols. Peabody, Mass.: Hendrickson, 1997.

———. *Theologisches Handwörterbuch zum Alten Testament*. 2 vols. Munich: Chr. Kaiser Verlag; Zürich: Theologischer Verlag, 1971–1976.

Jenson, Philip Peter. *Graded Holiness: A Key to the Priestly Conception of the World*. JSOTSup 106. Sheffield: Sheffield University Press, 1992.

Jeremias, Jörg. *The Book of Amos: A Commentary*. Translated by Douglas W. Stott. OTL. Louisville: Westminster John Knox, 1998.

Ji, Won Yong. Review of *The Silence of God: The Answer of the Buddha*, by Raimundo Panikkar. *ConJ* 17, no. 1 (1991): 93–95.

Johnson, Aubrey R. *The Cultic Prophet and Israel's Psalmody*. Cardiff: University of Wales Press, 1979.

Johnson, Bo. "Form and Message in Lamentations." *ZAW* 97, no. 1 (1985): 58–73.

Johnston, Philip S. *Shades of Sheol: Death and Afterlife in the Old Testament*. Leicester: Apollos, 2002.

Jones, Lindsay, ed. *Encyclopedia of Religion*. 2nd ed. 15 vols. Detroit: Macmillan Reference, 2005.

Kaiser, Otto. *Isaiah 13–39: A Commentary*. Translated by R. A. Wilson. OTL. London: SCM Press, 1974.

Kakalis, Christos, Jeff Malpas, and Alberto Pérez Gómez. *Architecture and Silence*. Routledge Research in Architecture. London: Routledge, 2020.

Kalimi, Isaac. "'Go, I Beg You, Take Your Beloved Son and Slay Him!': The Binding of Isaac in Rabbinic Literature and Thought." *RRJ* 13, no. 1 (2010): 1–29.

Kaufman, Stephen A. "An Emphatic Plea for Please." *Maarav* 7 (1991): 195–98.

Kaufmann, Yehezkel. *The Religion of Israel: From Its Beginnings to the Babylonian Exile*. Translated by M. Greenberg. London: Allen & Unwin, 1960.

Kenny, Colum. *The Power of Silence: Silent Communication in Daily Life*. London: Karnac, 2011.

Kessler, John. "Curse, Covenant, and Temple in the Book of Haggai." In *Covenant in the Persian Period: From Genesis to Chronicles*, edited by Richard Bautch and Gary N. Knoppers, 229–54. Winona Lake, Ind.: Eisenbrauns, 2014.

———. "Diaspora and Homeland in the Early Achaemenid Period: Community, Geography and Demography in Zechariah 1–8." In *Approaching Yehud: New Approaches to the Persian Period*, edited by Jonah L. Berquist, 137–66. SemeiaSt 50. Atlanta: Society of Biblical Literature, 2007.

———. "Images of Exile: Representations of the 'Exile' and 'Empty Land' in Sixth to Fourth Century BCE Yehudite Literature." In *The Concept of Exile in Ancient Israel and Its Historical Contexts*, edited by Ehud Ben Zvi and C. Levin, 309–51. BZAW 404. Berlin: de Gruyter, 2010.

———. *Old Testament Theology: Divine Call and Human Response*. Waco, Tex.: Baylor University Press, 2013.

———. "Patterns of Descriptive Curse Formulae in the Hebrew Bible, with Special Attention to Leviticus 26 and Amos 4:6-12." In *The Formation of the Pentateuch: Bridging the Academic Cultures of Europe, Israel, and North America*, edited by Jan C. Gertz, Bernard M. Levinson, Dalit Rom-Shiloni, and Konrad Schmid, 943–84. FAT 111. Tübingen: Mohr Siebeck, 2016.

Khatchadourian, Haig. *How to Do Things with Silence*. Philosophical Analysis 63. Berlin: de Gruyter, 2015.

Kidner, Derek. *Psalms 1–72*. TOTC. Downers Grove, Ill.: InterVarsity, 1973.

Kim, Min-Sun. "Perspectives on Human Communication: Implications for Transculture Theory." In *Transcultural Realities: Interdisciplinary Perspectives on Cross-Cultural Relations*, edited by Peter Nwosu, Molefi K. Asante, and Virginia Hall Milhouse, 3–31. Thousand Oaks, Calif.: Sage, 2001.

Kiuchi, Nobuyoshi. *Leviticus*. ApOTC 3. Nottingham: Apollos, 2007.

Klawans, Jonathan. *Impurity and Sin in Ancient Judaism*. New York: Oxford University Press, 2000.

Klein, Ralph W. *1 Samuel*. WBC 10. Waco, Tex.: Word, 1983.

Knibb, Michael A. "Life and Death in the Old Testament." In *The World of Ancient Israel: Sociological, Anthropological and Political Perspectives*, edited by R. E. Clements, 395–415. Cambridge: Cambridge University Press, 1989.

Knierim, Rolf P. "On the Task of Old Testament Theology." In *A Biblical Itinerary: In Search of Method, Form and Content: Essays in Honor of George W. Coats*, edited by Eugene E. Carpenter, 153–66. JSOTSup 240. Sheffield: JSOT Press, 1997.

Knohl, Israel. "Between Voice and Silence: The Relationship between Prayer and Temple Cult." *JBL* 115 (1996): 17–30.

———. *The Sanctuary of Silence: The Priestly Torah and the Holiness School*. Minneapolis: Fortress, 1995.

Koehler, Ludwig, Walter Baumgartner, and Johann J. Stamm. *The Hebrew and Aramaic Lexicon of the Old Testament*. Translated and edited by Mervyn E. J. Richardson. 4 vols. Leiden: Brill, 1994–1999.

Korpel, Marjo C. A., and Johannes C. de Moor. *The Silent God*. Leiden: Brill, 2011.

Kraus, Hans-Joachim. *Psalms 1–59*. Translated by Hilton C. Oswald. CC. Minneapolis: Fortress, 1993.

———. *Psalms 60–150*. Translated by Hilton C. Oswald. CC. Minneapolis: Fortress, 1989.

Kurzon, Dennis. *Discourse of Silence*. Amsterdam: John Benjamins, 1998.

Laato, Antti, and Johannes C. de Moor, eds. *Theodicy in the World of the Bible*. Leiden: Brill, 2003.

Laird, Martin. *Into the Silent Land: A Guide to the Christian Practice of Contemplation*. Oxford: Oxford University Press, 2006.

Lang, Bernhard. "Afterlife: Ancient Israel's Changing Vision of the World Beyond." *BRev* 4, no. 1 (1988): 12–23.

Laytner, Anson. *Arguing with God: A Jewish Tradition*. Northvale, N.J.: Aronson, 1990.

Levenson, Jon D. *Creation and the Persistence of Evil: The Jewish Drama of Divine Omnipotence*. Princeton: Princeton University Press, 1994.

———. *Resurrection and the Restoration of Israel: The Ultimate Victory of the God of Life*. New Haven: Yale University Press, 2006.

———. *Sinai and Zion: An Entry into the Jewish Bible*. NVBS. San Francisco: HarperSanFrancisco, 1987.

Lévêque, Jean. *Job et son Dieu: Essai d'exégèse et de théologie biblique*. 2 vols. Paris: Gabalda, 1970.

———. *Job ou le drame de la foi: Essais*. LD 216. Edited by Maurice Gilbert and Françoise Mies. Paris: Cerf, 2007.

———. "Silence de Dieu, silence de l'homme." *PeP* 60 (1974): 10–18.

Levine, Baruch A. *Leviticus: The Traditional Hebrew Text with the New JPS Translation*. JPSTC. Philadelphia: Jewish Publication Society, 1989.

———. "Silence, Sound, and the Phenomenology of Mourning in Biblical Israel." *JANESCU* 22 (1993): 89–106.

Lewis, C. S. *The Last Battle*. New York: HarperCollins, 1994.

Liddell, Henry George, Robert Scott, and Henry Stuart Jones. *A Greek-English Lexicon*. 9th ed. with rev. sup. Oxford: Clarendon, 1996.

Lipschits, Oded. "The Babylonian Period in Judah: In Search of the Half Full Cup." *JHebS* 7 (2007): 40–49.

———. *The Fall and Rise of Jerusalem: Judah under Babylonian Rule*. Winona Lake, Ind.: Eisenbrauns, 2005.

———. "Shedding New Light on the Dark Years of the 'Exilic Period': New Studies, Further Elucidation and Some Questions Regarding the Archaeology of Judah as an Empty Land." In *Interpreting Exile: Displacement and Deportation in Biblical and Modern Contexts*, edited by Brad E. Kelle, Frank R. Ames, and Jacob L. Wright, 57-90. AIL 10. Atlanta: Society of Biblical Literature, 2011.

Lipschits, Oded, and Joseph Blenkinsopp, eds. *Judah and the Judeans in the Neo-Babylonian Period*. Winona Lake, Ind.: Eisenbrauns, 2003.

Lohfink, Norbert. "Enthielten die im Alten Testament bezeugten Klageriten eine Phase des Schweigens?" *VT* 12, no. 3 (1962): 260–77.

Longman, Tremper, III. *Psalms: An Introduction and Commentary*. TOTC 15–16. Downers Grove, Ill.: IVP Academic, 2014.

Longman, Tremper, III, and Peter Enns, eds. *Dictionary of the Old Testament: Wisdom, Poetry and Writings*. Downers Grove, Ill.: IVP Academic, 2008.

Loretz, Oswald. "Der Altorientalische rechtliche Hintergrund der biblischen 'Klage des Einzelnen': 'Fortschrittsglaube' in der kanonischen Auslegung des Psalters." In *Textarbeit: Studien zu Texten und ihrer Rezeption aus dem Alten Testament und der Umwelt Israels*, ed. Klaus Kiesow and Thomas Meurer, 285–310. AOAT 294. Münster: Ugarit-Verlag, 2002.

Lust, J. "Gentle Breeze or a Roaring Thunderous Sound: Elijah at Horeb, 1 Kings 19:12." *VT* 25, no. 1 (1975): 110–15.

MacCulloch, Diarmaid. *Silence: A Christian History*. New York: Viking, 2013.

Martin, Troy W. "Concluding the Book of Job and YHWH: Reading Job from the End to the Beginning." *JBL* 137, no. 2 (2018): 299–318.

Martin-Achard, Robert. *From Death to Life: A Study of the Development of the Doctrine of the Resurrection in the Old Testament.* Translated by J. P. Smith. Edinburgh: Oliver & Boyd, 1960.

Matthews, Victor H. "The Anthropology of Clothing in the Joseph Narrative." *JSOT* 20, no. 65 (1995): 25–36.

Mays, James Luther. *Amos: A Commentary.* OTL. London: SCM Press, 1969.

McCarter, P. Kyle, Jr. *1 Samuel.* AB 8. New York: Doubleday, 1980.

McDonald, William J., et al., eds. *New Catholic Encyclopedia.* 2nd ed. 15 vols. Detroit: Gale, 2003.

McKane, William. *Jeremiah 1–25.* ICC. Edinburgh: T&T Clark, 2014.

McKenzie, Steven L. *The Trouble with Kings: The Composition of the Book of Kings in the Deuteronomistic History.* VTSup 42. Leiden: Brill, 1991.

Medubi, Oyinkan. "A Cross-Cultural Study of Silence in Nigeria: An Ethnolinguistic Approach." *JMD* 5, no. 1 (2010): 27–44.

Mercer, Samuel. "The Destiny of the Righteous in Israel." *AThR* 4 (1921): 185–91.

Meyers, Carol L., and Eric M. Meyers. *Haggai, Zechariah 1–8.* AB 25b. Garden City, N.Y.: Doubleday, 1987.

Middleton, J. Richard. "Does God Come to Bury Job or to Praise Him? The Significance of YHWH's Second Speech from the Whirlwind." *StMR* 239 (2017): 1–27.

Milgrom, Jacob. *Leviticus 1–16: A New Translation with Introduction and Commentary.* AB 3. New York: Doubleday, 1991.

———. "The Priestly Doctrine of Repentance." *RB* 82, no. 2 (1975): 186–205.

Miller, Cynthia L. "Silence as a Response in Biblical Hebrew Narrative: Strategies of Speakers and Narrators." *JNSL* 32 (2006): 23–43.

Miller, Patrick D. *They Cried to the Lord: The Form and Theology of Biblical Prayer.* Minneapolis: Fortress, 1994.

Milne, A. A. *The Complete Tales and Poems of Winnie-the-Pooh.* Rev. ed. New York: Dutton's Children's Books, 2001.

Morrow, William S. "The Affirmation of Divine Righteousness in Early Penitential Prayers: A Sign of Judaism's Entry into the Axial Age." In *Seeking the Favor of God, Volume 1: The Origins of Penitential Prayer in Second Temple Judaism*, edited by Mark J. Boda, Daniel K. Falk, and Rodney A. Werline, 101–17. Atlanta: Society of Biblical Literature, 2006.

———. "Consolation, Rejection, and Repentance in Job 42:6." *JBL* 105, no. 2 (1986): 211–25.

———. *Protest against God: The Eclipse of a Biblical Tradition.* HBM 4. Sheffield: Sheffield Phoenix, 2006.

Muers, Rachel. "Silence and the Patience of God." *MT* 17 (2001): 85–98.

Mulder, Martin J. *1 Kings*, vol. 1: *1 Kings 1–11*. Translated by John Vriend. HCOT. Leuven: Peeters, 1998.

Muñoz, Kristine L. *Transcribing Silence: Culture, Relationships, and Communication*. Walnut Creek, Calif.: Left Coast Press, 2014.

Neher, André. "Speech and Silence in Prophecy." *DlD* 6, no. 2 (1977–1978): 61–73.

Newell, B. Lynne. "Job: Repentant or Rebellious." *WTJ* 46, no. 2 (1984): 298–316.

Newsom, Carol A. *The Book of Job: A Contest of Moral Imaginations*. Oxford: Oxford University Press, 2003.

———. "Considering Job." *CurBR* 1 (1993): 87–118.

———. "Re-Considering Job." *CurBR* 5, no. 2 (2007): 155–82.

———. *Songs of the Sabbath Sacrifice: A Critical Edition*. Atlanta: Scholars Press, 1985.

Ngwa, Kenneth Numfor. *The Hermeneutics of the "Happy" Ending in Job 42:7-17*. BZAW 354. Berlin: de Gruyter, 2005.

Niditch, Susan. *The Symbolic Vision in Biblical Tradition*. HSM 30. Chico, Calif.: Scholars Press, 1983.

Noll, Sonja. *The Semantics of Silence in Biblical Hebrew*. SSLL 100. Leiden: Brill, 2020.

Noort, Edward, and Eibert J. C. Tigchelaar. *The Sacrifice of Isaac: The Aqedah (Genesis 22) and Its Interpretations*. TBN 4. Leiden: Brill, 2002.

O'Brien, Julia M. *Nahum, Habakkuk, Zephaniah, Haggai, Zechariah, Malachi*. AOTC. Nashville: Abingdon, 2004.

O'Connor, Kathleen M. *Lamentations and the Tears of the World*. Maryknoll, N.Y.: Orbis Books, 2002.

Oeming, Manfred. "'Ihr habt nicht recht von mir geredet wie mein Knecht Hiob': Gottes Schlusswort als Schlüssel zur Interpretation des Hiobbuchs und als kritische Anfrage an die moderne Theologie." *EvT* 60, no. 2 (2000): 103–16.

Oeming, Manfred, and Konrad Schmid. *Job's Journey: Stations of Suffering*. CSHebB 7. Winona Lake, Ind.: Eisenbrauns, 2015.

Oh, Abraham Sung-Ho. "Early Jewish Understanding of the Sacrifice of Isaac." *KJCS* 93 (2014): 5–24.

Ollenburger, Ben C. "If Mortals Die, Will They Live Again?: The Old Testament and Resurrection." *ExAud* 9 (1993): 29–44.

Olyan, Saul M. "Some Neglected Aspects of Israelite Interment Ideology." *JBL* 124 (2005): 601–16.

———. "Why an Altar of Unfinished Stones? Some Thoughts on Ex 20,25 and Dtn 27,5-6." *ZAW* 108 (1996): 161–71.

Painadath, Sebastian. "The Transforming Power of Contemplative Silence." *Concilium* 5 (2015): 33–43.

Parry, Robin A. *Lamentations*. THOTC. Grand Rapids: Eerdmans, 2010.

Paul, Shalom M. *Amos*. Minneapolis: Fortress, 1991.

Pedersen, Johannes. *Israel: Its Life and Culture*. SFSHJ 28–29. Atlanta: Scholars Press, 1991.

Pelham, Abigail. "Job's Crisis of Language: Power and Powerlessness in Job's Oaths." *JSOT* 36, no. 3 (2012): 333–54.

Pelletier, A. *Lettre d'Aristée à Philocrate*. SC 89. Paris: Cerf, 1962.

Penchansky, David. *What Rough Beast? Images of God in the Hebrew Bible*. Louisville: Westminster John Knox, 1999.

Pinker, Aron. "Sheol." *JBQ* 23, no. 3 (1995): 168–79.

Prideaux, Andrew. "Job 42:7-17, and the God of the Happy Ending." *RTR* 71, no. 3 (2012): 170–84.

Propp, William Henry. *Exodus 1–18: A New Translation with Introduction and Commentary*. AB 2. New York: Doubleday, 1999.

Provan, Iain. *Lamentations*. NCBC. Grand Rapids: Eerdmans, 1991.

Rad, Gerhard von. *Genesis: A Commentary*. Rev. ed. OTL. Philadelphia: Westminster, 1972.

Renaud, B. "Purification et recréation, le 'miserere' (Ps 51)." *RevScRel* 62, no. 4 (1988): 201–18.

Rendtorff, Rolf. "Alas for the Day: The 'Day of the Lord' in the Book of the Twelve." In *God in the Fray: A Tribute to Walter Brueggemann*, edited by Tod Linafelt and Timothy K. Beal, 186–97. Minneapolis: Fortress, 1998.

Renkema, Johan. *Lamentations*. HCOT. Leuven: Peeters, 1998.

Richardson, Michael, and Kyla Allison. "Affect and the Unsaid: Silences, Impasses, and Testimonies to Trauma." In *Qualitative Studies of Silence: The Unsaid as Social Action*, edited by Amy Jo Murray and Kevin Durrheim, 236–53. Cambridge: Cambridge University Press, 2019.

Roberts, J. J. M. *First Isaiah: A Commentary*. Hermeneia. Minneapolis: Fortress, 2015.

———. *Nahum, Habakkuk, and Zephaniah: A Commentary*. OTL. Louisville: Westminster John Knox, 1991.

Robinson, Bernard P. "Elijah at Horeb, 1 Kings 19:1-18: A Coherent Narrative?" *RB* 98 (1991): 513–36.

Rogland, Max. "Elijah and the 'Voice' at Horeb (1 Kings 19): Narrative Sequence in the Masoretic Text and Josephus." *VT* 62, no. 1 (2012): 88–94.

Römer, Thomas. *Dark God: Cruelty, Sex, and Violence in the Old Testament*. New York: Paulist, 2013.

Ross, Alex. "Searching for Silence: John Cage's Art of Noise." *New Yorker*, October 4, 2010. https://www.newyorker.com/magazine/2010/10/04/searching-for-silence.

Routledge, Robin L. "Death and Afterlife in the Old Testament." *JEBS* 9, no. 1 (2008): 22–39.

Rowley, H. H. *Job*. NCB. London: Nelson, 1970.

Rudolph, Wilhelm. *Micha, Nahum, Habakuk, Zephanja*. KAT 13, no. 3. Gütersloh: Gütersloher Verlagshaus, 1975.

Sadler, Paul M. "Learning to 'Read the Air': Three Ways to Improve Communication in Cultures Where Silence Is Golden." *EMQ* 51, no. 4 (2015): 388–92.

Sakenfeld, Katharine Doob. *Faithfulness in Action: Loyalty in Biblical Perspective*. OBT 16. Philadelphia: Fortress, 1985.

———, ed. *New Interpreter's Dictionary of the Bible*. 5 vols. Nashville: Abingdon, 2006–2009.

Salters, Robert B. *A Critical and Exegetical Commentary on Lamentations*. ICC. London: T&T Clark, 2010.

Sarah, Robert and Nicolas Diat. *The Power of Silence: Against the Dictatorship of Noise*. Translated by Michael J. Miller. San Francisco: Ignatius, 2017.

Sarna, Nahum M. *Genesis: The Traditional Hebrew Text with New JPS Translation*. JPSTC. Philadelphia: Jewish Publication Society, 1989.

Sarot, Marcel. "Theodicy and Modernity: An Inquiry into the Historicity of Theodicy." In *Theodicy in the World of the Bible*, edited by Antti Laato and Johannes C. de Moor, 1–26. Leiden: Brill, 2003.

Schart, Aaron. "Deathly Silence and Apocalyptic Noise: Observations on the Soundscape of the Book of the Twelve." *VEccl* 31, no. 1 (2010): article #383, 5 pages. https://doi.org/10.4102/ve.v31i1.383.

Schipper, Jeremy. "Healing and Silence in the Epilogue of Job." *WW* 30, no. 1 (2010): 16–22.

Schmid, Konrad. "Abraham's Sacrifice: Gerhard Von Rad's Interpretation of Genesis 22." *Int* 62, no. 3 (2008): 268–76.

Seibert, Eric A. *Disturbing Divine Behavior: Troubling Old Testament Images of God*. Minneapolis: Fortress, 2009.

Sellin, Ernst. *Das Zwölfprophetenbuch*. KAT 12. Leipzig: Deichertsche Verlagsbuchhandlung, 1922.

Sifianou, Maria. "Silence and Politeness." In *Silence: Interdisciplinary Perspectives*, edited by Adam Jaworski, 63–84. Berlin: de Gruyter, 1997.

Sim, Stuart. *Manifesto for Silence: Confronting the Politics and Culture of Noise*. Edinburgh: Edinburgh University Press, 2007.

Ska, Jean Louis. "Gn 22, 1-19: Essai sur les niveaux de lecture." *Bib* 69 (1988): 324–39.

———. *"Our Fathers Have Told Us": Introduction to the Analysis of Hebrew Narratives*. SubBi 13. Roma: Pontifical Biblical Institute, 1990.

Sklar, Jay. *Sin, Impurity, Sacrifice, Atonement: The Priestly Conceptions*. HBM 2. Sheffield: Sheffield Phoenix, 2005.

Skolnik, Fred, and Michael Berenbaum, eds. *Encyclopedia Judaica*. 2nd ed. 22 vols. Detroit: Macmillan Reference, 2007.

Smith, Henry P. *Samuel I and II*. ICC. Edinburgh: T&T Clark, 1898.

Smith, Mark S. "The Literary Arrangement of the Priestly Redaction of Exodus: A Preliminary Investigation." *CBQ* 58 (1996): 25–50.

Snow Flesher, Leann, Carol J. Dempsey, and Mark J. Boda, eds. *Why? . . . How Long? Studies on Voices of Lamentation Rooted in Biblical Hebrew Poetry*. LHBOTS 552. London: Bloomsbury, 2015.

Soggin, J. Alberto. *The Prophet Amos: A Translation and Commentary*. Translated by J. Bowden. OTL. London: SCM Press, 1987.

Speiser, E. A. *Genesis*. AB 1. New Haven: Yale University Press, 2008.

Sprinkle, Joe M. *The Book of the Covenant: A Literary Approach*. Sheffield: JSOT Press, 1994.

Spronk, Klaas. *Beatific Afterlife in Ancient Israel and in the Ancient Near East*. AOAT 219. Kevelaer: Butzon & Bercker, 1986.

Sternberg, Meir. "The Bible's Art of Persuasion: Ideology, Rhetoric, and Poetics in Saul's Fall." *HUCA* 54 (1983): 45–82.

———. *The Poetics of Biblical Narrative: Ideological Literature and the Drama of Reading*. Bloomington: Indiana University Press, 1985.

Streng, Frederick John. "The Ontology of Silence and Comparative Mysticism." *PT* 27 (1983): 121–27.

Suriano, Matthew. "Sheol, the Tomb, and the Problem of Postmortem Existence." *JHebS* 16 (2016): article #11, 31 pages. https://doi.org/10.5508/jhs.2016.v16.a11.

Sweeney, Marvin A. *I & II Kings: A Commentary*. OTL. Louisville: Westminster John Knox, 2007.

———. *The Twelve Prophets*. Berit Olam. 2 vols. Collegeville, Minn.: Liturgical Press, 2000.

———. *Zephaniah: A Commentary*. Hermeneia. Minneapolis: Fortress, 2003.

———. "Zephaniah: Prophet of His Time—Not the End Time!" *BRev* 20, no. 6 (2004): 34–40, 43.

Tam, Ekman P. C. "The Silence of Ch'an and the Experience of God: A Christian Reflection." *CSQ* 32, no. 4 (1997): 499–514.

Tate, Marvin E. *Psalms 51–100*. WBC 20. Dallas: Word, 1990.

Thomas, Heath. *Habakkuk*. THOTC. Grand Rapids: Eerdmans, 2018.

Toorn, Karel van der, Bob Becking, and Pieter W. van der Horst, eds. *Dictionary of Deities and Demons in the Bible*. 2nd rev. ed. Grand Rapids: Eerdmans, 1999.

Torresan, Paolo. "Dumah, demamah e dumiyyah: Il silenzio e l'esperienza del sacro nella Bibbia Ebraica." *BeO* 46, no. 2 (2004): 85–101.

———. "Silence in the Bible." *JBQ* 31, no. 3 (2003): 153–60.

Trites, Allison A. *The New Testament Concept of Witness*. SNTSMS 31. Cambridge: Cambridge University Press, 1977.

Uffenheimer, Benjamin. "From Prophetic to Apocalyptic Eschatology." In *Eschatology in the Bible and in Jewish and Christian Tradition*, edited by Henning Graf Reventlov, 200–217. Sheffield: Sheffield Academic, 1997.

Van der Merwe, Christo H. J. “Is There Any Difference between ירא מן, ירא מפני, and ירא את?” *JNSWSL* 18 (1992): 177–83.

VanGemeren, Willem A., ed. *New International Dictionary of Old Testament Theology and Exegesis*. 5 vols. Grand Rapids: Zondervan, 1997.

Vaux, Roland de. *Ancient Israel: Its Life and Institutions*. Translated by John McHugh. 2 vols. New York: McGraw-Hill, 1961.

Vawter, Bruce Francis. “Intimations of Immortality and the Old Testament.” *JBL* 91 (1972): 158–71.

Vlaardingerbroek, Johannes. *Zephaniah*. HCOT. Leuven: Peeters, 1999.

Vuilleumier, René, and Carl-Albert Keller. *Michée, Nahoum, Habacuc, Sophonie*. CAT 11b. Neuchâtel: Delachaux & Niestlé, 1971.

Walker, Susan, ed. *Speaking of Silence: Christians and Buddhists on the Contemplative Way*. New York: Paulist, 1987.

Walsh, Jerome T. *1 Kings*. BeOl. Collegeville, Minn.: Liturgical Press, 1996.

Walters, Stanley D. “I Talk of My Sin (to God) (and to You): Psalm 51, with David Speaking.” *CTJ* 50, no. 1 (2015): 91–109.

Waltke, Bruce K., and Michael O’Connor. *An Introduction to Biblical Hebrew Syntax*. Winona Lake, Ind.: Eisenbrauns, 1990.

Walton, John H. *Job*. NIVAC. Grand Rapids: Zondervan, 2012.

Weil, Simone. *Waiting for God*. New York: Harper & Row, 1973.

Weiser, Artur. *The Psalms: A Commentary*. Translated by Herbert Hartwell. OTL. Louisville: Westminster John Knox, 1962.

Wenham, Gordon J. *Genesis 1–15*. WBC 1. Waco, Tex.: Word, 1987.

———. *Genesis 16–50*. WBC 2. Dallas: Word, 1994.

Westermann, Claus. *Lamentations: Issues and Interpretation*. Minneapolis: Fortress, 1994.

———. *Praise and Lament in the Psalms*. Translated by Keith R. Crim and Richard N. Soulen. Atlanta: John Knox, 1981.

Wiesel, Elie. *The Trial of God (as It Was Held on February 25, 1649, in Shamgorod): A Play in Three Acts*. New York: Random House, 1979.

Wildberger, Hans. *Isaiah 28–39*. Translated by Thomas H. Trapp. CC. Minneapolis: Fortress, 2002.

Wilkinson, Lois, and Yumiko Olliver-Gray. “The Significance of Silence: Differences in Meaning, Learning Styles, and Teaching Strategies in Cross-Cultural Settings.” *Psychologia* 49, no. 2 (2006): 74–88.

Williams, Ronald J., and John C. Beckman. *Williams’ Hebrew Syntax*. 3rd ed. Toronto: University of Toronto Press, 2007.

Wilson, Marvin R. *Our Father Abraham: Jewish Roots of the Christian Faith*. Grand Rapids: Eerdmans, 1989.

Winner, Lauren F. *Mudhouse Sabbath: Seven Ways of Christian Formation Inspired by the Jewishness of Jesus*. Brewster, Mass.: Paraclete Press, 2009.

Wolff, Hans Walter. *The Anthropology of the Old Testament*. Translated by Margaret Kohl. Philadelphia: Fortress, 1973.

———. *Hosea: A Commentary on the Book of the Prophet Hosea*. Translated by Gary Stansell. Hermeneia. Philadelphia: Fortress, 1974.

———. *Joel and Amos*. Translated by W. Janzen. Philadelphia: Fortress, 1977.

Wray Beal, Lissa M. *1 & 2 Kings*. ApOTC 9. Nottingham: Apollos, 2014.

Wright, Christopher J. H. "What Happened Every Seven Years in Israel: Old Testament Sabbatical Institutions for Land, Debts and Slaves." *EvQ* 56 (1984): 193–201.

Yamauchi, Edwin M. "Life, Death, and the Afterlife in the Ancient Near East." In *Life in the Face of Death: The Resurrection Message of the New Testament*, edited by Richard N. Longenecker, 21–50. Grand Rapids: Eerdmans, 1998.

Yebra Rovira, Carmen. "Dios y Elías, su profeta, en 1 Reyes 19." *EstBib* 64, no. 3–4 (2006): 447–71.

AUTHOR INDEX

Aejmelaeus, Anneli, 210
Albertz, Rainer, 187n92, 207n31, 208n40
Alexander, T. Desmond, 196n1, 199n21, 199n29, 201n40
Allison, Dale C., 171n39, 183n27, 204n73, 214n29
Alter, Robert, 172n2, 175n21
Andersen, Francis I., 177n43, 179n55, 182n20, 182n21, 186n73, 217n65, 217n69, 218n87
Auld, Graeme, 104, 203n66

Báez, Silvio José, 3, 80, 169n23, 171n35, 172n44, 185n52, 187n89, 194n30, 195n44, 197n6
Balentine, Samuel E., 128, 179n56, 179n58, 204n3, 206n17, 206n18, 207n26, 207n29, 208n39, 211n81
Barr, James, 91, 199n23, 208n45, 208n50, 209n52, 209n53
Ben Zvi, Ehud, 182n16, 182n19, 186n78, 187n93, 196n59
Berlin, Adele, 172n2, 181n13, 184n46, 190n27, 190n30
Blenkinsopp, Joseph, 187n93, 207n30, 215n44
Boda, Mark J., 179n59, 180n65, 180n68, 184n40, 184n41, 187n1, 188n4, 190n28, 191n35, 191n36, 191n46, 191n47, 202n50, 204n5, 208n45
Broyles, Craig C., 114, 118, 191n32, 206n24, 208n43, 208n44
Brueggemann, Walter, 169n21, 182n14, 190n26, 210n57

Calvin, Jean, 189n19
Carlson, Rolf A., 146, 213n18, 216n49, 216n50, 216n52
Childs, Brevard S., 173n4, 189n5
Clines, David J. A., 154, 214n35, 216n56, 217n61, 217n63, 217n66, 217n67, 218n78, 218n87, 219n94, 219n95
Cook, Stephen L., 91, 176n30, 196n1, 197n9, 198n11, 198n18, 199n20, 199n25, 199n27, 199n28, 200n36
Craigie, Peter C., 128, 207n35, 211n80
Crenshaw, James L., 188n5, 191n33, 204n3, 205n13

Dobbs-Allsopp, F. W., 184n40, 190n27, 190n29, 190n30, 191n33, 191n34
Driver, S. R., 185n55, 185n61, 212n2, 212n3

Ebach, Jürgen, 151, 154, 156, 170n30, 190n25, 217n71, 217n72, 219n98, 219n106
Eichrodt, Walther, 172n46
Eidevall, Göran, 4, 65, 170n25, 191n40, 194n29, 214n34

Exum, Cheryl T., 22, 172n2, 173n5, 173n7, 175n19, 175n23, 176n34, 177n40, 177n41

Firth, David G., 174n12, 175n21, 175n22, 177n35, 177n38
Fischer, Georg, 187n88, 192n6, 206n17, 210n64
Fox, Michael V., 216n58, 218n92, 219n97
Freedman, David Noel, 177n43, 179n55, 186n73
Fretheim, Terence E., 173n7, 180n63, 180n67, 188n1

Gerstenberger, Erhard, 193n21, 195n37, 208n47, 211n74, 211n75, 211n76
Goldingay, John, 76, 104, 128, 189n15, 190n20, 193n19, 193n24, 194n31, 194n35, 194n36, 195n38, 195n43, 195n46, 196n1, 198n16, 198n17, 199n30, 200n31, 200n38, 203n67, 203n69, 211n78
Groenewald, Alphonso, 119, 171n37, 208n47
Gruber, Mayer I., 172n45, 184n48, 218n86
Gunn, David M., 172n2, 173n7

Hadjiev, Tchavdar S., 177n42, 214n24, 214n25, 214n27, 216n55
Ham, T. C., 153, 218n80, 218n81, 218n83
Hartley, John E., 152, 217n61, 217n65, 217n67, 218n75, 218n76, 218n82
Hayward, Robert, 105, 204n70, 204n71, 204n72, 204n73, 204n74
Hertzberg, Hans Wilhelm, 173n6, 174n10, 175n20
Heschel, Abraham, 99, 202n47
Heschel, Susannah, 99
Hillers, Delbert R., 184n40, 185n52, 186n70, 190n27
Holladay, William L., 179n60, 180n64
Horn, Friedrich W., 196n53
Hossfeld, Frank-Lothar, and Erich Zenger, 79, 81, 187n90, 190n20, 193n20, 193n21, 193n24, 194n33, 194n34, 194n36, 195n39, 195n41, 195n43, 195n47, 195n48, 203n67, 210n58, 211n68

Jenson, Philip Peter, 101, 200n35, 202n49, 202n51, 202n52, 202n53
Jeremias, Jörg, 177n42, 179n55, 186n72
Johnston, Philip S., 176n30, 197n1, 198n11, 198n14, 108n15, 199n24

Kaiser, Otto, 196n58, 198n15, 199n30
Kaufmann, Yehezkel, 101–2, 202n56, 203n58
Kessler, John, 171n40, 172n47, 175n24, 180n70, 181n8, 186n77, 186n78, 187n93, 191n33, 191n43, 192n2, 200n35, 205n9
Knohl, Israel, 102, 183n27, 203n57, 203n58, 204n73
Korpel, Marjo C. A., and Johannes C. de Moor, 4, 168n9, 169n21, 170n24, 172n1, 189n10, 190n26, 205n11, 205n14
Kraus, Hans-Joachim, 57, 189n11, 190n23, 193n19, 193n22

Levenson, Jon D., 91, 193n13, 199n21, 199n25, 199n26, 207n32
Lévêque, Jean, 156, 171n39, 206n15, 217n61, 217n64, 217n69, 218n78, 218n84, 218n85, 218n89, 219n107
Levine, Baruch A., 183n29, 184n44, 184n46
Lipschits, Oded, 187n93, 191n48

Martin, Troy W., 154, 218n93, 219n95
Mays, James Luther, 178n47, 178n52, 179n55, 185n57, 185n61
McCarter, P. Kyle, Jr., 175n22, 175n25, 177n38
Middleton, J. Richard, 153, 156, 212n4, 213n15, 217n70, 218n78, 218n83, 218n91, 219n105
Milgrom, Jacob, 188n1, 188n2, 202n50, 211n82
Miller, Patrick D., 180n61, 189n9, 194n36, 195n40, 204n5, 207n24, 207n26
Morrow, William S., 114, 116, 118, 154, 188n4, 206n21, 206n22, 206n23, 206n24, 207n25, 207n26, 207n27, 207n33, 207n37, 208n39, 208n40, 208n42, 208n48, 208n49, 209n51, 209n56, 210n56, 210n57, 210n61, 210n62, 211n73, 219n96
Muñoz, Kristine L., 170n33, 171n34, 177n37

Neher, André, 130, 206n15, 212n83
Newsom, Carol A., 183n27, 204n73, 204n74, 216n56, 216n57, 216n59, 218n78, 218n80, 219n96
Noll, Sonja, 4, 168n14, 169n14, 170n26, 170n27, 170n28, 171n34, 172n41, 172n42, 181n7, 191n41, 192n9, 197n4, 197n6, 204n6, 214n33

Oeming, Manfred, 149, 155–56, 216n56, 216n58, 217n67, 217n68, 218n77, 219n97, 219n99, 219n102, 219n103, 219n104
Olyan, Saul M., 90, 198n19, 203n62, 203n64, 203n65

Parry, Robin A., 190n27, 190n30, 191n30
Paul, Shalom M., 177n42, 178n48, 179n55, 183n36, 185n56, 185n59, 186n69, 186n71, 186n73, 187n90
Provan, Iain, 184n42, 190n27, 190n29, 191n31

Rad, Gerhard von, 212n2, 212n7
Renkema, Johan, 190n27, 190n30, 191n46
Roberts, J. J. M., 180n3, 199n30
Robinson, Bernard P., 213n17, 214n23, 214n24, 214n28, 214n36, 216n48, 216n53
Routledge, Robin L., 197n1, 198n14, 198n17, 199n29, 201n38

Salters, Robert B., 184n42, 184n47, 190n27
Sarna, Nahum M., 133, 212n7
Sarot, Marcel, 107, 204n2, 204n4
Schart, Aaron, 170n31, 177n44, 181n5
Schmid, Konrad, 149, 201n45, 212n5, 213n16, 216n56, 216n58, 217n67, 217n68, 218n77, 219n97, 219n99, 219n102, 219n103, 219n104
Sim, Stuart, 167n3, 168n11, 169n17, 170n33
Ska, Jean Louis, 135–36, 172n2, 213n12, 213n13, 213n14
Speiser, E. A., 6, 133, 171n36, 212n6
Sternberg, Meir, 172n2, 174n13, 177n37
Suriano, Matthew, 197n1, 198n17, 199n29, 201n40
Sweeney, Marvin A., 34, 181n4, 181n12, 181n13, 182n17, 185n54, 213n17, 214n30, 214n36, 215n40

Tate, Marvin E., 128, 193n23, 193n24, 203n68, 207n35, 211n80
Torresan, Paolo, 3, 169n22

Vaux, Roland de, 203n62
Vlaardingerbroek, Johannes, 181n12, 182n18, 185n63

Walsh, Jerome T., 139, 213n20, 213n21, 214n24, 214n32, 215n37, 215n39, 215n43
Walton, John H., 216n58, 217n64, 217n66, 218n90
Weil, Simone, 2, 168n6
Weiser, Artur, 193n24, 211n77
Wenham, Gordon J., 201n42, 213n11
Westermann, Claus, 118, 128, 190n27, 194n25, 208n41, 208n49, 209n51, 209n52, 209n53, 209n56, 210n60, 211n70, 211n71, 211n79
Wildberger, Hans, 196n53, 196n54
Wilson, Marvin R., 202n48
Winner, Lauren, 202n48
Wolff, Hans Walter, 178n50, 178n53, 185n67, 186n72, 197n7
Wray Beal, Lissa M., 147, 213n22, 214n31, 216n54

SUBJECT INDEX

Aaron, 6, 124, 198n13, 210n67
abandonment, divine, 22, 31, 53, 57, 68, 113, 123, 127–28, 146, 156, 160, 193n17, 207n27
Abraham, 6, 108, 124, 131, 137, 143, 148, 198n13, 202n47, 202n48, 205n13, 213n11; bosom of, 90, 199n22; Cycle, 132; obedience of, 132–36, 212n1; prayer of, 27, 155; sacrifice of, 134, 212n5, 213n16
absence: of activity, 4, 13, 76, 83, 90, 102, 104, 113, 143, 160; of God, 17, 37, 54, 93, 131, 209n51, 209n54; of praise, 61, 90; of sound, 1, 2, 4, 8, 17, 26, 44, 48, 50, 52, 66, 94, 96, 103–4, 109, 143, 160, 209n51; of words, 4, 13, 96, 113, 127
acceptance or assent, 2, 18, 40, 45, 66–67, 154, 157
accursed: *see* curse
Achan, 40, 174
acrostic, 42, 64, 183n38, 184n38
Adversary, 150, 155, 217n64
affliction, 23, 32, 62–63, 114–15, 148, 150–52
afterlife, 94; and Sheol, 87; in Psalms, 196n1, 198n16, 198n17, 199n31, 201n38; in the ancient Near East, 87, 176n30, 197n1, 197n2, 198n11, 201n38
Agag, 174
agitation, 76, 123, 178n50
agony, 57, 113
agriculture, 24, 49, 53, 69, 83, 116
Ahab, 138–40
Ahaz, 195n51, 196n51
Ahijah, 18, 175n18
Ahimelech, 17–20
aid, 81, 85, 113, 115–18, 123, 192n7, 196n51, 208n40
Aqedah, 212
alien, 49, 69, 112
alienation, 9, 13–14, 19, 26, 32–33, 53–55, 71, 115, 160–61
allusion, 2, 9, 65, 103, 119, 126, 140, 146, 201n38, 201n44, 209n56, 210n67; to funerary practices, 43, 46, 89; to silence, 58, 61, 94, 105, 171n38
alone, in silence, 63, 65, 67, 129, 131, 135, 157
altar, 44, 51, 98, 100, 102–4, 174n9, 203n62, 203n64
Amalekite, 16, 174n13, 174n14
ancestors, being gathered to one's: *see* Sheol
anguish, 22, 122–23, 125, 128, 175n23
animals, 4, 34, 49, 62, 98–101, 153, 187n81, 196n58, 201n43, 210n66
apostasy, 30, 36, 140
ark of the covenant, 100–101
army, 45, 72; Assyrian, 84; Egyptian, 71, 73; Israelite, 15, 16, 20–21
assemblies, 27, 62, 90, 95–96, 171n39

Assyria, 62, 195n49, 196n51; invasion and conquest, 81–82, 84–85; leadership, 81, 84; military, 6, 84
authorship, Davidic, 59, 188n5
awaiting: *see* waiting

Baal, 29, 138–40, 143, 146–47, 213n18, 213n19
Babylon, 48, 50, 52, 66, 68, 95–96, 102
Babylonian conquest, 27, 42, 48, 52, 68
Babylonian rule, 51, 68, 187n93, 191n48, 202n56
Babylonians, 32, 37–38, 41, 62, 205n10
Bathsheba, 59
beasts, 62, 83, 98, 153
belief, 27, 68, 117–18, 137, 140, 147, 185n60, 198n15, 199n31, 200n32
Bethel, 68, 186n74
biblical: Hebrew, 13, 169n14, 170n25, 170n32, 208n45, 208n50, 209n52, 209n53; narrative, 72, 172n2, 173n7, 175n21, 176n33, 176n34; writers, 4, 108, 110–11, 113–14, 117–18, 136, 201n40
blame, 15, 16, 60, 64, 114, 119, 121–22
blasphemy, 150, 156–57, 218n75
blessing: divine, 14, 17, 40, 75, 81, 124, 132, 135, 155; Priestly, 77, 105, 210n67
bloodguilt, 59, 94
bloodshed, 58–60, 190n21
bones, 57, 88–89, 92, 197n8, 200n35
breath, 37, 67, 88, 97, 134, 194n25
bride and bridegroom, 49–50
burial, 28, 46, 88–91, 96, 140, 186n68, 197n9, 199n19
burning, 29, 44, 46, 49, 100–101, 132, 142, 144, 179n60; as burial practice, 45, 89, 132; bush, 100, 142; of incense, 46, 98, 101
burnt offering, 15, 30, 62, 100, 103, 132–34

cacophony, 77, 143
calm, 1, 4, 8, 53, 65, 73, 78–80, 82–83, 85, 119, 128, 142, 196n51
Canaan, 89, 100, 145, 200n32
canon, 55, 97, 111, 154, 157
catastrophe, 9, 33, 48, 53–55, 62, 71, 150
cessation, 4, 8, 53, 62, 73, 88, 148; divine, 63–64, 67, 121; of activity, 1, 4, 8, 46, 50, 53, 62, 73, 88, 98–99, 160; of sound, 1, 4, 8, 49, 60, 66, 73–74, 99, 160
chaos, 8, 37, 77, 82, 85, 116, 160, 210n61
character: of God, 56, 64–65, 68, 108, 110–11, 131, 191n36, 204n5, 205n13, 210n61; personal, 10, 14, 21–22, 141, 173n5, 173n7
characters, of Scripture, 15, 39, 114–15, 131, 135–36, 149, 216n59
chariots, 16, 72, 73, 105, 147
child, 1, 5, 78–81, 123, 132, 134, 137, 151, 195n40
Christian: interpretation, 10, 90, 99, 132, 199n22; practice, 7, 100, 169n18; theology, 7, 90, 100, 187n1, 199n22, 202n48; tradition, 3, 7, 132, 182n14
clamor, 44, 51
cleanness, 200n35
cleansing, 59, 60, 70, 111
clothing, 9, 21, 96, 176n33
comfort, 24, 79, 81, 90, 114, 151, 153
comforters, of Job, 44, 149, 151
commandments, 15, 17, 109, 138, 144, 178n55, 209n55
community, 13, 24, 26–29, 32, 62, 64–65, 69, 91, 107–8, 114–15, 148–49, 180n3, 204n73, 207n28; as reader of the Psalms, 74, 76–77, 119, 124–25, 208n39; of faith, 3, 10, 71, 77, 137, 160, 162; of Israel, 9, 68, 125, 181n8, 200n35, 208n39
compassion, 32, 53, 64, 65, 68, 151
complaint, 31, 37, 38, 41, 64, 108, 110, 113–14, 118–19, 151, 179n58, 179n59, 180n68, 205n15, 206n24, 211n76
confession, 31–32, 101, 108, 179n58, 188n4, 205n15, 206n17; of sin: *see* sin, confession of
confidence, 15, 76, 78, 83, 99, 111, 124, 139–40, 143; expressions of, 30, 119, 122, 126–27, 130, 192n1, 193n24; hopeful, 71, 73, 122, 126, 128, 130–31; silent, 73, 75, 84, 196n58
consecration, 33, 37, 39, 97–98
consolation, 153, 219n95, 219n96
conspiracy, 17–18, 29
contemplation, 157, 169n18, 169n20

conviction, 9, 10, 22, 27, 117, 126–28, 155, 160, 205n12
corpse, 46–47, 89, 92, 96, 100, 132, 199n19
counsel, 3, 20–22, 24, 31–32, 67, 78, 81–82, 153, 160, 174n17, 175n25, 176n29, 179n55, 195n51
courage, 72, 74, 137
covenant, 30, 128, 175n24, 177n45, 197n2, 203n64, 208n39; breaking of, 27–29, 138, 144–45, 177n45; Sinaiatic, 27, 29, 99, 138, 144–45
creation: as natural world, 10, 34, 153, 207n32; God's act of, 37, 97, 201n43; of biblical literature, 186n77
crisis, 75, 81, 135, 217n72, 218n74, 218n75; national, 27, 81, 195n51; personal, 9, 75, 77, 80, 82, 116, 119, 148, 157, 211n76
cult, 102, 132, 183n27, 202n50, 211n74
culture, 5, 44, 87, 93, 102, 167, 169n16, 170n28, 170n33, 171n34, 175n24, 184n40, 198n11, 198n17
curse, 24, 47, 76, 149–50, 152, 175n24, 177n45, 186n70, 218n75

darkness, 25, 36, 63, 122, 129, 167n3; and death, 47–48, 93; and Sheol, 21, 66, 91; and silence, 14, 17, 54, 66, 160
David, 14, 50, 60, 94, 195n36, 201n44; and divine punishment, 19, 55; and kingship, 53, 173n7, 195n51; and Psalms, 56, 59, 188n5, 189n13, 189n19, 194n36, 208n46; and Saul, 15, 17–18, 20, 173n7, 175n25, 177n39; and Tamar, 8, 61
Day of Atonement, 68, 92, 202n50
Day of the Lord, 33, 36, 181n12, 182n14
dead, realm of the: *see* Sheol
death, 45, 54, 90–92, 132, 150, 176n30; and afterlife, 87, 89, 93–96, 197n1, 197n2, 197n3, 198n11, 198n14, 198n16, 198n17, 199n21, 199n22, 199n29, 199n31, 200n31, 200n32, 200n35; and life, 56, 126, 211n82; and Psalms, 56, 59–61, 89, 93–94, 116, 119, 125–26, 190n24, 194n25, 196n1, 198n17, 200n31, 201n38; and Saul, 14, 19, 21–22; and silence, 3, 6, 9, 14, 48, 52, 58, 60–61, 69, 87–88, 94–96, 170n31, 177n44, 181n5; threat of, 19, 21, 23, 25, 28, 46, 60–61, 68, 94, 116, 119, 125–26, 137, 190n21, 198n17, 210n61
defilement, 92, 103–4, 106, 197n8, 200n36
deliverance, 94, 124–25, 127, 190n21, 190n24, 193n24; and judgment, 29, 33, 35, 38; from bloodguilt, 58–61; God's acts of, 33, 35, 37–38, 40, 66, 71–73, 81–82, 84–85, 126, 128, 143; of Israel, 22, 59, 72–73, 81, 117, 143; requests for, 59–61, 111, 113, 117–18, 120, 122; waiting for, 40, 66–67, 71–72, 75–77, 110, 128
deliverer, 71, 117–18, 121, 210n61
dependence, 14, 76, 78, 82, 99, 208n47, 217n64
desolation, 42, 44–45, 48–49, 51–52, 69
despair, 21–22, 25, 42, 47, 54, 63–64, 121, 124–26, 128–29
destiny, 70, 90–91, 94, 188n3, 199n20
destruction, 16, 20, 36, 38, 40, 43, 96, 112, 143, 174n14; national, 23, 30–32, 37, 42, 45, 48, 52, 62, 66, 82, 109, 119; of Jerusalem, 6, 42–45, 47–48, 51–53, 69, 161, 178n47, 184n42; personal, 29, 63, 88, 122, 211n76
Deuteronomistic: History, 14, 138, 173n3, 213n17; writer(s), 138, 141
dialogue, 18, 46, 133–34, 149, 151–52, 154, 179n58, 205n15, 216n59, 217n61, 217n72, 218n73
disaster, 23–24, 27, 29, 41, 44, 48, 68, 81, 103, 116, 136
disobedience, 14, 22, 28, 49, 137, 212n4
distancing, 30, 94, 96, 115, 123, 136, 161, 206n19
distress, 20–22, 58, 64, 65, 70, 111–12, 114, 116, 118, 120, 122–23, 125–26, 130, 161, 178n50, 206n24, 208n43
divine-human relationship, 7, 9–10, 13, 26, 31–33, 54–55, 62, 65, 70, 78, 80, 87, 160–61, 179n58, 206n15, 208n39
Doeg, 18–20, 175n20
doubt, 9, 123, 136, 212n1
drama, 22, 136, 172n2, 179n58, 205n15, 207n32, 217n64, 217n69, 218n78, 218n84, 218n85, 218n89, 219n107; of Job, 152, 154; three-act, 112–17, 119, 122, 125, 128–31, 144

dramatis personae, 39–40, 114, 135
dreams, 17–18, 20–21, 145
dust, 23, 45, 63, 88–89, 142, 219n95
dwell, 26, 54–55, 77, 82, 85, 88, 93, 95–96, 154, 160
dwelling: of God, 34–35, 38, 74, 178n49, 182n25; of humans, 44, 49, 51, 83, 89–90, 148, 187n86
dynasty, 14–16, 22, 138, 173n7, 195n51

earthquake, 6, 138, 141–43, 146–47
Egypt, 40, 48, 53, 71–73, 81, 89, 100, 102, 109, 113, 117, 132
Elihu, 149, 151, 217n62
Elijah, 6, 131, 148, 161, 213n17, 213n20; and Moses, 144–46; and the voice of God, 137–47, 194n30, 214n24, 214n28, 215n36, 215n41, 216n53; Cycle, 141–44
Eliphaz, 142, 149, 217n60
Elisha, 6, 16, 147–48
Elohim, 133–34
emotions, 28–29, 42, 66, 117, 119, 122–23, 137, 150
encouragement, 28, 68, 72–73, 75, 77–78, 188n5, 192n12
enemies, 36, 59, 72, 75–77, 99, 113–15, 119, 122, 124, 207n28
ephod, 17, 20, 175n17
eschatological, 36, 181n12
eschatology, 182
estrangement: *see* alienation
ethos, 2, 5–6, 80, 133
evil, 61, 91, 116, 121, 130, 173n5, 191n33, 204n1, 206n20, 207n32; deeds, 62, 69, 78, 108–9; God's response to, 33, 37, 62, 108–13, 205n15; spirit, 17, 49
evildoers, 37–38, 40, 42, 77, 91, 94–95, 108–10, 148
exile, 190n30, 192n48, 199n31; and prophecy, 23, 43, 50, 52; period of, 51–56, 68, 113, 119, 178n47, 184n40, 186n78, 187n93, 191n45, 191n48, 202n56
exodus from Egypt, 40, 71, 73, 124, 143
expectation, 6, 73, 130
expected sounds or actions, 4, 5, 8, 48, 65, 109, 113, 120

failure: of God to act, 106, 108, 118, 120, 122; of Saul, 14, 16, 22, 177n39; personal, 8, 26, 31–32, 106, 135, 179n55, 216n51
faith, 68, 73, 113, 130, 139, 157, 206n15, 206n24, 208n43, 208n44; community of: *see* community, of faith; expression of, 85, 108, 127–28, 213n11; of Abraham, 132, 136–37, 202n48, 213n11
faithful, people, 28, 78, 108, 110–11, 113, 118–19, 140, 156, 161
faithfulness: of God, 60, 63–65, 135, 192n1, 200n38; to God, 70, 131, 138, 160
false prophets, 25, 27, 178n54
famine, 13, 24–26, 30, 49, 116, 132, 160, 175n24, 177n45, 179n55
fasting, 43, 68–70
fate, 40, 90–92, 115, 173n7, 175n19, 199n22
feasts, 37, 50, 98
festivals, 23–24, 44–45, 50–51, 62, 70, 203n63
forgiveness, 13, 30–32, 55, 57–61, 64–65, 70, 94, 145, 189n9
forsakenness, 119, 121, 123, 125, 127, 137, 140, 186n78
fortress, 77, 129, 157
friends, of Job, 150, 154–56, 218n72
fruitfulness, 82–83
frustration, 54, 77, 137, 141, 146
futility, 19, 22, 30–31, 37, 62
future, 32, 126, 128, 147, 211n72

garden, 44, 51, 146, 199n23, 200n34
garments, 17, 43, 101, 176n33
gates, 43, 51, 69, 90, 115
gathered to one's ancestors: *see* Sheol
genre, 114, 128, 131, 148
gentiles, 90, 199n22
Gideon, 15–16
gladness, 49, 58, 61, 70, 105
glory, 63, 73, 96, 105, 140, 145
gods, 17, 28, 29, 37, 56, 84, 109, 138, 174n17
Goliath, 18
goodness, of God, 53, 64, 77–78, 99, 119, 129, 131, 145, 148
grace, 13, 32, 64–65, 68, 82, 109, 110, 124–25, 145
grave, 72, 89; as Sheol, 87, 89, 91, 94–96, 200n38; danger, 72, 80, 116–17; silence of, 61, 70, 87, 94, 200n38

grief, 50, 64, 68, 73, 77, 94, 128, 151; and mourning, 33, 42–43, 53, 93; expressions of, 33, 42–43, 45, 93, 184n44
guidance, 32, 42, 184n43
guilt, 19, 25, 57–58, 60–61, 114, 124, 152, 173n5, 174n14, 189n19, 190n19

habitation, 35, 38, 49, 69, 83, 187n86
healing, 53–54, 60, 94, 113, 119, 125, 131, 155, 161, 219n101
hearing, 2, 13, 48, 134, 137, 146, 155, 167n3, 218n73; and seeing, 153, 219n94; and silence, 7, 9, 142; of the word(s) of God, 6, 13, 24, 26, 160–61, 179n55, 215n36
heaven, 34, 39, 41, 44, 88, 96, 139, 141, 149–50, 152, 154, 171n39, 182n25, 197n2
Hezekiah, 6, 81, 84–85
history, 14, 36, 55, 103, 124, 168n11, 169n20, 187n92, 195n43, 195n49; of Israel, 55, 103, 194n35, 208n39; of textual composition, 148, 210n64, 213n17
holiness, 54, 97, 100, 102, 106, 130, 200n35, 202n49, 202n51, 202n52, 202n53, 203n57, 203n64, 211n82
Holocaust, 206n19
holy, 81, 92, 97, 104–5, 200n34, 203n63; dwelling, 34, 38, 182n25; of holies, 100–101; place, 9, 100–102; temple, 33, 37
Holy Spirit, 196n53, 201n42
honor, 5, 30, 77, 106, 135, 151
hopeful, 63, 78, 190n29, 191n42
hopelessness, 109, 175n23, 176n34
hoping, 22, 61, 66–67, 94, 110, 130
Horeb, 137, 139–45, 213n17, 214n23, 214n24, 214n28, 215n36, 216n48, 216n53
human, 9, 13, 46, 48, 66, 83, 91–92, 101, 104, 108–10, 114, 131–32, 137, 141–42, 145–46, 156–57, 171n34, 171n40, 172n1, 179n55, 200n35, 215n37; beings, 34, 44, 49, 88, 93, 99, 106, 135, 183n31; experience, 42, 87, 93, 106; life, 49, 183n31; person, 2, 87–88, 161, 193n25, 194n25, 201n43, 216n50; silence, 2, 5, 6, 23, 32, 57, 106, 160, 189n12; suffering, 106–7, 111–12, 115, 148
humanity, 37, 54, 90, 111, 131, 183n31, 203n58
humiliation, 20, 43–44, 124, 139
humility, 153
hunger, 1, 25, 50, 79–80

ideology, 4, 14, 97, 172n2, 174n13, 188n4, 198n19
idolaters, 37, 197n8
idols, 37, 66, 109, 196n56
image, 3, 7, 9, 21, 24, 29, 37–38, 48–49, 69, 73, 75, 77, 80–81, 88, 117, 123–24, 142, 151–53, 159–60, 191n44, 194n34, 198n15, 214n24, 214n29, 215n37; of death, 47, 52, 61, 88–89, 92–93, 96; of exile, 52, 53, 186n78, 187n93; of God, 39, 41, 74, 79, 192n1, 205n13
imperative, 123, 210n63, 212n8; form, negative, 119, 120, 125, 180n69, 206n24, 209n55, 209n56; silence, 35, 41, 47, 76, 194n27
impurity, 92, 183n31, 200n35, 202n50, 211n82
inaccessibility, 18, 123, 150, 152
inaction, 8, 38, 110, 113–14, 120, 129–31, 205n8, 209n51
incense, 46, 62, 98, 100–101, 105, 200n34
incomprehensibility, 210n56; of God, 113, 115, 117–20, 124–25, 129, 131–32, 157, 161, 209n53; of silence, 108, 115, 117, 119, 125, 129, 161
incomprehension, and silence, 136, 151, 157
indifference, 8, 107–8, 111–14, 210n62
iniquity, 30, 40, 56–57, 62, 114, 127, 130
injustice, 23, 56, 61, 78, 110, 117, 119
innocence, 19, 59, 60, 111, 117, 119, 122, 125, 130, 148, 152, 195n37, 207n35, 210n65
integrity, 117, 125, 149–50
intercession, 55; of Moses: *see* Moses, intercession of; prophetic, 26–29, 31, 179n56, 180n63
interpreters of Scripture, 34, 90, 132, 140, 173, 192n12, 212n2, 219n94

intertestamental: literature, 7, 95, 97, 176n30, 213n20, 217n64; period, 104, 183, 199n22
Isaac, sacrifice of, 6, 132–35, 212n1, 212n2, 212n4, 213n11
Ishmael, 134, 198n13
isolation, 115, 132–36, 148, 157, 175n23, 176n34, 188n3

Jacob, 8, 44, 74, 136, 193n20, 198n13
jealousy, 17, 19, 140
Jehoiakim, 60, 179n60
Jehu, 148
Jephthah, 19
Jerusalem, 25, 27, 38, 43, 49, 52, 58, 60, 63, 68, 70, 74, 81, 84, 98, 187n93, 191n48; destruction of: *see* destruction, of Jerusalem; restoration of: *see* restoration, of Jerusalem; temple in, 51, 69, 75, 105, 118, 161, 171n39, 178n47, 178n49, 182n25, 203n59, 204n73
Jesse, 18
Jesus, 99, 202n48, 219n98
Jezebel, 137, 139–40, 146
Joab, 94
Jonathan, 15–20, 214n36
Jordan River, 140
Joseph, 23, 50, 89, 123–24, 176n33
Josephus, 216n53
joy, 57, 129, 198n17; and gladness, 58, 61, 70; sounds of, 24, 50, 58, 68, 84, 184n44
Judah, 20, 25–26, 43, 53, 61, 68, 70, 81, 98, 109, 175n21, 178n49, 186n68, 186n77, 192n48; conquest of, 32, 42, 44, 48, 51–52, 69, 84, 187n93, 191n48; judgment of, 36–37
Judaism, 99, 114, 183n31, 188n4, 196n1, 199n22, 207n36, 212n4
Judea, 48, 52
Judean, 37, 52, 187n93
judgment, divine, 9, 21, 32, 55, 57, 62, 103, 107, 148, 160, 174n13, 199n22, 214n24; and silence, 23, 35, 37–42, 45–54, 66–70, 93, 108–10; in Psalms, 50, 67, 76, 80, 94–95, 108–10, 121; in the Prophets, 24, 26, 29, 31, 33, 35–54, 68–70, 83, 178n47, 178n49, 182n22, 183n31, 196n51
justice, 37, 61, 93, 118, 208n38; and righteousness, 23, 26, 62, 82–83, 111; of God, 60, 64, 78, 82, 107, 111, 117, 145, 153, 191n33, 204n3

kindness, 65, 69, 110
kingship, 16, 17, 173n7, 208n39
knowledge, 50, 93, 128, 131, 135, 153, 155–56, 161

lament, 32, 41–42, 44, 49, 51, 70, 114–15, 146, 180n65, 184n40, 190n29, 207n29, 218n75; and praise, 209n51, 209n52, 209n53, 209n56, 210n60, 210n67, 211n70, 211n71, 211n79; and repentance, 30, 45, 67, 188n4; psalms of, 30, 64, 77, 126, 128, 191n32, 192n1, 193n23, 208n39, 209n55, 210n67
laws, 103–4, 109, 117, 138, 176n32, 208n38
Letter of Aristeas, 104–5, 171n39
Levant, 84, 207n31
Leviathan, 124, 153
liturgy, 34, 56, 64, 118, 179n59, 180n65, 180n3, 181n3, 184n40
loss, 17, 43, 49, 55, 68, 116, 122, 149, 150, 167n3, 198n17; of access to God, 14, 22, 24, 26, 160, 179n55; of expected sound(s), 51, 52, 54, 93–94
loyalty, 27, 31, 65, 118, 191n37, 217n64

magic, 48–49, 102, 174n15, 174n16, 176n28
majesty, 73, 106, 144
manifestation, of God, 41, 45, 104, 142, 145–47
Masoretic Text, 7, 104, 147, 188n5, 195n41, 216n53
medium, 20–22, 176n28, 200n36
mercy: divine, 13, 44–45, 56, 65, 70, 82, 110, 128, 145, 151; human, 62, 69
Midianites, 15–16
mirth, 50–51
misery, 14, 56, 95, 108, 148, 151
Mizpah, 52
monarchy, 14, 174n9, 174n11
Moses, 40, 49, 71–72, 97, 100, 103, 124, 192n12, 198n13; and Elijah, 138–47; intercession of, 27–30, 145
motif of silence, 4, 7, 9, 17, 25–26, 33, 39, 42, 73, 77–78, 91–92, 156–57

mourning: *see* grief, and mourning
murder, 18, 59, 60, 77, 194n26

narrative, 7, 8, 13–14, 16–17, 35, 55, 85, 103, 110, 123, 131, 133, 136, 149, 154, 170n32, 171n39, 172n2, 181n7, 185n62, 192n7, 213n13; of Abraham, 134; of Elijah, 141, 143–44, 148, 213n17, 215n44, 216n53; of Saul, 21–22, 138, 173n7, 174n14, 175n25, 176n31; of the exodus, 71–72, 124
narrator, 14–15, 17, 19–21, 84, 102, 104, 138–40, 142, 148, 150, 152, 154, 157, 170n32, 173n5, 173n7, 174n14, 176n31, 184n42, 214n24
Nathan, 59
nations, 36–39, 41, 48–49, 69, 74–75, 78, 84, 96, 109, 181n12, 193n19, 193n20
netherworld: *see* Sheol
New Testament (NT), 7, 10, 99, 109, 162, 171n39, 176n30, 183n27, 196n53, 201n42, 213n20, 217n64
Nob, 18–21
nonverbal communication, 7, 8, 44, 172n45, 184n44, 184n48, 193n15, 207n26, 218n86
Northern Kingdom (NK), 22, 26–27, 41, 45, 62, 81, 84, 109, 139, 178n49, 185n60, 186n77, 195n51
nurture, 78–79, 81, 159

oath, 19, 46, 135, 152, 175n24, 218n72, 218n75
obedience, to God, 10, 14, 22, 56, 82, 132, 135–37, 177n42, 178n55, 179n55, 212n1, 212n4, 214n24
Old Testament (OT), 90, 174n14, 188n1, 188n2, 199n22, 203n63, 205n13, 219n98
omnipotence, 111, 116, 207n32
oppression, 33, 61–62, 78, 117–19, 133, 162, 177n43, 196n56, 205n13, 210n65, 212n7
oppressors, 23, 38, 40, 84, 111

pain, 28, 113, 123–24, 126, 129, 136
parallelism, 57, 215n43
parashah petuchah, line break, 7
parashah setumah, space, 7
parousia, 110
peace, 2–3, 25, 52, 63, 66, 69, 76, 84, 92, 116, 121, 124, 150, 156, 163, 181n12, 193n20, 196n58, 201n44; and death, 90, 94–95, 150; and quiet, 1, 8, 77, 82, 99, 112; and security, 73, 81, 128–29, 178n54; and stillness, 73, 80, 83, 151
penitence, 9, 30, 31, 56, 66–67, 184n40, 184n41, 188n4
penitential prayer, 30, 56, 58, 60–61, 63–64, 184n40, 188n4, 191n36
Persia, 52, 68, 125, 175n24, 181n8, 200n32, 213n16
pestilence, 30, 46, 49
Philistines, 15–16, 18–21, 103
piety, 18, 64, 114, 148–50, 185n60, 208n40, 215n36
poetry, 131, 149, 208n45, 211n74
polysemy, 43, 73
presence of God, 35, 37, 40, 52, 59, 83, 90, 100, 104, 140, 143, 145, 147, 161, 162
priestly garments, 17, 20, 101
priests, 14–21, 34, 36, 44, 51, 68, 72, 74, 97, 100–102, 105, 115, 127, 130, 174n9, 175n18, 175n25, 202n55, 203n58, 207n28, 208n40
promises of God, 40, 66, 81, 85, 108, 113, 125, 127, 132, 134–35, 137, 173n7, 177n45, 211n76
prophetic word, 24, 52, 178n47, 215n36, 215n42
prose, 45, 131, 149
protest against God, 110, 113–20, 122, 124, 126, 129, 161, 206n16, 206n21, 206n22, 206n23, 206n24, 207n25, 207n26, 207n27, 207n33, 207n34, 207n37, 208n39, 208n40, 208n42, 208n48, 208n49, 209n51, 209n55, 209n56, 210n57, 210n61, 210n62, 211n73
providence, 107, 151
psalms: of Ascents, 78; of direct protest, 209n56, 210n61, 211n73; of indirect protest, 209n56; of lament, 30, 64, 77, 126, 193n23, 209n56, 210n67; of plea, 126, 209n56; of protest, 122, 210n62; of thanksgiving, 125–27
purity, 36, 66, 92, 100, 183n31

Queen of Heaven, 28, 180n62
quietness, 66, 71, 76, 81, 83, 99

Rabshakeh, 84–85, 196n59
readers, 11, 54, 71, 120, 131, 134–36, 157, 159–60, 163; (or hearers) of the biblical text, 14–15, 19–21, 25, 29, 34, 40–41, 46, 48, 53, 75, 105, 122–23, 129, 133, 142, 145, 147–50, 152, 154–55, 162, 176n31, 177n39, 182n26, 184n42, 216n59; Christian, 7, 10, 25, 55, 99
reading, of the biblical text, 7, 80, 135, 137, 141, 147, 172n2, 173n3, 180n64, 208n46, 211n77, 213n16, 214n24, 215n38, 219n93
realm of the dead: *see* Sheol
rebelliousness, 26, 29, 56, 71, 75, 200n34, 218n82
rebuke, 24, 36, 108, 153, 156, 192n12
recompense, 94, 96, 108, 113
redemption, 42, 53
refuge, 74, 77, 121, 192n1
rejection, 2, 15, 124, 132, 147, 160, 168n11, 219n96; of God by humans, 13, 22, 53, 140, 173n7; of humans by God, 14, 17–18, 22, 30, 40, 172n1, 173n7, 209n53
relationship: between Israel and God, 24, 26, 53, 65, 67, 118, 138, 145; divine-human: *see* divine-human relationship; interpersonal, 79, 134, 139, 161, 194n36, 196n58; intertextual, 15, 46, 73, 117, 138, 141, 149, 174n13, 186n77
remembrance, 44, 50, 64, 69, 95, 126, 202n54
renewal, 9, 42, 53–56, 58, 61, 63, 69–71, 78, 83–84, 135, 137, 140, 155, 157, 187n1
repentance, 29, 31, 36, 42, 59, 63, 110, 154, 177n45, 187n1, 188n2, 188n3, 202n50, 219n96; and silence, 9, 32, 55–57, 62, 67, 70, 109, 155, 161; calls for, 26, 36, 56; prayers of, 20, 30, 45, 56–57, 59
reproach, 67, 119–20, 151, 161, 194n33
rescue, 59, 62, 80, 94, 116, 124–25, 178n47
resentment, 77
resolution, 41, 58, 116, 129, 131–32, 135, 141, 147, 157, 205n15, 207n31
restoration, 71, 77, 131, 135, 154; of Jerusalem, 53, 68–69, 161, 199n21; of relationship, 54–55, 62, 64, 67, 70, 145
resurrection, 90, 197n2, 198n10, 199n21, 199n22, 199n25, 199n26
rhetoric, 21, 34, 48, 119, 171n39, 174n13, 197n2
righteous, 23, 38, 59, 78, 83, 90–91, 94–95, 109–10, 113, 121, 124–25, 148, 199n20, 199n22, 200n35, 210n65, 211n76
righteousness, 23, 26, 62, 70, 82–83, 111, 117, 188n4, 196n58
ritual, 35, 43–46, 92, 100, 102–3, 118, 131, 183n31, 202n55, 203n62
ruin, 23, 44–45, 49–51, 83

sabbath, 23, 44, 51–53, 62, 97–100, 103, 105, 161, 171n39, 183n27, 201n43, 202n47, 202n48, 203n63, 204n73, 204n74, 214n29
sacred, 18, 34–35, 39, 41, 87, 106, 175n24, 188n5, 203n62; space, 97, 100–105, 141, 143, 146; time, 97–99
sacredness, 9, 96, 100, 102, 104, 106, 156, 200n35
sacrifice, 15, 19, 23, 29, 33–35, 37, 62, 98, 100, 103, 105, 108, 132–34, 137, 171n39, 174n8, 174n9, 174n14, 183n27, 200n34, 202n50, 204n73, 204n74, 212n1, 212n5, 213n11, 213n15, 214n29
salvation, 32, 36, 38, 58, 63, 65–66, 81–82, 127, 129–30, 157, 211n76
Samaria, 47, 81, 84, 148, 185n62
sanctity, 103–5, 183n31
sanctuary, 44, 51, 68, 203n57, 203n58, 203n63
Sarah, 132, 134–35
Satan: *see* Adversary
Saul, 6, 13–27, 138, 160, 173n5, 173n7, 174n9, 174n13, 174n14, 175n18, 175n19, 175n21, 175n23, 175n25, 176n27, 176n32, 176n34, 177n36, 177n39, 177n40, 179n41
scripture, 30, 80, 111, 113, 136–37, 160, 173n4, 192n3, 205n12
security, 9, 136, 178n54; and silence, 71, 73–74, 78, 81, 83, 196n58; and trust, 156, 160
Sennacherib, 81, 195n49
separation, 3, 53, 76, 92–96, 152, 203n85
shades, 89, 95–96, 176n30, 197n1, 198n11, 198n14, 198n15, 199n24
Sheol, 9, 21, 45, 61, 66, 87–96, 106, 125, 150, 176n30, 197n1, 198n11, 199n20,

199n24, 199n29, 200n35, 200n38, 201n39, 201n40
Shiloh, 6
simile, 79–80, 195n40
sin, 43, 62, 92, 100, 172n1, 180n65, 183n31, 202n50; confession of, 30–31, 40, 55–58, 64, 67, 70; effects of, 58–60, 189n19, 209n56, 210n56; forgiveness of, 17, 31, 55, 58, 61, 64, 70; punishment for, 30, 47, 67, 113, 177n45, 191n44, 209n56
Sinai, 27, 29, 97, 138–46, 193n13, 208n39, 215n44
sleep, 38, 49, 80, 89–93, 159, 165, 201n44
Sodom and Gomorrah, 27, 62, 134
solitude, 3, 133, 136, 159, 164, 168n11
Solomon, 94
songs, 23, 47, 50–51, 58, 61–62, 84, 105, 171n39, 183n27, 185n67, 192n1, 194n35, 204n73, 204n74, 214n29
Songs of Sabbath Sacrifice, 105, 171
sorrow, 3, 32, 43, 45, 49, 53, 94, 122–23, 190n29, 198n17
sounds, 2, 5–6, 13, 28, 36, 104, 133, 165, 170n25, 191n40, 194n29, 214n34; expected, 4, 48–51, 69, 93, 98–101, 109, 161–62; of life, 48–49, 52, 54, 68–70, 83, 93; of worship: *see* worship, sounds of
soundscape, 5, 23, 36, 50, 53, 55, 58, 61, 69, 77, 83–84, 92–93, 98–101, 122–23, 134, 149–52, 170n31, 180n61
Southern Kingdom (SK), 52, 62, 68, 84, 125, 137, 181n8, 186n77, 186n78, 191n48
spirit, 21, 49, 77–78, 100, 104, 201n42, 208n47; human, 6; of God, 17, 22, 82–83, 97, 105, 196n53
spirituality, 7, 9, 157, 160, 169n20
steadfast love, 63–65, 130, 145
stillness, 1, 3–4, 8, 38, 65–66, 71–85, 92, 142–43, 146–47, 151, 157, 159–62, 191n38, 194n29, 194n30, 196n58, 204n74, 214n34
stones, 17, 96, 103–4, 203n62, 203n64, 203n65
strongholds, 44, 76, 185n62
suffering, 9, 17, 22, 57, 61–70, 94–95, 106–30, 148, 150, 156, 160–61, 171n37, 204n3, 206n19, 209n56, 211n76, 216n56

tabernacle, 9, 35, 44, 51, 97–102, 105, 161, 202n49, 202n51, 202n54, 202n55
Tamar, 8, 61
teaching, 62, 66, 156, 202n55
temple, 9, 27, 29, 33, 35, 37–38, 47, 51, 68–69, 74–75, 94, 97, 100–105, 115, 118, 161, 171n39, 175n24, 178n47, 178n49, 182n25, 183n27, 185n67, 188n4, 203n59, 204n70, 204n71, 204n72, 204n73, 204n74, 208n39
terror, 25, 48, 91, 95, 124, 176n34
testimony, 24, 26, 84, 200n38, 210n57
thanksgiving, 94, 101–2, 126, 192n1, 193n23, 200n38
theodicy, 7, 107–8, 130, 148, 191n33, 202n50, 204n1, 204n3
theological reflection, 94, 114, 206n19, 213n20
theology, 7, 63–64, 74, 85, 90, 107, 113, 156, 200n35
theophany, 139–47, 215n37, 216n48
tomb, 88–96, 197n1, 198n15, 199n19, 200n34
torah, 178n55, 184n43, 187n1, 203n57
translation, of Hebrew into English, 11, 18, 25, 57, 65, 76, 79, 88, 103–4, 138, 140–42, 146, 150, 154–56, 176n28, 177n, 183n37, 193n25, 194n27, 194n29, 201n43, 204n70, 204n74, 211n72, 214n36, 219n95
trauma, 6, 155, 171n37
trust, in God, 15, 64, 70–85, 104, 115, 122, 126–32, 136, 156, 160–61, 192n12, 196n51, 212n2

uncircumcised, 16, 95
unfaithfulness, 9, 147
Uriah, 59–60
Urim and Thummim, 17, 18, 20, 93, 174n17

victim, 8, 41, 61, 75, 118, 132
victory, 19, 72, 78, 175n18, 199n21, 201n44
vindication, 19, 37–38, 40–41, 78, 113, 117, 119, 207n35
violence, 91, 94–95, 110, 112, 114, 118, 143, 151, 153, 155–56, 205n13

vision, 25, 32, 42–43, 47, 56, 186n76, 189n9, 197n1, 214n35
visions, 24, 26, 38, 145, 173n5, 185n64
vows, 104, 175n20, 175n24

wailing, 9, 24, 28, 36, 43, 45, 47, 49, 51, 83, 172n43, 185n67, 190n21
waiting, 2, 6, 15, 42, 65–82, 104, 110, 124, 130, 157, 161, 168n6, 169n20
weakness, 25, 31, 44, 90, 111, 123, 151
worship, 17, 34, 84, 109, 113, 118, 131, 134, 181n3, 201n38; location of, 35, 94, 100, 105, 127, 171n39, 183n27, 187n90; of other gods, 28–29, 56, 138–39, 144, 183n27; sounds of, 23, 47, 51, 70, 93–94, 96, 171n39
worshippers, 101, 104, 138

Yehud: *see* Southern Kingdom

Zadok, 14
zeal, 140
Zion, 27, 75, 81, 104, 178n49, 184n42, 193n13; daughter(s) of, 43–45; song(s) of, 50–51, 74
zone(s) of holiness, 100–102
Zophar, 149, 217n60

SCRIPTURE INDEX

Genesis
- 1:1–2:4 97
- 1:14 97
- 1:31–2:1 97
- 2:2-3 97
- 2:3 98, 201n43
- 2:7 88, 194n25
- 3:8 146
- 3:8, 10 141
- 3:19 45
- 4:6 120
- 4:8-10 118
- 4:10-11 189n14
- 4:12 25
- 4:12, 14 25
- 6:12 34
- 6:12, 17, 19 34
- 6:13 185n66
- 7:7 35
- 8:20 133
- 11:30 116
- 12:1–25:11 132
- 12:1-3, 7 132
- 15:1-17 132
- 15:1 215n42
- 15:1-2 118
- 15:4 143
- 15:15 94
- 17:1-8 132
- 17:7 118
- 18:16-33 27, 207n34
- 18:17 27, 31
- 18:19 117
- 18:22 35
- 18:23 124
- 18:25 34
- 19 125
- 20:7 27, 155
- 20:17 155
- 21:8 79
- 21:12 132
- 22 6, 8–9, 131–37, 148–49, 212n1, 212n5, 213n16
- 22:1-2 133
- 22:5 137
- 23:4, 6, 9, 20 89
- 23:8 28
- 24:21 183n30, 192n8
- 24:40 118
- 25:8 198n13
- 25:17 88, 198n13
- 25:21 116
- 25:22 176n29
- 27:7 35
- 29:31 116
- 31:44 41
- 32:22-32 136
- 33:40 194n25
- 34:5 183n30
- 34:5, 25-31 8, 61, 160
- 35:1 35
- 35:29 88, 198n13

37–39 176n33
37:21 59
37:22 59
37:28 124
37:34-35 43
37:35 90
39:19 124
41:32 154
42:38 94
44:18 124
47:30 89
49:4 103
49:9 38
49:18 157
49:30 89
49:33 88, 198n13
50:5, 13 89
50:25 89

Exodus
2:19 59
2:23 116–17
3:1-4 142
3:1-12 143
3:5 100
3:7-8 124
3:8 59
4:21 110
4:22 118
6:6 59, 117–18
6:7 118
7:3 110
9:3 57
9:16 34
10:13, 19 143
13:19 89
14 73
14:4, 17 110
14:10-12 72
14:13-14 40, 72
14:13-15 73
14:14 8, 71, 73, 161
14:18-19 73
14:21 143
14:30 118
15 73
15:5 198n15
15:10 143
15:16 8
15:22 73
16 139
16:1 73
16:33 35
17:1 73
17:1-4 146
18:4, 9 59
18:8 117
18:10 59
18:15 176n29
19–24 144, 147
19:16-25 144
19:18 143
19:18-24 143
19:19 143
19:22, 24 39, 41
20:1–23:33 144
20:5 140
20:8-10 98
20:8-11 99
20:13 194n26
20:18 25
20:24 203n64
20:25 103–4
21:23 194n25
22:2 189n14
22:22-24 117
23:10-11 53
23:12 98
24:3 143
24:12-18 144
24:15 144
24:15-16 97, 143
24:18 145
25:22 100
26:1, 31, 36 101
26:33-34 97
26:35 100
27:21 35, 100
28:6, 15, 39 101
28:14 101
28:22, 29 101
28:30 93
28:33-35 202n54
28:35 35
28:36 101
28:41 97
29:25 101, 133

29:45 118
30:18 100
30:33, 38 98
30:36 142
31:12-15 98
31:14 103
31:16-17 99
31:18 144
32–34 144–45, 215n47
32:1 144
32:10 28, 31
32:10-14 56
33:10, 22 140
32:11-13, 31-34 55
32:11-14 27
32:19-20 146
32:20–34:35 145
32:20 142
32:25-29 56
32:30–34:35 145
33:4-6 188n3
33:10 140
33:12–34:9 145
33:17-21 140
33:19 110
34:6 65
34:6-7 64, 110
34:7 124, 189n6
34:9 55
34:21 98
34:28 145
35:2 98
35:35 101
39:25 101
39:27 101
40:9 97

Leviticus
1:3 118
1:3, 10, 13 133
4:6-7, 17 100
4:32-35 100
5:1 61, 160
7:18 189n7
8:5-9 93
8:33, 35 101
9:22 101
10:3 6, 43, 172n43, 183n37
10:3b 8, 183n29
10:7 101
10:16-20 130
12:6 101
14:11, 23 101
15:30 118
15:31 68
16 92
16:15-17 100
16:21 101
18:21 137
19:15 117
19:15a 117
19:29 103
19:31 92, 176n32, 200n36
20:2 137
20:6, 27 176n32
20:27 22
21:11 92, 200n35
21:22 98
23:2, 4, 37 97
23:3, 32 98
23:3, 7 98
24:15 150
25:2-7 53, 99
25:18 196n57
26 177n45
26:14-39 177n45
26:31, 34, 43 69
26:32 185n49
26:33 49
26:36 141
26:40-45 64, 67–68
26:45 183n35

Numbers
3:31 100
4:5-14 101
4:7 100
5:19-22 101
6:1-5 68
6:7 92, 200n35
6:23-26 101
6:24-26 124
7:89 100
9:2-3, 13 97
10:10 97
10:35 38
11:2 27
11:10-15 146

11:16 73
11:31 143
12:6-8 145
12:11-13 55
13:30 180n1
14:9 192n4
14:13-19 55
14:13-20 27
14:18 189n6
14:18-19 110
14:21 34
14:26-35 56
17:11 39
18:15 34
19 92
19:11, 13-14, 16 92, 200n35
20:9-13 146
20:20 57
20:24 198
20:29 43, 88
21:34-35 192n5
23:10 94
23:24 38
24:9 38
27:13 198n13
27:21 176n29
28:2 97
29:7-11 92
29:39 97
30:1-15 109
30:3, 7 183n28
30:4 8
35:25, 31-33 60

Deuteronomy
1:17 117
1:20-21 192n5
1:21 192n4
3:1-3 192n4
3:2 192n4
4–5 147
4:7 124
4:9-14 144
4:10-11 140
4:11-12, 15, 33-36 143–45
4:12 144
4:24 140
4:25-31 64
4:25 28
4:26 41
4:28-32 177n45
4:30 82
4:31 75, 193n17
4:33, 36 143
5:4-5, 22-26 143–45
5:5 140
5:6-10 138
5:10 110
5:12-15 98
5:22-23 144
5:22-26 143
5:25-27 144
5:25 141
6:15 140
7:24 73
8 178n55
8:1-3 178n55
8:2, 4 139
9–10 147
9:7–10:11 144, 215n47
9:9, 11, 18, 25 145
9:16-29 55
9:18 28
10:1-11 145
10:10 145
10:18 117
12:10 196n57
12:12 118
13:14 154
16:19 117
16:20 117
17:6 41
18:10-12 176n32
18:11 93
20:1-4 72
20:2-4 192n5
21:3 210n66
22:8 59
22:24, 27 118
23:14 117
24:17 118
25:19 191
26:1 102
26:3-11 101
26:15 182
27:6 103
27:19 117

28 14, 177n45
28:15–29:1 177n45
30:1-5 64
30:1-10 177n45
30:1 82
30:3 110
30:19 41
31:5-6 192n5
31:6-8 75
31:6 193n17
32:16 28, 90, 92
32:22 90
32:24 177n45
32:48-52 140
32:50 198n13
33:29 118
34:1-4 140
34:5 140
34:8 43
34:10-12 138, 145
Joshua
1:5 75, 125
3:5 183n31
3:11, 13 34
7 174n13, 175n24
7:6 43–45, 184n45
7:19-23
8:1 192n5
8:29 186n69
8:30-31 103
10:7-8, 24-25 192n5
10:8, 25 192n4
10:11 35
10:12 8
10:27 186n69
11:5-7 192n5
18:3 193n18
23:14 34
24:27 41
24:32 89
Judges
2:10 90
2:12 28
3:9, 15 116
3:19 8, 180n1
5:4 143
6:13 108
7 15
7:2 16
7:22 16
9:21 35
11:29-40 19
11:37-38 43
13:2 116
16:2 183n30
18:5 176n29
18:19 8, 192n8
Ruth
1:16-17 28
1 Samuel
1–12 14
1:3 100
1:15 77, 194n32
1:22-24 79
2:27-36 14
3 161
3:1 24
3:11-14 14
3:18 18, 40
4:3 207n34
4:8 59
4:12 44, 184n45
5:6, 11 57
7:8-9 116
7:15-17 14
8–12 14, 173n4
8–31 13
9 24
9:5-6 24
9:5-17 22
9:9 176n29
9:13 174n9
9:15–11:15 14
9:19–10:8 18
10:1 22
10:3-9 22
10:16 8
10:22 176n29
10:27 183n30
12:5-6 41
12:8 116
12:16 73
13 14, 16–17
13–31 13, 173n5
13:1-14 14–15
13:11-12 15

13:13 15
13:13-14 22, 173n7
14 16
14:18-19 175n18
14:24, 29 19
14:36-37 19
14:41-42 18
14:47-48 173n5
15 14
15:1-3 16
15:8-9 16
15:10-11 22
15:10-12 16
15:11 27
15:16 74
15:17-21 16
15:22-29 17
15:23b-28 17
15:27-31 22
16:14 17, 22
17:1-58 17
17:24 35
17:26 67
18:10 17, 188n5
18:11, 17, 21-25 17
18:12, 29 17
18:14-16 20
19:2, 10, 11-15 17
20:23 41
20:31 17
21–22 18
21:2 17
21:2-3 18
21:7 18
22:8, 13 17
22:9-11 18
22:14-15 18
22:16-19 19
25:26 189n14
28 24, 26, 92
28:6 17
28:6, 15 6, 22
28:13, 19 90
28:15 93, 95, 160
28:19 22
31:11-13 89
31:12 46

2 Samuel
1:2 44, 184n45
1:16 18914
1:17-27 188n5
5:3 35
6:8 39
7:1-2 201n44
7:1-13 100
7:4 215n42
7:8-17 173n7
7:12 90, 92, 94
11–12 55, 189n18
12:16, 20 184n45
12:23 90
13:13 67
13:19 43, 184n45
13:20 8, 192n8
13:21 8, 61, 160
13:31 45
15:32 184n45
16:1 185n65
19:19 189n7
21:1-9 175n24
21:5 73
21:11-14 89
22:2-51 188n5
22:43 142
24:15-17 19
24:24-25 15

1 Kings
1:21 90, 92
2:2 34
2:5 95
2:9, 32-33 95
2:6 94
2:26-27 14
6:1-36 102
6:7-8 103
6:7 9, 102
6:8 104
6:11 215n42
11:20 79
11:21 90, 92
13:24-25, 28 186n69
14:20 90, 92
15:24 90, 92
16:31-32 139

16:31 139
17–19 138, 147–48, 213n18
17:1-7 139
17:15-17 140
18 146
18:21 139
18:23-24a 139
18:24 143
18:28-29 139
18:45 143
19 9, 131–32, 137–49, 155, 194n30
19:3-4, 10, 14 140
19:8 139
19:9-10 145–47
19:9-18 140
19:9 140
19:10, 14 138, 140
19:11-12 142, 145, 215n46
19:11-13 142–43
19:11-18 161
19:11 140
19:11, 13 140
19:12-13 143
19:12 6, 141–42, 146
19:15-17 147
19:15-18 147
19:16 148
21:10, 13 150
22 149
22:5-28 178
22:5-40 39
22:5, 7-8 176n29
22:24 67
28 20–22

2 Kings
1 148
1–2 138
1:8 148
2:1, 11 153
2:3, 5 6
2:9-12 140, 216n55
2:11-12 141
2:12 147
3:26-27 19
6:15-17 16
6:15-23 147
6:16 192n4
6:16-17 16
7 192n7
9:6-7 148
9:25-26 186n69
13:13 90, 92
13:21 8
17 116
17:7-18 47, 109
17:13 179n57
18:1-6 84
18:28-35 84
18:30 196n55
18:36 6, 8, 84, 192n8
19:1-7 85
22:17 28
22:20 89–90, 94
23:10 137
23:14, 20 197n8
23:16 92, 200n35
24:1-7 116
24:2 179n57
24:3-4 60
25:11 52
25:21b 52

1 Chronicles
4:40 83
5:1 103
10:13 22
13:11 39
16:4 46
16:30 34
17:11 94
21:28 15
28:1-19 102
28:14-18 102
28:20 75
29:1-5, 6-9 102

2 Chronicles
15:3 202n55
16:5 99
16:9 25
18:23 67
21:16 182n24
24:20-21 219n98
28:20 192n4
30:27 182n25

34:25 28
34:28 94
36:20-21 52

Ezra
2:63 98
4:4 193n16
9 56
9:3-4 44, 185n49
9:6-7, 15 56
9:6-15 206n19
9:7 56
9:11 179n57
9:13 56

Nehemiah
4:11 99
5:8 183n28
8:11 8, 180n1
9 56
9:1 184n45
9:17 65
9:19, 31 125
9:32 56
13:15-16 98

Esther
4:3 43

Job
1–2 39, 155
1:1–2:13 149
1:5 150
1:7 149
1:8 154, 179n57
1:11 150
1:12 150
1:13-19 150
2:2-3 149
2:3 154
2:5 150
2:6 150
2:7-8 150
2:7 155
2:9 150
2:10 151
2:11-13 151
2:12-13 44, 184n45
2:13 45
3–37 217n70
3–31 155
3–7 154
3 217n70
3:1–37:24 151–52
3:1–31:40 152
3:1–27:12 149
3:1-26 149
3:10b 150
3:11-19 150
3:13 151
3:24 57, 123
4:1–27:23 149
4:1–21:34 217n60
4:16 142
5:17-18 66
6:24 151, 192n8
7:9 90
7:21 45, 189n6
8:6 38
9:14-19 152
9:20-23 152
9:27-35 151
10:1-7 151
10:21-22 90
11:3 151
13:5, 19 151
13:13 8, 151
14:12 93
16:10 67
16:12-14 151
16:15 184n45
17:6 151
17:13 90
19:3, 13-19 151
19:13 123
21:5 8, 44, 185n49
22:1–27:23 217n60
23:1-7 151
23:2 57
24:4 210n65
26:5 89, 176n30
27:4 189n8
28 149
29:1–41:34 149
29:7-10 151
29:21 151, 157
30:10 123
30:27 150–51
30:29 187n80
31:1-40 152

31:40 218n76
31:40b 152
33:31, 33 151
34:29 151
36:16 196n52
37:1-13 153
38–42 154
38:1–42:6 149, 152–54
38–41 147, 154
38:1–40:2 152
38 152
38:2 152
38:4-6, 18 153
38:6, 19, 24-25, 28-29, 33 153
38:8-11, 31-32 153
38:16-17, 22 153
38:39-41 153
39:1-2 153
40:1-2 153
40:3-5 152, 217n70
40:3 152
40:4 8
40:6–41:34 152, 217n70
40:6-14 153
40:8 152
40:15-24 153
41:1-34 153
41:1 124
42:1-6 149, 152–53
42:1 152
42:2 154
42:3-6 80, 154, 219n96
42:6 153–54, 217n70
42:7-17 149, 154, 219n100
42:7-16 155
42:7-8 154
42:7 124, 152, 154–55
42:10-17 154
42:10 154

Psalms
2–89 119
2 75, 81, 193n14
3 64, 117, 126
4 75, 120, 123, 172n43, 196n55, 196n57
6 60, 64, 88, 90, 94, 119–20, 123–28, 211n73
7 38, 45, 117, 119
9 117, 119
10 38, 108, 115, 117, 120, 124, 126, 150
12 38, 110, 115, 119, 193n14, 211n76
13 77, 93, 115, 118–20, 122, 124, 126–28, 161, 211n73
14 74
15 115
16 75, 89, 161
17 38, 108, 117, 123, 207n35
18 119, 143, 188n5, 192n1
19 192n1
20 115, 120
22 45, 57, 88–90, 113, 115, 120–21, 123–28, 161, 211n73
23 75
25 64–65, 117, 124
26 108, 113, 117, 119, 121, 182n25, 194n25
27 64, 75, 117, 120–21, 123–26, 128, 157, 161
28 8, 74, 94, 112, 119–21, 123–24, 126, 192n1, 210n62
29 74
30 60, 75, 88–90, 94, 115, 117, 119, 123, 125–26, 190n24, 194n25, 198n15
31 64, 115, 123–24, 126, 128, 157, 192n1, 201n38, 211n67
32 55–58, 61, 70, 160, 192n8
33 34, 58, 70, 157
34 95, 117
35 38, 112, 117, 119–24, 194n25, 210n62, 211n76
36 65
37 8, 40, 66, 78, 95, 110, 119–20, 125, 128, 157
38 58, 66, 121, 123, 126, 128, 157
39 59–60, 66–67, 112, 120, 122–24, 128, 157, 185n65, 192n8, 210n62
40 121, 119, 124, 157, 185n49, 198n15

41 117, 119, 194n25
42 77, 80, 120–22, 194n25
43 80, 117, 120–21
44 38, 52, 115, 119–21, 124, 187n80
46 40, 51, 74–75, 78, 81, 193n14
48 27, 51
49 27, 94, 120, 199n31
50 8, 47, 108–9, 124, 143, 161, 193n14, 205n50
51 55–61, 65, 68, 70, 189n13, 189n16, 190n23
52 93
54 126
55 119, 124
56 126, 190n24
57 123
58 117
59 59, 108
60 193n14
61 161
62 6, 8, 66, 74–78, 80, 108, 129, 157, 192n1, 195n45
63 90, 198n15
64 40, 108, 126
65 104
66 34, 123, 127
68 35, 90, 124, 182n25
69 117, 121, 123–24, 208n47
70 119, 120, 124
71 89, 90, 115, 120–21, 123, 192n1
72 119, 123
73 40, 95, 108, 110, 119, 191n33, 195n43, 199n31
74 38, 52, 113, 119–22, 124
75 117, 193n14
77 143
78 28, 192n1
79 52, 119–20
80 117, 119–20, 122, 211n67
81 123, 193n14
82 38
83 83, 112, 119, 123–24, 193n14, 210n62
86 65, 90, 115, 119, 123
88 60, 88–90, 94, 115, 119–24, 176n30, 190n24, 198n15
89 52, 65, 89–90, 119–20, 122, 124, 192n1
90 77, 119–20
91 74–75, 193n14, 211n76
92 192n1
94 88, 93, 120, 190n24, 191n42, 197n5
95 192n1, 193n14
97 143
98 183n35
101 117, 189n8
102 52, 115, 119–24
103 13, 45, 65, 110
105 124, 193n14
106 52, 122
107 24, 153
109 25, 112, 117, 119, 123–24, 210n62
110 75, 81, 193n14
113 116–17, 119
115 9, 88, 93–94, 120, 122, 190n24
116 75, 94, 117–18, 125–26, 190n24
117 78
118 117
119 120–21, 211n67
120 189n8
121 75
130 66, 80, 90, 110, 115, 128, 130, 157
131 8, 75, 78–81
132 81, 193n14
133 36
137 50, 119
139 118, 177n35
140 119
141 121
142 117, 123
143 44, 90, 115, 119, 121, 124, 185n49
145 65, 94, 118
147 121
148 153
Proverbs
2 89, 176n30

3 66, 196n55
4 74
5 66
9 90, 176n30, 192n8
12 41, 154
13 129
13 66
14 74
17 148
18 210n65
19 123
20 157
21 90, 95, 176n30
24 61, 160, 193n18
29 196n52
30 116

Ecclesiastes
3:19 88
4:6 196n52
6:5 196n52
9:10 90
9:17 196n52
11:5 88
12:7 88

Isaiah
1:7 49
1:10-17 62
1:12-15 23
1:15 189n14
2:1-4 27
2:3 184n43
2:10-18 36
3:6 184n45
4:1 67
4:6 74
5:7, 23 116
5:11-13 50
6:1-6 34
6:1-13 39
6:4 25
6:11 49
7:1-6 195n51
7:2 25
7:4 83, 192n4
7:7-10 196n51
7:14 191
7:17-25 196n51
8:5-22 196n51
8:17 157
8:19 93
9:4 36
10:2 210n65
10:5-11 37
10:26 182n24
11:8 79
12:2 196n55
13–14 38
13:7 193n15
13:22 48–49, 187n80, 187n86
14:7 83, 191n42
14:9-20 96
14:9-11, 15-20 95
14:9-11 93
14:9 89, 176n30
14:10 90
14:12-17 9
14:15 90, 198n15
14:16-20 88
14:19 186n69
14:20 89
16:9 123
16:10 99
17:10 192n1
18:4 83, 191n42
19:1 25
19:3 93
19:22 53
19:25 42
22:4, 12 123
22:12 43
22:16 89
23:2 8
24–27 36
24:7-8 50
24:8 99
24:20 24
25:4 74
25:9 157
26 199n30
26:4 192n1, 196n55
26:8 157
26:13-14 90
26:13 46
26:14, 19 176n30
26:14 89
26:19 45, 89, 91
26:20-21 40–41
26:20 68

28:9–33:24 81
28:21 183n31
28:25 79
28:28 142
29:6 153
29:9 24
29:13 123
29:21 210n65
30:1-18 81
30:1-4 81
30:12 196n56
30:15-17 82
30:15 82–83, 196n52
30:18 82, 110
30:27 143
31:1 196n56
31:4 38
32 82
32:15-18 83
33:2 157
33:8 69
33:15 116
34:3 186n69
34:13 187n80
34:14 48
35:4 192n4
35:7 187n86
35:10 50, 123
36:21 192n8
37:6 192n4
38:3 123
38:4 215n42
38:10-20 126
38:11 93
38:17 89
38:18 88, 90, 94, 198n15
40–55 38, 41, 209n52
40:1-2 53, 68, 191n45
40:9 192n4
40:24 153
40:31 157, 161
41:2, 25 182n24
41:16 153
41:17 125
42:13 38, 182n24
42:14 8
42:17 196n56
43:6 118
44:23 89
47:1 44, 184n45
47:3 67
47:5 9, 66
47:6 103
48:1 46
49:7 41
49:15 123
49:23 157
50:6 67
50:10 196n55
51:3 84
51:9 182n24
51:11 123
51:14 89
52:10 41
52:10, 15 41
52:13-14 44
52:14 185n49
52:15 8
53:7 40
53:8 93
53:12 189n6
54:6-7 68, 191n45
54:7 53
54:8 65, 110
56:2, 6 103
57:20 83
61:9 41
62:1 83
62:2 41
63:7–64:11 119
63:7-9 118
65:2-6 200
65:4 89, 92
65:11 70
65:19 84
65:20 94
66:18 41
Jeremiah
1:4 215n42
1:8 113
1:11-12 185n66
1:18 113
2:5 123
2:12 185n49
3:21 123
4:7 38

4:19 123, 192n8
4:27 186n79
5:1 25
5:13-14 178n54
5:28 116
6:8 49, 186n79
6:24 193n15
7:4, 10 29
7:5-7 29
7:14 196n56
7:16-20 13, 27–29
7:16 26, 31
7:25 179n57
7:34 49
8:1-2 197n8
8:19 28
8:20–9:2 146
9:10 123, 187n87
9:11 186n79, 187n80
9.19 51
10:22 186n79, 187n80, 187n86
11:1-17 29
11:1-8 29
11:4 26
11:9-13 29
11:11, 14 29
11:11 29
11:13, 17 29
11:14-17 13
11:14 29, 31
11:15-17 29
11:18–12:6 146
11:18-23 205n15
11:18-20 179n58
11:19 93
11:22-23 29
12:1-6 115, 179n58, 205n15
12:6 113
12:10-11 49, 186n79
14:1–15:9 30
14:1–15:4 179n59
14:7-10 30
14:7-9, 19-22 30
14:8 30
14:9b, 21b 30
14:10-11 30
14:10, 12 30
14:10 30
14:11-16 13, 26, 30–32
14:11 30–31
14:12 31
14:13-14 178n54
14:16 186n69
14:21 30
15:1-9 30
15:1-4 13, 26, 30–32
15:1-2 32
15:1 30
15:10-21 179n58
15:10-18 146
15:10 205n15
15:15-18 115
15:18 113
15:22 30
16:9 49, 99
17:4 124
17:11 95
17:14-18 179n58
17:17 74
18:1-11 31
18:16 185n49
18:18-23 146, 179n58, 205n15
18:18 184n43
18:19-20 113
18:20 113
20:7-18 146
20:7-13, 14-18 205n15
20:7-13 179n58
20:7-10 115
22:3 59
22:19 186n69
23:6 196n57
23:16-22 178n54
23:18, 21-22 149
23:19 153
24:10 177n45
25:4 179n57
25:10 49–50, 52, 141
25:11-12 53, 161, 191n45
25:11 68
25:12-14, 26 38
25:30 182n25
25:38 38
26:25 28
27:18 28
29:10 68, 191n45

29:17 177n45
30:10 83
30:23 153
31:9 118, 123
32 41
32:35 137
32:37 196n57
32:43 186n79
33:11 49
36 179n60
36:30 186n69
38:4 193n16
38:6-13 113
40:9 192n4
40:40 185n65
42:1-22 27
42:1-17 31
42:5 41
43 113
44:6 186n79
45:3 123
45:5 34
46:27 83
47:6 83
48:2 61
48:36 123
49:17-18 49
49:17, 20 185n49
49:19 38
50–51 38
50:9 182n24
50:13 48, 185n49
50:39 187n83
51:1, 11 182n24
51:7 34
51:13 185n66
51:43 48
51:51 67
52:3a 52
52:16 52

Lamentations
1 63
1:4 51
1:14 191n44
1:16 123
1:22 123
2 42, 63
2:1-8 44–45
2:6-7 51
2:9-10 42
2:9 42
2:9b 32
2:10 6, 9, 42–45, 47, 53, 57, 200n37
2:11, 18-19 9
2:17 42
2:18 43
2:19 77
2:22 36, 51
3 42, 55, 70
3:1-30 161
3:2 57
3:6 90
3:16-17 52
3:17-18 63
3:19-33 63–68, 190n29
3:21, 24, 29 67
3:22-23 67
3:22, 32 68
3:22 65
3:25-30 68
3:25-26 9, 67, 157, 161
3:26, 28 57, 67–68
3:26 65–67
3:28 40
3:30 67
3:31 68
3:33 68
3:40-42
3:49-50 9
4:3 187n80
4:18 185n66

Ezekiel
1:4 153
3:16 215n42
3:18, 20 95
4:17 44, 185n49
5:8 183n35
5:16 177n45
6:5 197
6:14 49, 186n79
7:2, 6 185n66
7:16 123
7:21 103
7:27 186n79
8:6 123

9:8 43
9:9 189n14
11:13 43
12:20 186n79
13:5 27, 36
13:11, 13 153
14:13, 21 177n45
15:8 186n79
16:5 186n69
16:26 28
16:42 83
20:9, 14, 22, 41 183n35
21:25 185n66
22:16 183n35
22:30 27
23:22 182n24
23:33 186n79
23:37, 45 95
24:6 189n14
24:16 17 43
26:13 99
26:16 45, 185n49
26:20 89, 94
27:28-31 44, 184n45
27:30-31 43
27:35 44
28:25 183n35
29:11 48
31:16-30 94
31:16 198n15
32:10 44, 185n49
32:21 93
32:24-29 95
32:25 93
33:6, 8 95
33:28-29 186n79
34:27 196n57
36:34-35
36:34 186n79
38:17 179n57
38:23 183n35
39:21 41
39:27 183n35
44:10 123
44:25 92, 200n35

Daniel
8:17, 19 185n66
9 56
9:2 53, 191n45
9:4 56
9:6, 10 179n57
9:19 124
12:1-2 91, 199n30
12:4 178n51
12:12 93

Hosea
1:8 79
1:11 36
2:11 51, 99
3:3-5 178n53
3:4-5 53, 68
3:5 53, 191n45
4:2 189n14
5:5-6 25
5:14 38
6:1-4 30
9:5 51
11:1 118
11:8-9 31
13:7-8 38
14:1-2 56
14:1 161

Joel
1–2 116
1:13-14, 19-20 27
2:12-17 27
2:12-14 9, 56
2:12 44
2:13-14 82
2:13 65
2:19-29 27
4:7 38

Amos
1–6 26
1:2 178n49
2:1 89
2:6b-7 23
2:14-15 23
3:1 23, 25
3:7 179n57
3:13-15 41
3:15 23
4:1 23, 25, 185n62
4:2-3, 12 23
4:3 186n69
4:6-12 26, 116, 175n24

4:6, 8-11 26, 56, 82
4:8 25
5:1-5, 16-20 23
5:1 23, 25
5:4-6, 14 26
5:7, 12 116
5:7 23
5:12 210n65
5:13 8, 43, 172n43
5:18-20 36
5:19 35
5:21-24 23, 62
5:23-24 23, 47
5:24 26
6:1-14 45
6:4-7 50
6:4-6 23
6:5 23, 47, 188n5
6:6b 23
6:7-11 23
6:9-10 23, 42, 45–48, 53
6:10 8, 35, 41, 47, 180n1, 186n75
6:12 23
7:1-6 26–27
7:1-3 185n64
7:4-6 185n64
7:7-9 185n64
7:8-9 23
7:16 25
8 179n55
8:1-3 45–48, 53
8:2-3, 9-14 23
8:3 8, 35, 42, 180n1, 183n36
8:4-6 23
8:4 23, 25
8:5 99
8:10 23
8:11-12 13, 23–26, 178n55
8:11 25, 160
9:1-4 23
9:14 69

Jonah
1:1 215n42
2:4, 7 94
4:2 65

Micah
1:8 49, 187n80
3:5-7 26
3:9, 11 116
4:1-5 27
5:1 67
5:8 38
6:12 189n8
7:1 185n65
7:3 116
7:7 157, 161
7:16 8, 41
7:18-20 110
7:18 189n6

Nahum
2:10-12 38
3:1 189n14
3:5 41

Habakkuk
1–2 205n10
1:2–2:4 125
1:2-4 37
1:2-3, 13 113
1:2, 13 110
1:2 118
1:5-11 37, 205n10
1:12-17 37
1:13 110
2 41
2:1-20 37
2:1-17 37
2:1-4 110
2:3 185n66
2:5-17 37–38
2:8, 12 189n14
2:9 59
2:18 196n56
2:19 38, 66
2:20 8, 33–35, 37–38, 41, 45, 53, 181n3, 182n25
3 116, 182n21
3:1-19 37
3:2-19 37
3:9 182n24
3:17-19 130
3:16 191n42

Zephaniah
1:2–2:15 36
1:4-9 36
1:4b-6 36

1:7-8 35
1:7 33, 34, 36–37, 53
1:8-9 36
1:10–2:4 36
1:12b, 17-18 36
1:12b 109
2:1-4 36
2:13-14 49
3:8-20 36
3:17 73

Haggai
1:1-11 175n24
1:1 215
1:12 35
1:14 38
2:10-14 202
2:11 184

Zechariah
1–8 38, 181n8
1–6 69
1:1-6 38
1:6 179n57
1:7–6:15 38
1:11 83
1:12 53, 161, 191n45
2 38
2:1-4 38
2:9 38
2:11 42
2:12 182n22
2:13 8, 33–35, 38–39, 41, 45, 53
2:17 181n3
4:1 38
4:10 25
6:8 191n42
7–8 55, 68–70, 84
7:1–8:23 38
7 68
7:3 68
7:3, 5 68
7:5 161, 191n45
7:7 69
7:10 69
7:14 44, 49, 69, 185n49
8:4-8 70
8:16 69
8:19 68, 70
9–14 38
9:13 182n24
9:14 153
10:11 198n15
13:7 182
14 192n7

Matthew
11:14 213n20
16:14 213n20
17:3-4, 17-27 213n20
23:35 219n98
24:47-49 213n20
26:62-63 171n39
27:12-14 171n39

Mark
14:60-61 171n39
15:4 171n39

Luke
1:17 213n20
9:8 213n20
11:5-10 161
11:51 219n98

John
19:9 171n39

Romans
2:4-5 109
2:4 161

1 Corinthians
10:1-11 10
14 171n39

1 Thessalonians
4:13 94

1 Peter
2:1-10 10
3:10 10

2 Peter
3:8-9 161
3:9 110

Revelation
8:1 34, 171n39

HEBREW INDEX

'azin, to give ear, 117
'iy, hyena, 187n83
'al-tiphga', do not intercede, 28
'al-titpallel, do not pray, 28
'emunah, faithfulness, 65
'anaḥah, moaning, 123
'asaph, to gather, 89
'aphar, dust, 89
'esh, fire, 143
'esheth ba 'alat 'ob, medium, 176n28

baṭaḥ, and *beṭaḥ*, to trust, experience security, object of trust, 81, 83, 196n58
beki, weeping, 123

gawa', cessation of breath, 88
goyim, nations, 41

dabar, word, 143, 215n43
**damah*, to be silent, still, 8
**damam*, to be still or silent, 8, 40, 43, 65, 73, 78–79, 141, 190n21
demamah, stillness, 8, 141–42, 147, 169n22, 215n36, 215n38
**doum*, to be silent, 8
dumah, silence, 88, 93, 169n22
dumam, quietly, 65–66, 191n38
dumia, in silence, 76, 194n29
dumiyah, silence, rest, 8, 169n22
**daqaq*, grinding of a substance into fine powder, 142, 215n36
daqqah, a substance ground into fine powder, 138, 141–43, 146–47, 215n36

hagig, sighing, 123
**hamah*, to agitate, 123
hekal, temple or palace, 182n25
hashqeṭ, quietness, 83, 196n58

wcha 'abadti, banish, 50
weyiddom, he shall be silent/still, sit silently, 65, 191n38
wayyishboth, resting, 98

**za'aq*, to cry out, 116

**ḥillel*, to profane, 103
ḥaṭa', sin, 56
ḥesed, steadfast love, 65
**ḥarash*, to restrain, be silent, 8, 73, 123, 183n30, 192n9, 204n6, 210n62

ṭouv, goodness, 145

**yadah*, to confess sin, 56–57
**yaḥal*, to hope, 80
**ya'an*, to answer, 152
**yatzav*, to take a stand, 73
**yatza'*, to break forth, 39
**yara'*, to fear, 35, 73
**yarad*, to descend, 90, 91

kavod, glory, brilliance,

lamah, why, 120

le'ene' hagoyim, before the eyes of the nations, 183n35
liphne, before (spatial or cultic), 35

ma'kov, pain, 123
midamim, from silence, 60
middamim, from bloods, 60
maweth, death, 89
mah, why, 120
maḥaseh, refuge, 74
mimme'on qodsho, from his holy dwelling, 38
min hasse'ara, out of the whirlwind, 153
miphne, before, because of (causal), 34–35, 180n1, 181n11
mippenei ḥata 'einu, because of our sins, 206n19
**mashak*, to drag away, 124
meshuvotenu, (our) apostasies, 30
mishpaṭ, justice, 117
matay, when, 120
mitok ha'esh, out of the midst of the fire, 215n46

**nabaṭ*, to look down, 117
niḥam, to repent, 153
nouaḥ, quietness, 66, 191n42
naḥat, quietness, peace, 196n52
nekonah, rightly, correctly, 154
nephesh, inner being, 78, 193n25, 194n32
netzaḥ, forever, 120
**natzal*, to rescue, deliver, 66, 191n42, 59

**sakat*, to be quiet, 8

'ad-'anah, how long, 120
'ad-mah, how long, 120
'ad-matai, how long, 120
'al-mah, why, 120
'awon, sin, 56–57
'avonenu, our sins, 30
**'azav*, to forsake, 123, 186n78
'olah, burnt offering, 133
**'amad*, stand, 140

**paga'*, to intercede, 28–29
**palaṭ, to deliver, 124*
**pillel*, to pray, 28
**paqad*, to visit, appoint, 10
parashah petuchah, line break, 7
parashah setumah, space, 7
**peretz*, to break out, 39, 41

tzedaqah, righteousness, 117
tzedeq, righteous, righteousness, 117
**tza'aq*, to cry out, 123

qever, grave, 89
qevurah, grave, 89
**qiddesh*, to consecrate, 97
qahal, assembly, 90, 95
qayitz, ripe summer fruit, 185n65
qol, sound, 142
qol demamah daqqah, sound of finely ground stillness, 138, 141–43, 146–47, 215n36
**qoum*, to rise up, 10, 38

qetz, end, 185n66
qetzeph, wrath, 39
**qara'*, to call, 117, 123

**ra'ah*, to behold, 40–41, 73, 117
ruaḥ gedolah, great wind, 143
remia, deceit, 189n8
rinna, cry, 28
ra'ash, earthquake, 143
**raphah*, to be still, 74–75
repha'im, shades, 89, 176n30, 198n12
rasha', sin, 56
rish'enu, (our) wickedness, 30

**satar paneka*, to hide one's face, 124

she'agah, groan, 123
**shabat*, to cease, 98–99
**sheva'*, to cry, 123
**shouv*, to return, 56, 81
shaḥat, pit, 89
**shakaḥ*, to forget, 123
**shakan*, to sleep, 90
shalom, peace, tranquility, stillness, well-being, 83
**shama'*, to hear, 117
**shamam*, to be appalled, to be desolate, 185
shemamah, desolation, 49
she'arim, gates, 90
**shaqaṭ*, to be quiet, 8, 66, 81, 83, 191n42
**shataq*, to grow silent, 8

tehomoth 'eretz, depths of the earth, 89
taḥtiyoth 'eretz, depths of the earth, 89
tepilla, prayer, 28
tiqwah, hope, 75